DATE DUE

OC 1 '04		
OC 3 05		

DEMCO 38-296

Kid-Friendly Parenting with Deaf
and Hard of Hearing Children

Clerc Books
Gallaudet University Press
Washington, D.C.

Clerc Books
An imprint of Gallaudet University Press
Washington, DC 20002

Published 1995. Second printing 1997
Printed in the United States of America

Library of Congress Cataloging-in-Publication Data

Chapman Weston, Denise.
  Kid-friendly parenting with deaf and hard of hearing children /
Denise Chapman Weston, Daria J. Medwid.
      p.   cm.
  Includes bibliographical references.
  ISBN 1-56368-031-9 (alk. paper)
  1. Parents of handicapped children.   2. Children, Deaf—Family
relationships.   3. Hearing impaired children—Family relationships.
4. Parent and child.   5. Child rearing.   6. Creative activities and
seat work.   I. Medwid, Daria J.   II. Title.
HQ759.913.C53   1995
649'.1512—dc20   95-25434
                                                          CIP

Grateful acknowledgment is made to Jeremy P. Tarcher Inc. and G.P. Put-
nam's Sons for permission to reprint and adapt activities from *Playful Par-
enting: Turning the Dilemma of Discipline into Fun and Games* by Denise
Chapman Weston and Mark S. Weston. Copyright 1993 by Denise Chapman
Weston and Mark S. Weston. Reprinted by permission of Jeremy P. Tarcher,
Inc. / G.P. Putnam's Sons.

Cover design by Dorothy Wachtenheim
Interior design by Alice Fernandes-Brown
Cover photo by Chun Louie, Gallaudet University

We dedicate this book to the parents, children, and deaf individuals with whom we have worked . . . and to those with whom we haven't. You are, and continue to be, an inspiration.

Contents

• • • •

Acknowledgments

· · · ·

We are grateful to the following schools and agencies for allowing us to grow and mature in our professional life: The Hayden Hearing Impaired Program, South Shore Mental Health, The South Shore Educational Collaborative, Regional Educational and Diagnostic Services, Austine School for the Deaf, Arizona State School for the Deaf and Blind, Rhode Island School for the Deaf, and The Learning Center for Deaf Children.

We extend our appreciation to all of the supervisors, consultants, and teachers who have taught us, and to all of the supervisees and students who have given us the opportunity to teach.

For those who have contributed directly to the task of turning our ideas into this book, we give a heartfelt thanks—the authors of the chapter introductions (Mervin Garretson, Rosalyn and Jack Gannon, John Adams, Max and Della Fitz-Gerald, Neil and Susan Burgess, Ruthann and Michael Schlang, Kim Kelly, Terrell Clark, I. King Jordan, and Judith Gansberg), Allen Beal, Rachel Cane, Bernard Bragg, Jim Bombacino, Chris Pacheco, McCay Vernon, Kendra Timko, Carolyn Jones, The Massachusetts Parents Association for the Deaf, Ivey Pittle Wallace, and the staff at Gallaudet University Press.

Daria gives her thanks to her (adult) family in Boston—their love, support, belief, and humor are my sustenance. Love to Susan, Paul, Michelle, Denise, Mark, and especially, Jerry, who gives in shamanic ways.

To my family in Pittsburgh (Natalie, Bob, Bobby, Jij, Dom, Gina, Dominic, Sunny, Tasha, Raymond, Tanya, Adam, Gia, Alex, Anthony, Tessa, and Nicco)— they have given me a rich and loving history and a hopeful future full of wonderful nieces and nephews.

To Cheri, Marcus, and the dance community, who have helped to keep me sane through movement and friendship. To Jonas and Blaine, who have helped start me on an important journey. To Savina, Diane, Neil, Luc, and Jeffrey, whose guidance and friendship goes beyond time and place. To the Deaf people and their families I have come to know—it has been an honor to be a part of your lives.

And lastly, to Denise—just a phone call, a book, or a laugh away.

Denise sends warm thanks to the incredibly great people at Jeremy Tarcher Inc. and Putnam Publishing for permission to reprint and adapt some of the activities from *Playful Parenting*.

A special thanks to those who taught me how to play, including my parents Audrey and Cliff Chapman, my brother Jerry, and all the great playmates I had through the years.

A big thanks to the numerous camps for Deaf children in which I have worked over the years. And my biggest thanks to the campers who started me off on the right foot (actually hand!) to learn to sign.

To my partner for life, co-author of *Playful Parenting* and all-around great guy and dad Mark. Thanks for your patience and playfulness.

To my really great kids Arielle and Emily, who have taught me the true meaning of parenthood. What a lucky Mommy to have girls like you two!

And to Daria—it's so nice to have a friend who doubles as a co-author. Thank you for sharing your wisdom with me and now with others.

CHAPTER

1

Introduction

• • • •

WHY THIS BOOK WAS WRITTEN

"Wouldn't it be nice if all of our children came home from the hospital with a 'how to' instruction book?" asked a single mother of a seven-year-old deaf child.

"Yeah—like you could turn to the chapter on how to stop your child from throwing tantrums and by simply following the directions in the book—presto—she turns into an exemplary child!" remarked a father of a four-year-old.

These are not unusual comments from parents of deaf children in our counseling sessions. We have often been asked if we know of a good book that could help parents manage specific behavior problems with their deaf child. Our answers have always been the same—yes, there are good parenting books, and no, none of them focus on the specific difficulties related to deafness and behavior problems.

Throughout our work as psychotherapists specializing in deafness, we have encountered numerous good books written about relations between parents and their deaf infants; these books help parents work through feelings related to having a deaf child and explain the educational choices that are available for deaf children. Little has been written to assist parents of deaf or hard of hearing children in managing day-to-day child behavior problems.

Although parents can find golden nuggets of information in various books, articles, and research projects prepared by skilled researchers and practitioners specializing in deafness, the typical parent doesn't have access to these sources. Parents are busy with a host of responsibilities and have scant time to seek such information.

Thus, we chose as our mission to gather vital information for parents of deaf children and to deliver it in the form of a book—a comprehensive instruction manual that includes practical and easy-to-understand suggestions about how to parent a deaf child from age three to age twelve.

We have taken everyday childhood behavior problems that require parental attention and have addressed their resolution in the form of concise explanations, techniques, fun ideas, and playful activities. Since we cannot pretend to have the last word on every behavior of a deaf child or every challenge of raising a deaf child, we invited a team of experts to offer their knowledge to parents. These people are parents of deaf and hard of hearing children, university professors, researchers, psychologists, authors, counselors, deaf adults, and other helping professionals who have been exploring the field of deafness (or living it) for many years.

This book is about what to do after you have begun to accept your deaf child for who she is. If you feel you have not adequately begun this acceptance process, then you should take a look at some of the helpful books available on this topic. One such book that we suggest is *You and Your Hearing Impaired Child,* by John W. Adams (Clerc Books, Gallaudet University Press, 1988).

We realize, however, that acceptance and understanding is a life-long process. With each new child and/or family development, there may be new questions, old feelings, and challenges to be faced. In fact, many parents who feel that they have dealt with accepting their child's deafness are often surprised to have old questions and fears re-emerge when, for instance, the child starts school, begins to communicate faster (in sign language), or starts puberty. With that in mind, we will give consistent reminders as to how parents' feelings and levels of acceptance influence the deaf child.

Sometimes parents are looking for new ideas, tools, and immediate techniques. As one parent of a deaf seven-year-old exclaimed, "I'm all feelinged out! I've gone through parent-infant programs and seen a few therapists. Now I want to deal with the tantrums, the messy rooms, and the fresh talk."

We hope this book helps you do just that.

WHO SHOULD USE THIS BOOK

This book is for the family who has a child with any hearing loss that significantly affects communication. We use the term "deaf" child in its broadest sense and that definition is not based on any strict auditory status (mild, moderate, severe, profound) or cultural affiliation (Deaf, hearing).

We recognize that the greater the hearing loss in the child, the more communication enters as a factor in a mixed (deaf/hearing) family. Significant adjustments must occur when the child relies solely on vision and the family is used to auditory communication. Ongoing communication problems can result in behavioral difficulties for the deaf child. For this reason, we hope that this book can be of particular value to a family facing these challenges.

Deaf parents of deaf children will also find many of the parenting techniques and activities useful for child behavior problems. The strong visual/tactile/action-oriented activities are designed to appeal to any deaf child. We recognize that the majority of deaf parents do not have the same communication and cultural differences to negotiate with their deaf child that hearing parents do. Therefore, the information we provide that is specific to deaf/hearing issues will obviously not apply.

DEFINING PROBLEM BEHAVIORS

Most childhood behaviors are developmental and can be expected; for example bed-wetting in two-year-olds, tantrums in two-to-five-year-olds, high sensitivity to being accepted by peers in seven-to-ten-year-olds, nightmares, crying, oppositional behavior, and lying. Time, consistency, and understanding will usually help children navigate difficulties.

We suggest that you familiarize yourself with which behaviors to expect at which ages and in which different social environments/situations. John W. Adams's book, *You and Your Hearing-Impaired Child* (Clerc Books, Gallaudet University Press, 1988), gives concise descriptions of predictable age-related behaviors in deaf children. In addition to the Adams book, you will find that you can use the beginning sections of each chapter of this book to find out how certain situations and transitions (such as confusing communication, divorce, lack of neighborhood friends, change of schools, or over-permissiveness) can naturally result in behavior problems.

Most of all, use your own judgment and that inner voice that says, "Something is not working here." If a specific behavior problem is present for a long period of time (three to six months), if you lose your patience regularly, if your child expresses ongoing frustration or unhappiness, and if behaviors intensify, you may need some additional help and new ideas. It may be enough to get a fresh perspective from other parents or from ideas presented in a book such as this one. If you don't experience adequate change or relief, consider seeking extra support services (see chapter 2).

How We Developed Our Approach to Solving Behavior Problems

The Power and Possibilities of Play

In working with deaf children, we have come to recognize that traditional "talk" therapy is often not the answer. Since the deaf child faces communication challenges daily, encouraging her to describe her emotional pain or difficulties exclusively through "talk" is insensitive and unproductive. This holds true for hearing children as well.

Talking is not necessarily a child's first choice for communicating thoughts and feelings. But play is! Play is a child's friend. Try to talk to any child for fifteen minutes while you are both just sitting in chairs. Watch her eyes, body, hands, and feet. You will probably observe the child itching to explore. Now, pull out a game, a ball, a book, or crayons and watch her. The eyes light up, she excitedly moves to the materials, and for the moment you can sense her comfort—she feels at home.

As play therapists, we have offices filled with puppets, art supplies, dolls, board games, sports-related gear and whatever paraphernalia might appeal to a child. Our goal is to make the child comfortable enough to allow us to help her identify and overcome her problems and experience some relief.

We have spent a good portion of our workdays on our hands and knees, telling children stories, talking with puppets, coloring, painting, or throwing a ball. We have found it exhausting but at the same time revitalizing to view the world through the excitement and freshness of a child's eye; with all her curiosity, delight in discovery, and boundless energy.

Play has a wonderful appeal and benefit to any child and especially a deaf child since it accesses visual, action-oriented, and experiential forms of communication. These help the child to express her thoughts and feelings, learn about social roles and responsibilities, confront obstacles in life, and employ skills to solve everyday difficulties.

Time and time again we have observed how play offers adults a window into a child's world and provides an arena for family communication. When a child steps into play, she displays who she is, what she thinks and dreams about, how she thinks, and what worries her.

When you participate in the deaf child's play you can both observe and interact with her imagination, language, emotions, movements, memory, and thinking. Because play allows the child to feel in control, she can be an initiator and a leader more than in daily living activities. When the child feels at ease she will be more likely to explain things, to respond to questions, to laugh at your and her mistakes, to repeat herself, to ask you for clarification, and to tell you her heartfelt concerns. In the context of play, a parent can more easily teach and offer ideas that help the child in her development.

Consider the following vignette of a deaf child playing with bubbles while staying in bed due to illness.

> "Look, Mommy, balls, baby balls (bubbles)."
>
> *"Oh, you call the b-u-b-b-l-e-s 'baby balls.' What are they doing?"*
>
> "The ones flying outside are the happy ones and the ones that stay in here are not."
>
> *"I'm sorry, I did not understand you—the ones outside are happy?"*
>
> "Yes, look they are dancing."
>
> *"Oh, look, that one dancing outside—is she happy? How do you know?"*
>
> "Because she likes to go outside like me and look she is jumping!!"
>
> *"Yes, look, all of the baby bubbles are jumping outside, like people when they are happy—what about the rest that stay inside—are they happy, too?"*
>
> "Huh?"
>
> *"These here, are they happy?"*
>
> "No, they don't like being sick, they want to dance!"
>
> *"Well, maybe we can make a tent for all of the sick baby bubbles and you can keep them company until you are all better."*

In this vignette there are a number of things that occur—the deaf child asks the parent to join her, the parent notes a new word "bubble" in a nonthreatening way, the parent asks for clarification, the child repeats herself without a struggle, the child visually notes differences between the happy (dancing) bubbles and the sad ones, the child connects a feeling to a cause (sad about being sick and happy when she goes outside), and the mother designs a way to address sad feelings. It's amazing what can happen in a simple few minutes of play!

Play makes communication that much easier, more fun, and can help establish relationships between people regardless of differences. Play can provide a shared visual and experiential focus to assist a parent and a deaf child when they hit a communication block. It can help with explanations and offer a concept or action that can be referenced later. For example, if a young deaf child is going to the hospital to have ear tubes inserted, her mother can play "hospital" with a stuffed animal to explain the procedure. In the doctor's office the mother can say, "Remember when we looked at the rabbit's ears? That's just what the doctor will do to you."

In order for a child to grow, play must be connected to language. To this end, we strongly advocate that your family choose a communication method (see chapter 5) that works for your deaf child and commit yourselves to using it. Successful communication between parents and their deaf child allows for clear explanations about any of her problems or misbehaviors, the effect she has on others, and alternative ways of handling herself in future situations.

Play goes hand-in-hand with communication—play can increase language development in deaf children and language development can help in advancing play. Play, a very active and hands-on experience, can be used symbolically by a deaf child to understand the world around her.

In summary, deaf children and their families can use play to better understand each other. Parents are the key figures in responding to their child's needs and, with some guidance, should be able to help their child solve everyday difficulties. Parents can be taught to use play techniques to work through common family and child behavior problems. Hence, this book offers over 300 play activities that you can do with your child to solve problems, enhance communication, and strengthen relationships. Step into the world of play and you step into a world of imagination and possibilities.

Family Problem-solving

Play is one of the methods that we, as psychotherapists, use to work through problems. We also strongly believe in the power of the family and its influence as a guiding force in children's lives. In family therapy, we invite all members of a child's family to work through a problem.

We had one case where a bright, six-year-old deaf child was aggressive, overactive, and performed poorly in school. Her parents complained that they had "no control" over her and were at their "wit's end." In this particular case, we identified the aggression and "loss of control" issues as not belonging to the child alone, but rather as an integral component of the family "culture." Change came about when the entire family worked together to resolve the problem at hand by using nonaggressive ways to communicate their feelings.

We favor a family approach because it relieves both child and parent of blame, while encouraging everyone to share responsibility for the problem and for correcting it. When parents and children take an active part in finding and carrying out a solution to their problems, the family members lose that sense of helplessness and loneliness. An environment needs to be created where family members, parent and child alike, are trained to become the experts and skilled problem-solvers of their own difficulties. This ultimately should increase their sense of confidence in their ability to influence their own lives.

HOW TO USE THIS BOOK

Chapters 2, 3, and 4 offer ideas for enhancing parenting skills. Chapter 2 focuses on ways to support the parent of a deaf child, techniques that improve communication, and special resources and assistance available to anyone raising a deaf child. Chapter 3 focuses on specific techniques you can use to define limits of behavior, and that might help you avoid power struggles with your child. Chapter 4 addresses more general parenting techniques that foster behavioral changes.

Although the amount of information in these chapters may appear overwhelming, we have attempted to condense these techniques to make them easy to learn, apply, and integrate into your present parenting style. We have designed the book so that you can quickly turn to the parent skill chapters to look up a technique to assist you in solving a problem.

We have grouped the next eleven chapters together by family challenges (such as communication problems, cultural diversity, and family unity) or behavior problem themes (such as moodiness, poor self-concept, and irresponsibility). After familiarizing yourself with chapters 2 to 4, scan the table of contents and pick out problems that you might wish to prevent or solve, then turn to the chapter that discusses these problems.

As noted earlier, beginning with chapter 5, we include an introduction to the defined problem or challenge written by a knowledgeable person in the field of deafness. These experts come from diverse backgrounds and from different areas of the country. After each introduction, we address the specific problems by first giving you clear and simple explanations of what the problem(s) might look like. Following that, we provide background information on each of the behavior problems and then activities you can use as preventative or remedial interventions.

We recognize that every family is different. Some families prefer extensive structure and resources, while others require less and prefer to be more spontaneous. Therefore, we have designed this book so that a more structured parent can read through and practice the introductory steps thoroughly and use the worksheets located in the appendices. The less structured parent can simply choose an activity and use it as an enriching family experience.

We hope this book will prove to be a long-term reference that you will turn to in the course of your deaf child's ever-changing life and challenges. You will likely be confronted with many parenting challenges throughout your child's lifetime.

Although we have written this book for you, the parent, the methods, techniques, and problem-solving activities are designed to be "child-friendly." Just as we strive in family therapy sessions to include children in the family process of understanding and dealing with the problems at hand, we have designed the concepts and problem-solving activities in this book to appeal to children. We hope this book will serve as a good resource for planning family activities.

We combine guidance with fun, family-tested, child-approved approaches to parenting and problem-solving. Challenging childhood behavior problems don't always have to result in punishment. Our goal with this book is to offer possibilities for positive and enjoyable ways to solve problems.

Usage Notes

1. A handful of the activities include some auditory aspects (music, for example). In those activities we will note that they may be most appropriate for a hard of hearing child.

2. When we are speaking specifically about Deaf culture or people who identify themselves as culturally Deaf, we will use the capital "D." In all other cases, a lowercase letter "d" (deaf) will be used.

3. We may refer to a "young" or an "older" deaf child at times. Generally, our reference to a "young" deaf child will mean one below the age of six, and "older" will mean aged six to twelve. We will note a child's specific age when we want to make distinctions for the purpose of explaining developmental markers or appropriateness of parenting techniques or problem-solving activities.

4. We suggest that you read through the first three chapters of this book and choose those parenting techniques that best suit your personal parenting style. It is certainly not possible to use all the techniques at once, so test out a few and see which ones fit you.

5. Throughout the book, we may suggest a few methods described in the parenting skills chapters to further help you solve a problem. You can refer back to chapters 2 to 4 to refresh your memory regarding these specific techniques.

6. When we present the activities, we will note what materials are needed, what age-group the activity best serves, and what vocabulary words or concepts would be useful for the parent to use to teach and practice with the deaf child. When we suggest a specific ASL word or concept, we will put that word into small capital letters, such as VOICE-OFF. The suggested vocabulary in activities is just a starting place and is not meant to be a linguistic exercise. If you have trouble describing something to your child or do not know the signs for concepts (such as *responsibility* or *privacy*), ask a deaf adult or a teacher of deaf children to help you find the best way to do this.

7. We believe that your deaf child will mature behaviorally if she learns the necessary vocabulary to define and explain things such as feelings, Deaf culture, pride, human rights, privacy, and family relationships. We expect

that a family would incorporate the suggested words/signs into a communication style that makes sense to the deaf child.

8. You will notice that we alternate between referring to the child as "he" and "she" in this book. This is our method of choice for writing with gender equity in mind.

9. We do not presume to know "the" right way to raise a deaf child. We certainly don't know how to raise *your* deaf child. Furthermore, all of our years of experience can only give us a glimpse of what life is really like for a deaf person. But we have tried to be informative and accessible to parents by presenting our own insights drawn from readings, observations, years of professional experience, and conversations with deaf adults and deaf children and their families. We welcome your feedback to better understand how to make this book more child-friendly, Deaf-friendly, and parent-friendly.

CHAPTER

2

Raising a Deaf or Hard of Hearing Child

• • • •

Hearing parents of deaf children can be expected to feel perplexed about how to raise their deaf child. They have images, wishes, and expectations, and, unless they have deaf family members, they never consider that they may have a deaf child. Not only might they not have had the experience of meeting deaf children, they may never have met a deaf adult. Or their experience may have been filled with myths, questions, and benign disinterest.

Parenting is a complicated process that can be both joyous and a struggle. The struggles of parenthood can be handled more easily when a parent has knowledge of specific parenting techniques, of what to expect in raising a deaf child, and of how to get support when dozens of questions and feelings arise.

A deaf child and his family will experience many of the same developmental joys and problems experienced by an all hearing family. There will be arguments and agreements, oppositional behavior and teamwork, parent embarrassments and pride, and happiness and loss. However, the deaf child's family must always deal with the child being different from other (hearing) family members and different from the hearing majority.

The deaf child's individual developmental needs (and therefore the child's behavioral experiments and problems) will be basically the same as a hearing child's except for one major difference—communication. Attachment, friendships, self-esteem, confidence, academic standing, frustration, tolerance, problem-solving, and intimacy will be affected by the deaf child's ability to understand and to be understood when communicating. For this reason, much of the information contained in this book stresses and gives structures to communication nuances that affect problem-solving, development, and discipline.

While many parents can succeed in eighteen-plus years of intuitive child-rearing, this process can be made easier with more knowledge. That knowledge may come from a neighbor, a family member, a magazine article, a teacher, the family doctor, or from a book such as this. A repertoire of knowledge and techniques can help a parent to feel prepared, supported, and a little less "crazy" during those moments of need.

This is especially important when a parent is being introduced to the added factor of deafness for the first time. It is quite a task to learn how to honor the deaf child's different needs while simultaneously treating him like any other child. This is a difficult balance to maintain, and in their best efforts, parents might confuse these two.

SUPPORT FOR THE PARENTS OF THE DEAF CHILD

Adjusting to a Difference in the Family over a Lifetime

Following the diagnosis of deafness in their child, it is important for hearing parents to get support from other sensitive adults and professionals. A parent has a right to express feelings and fears. High parental stress means less ability to respond spontaneously to the child.

Deaf parents of a deaf child will have less of an adjustment—they understand deafness through their own lives. However, in some circumstances, a deaf parent may be shocked that his child is deaf, especially when the parent believes his own deafness was not genetic in nature and therefore expects a hearing infant. The deaf parent may also be surprised and disappointed if he expected and looked forward to having a deaf child and the child is hearing.

Early in the child's life, a parent will attribute meaning to being "deaf." That interpretation will have an impact on parental feelings and interactions with the child. If a parent views his child as unique rather than flawed, the child will develop a more healthy view of himself.

Often delays in the diagnosis of deafness by pediatricians begin a cycle of parents being put in an uncertain position—they begin to doubt themselves. Later, the parents may find themselves furious at the doctor for mislabeling their child and disbelieving them. Some parents have voiced their feelings that they welcomed the delay in diagnosis because it allowed them to believe, if only for a while, that their child could hear. In any case, delays in diagnosis cause delays in intervention, and the child may miss out on reasonable and satisfying communication.

As hearing parents, a diagnosis of deafness may shock and sadden you. You may feel numb and guilty. You may feel lost and isolated. Some parents may feel that their child is developmentally disabled or seriously impaired. These are all common and natural feelings. With support and knowledge, hearing parents can do a wonderful job of raising a deaf child. However, parents' feelings may often vacillate.

Parents may struggle with difficult feelings and vulnerabilities at different stages in their deaf child's development; for instance, when the child starts school, when he develops greater (sign) language capacities, when the child begins adolescence, and when planning begins for graduation from high school and turning eighteen.

Hearing parents of deaf children need ways to express their expectations at each stage of the child's development. While sorting out these expectations, a parent may need to make adjustments to match the child's realistic needs and progress.

Often parents of a deaf child have difficulty finding other adults who will care for their child. Deafness may make many hearing relatives, neighbors, and baby-sitters nervous and unwilling. Thus both the parent and the child become isolated.

Being deaf in and of itself does not create problems, but the context in which deafness occurs does—for example: hearing culture norms; a hearing family who, through no fault of their own, has never met a deaf individual; extended family members who don't know how to be supportive; or hearing professionals who make decisions for deaf individuals and their families. How all of these contexts define deafness will make it easier or harder for the child and his family to adapt and develop.

Parents need to continually balance supporting a deaf child through the challenges the child faces with helping the child to understand his capabilities, differences, and limitations. This may make a hearing/deaf family's development seemingly more tedious and slower than an all-hearing or all-deaf family's development.

Because you can't see deafness, it is often called an "invisible" difference. For this reason, parents may continually wish and practice with their child how to "pass" for hearing.

With the general hearing public, parents are often put in the position of the main spokesperson, advocate, healer, and teacher for their child. In addition, all parents receive their share of advice and criticism from insistent professionals and family members.

Each member of the family may have his own view of what deafness means and how to interact with the deaf child. The parents set the tone. Often each of the parents has distinctly different views on what the child needs. As with any child-rearing issue, the parents must resolve and negotiate their differences. This takes time and requires compromise. Don't do this in a vacuum—make decisions based on what is best for the child, not what is easiest. Gather as much information as possible (through teachers, deaf adults, books, and other parents) to help you weigh options. If need be, consider seeing a counselor (who understands deaf individuals) to help in this process.

The SOS Plan for Parents

Parents have taught us again and again how many adjustments and challenges they face throughout their children's lives. The phrase, "I would never have made it through that if it weren't for . . ." is frequently heard. What this indicates is that parents need help and support from other people.

What your own SOS plan looks like will depend on your personality, contacts, and social supports. Here are some ideas.

1. Join a parents of deaf children group or start your own. Begin with other parents in your child's school.

2. Make several lists of people you can call in times of need. Include close friends (who let you cry on their shoulder), professional agencies that can provide resources, any crisis numbers for counseling centers or parent hotlines, appropriate clergy from your particular place of worship, and professionals involved in your child's life.

3. Take breaks, however small. Take bath breaks, nap breaks, weekend breaks, vacation breaks—but take them. Your rejuvenation will help keep you sane and allow you more tolerance to get through even the toughest moments. Explore respite services offered through children's advocacy groups, mental health programs, and state agencies.

4. Don't give up those hobbies you enjoy. Continue to garden, knit, cook, can, build things, take photographs, and paint. Even a small amount of time devoted to these pursuits is worth it. Consider teaching your child your hobby so you can do it together.

5. Exercise regularly. Keep your lungs, heart, and blood fresh and wash away some worries.

6. In times of need, people find solace in their spiritual life. This can mean attending church, temple, or mosque, or simply reading spiritual teachings. Some people like to meditate. If you are actively involved in a faith community, you will probably find people willing to offer support, child-sitting, or services to your family.

7. Whether you have a partner or are a single parent, do not skimp on time spent talking to other adults. You can even teach your children the phrase "adult time" to let them know that there are some things that are family matters and others that just involve the adults in the family or family network.

I Wonder, I Wish, I Worry, and What Is . . .

Every parent raising a child has questions, wishes, worries, and observations. You deserve an opportunity to freely explore your own feelings and thoughts no matter what they are. And your child needs you to be a keen observer of what makes him happy. The first three "w's" are what you as a parent think and feel about the development of your deaf child and the fourth "w" is using your child's progress, self-satisfaction, complaints, and joys as markers for decision-making.

Here follows an outline of what kinds of things fall under the headings of the four "w's."

I Wonder: Here are some of the questions a parent has throughout his deaf child's life.

- I wonder if my child is developmentally disabled?

- I wonder what kinds of schools they have for deaf children?

- I wonder what communication mediums are used with deaf children?

- I wonder how he will meet and date other deaf children?

- I wonder if I should consider sending him to a residential school?

- I wonder what kind of careers deaf people can expect to have?

Don't let these questions roll around in your head, make you ashamed, or keep you up at night. Note them, write them down, and talk, talk, talk. For your concrete questions, ask people who are knowledgeable in the field of deafness. For the questions that seem silly to you, ask trusted friends first. Next, find people knowledgeable about deafness (another parent, a deaf adult, or a concerned professional).

I Wish: These are the secret thoughts that parents have from before their children are born and throughout their children's lives. They emerge from the parents' experiences, upbringing, exposure to other deaf people, and natural sense of the future. It is normal for wishes to go beyond what is observed— this is the stuff that daydreams are made of. And there are levels of wishes— there are the ones that are always spoken, "I want the best for my child," and the ones that parents are ashamed of or that are very deep inside of them and unacknowledged, "I wish my child were hearing, then there wouldn't be all this trouble," or, "I hope my child never leaves me," or, "I hope he doesn't date other deaf people." There is not a person alive who doesn't have disturbing thoughts and wishes that run contrary to who they consider themselves to be.

Acknowledge these wishes as just that—wishes, hopes, dreams. When they support the child towards self-satisfaction, confidence, and happiness, they are worth enacting. When your child is struggling, unhappy, or defeated, these wishes should remain wishes not actions or plans. Wishes are things that are best discussed (at least initially) in a confidential place with other parents, with a spouse or trusted friend, or with a mental health professional who is bound by a confidential oath.

Share with your child some of your previous wishes and dreams and that how, through time, you've come to understand and accept things more realistically. "You know, I sometimes used to wish I didn't have to learn sign language because it was so difficult, but now I am happy we communicate so much better" or "I wanted you to get a good educational experience, but I guess that school wasn't the right fit for you." Remember to add that sometimes making the right decision takes time. Be sure that these wishes do not paint the child as "faulty." Examples of wishes only to be shared with other trusted adults are, "I wish I'd never had children" or "I wish my child were hearing" or "I hope that an operation will make him just like a hearing person."

I Worry: Sometimes it seems like one of the job requirements of parents is worrying. Worrying certainly serves the purpose of thinking through situations and contemplating difficulties. Examples of useful and helpful worrying are: thinking about your child's safety while with a sitter, planning for emergencies, worrying about the health of your child, teaching him good nutrition habits, and worrying about your child's isolation and seeking out social contacts for him. As you can see, worries based on the child's needs result in useful plans of action.

But that's not the way that all worries go. Often worries are constant companions to a parent and are unfounded in fact, unconnected to positive action. Parents of deaf children often worry about their child's safety. This is vital and understandable. The key, however, is to teach a child how to keep himself safe. In other words, if you are worried about your child riding a bike, teach him how to use his visual skills, supply him with extra mirrors, and have him ride in safe areas.

It is often useful to turn a worry into a wonder. What this means is taking a worry, "I worry that he will get hurt on a bike" and develop questions: "I wonder what can be done so that he can ride a bike like others?" "I wonder what other deaf children do?" "I wonder if a deaf adult can tell me what they did as a child?" In this way you can find solutions to the worries and find out new information to pass along to your child.

What Is: This includes your observations of your child, your assessment of his happiness, the discussions you have with him to get his point of view, the observations of his teachers, and the end results of plans. "What is" must always be balanced with what you wonder, wish, and worry. If you wonder whether you should send your child to a residential school, then observe his social contacts, talk to his teachers, and ask him what he would like. If you wish that your child had more deaf friends but he associates primarily with hearing children, then observe his interactions, ask him about his friendships and his wishes. And if you worry that your child will become prematurely interested in sexual exploration, then notice his interests, the groups of friends he has, his behavior in school, and ask him what he knows about the topic.

What we have described here is much easier to write about than to do. But you can use this as a guideline for how to approach your deaf child's development. Always remember to discuss issues with your child to solicit his point of view. He, too, will have wonders ("Can I go to college?"), wishes ("I wish my family were all-deaf"), worries ("I don't think the store clerk will understand me"), and what is ("I guess I can be the manager of the team if I don't like to participate in sports"). Your child may have some valuable insights to offer as well as his own misconceptions. For example, some deaf children believe that in adulthood or adolescence they will become hearing. Such a wish or wonder requires clarification and, of course, exposure to positive images of successful deaf adults.

Strong Emotions Everywhere

The hearing family that includes a deaf child must make a communication decision for their family that allows the deaf child to be a part of the daily family workings. You, as parents, will undoubtedly meet avid supporters of oral-only, signing, cued speech, and other modes of communicating. The strong emotions of ASL supporters have been born from deaf individuals who may have experienced years of frustration and negative feelings related to being forced to speak. These people often tell of the relief, the gains, and the pride they feel when using American Sign Language in the Deaf community. The oral-only (and cued speech) supporters are predominantly hearing individuals who believe that in order for the deaf child to excel he must learn to speak.

Amid the flurry of learning about deafness, parents can easily become overwhelmed by these opinions. Parents may experience feelings of confusion, depression, isolation, guilt, and impotence.

Throughout a deaf child's life, hearing parents will probably have to cope with many difficult feelings; for instance, when a parent is shocked by the child's deafness, when the child does not live up to a parent's expectations, when a parent continually hopes that the child will be able to act hearing, or when the extended family and larger community proves insensitive or unkind. Often these feelings recede and emerge again at different developmental times in the child's life.

Some extended families are invaluable in raising a deaf child, while others add to the pressures of the parents by criticizing, avoiding, or demeaning a parent.

Filing Away

When we are confronted with strong opinions we can become confused and lose a sense of ourselves. As a parent of a deaf child, you may be told what you are doing is wrong, you may be forcefully told to use a certain communication system, and you may be given erroneous information. Whatever the case, you will have to make sense of these opinions yourself.

When a person gives you information in a very emotional way or with great force, try not to become reactive. Don't respond emotionally or become overwhelmed and defensive. Listen and file. Take note of what the person says and how that makes you feel and why. Reflect on how they came to have their beliefs and how that relates to your family's and child's situation.

If you can file their opinions mentally, do so. If not, take a moment right after the interaction to make some notes on paper and literally make files of opinions, ideas, and suggestions. Later, when you have some more objectivity or after you have gathered numerous opinions, read over your notes and see what this teaches you about you and your child's situation.

You may discover that you become overwhelmed when presented with a particular kind of person. You may see that deaf adults have similar experiences. You may learn from other parents who have circumstances similar to or very different from your own. When you meet parents, deaf adults, or professionals you trust, then ask them to help you better understand these strong opinions you have encountered.

DEVELOPING GOOD COMMUNICATION

Since communication is a vital ingredient in raising any child and is particularly tricky when raising a deaf child, we are devoting not just this section but an entire chapter to the subject of developing good communication in your family. In chapter 5 we will focus on more specific communication choices that families face (signing, speechreading, cued speech, etc.) and how to integrate them into the daily life of your family. At this juncture we would like to offer general communication techniques for improving expressive and listening skills between you and your deaf child.

Effective Listening

Effective listening requires that you convey to your child a willingness to allow feelings to be expressed without lecturing or judging. It means listening with your eyes, ears, and heart; listening with interest to your child's thoughts and feelings. This approach communicates to your child that his thoughts and feelings are important to you when expressed in an acceptable fashion, while unacceptable expression (misbehavior) is not useful.

When we use the word "listening," it includes visual and/or auditory attention. In order to attend, acknowledge, and understand what is being said by a deaf child, it is imperative that "listening" occurs with the eyes.

This is not a natural skill for hearing people who have learned since childhood to rely much more heavily on their ears than their eyes. Therefore, you may need to retrain yourself to listen to your deaf child with your eyes.

Even if your child has strong speech skills and can be understood without your looking at him, he most likely needs to look at others to understand what is being said. By making eye contact with your child when he expresses himself, you "model" (see pgs. 22-24) listening attentively. In addition, you decrease the possibility that your child will experience you as disinterested, which can lead to an escalation of difficult feelings for him (frustration, loneliness, shame) and undesirable behavior (interrupting, demanding, crying).

How Parents Can Use Effective Listening

Effective listening can be achieved by always turning your head, finding your child's eyes, and concentrating on what his entire body is saying (see nonverbal communications on pgs. 26-27). It also involves clarifying messages and repeating messages in your child's words with his expressed feelings. If you don't get the message, ask for clarification by having your child repeat himself. Communication becomes very trying when hearing people do not understand what a deaf person has said but act as if they do. Misunderstandings between parent and child can be avoided when you are vigilant about clearly understanding your child's statements regardless of the circumstances. In return, your child should learn and practice asserting himself by insisting upon understanding what others say.

Listening means understanding and acknowledging others' thoughts and feelings. To do this you can become a sportscaster for your child's ideas,

Examples of Effective Listening

• • • • • • •

1. "I did not see what you said, come closer and say it again."

2. "I hear you saying that you're not tired at 8:30."

3. "I want to make sure I heard you correctly. You said . . ."

4. "Sometimes I miss what you say, and I want to know what you are trying to say, can you repeat yourself, please?"

5. "I guess you're too angry to talk right now."

6. To a child throwing a tantrum, "I understand that you feel angry, but I cannot accept that behavior . . ."

7. "Sorry, everyone was talking at once. Did you understand or do people need to repeat it and be reminded of our communication rules?"

8. "You said you wish your whole family was deaf—I wonder if you are feeling left out?"

thoughts, and feelings by giving a "play by play" account of what he is saying. By repeating what your child has expressed, you help your child to identify feelings and reassure him that you are listening. This minimizes struggles and opens the door for future discussions.

You may find that this technique is very difficult to use when your child is angrily expressing himself or if his requests are unreasonable. Keep in mind that when you listen with genuine consideration to his feelings, you are modeling for your child how to take part in a two-way conversation.

Sometimes a familiar gesture or phrase indicating that you understand what he might think or feel will provide comfort to your child. Of course, there will be times when you are at a loss for understanding your child's behavior. At these times, continue to ask fact- or feeling-finding questions to strengthen your ability to communicate with your child.

Family Council

The family council is a regularly scheduled meeting (usually weekly) during which all family members follow a format to update one another, share concerns, solve problems, recognize accomplishments, and make family plans.

Setting aside a special time on a weekly basis to sit down and talk and listen to one another is a comforting break from hectic routines. Such a meeting can be used to enhance aspects emphasized in this book, such as cooperation, democratic team spirit, supportiveness, and communication.

How Parents Can Use the Family Council

The family council is an excellent tool for setting up a clear and organized communication process in your family. This meeting can keep your deaf child updated on any incidental auditory information he may have missed, such as an overheard telephone call, an announcement on the radio, or a conversation held in an adjacent room. A family council meeting is useful for the deaf child who has a hectic transportation schedule or is in a residential school.

The topics discussed at these meetings can include solving problems, distributing chores, reviewing family responsibilities, sharing appreciation for one another, and planning family activities. It is very important that everyone understand that criticizing or disregarding one person's ideas is unacceptable. Everyone must feel safe to express personal feelings.

In the early stages, the meetings will be generated by the parents, but all members should share in the responsibility for running and contributing to the meetings. You can rotate the jobs of chairperson, secretary, and all other "officers." The meetings should be regularly scheduled and operate under rules agreed upon by everyone in advance. Rules should clearly and consistently prohibit yelling, blaming others, excluding others from the conversations, and speaking out of turn. One way to control turn-taking is to use a stuffed sock or soft ball to identify whose turn it is to speak. Only the person holding the ball is allowed to speak, and when that person is finished, he passes it to the next person who wishes to speak. This will help your deaf child keep track of the conversation.

Before the first meeting, you must decide on a mode of communication (see chapter 5) that allows all family members to be full and active participants. In addition to agreeing on a mode of communication, all family members should adhere to the communication techniques described in this chapter, such as mutual respect, empathy, modeling, "I" messages, and effective listening. Everyone should be familiar with these techniques in order to determine which best suit your family's style.

To ensure clear communication during the meetings, you can use a large board or piece of paper to list the agenda items for the meeting. You may even want to post a piece of paper in the house with the heading "Family Council Agenda" and the upcoming date. This allows all family members to jot down topics as they think of them. Your family meetings will be

---

Examples of How Parents Can Begin the Family Council

• • • • • • •

1. "Today's family council meeting will cover the topics of homework, Dad's late work nights, and what we want to do this weekend."

2. "Remember—no yelling, ignoring, blaming, or speaking out during someone else's turn to speak."

3. "Alex is the boss of the meeting today, which means Alex gets to go first. Alex, what is our agenda today?"

4. "Since Patty is away all week at school, let's use a portion of our meeting to do a weekly family update with her."

5. "We need to have an emergency family council meeting to discuss some urgent news." (This can be fun and exciting news or it can be a family crisis such as an illness or death.)

---

more effective and more fun if everyone abides by the ground rules set ahead of time.

"I" Messages: My View, My Feelings, My Opinion

An "I" message is a nonjudgmental and nonblaming form of communication in which an individual conveys his feelings about a situation. In an "I" message, a person takes responsibility for his point of view and does not speak for another person even if he knows the other person well.

Because the deaf child is bombarded with daily communication challenges, he could benefit by early training in stating his point of view and his needs. This is the foundation of assertion skills. Practice "I" messages by starting sentences with the following phrases, "I think . . .", "In my opinion . . .", "My view is . . .", "That made me feel . . .", or "I agree/disagree . . .".

In a neutral situation, a person using "I" messages practices stating likes/dislikes, opinions, and noting when he agrees or disagrees with someone else. He also practices developing an individual perspective and not "following the crowd." The deaf child who frequently misunderstands communication might develop a habit of nodding, pretending to understand, and following what others do to avoid being identified as not understanding.

In a problem situation, the person who feels discomfort with another's behavior is identified as the "owner" of the opinion, as opposed to the owner of the behavior. This means that he is responsible for sharing his thoughts and feelings about how a behavior causes his discomfort.

When the owner of the opinion expresses his thoughts and feelings in a non-accusatory manner, the owner of the behavior may be more willing to listen and to confront his part in it. When parents use "I" messages to describe how a child's behavior affects them, they show that they, too, have feelings, needs, and limits.

How Parents Can Use "I" Messages

When using this technique in your family to deal with problem situations, follow these three easy steps: First, label the behavior that is causing you discomfort; second, describe the effect it has on you; and, third, share with your family members how you feel about it. The deaf child benefits greatly from having a step-by-step process for stating his complaints. Practice using "I" messages in neutral situations to teach your child that describing a point of view or feelings does not have to occur only during conflict or under stressful conditions.

Most importantly, state the facts as you see them, without blaming others. You could say, for example, "When you wipe your dirty feet on the car seat it becomes stained and I feel angry." At first it may feel useless and awkward using statements such as these, rather than simply alerting the child to his bad behavior—"You're acting like an animal. Stop it or else!"

Using "I" messages instead of pointing a finger at your child and giving attention to the behavior decreases defensiveness and allows for further discussion and problem-solving. Over time you will find that "I" messages become more natural.

When you consider using "I" messages, think about how you respond to statements which blame you for your behavior. When you are told, "you better, you will, you are," etc., your first reaction is probably, "not me!" You naturally become defensive when you feel attacked or confronted by your weaknesses and misdeeds. On the other hand, when a problem is brought to your attention by a person who "owns" his feelings regarding it, you are less likely to feel judged and more likely to listen and to try to change rather than argue your position.

Modeling

Parental modeling is a lifelong process of teaching your child through personal demonstration. Messages get transmitted through our actions regardless of whether we are aware of them or not. The child of an engineer may learn

Examples of How to Use "I" Messages

• • • • • • •

1. "It makes me feel great when you say thank you and please."

2. "I felt frightened when you ran across the street like that. I got angry because you might have gotten hurt."

3. "I felt frustrated when you fell back to sleep after I woke you two times this morning."

4. "I know that you said you were sorry, but I am still losing my patience when you push me to get my attention."

sophisticated Lego™ construction from his father and may also learn from Dad to behave poorly when his constructions don't turn out to be perfect. This child learns a skill and a personal trait from his father, which obviously affects his behavior.

Think of yourself as constantly performing for your child in a picture show entitled "This Is How You Are Supposed to Act." While your deaf child may be a keen observer, he may not fully understand the context, reasons, and purpose of your behavior without an explanation. For example, imagine riding in the car with your children and hearing a news bulletin about car-jacking. Anxiously and swiftly, you lock your door and instruct others to do the same. Your hearing child may ask, "What's a car-jacking, Mom?" and you respond. In all of this your deaf child only sees a flurry of action and no context.

The parent of a deaf child must always ask, "Does my child understand the reasons for my behavior?" This sounds tedious and certainly cannot be done one hundred percent of the time. However, the more you can interject explanations, the more your child can understand how behaviors are related to causes and contexts. In the above example, you could wait until you stop at a red light and turn to your deaf child to explain, "The radio said many cars have been stolen; that is why I asked you to lock the doors; understand?"

Modeling (with interjected explanations for your deaf child when necessary) offers an active blueprint for your deaf child's behavior; but consistent use is difficult because, as humans, we make mistakes daily. Fortunately, our children learn as much from how we handle our mistakes as they learn from our more noble behaviors. Be sure that your child understands why you consider something a mistake. You may need to explain your intent, goal, or a rule that you broke in order for him to comprehend the whole picture.

How Parents Can Use Modeling

Modeling requires that you pay attention to the messages that your behavior communicates to your child. There are essentially two ways parents model these messages to their children. The first entails taking stock of your beliefs and values, such as being on time, saying "thank you," and standing up for what you believe in, and then determining how well your own behavior supports these beliefs and values.

The second is a process in which a parent identifies problem behaviors and then demonstrates (models) how those behaviors can be corrected. For instance, if your child has difficulty eating healthful foods, you might verbalize your own desires for junk food and then show how you handle these desires. For example, "Boy, I could really go for a double chocolate shake, but that isn't good for me so maybe I'll make a fruit shake instead; would you like one, too?" Notice that you shared with your child the internal dialogue that influenced your behavior. By sharing this, you make your child aware that you, too, have impulses that you must curb.

Support and teach your deaf child to question the reasons for your behavior. This will make clarification a team effort and improve his assertion skills. Take care not to silence your child. If you find yourself in a situation where you cannot immediately answer him, repeat the question and ask that you both remember it, "Why the locked doors? Hold onto that until we stop."

Planful Playing

This fun, child-oriented technique is derived from the enjoyable experiences and successes we have had playing with children. There are three types of planful playing—role playing, joining in play, and planned play. Planful playing aims at redirecting your child and teaching him better behavior in a fun, non-threatening manner.

Examples of How to Use Modeling
● ● ● ● ● ● ●

1. "I'm going to sit here and cool down so I won't yell."

2. To a child who doesn't eat vegetables: "These carrots are so crunchy and taste great dipped in a little salad dressing."

3. To a child who has trouble sharing: "Would you like to share my soda, I love sharing things with you."

As described in chapter 1, play is a form of communication and a window into our children's thoughts, feelings, and actions. When you join your deaf child in play, you can practice communication strategies like asking for clarification, repeating suggestions, and noting confusions that occur. Play time is a "child's" time, and he will be more open to constructive communication during play than during heated discussions.

How Parents Can Use Planful Playing

When your child invites you to play with him, seize the opportunity to explore issues relevant to solving daily challenges through play. Doll-house play, coloring, and make-believe play can uncover many important aspects of your child's thinking and give you opportunities to introduce new helpful ideas. You might join your child's play scene and interject a few new ways to resolve conflict between two angry stuffed animals. Help him put a frightened doll to bed. Have the deaf bear talk to the hearing bear. Confront some big, ugly monsters. In this play you learn much about your child's internal conflicts and assist him in managing them. Use the play later as a reference, "Remember how we put the bear to bed—he needed lots of hugs. Do you need that, too?"

Planned play is a technique in which you create fun situations to help your child improve his behavior. For example, play "beat the clock" at clean-up time—"Can you pick up your toys before the big hand reaches the twelve?" This will draw your child's interest to compete against the clock rather than competing for control with you.

Rather than nagging or threatening, you can playfully get your message across to your child. For example, an impromptu charade or mime might well illustrate your request for him to take the garbage out or you will "keel over and suffocate from the smell of the garbage." Or pin a fun note onto a misplaced item: "Help, I'm lost! Take me to my hamper home with the rest of my stinky friends."

Role-playing is a dramatic technique in which two or more persons act out assigned roles. It allows your child to practice problem-solving and look at himself from another point of view. You and your child can role-play a specific problem he recently had with a friend or a new situation he may encounter. By recreating an actual situation, your child gets first-hand practice in dealing with an issue. Misunderstandings and miscommunications can be decreased, allowing for deeper comprehension.

Have your child practice his new skills by acting out a problem situation. Ask your child to play a role other than his own so that he may experience the situation from another perspective. Through this safe medium, parents can direct these "mini-plays" and engage children in confronting fears, exploring personal difficulties, and examining their own and others' behaviors.

Examples of Planful Playing

● ● ● ● ● ● ●

1. To a child who fights with other children: "Let's practice solving an argument. You pretend to be playing by yourself and I'll come and bother you."

2. To a child who cannot explain why he is sad, "Let's draw a picture together of what makes us sad . . ."

3. A sign taped to your forehead says, "Beware! Mom's got a big headache! Pick up your stuff before she explodes!"

4. When a parent is in a hurry, "Look! The floor has turned to hot coals. Everything will burn if we don't pick it up fast!"

5. "OK, are the dolls in the play house deaf or hearing?"

Nonverbal Communication

A parent lifts his eyebrows and frowns slightly as his child picks up a breakable item. No words or sign language was used and yet the child knows immediately that he is doing something worrisome. Nonverbal communication (meaning not using vocal or signed language forms) is an integral part of communication, though it varies between cultures and families.

Nonverbal communication includes facial expressions, body movements, posture, eye contact, pupil dilation, clothing, or even a locked door. Nonverbal communication often reveals our true feelings. You may be telling your child that you are not nervous about him riding the school bus for the first time, but your shaking hands and uncertain gaze say something different. Since facial expressions and body language are essential elements of visual communication, it is vital that parents of deaf children examine and shape their nonverbal style of communicating.

How to Use Nonverbal Communication

When you communicate a message to your deaf child, assess whether your nonverbal actions are clear and support your feelings and values. You may want to establish a few consistent nonverbal signals for your face or body that represent the same message to your child. For example, folding your arms, pursing your lips, and crunching your brows will always mean to your child, "I don't like what you are doing." While a thumbs up, huge smile, and uplifted eyebrows can mean, "I am thrilled with your behavior."

Further, examine your child's nonverbal communication and attempt to label messages that seem to convey the same thing. Be sure to pay attention to your child if he disagrees with your interpretation. By understanding your child's nonverbal messages in a more detailed manner, you can plan your response.

Finally, keep in mind the importance of nonverbal cues and body language for deaf people. Consider the messages deaf people might pick up from these. Experiment with being more animated when you are speaking with a young deaf child (ages three to six). For this child use big gestures and consistent facial expressions to emphasize a message. As the child grows older, focus more on the details of your facial expressions and body positioning/posture.

If your child and family use sign language, be sure to become familiar with the various meanings of facial expressions and gestures. Many misunderstandings can be a result of not using or understanding the difference in linguistic rules between ASL and English.

Visual Aids and Assistive Devices

We have lumped fluorescent markers and teletype telephone devices together in this chapter because both can help parents deliver a message or assist a child in becoming more independent and responsible. Making the world more understandable to a deaf child is done by capitalizing on his visual and tactile capabilities.

Examples of Nonverbal Communication

• • • • • • •

A good way to examine your nonverbal communication can be done by looking into a body-length mirror and going through dialogues and feeling-packed conversations you would have with your deaf child. Look closely at your facial expressions and body language. Ask yourself if your expressions are effectively communicating your message.

1. Observe your eyes—do they look questioning? Stern? Confused? Pleading?

2. Observe your shoulders—are they slumped? Rigid? Pulled up to your ears?

3. Observe your posture—are you leaning towards your child? Away? Are your arms touching him?

4. Observe your signing or speech quality—is it harsh? Over-exaggerated? Hard to follow? Choppy?

Visual Aids

Visual aids are anything that can enhance a communicative message. They can be bold, eye-catching bulletin boards, calendars, symbols, signs, drawings, toys, or any item that stresses the message through vision. Teachers, politicians, advertisers, and even the weather reporters depend on visual aids to effectively transmit their message.

Parents of deaf children can overlook visual techniques since they are not a common way to communicate with a hearing child. For a deaf child, visual aids make communication clearer and easier to understand, and can assist you in determining whether your deaf child fully understands a concept.

How Parents Can Use Visual Aids

When you have an important message to communicate to your deaf child—*think visual!* Say to yourself, "How can I make this message visually accessible to my deaf child?" Hearing people need to be creative in thinking visually when communicating. Many of this book's communication techniques and play activities turn auditory instructions into kid-friendly visual experiences. "The Greenlight/Redlight Diet" on page 145 is a good example of a visually stimulating activity that uses color-coded labels (red, yellow, and green) on food items to help children remember which foods are healthful and which are not.

Assistive Devices

Special devices can make a world of difference to the smooth running of your family. Lights that flash when the phone or doorbell rings, someone speaks, or when an alarm clock goes off can be easily purchased and installed in your home. Of course, the teletype telephone device (TTY) is a must in making phone service available to a deaf child. There are many obvious benefits to having assistive devices in your home, such as enabling your child to wake up for school or to know when someone is at the door. The following is a list of companies that sell assistive devices for deaf people.

Gallaudet University Bookstore
800 Florida Avenue NE
Washington, DC 20002–3695
1–800–451–1073 (V/TTY); 1–202–651–5489 (Fax)

Harris Communications
6541 City West Parkway
Eden Prairie, MN 55344–3248
1–800–825–6758 (V); 1–800–825–9187 (TTY); 1–612–946–0924 (Fax)

Nationwide Flashing Signal Systems, Inc.
8120 Fenton Street
Silver Spring, MD 20910
1–301–589–6671 (V); 1–301–589–6670 (TTY); 1–301–589–5153 (Fax)

Examples of Visual Aids

· · · · · · ·

1. Remind your child that he has soccer practice every Saturday at 2:00 by drawing a big soccer ball on the calendar and writing the practice time on every Saturday in the month.

2. Put big, red paper X's on cabinets, doors, and belongings you don't want your younger deaf child to touch. Explain to your child what these red X's mean.

3. Use an hourglass timer to show your child how much time he has to get ready, finish a chore, or get into bed.

4. Charts with pictures or words can indicate duties or chores. For younger children you can use pictures with velcro on the back to change chores, lists, and graphs.

5. Use symbols to indicate good behavior/results (stars, smiley faces, checks, stickers).

6. Photographs can clarify a message. Use a photo to explain steps to a process, identify feelings, clarify chores, capture special events or successes, and create a running log of a particular subject.

Potomac Technology
One Church Street, Suite 402
Rockville, MD 20850–4158
1–800–433–2838 (V/TTY) to order a catalog

Weitbrecht Communications, Inc.
2656 29th Street, Suite 205
Santa Monica, CA 90405
1–800–233–9130 (V/TTY) to order a catalog

How Parents Can Use Assistive Devices

Consider these devices as tools that allow your child to feel competent, safe, and worthy. With a TTY, the child can call and answer the phone; with a flashing alarm, he can be responsible for waking himself; with a visual fire alarm, he can learn and practice safety procedures; and with a doorbell light, he can be aware of guests and greet them if he so chooses. These are daily events that need not be a mystery to the deaf child.

Examples of Using Assistive Devices

• • • • • • •

1. "Would you please call Grandma for me and ask her for Mrs. Smith's phone number?"

2. "OK, so remember your alarm is set for 7:00 and it is your responsibility to wake yourself up like we practiced."

3. "Now, let's review again what to do in case of an emergency."

4. "Who is at the door, Dominic?"

SPECIAL SUPPORT SERVICES AND LEGAL KNOWLEDGE

While raising a deaf child, parents often feel isolated and without support. Whereas, many parents support one another by sharing experiences, successes, and failures, often a parent of a hearing child does not have the same experiences as a parent of a deaf child.

The following resources are offered to specifically help you with many aspects of parenting your deaf child. In this section we also discuss supportive services. Feelings of loneliness and confusion can be eased by connecting with other parents who have needs similar to yours and with professionals who can help your family.

Support Services

One of the most comforting supports for a parent of a deaf child is the company of another parent of a deaf child. No one better understands the daily life of a family with a deaf child than another parent in the same situation. Depending upon the state in which you live, there are support groups and parent organizations that will give you important information, advice, and companionship in raising your deaf child. Many organizations have annual conferences, workshops, and classes in sign language.

How to Find Support Services in Your Area

The following national organizations offer supportive information to parents of deaf children. We've also included the address of NICD (National Information Center on Deafness) which serves as an information clearinghouse for deafness-related issues:

National Information Center on Deafness
Gallaudet University
800 Florida Avenue NE
Washington, DC 20002–3695
1–202–651–5051 (V); 1–202–651–5052 (TTY)

American Society for Deaf Children
814 Thayer Ave.
Silver Spring, MD 20910
V/TTY: 1–800–942–ASDC

John Tracy Clinic
806 W. Adams Blvd.
Los Angeles, CA 90007
1–213–748–5481 (V)
1–213–747–2924 (TTY)
1–800–522–4582 (V/TTY)

Professional Services

In this section, professional services are described by the terms "therapy," "counseling," or "psychotherapy." Parents may seek help for their child's or family's problems after they have continually tried to overcome difficulties and have had unsatisfactory results. Other parents might turn to therapists to help them process feelings and to cope with differences in their family.

Seeking therapy does not mean that you have failed. On the contrary, it is a very thoughtful decision that shows you believe there is something that still can be done to solve your difficulties. If you have decided to seek therapy, it is vital that you take the time to find a professional who is specifically trained in deaf-related issues, particularly if your child uses sign language. This may prove difficult, but it is not impossible.

It is much easier to find such a professional if you live in or near a big city or near deaf organizations, schools, or clubs. However, if you live in a rural or lightly populated area, you may have more difficulty. If you've thoroughly explored your area and are not successful in finding a therapist who specializes in working with deaf individuals and their families, you may have to do the next-best thing. This would mean finding a therapist who is flexible and willing to learn about your child's needs.

This therapist should consult with a professional who has ample knowledge about the communication needs of deaf individuals, use of interpreters, developmental needs of deaf individuals and their families, how communication affects the family system, impact of having deaf/hearing mixtures in families, and resources for deaf people. The therapist may need to consult through long-distance phone calls. Lastly, an interpreter would be vital for family meetings, even if the family has relatively smooth communication. The therapist needs to communicate with the deaf child and no family member should play an interpreting role.

Who Does Therapy with Deaf Children and Their Families?

The mental health professionals described below should be trained in working with deaf people or should have attended a school specializing in servicing or understanding deaf people. A professional must be able to communicate with the deaf child in order to provide treatment for him.

Psychiatrists (*medical doctors*): While psychiatrists most often work directly with families and individuals in therapy, they also are called upon simply to prescribe medications for those who need it. Though some psychiatric nurses are approved to dispense medications under supervision, psychiatrists most frequently prescribe psychoactive medications. When looking for a psychiatrist for your child, be sure to find one who works with children. Of all of the listed professionals, psychiatrists who specialize in working with deaf people are few and far between.

Psychologists (*Ph.D.*): A psychologist is not a medical doctor but has a doctorate degree in psychology. Psychologists provide direct service (group, individual, and family psychotherapy) in a number of settings. In addition, they can administer tests to children for IEP's or to help diagnose strengths and weaknesses. Some psychologists are specialists in areas such as neuropsychology or learning disabilities. If your child needs to be tested, seek out a professional who can communicate with him and who understands the possible differences between testing deaf children and hearing children.

Mental Health Counselors (*masters degree in counseling or education*): This professional can generally be found in schools, private practice, or in community mental health centers and can do direct treatment (group, family, and individual). Again, seek out a person who can address the deaf-related issues previously described.

Clinical Social Workers (*masters degree in clinical social work*): This professional constitutes the majority of mental health professionals found in outpatient clinics. He can perform direct service functions for hospitals, schools, community mental health centers, and in private practice. Like the psychologist, mental health counselor, and family therapist, he might have specialized training or experience. Seek out individuals who are competent in deaf-related issues and communication, in working with children, and in family issues.

Psychiatric Nurses (*registered nurses who have a masters degree in psychiatric nursing*): This professional is generally found in psychiatric hospitals but also works in outpatient settings. He may treat individuals, families, and groups and, under the supervision of a psychiatrist, may have special qualifications to prescribe psychiatric medications.

Marriage and Family Therapists (qualified specialists in family and marriage counseling, most with a masters or doctorate degree): While many professionals described above do family therapy, marriage and family therapists have specific training and certification in family work. Be sure that an interpreter is present for your child if necessary. The family therapist, even if fluent in sign language, should not be the interpreter for family meetings.

School Counselors (masters or doctorate degree in the counseling field): These professionals do individual or group work in the school or provide consultation to teachers and parents. Some are qualified to do school testing. Obviously, this counselor should be able to communicate with his deaf clientele.

Rehabilitation Counselors (masters degree in education and rehabilitation): This person is often important as a deaf child reaches adolescence. In many states, there are professionals who specialize in deaf rehabilitation or vocational counseling and help (through guidance and funds) the deaf individual actualize his goals in college, vocational training, or through on-site work programs.

To find a therapist who works with deaf children and their families, you can:

1. Ask your child's teacher, principal, or school counselor for a professional in your area;

2. Call a local university or college that has deaf-related programs for educators, professionals, and/or therapists; or

3. Check recognized state and national associations for deaf people. Most have lists of members who are qualified and sometimes specialize in a specific problem area.

What Should We Expect from Counseling/Therapy?

Sometimes you will seek extra support for your child or family and at other times recommendations for therapy might be made by professionals already involved with your family. Explore the reasons for any recommendations made to you by teachers, evaluators, or pediatricians. Often people working with your child will make recommendations for counseling/therapy based on the nature of the difficulty as compared to similar experiences with other children.

Mental health/rehabilitation professionals are bound by a confidentiality commitment. This means that what you discuss with them is strictly private unless you give written approval for them to talk with other individuals outside of their agency or if the child is a danger to himself or others. These professionals, however, will discuss cases within their agencies for supervisory reasons. If your child is being seen individually, the therapist cannot tell you specifically what your child has said unless your child gives approval. This does not mean that you will be kept in the dark, but rather that you will receive more general and synthesized information and updates.

At initial meetings, the professional might ask many personal and sensitive questions. These questions may seem unrelated to the immediate problem. However, a professional meeting you for the first time needs to know about your child's and family's history to put the problems into perspective. Tell the therapist if you don't like the manner or type of question.

A therapist/counselor might treat a family, an individual, or a few members of the family. This depends on what kind of problem is presented and what the parents and therapist negotiate. This can change over time.

Communication clarity should be a priority in counseling sessions. The therapist should be able to communicate with the deaf and hearing members of your family and utilize an interpreter when the deaf child cannot follow the group conversation. The therapist is the monitor of family meetings and cannot do that properly if he is asked to interpret. Therefore, a therapist should not interpret family meetings. Any facility which receives federal funds is mandated to provide an interpreter for the deaf child to have equal access to communication.

If your child is in school counseling, you can expect to be contacted if any concerns surface. The school counselor might have a regular system of updating parents. Talk with your child's school counselor to determine how you will keep one another updated. Be aware that the school counselor is bound by the same rules of confidentiality and can share general updates but cannot tell you specifically what your child said without the child's permission, unless it relates to safety issues.

In outpatient therapy/counseling you will make an agreement with the counselor to work on certain issues. Depending on the circumstances, the counseling may take a few months or it may be done over a longer period of time. In an effort to save money, insurance companies are limiting how long people may go to counseling. They generally will approve two- to three-month increments.

Usually counseling takes place weekly for fifty-minute meetings. The meetings are sometimes longer if the whole family is involved. As the problem lessens in intensity, treatment may be reduced in frequency and length of meetings, or ended completely. This is usually determined by a combination of opinions of the therapist, clients, or insurance companies.

Sometimes a therapist will suggest another evaluation or consultation from a psychiatrist, psychologist, or supervisor. He may want a specific type of evaluation for certain problem areas.

If you are dissatisfied, you should ask questions of the counselor/therapist. If you feel that this person is not adequately serving your family, you have a right to seek another professional. However, take the time to negotiate with the professional first. In therapy, the difficult feelings that arise might influence you to want to end treatment.

To find organizations that serve deaf and hard of hearing people in your area, consider contacting the National Information Center on Deafness (see pg. 31); buy the book, *Mental Health Services for Deaf People* (Barbara A. Willigan and Susan J. King, eds., University of California, 1992), which can be ordered through the Gallaudet University Bookstore; or get a TTY directory for your area. *The National Telephone Directory for TDD Users* (Telecommunications for the Deaf, Inc., published annually) may also be a handy resource to obtain from the Gallaudet University Bookstore.

The following is a list of organizations that serve all populations:

American Association for Marriage and Family Therapy
1717 K Street, N.W., Suite 407
Washington, DC 20026

American Family Therapy Association
2550 M Street, N.W., Suite 275
Washington, DC 20037

American Psychiatric Association
1700 18th Street, N.W.
Washington, DC 20009

American Psychological Association
1200 17th Street, N.W.
Washington, DC 20036

National Association of Social Workers
7981 Eastern Ave.
Silver Spring, MD 20910

National Register of Health Service Providers In Psychology
1200 17th Street, N.W.
Washington, DC 20036

Legal Rights of Deaf People

In the past few decades, state and federal legislatures have passed laws supporting the rights of deaf and hard of hearing individuals to equal (communication) access. Section 504 of the Rehabilitation Act of 1973, Public Law 94–142 or The Education for all Handicapped Children Act (1975, now the Individuals with Disabilities Education Act [1990]), and the Americans with Disabilities Act (1990) are legal cornerstones for deaf rights.

Section 504 of the Rehabilitation Act of 1973 reads that any facility receiving federal funds must not deny or discriminate against disabled individuals. A deaf person must be considered for a job or school for which he is qualified (and can perform with reasonable accommodation). In most cases, with deaf individuals, equal accessibility usually means the provision of qualified interpreting services, notetakers, aids, modification of alarm and telephone systems, TTYs and volume-controlled telephones, captions for films, and/or audiovisual systems which are sensitive to interpreting needs.

Hospitals, public schools, courts, state and federal agencies, mental health facilities and worksites are all affected by Section 504 if they receive federal funds. If a deaf person or parent of a deaf child believes that the appropriate services are not being provided then a grievance can be filed with the Regional Office for Civil Rights.

The Individuals with Disabilities Education Act was first passed in 1975 as a result of court cases addressing the public education of mentally retarded children. The result is that a deaf child is guaranteed a free and appropriate public education and, if necessary, special education services; the child and his parent's rights are protected; Individual Educational Plans are annually developed and must be in the parent's native language; and an appropriate communication medium for each child should be employed. A parent who is dissatisfied with the program or placement of his child can request a due-process hearing through the school officials.

The Americans with Disabilities Act (ADA) provides legal protections for deaf and disabled people in employment, access to public transportation, public accommodations, and telecommunications. In addition, the law stipulates that all state and local government agencies must make their services accessible to people with disabilities. This includes providing appropriate auxiliary aids (such as interpreters; loop, FM, and infrared systems; television decoders; and TTYs).

Qualified interpreters are a necessity in a number of situations. One can contact the local or state chapter of the Registry of Interpreters for the Deaf (RID) to obtain a list of certified or qualified interpreters. In the case of court or legal proceedings, an interpreter with RID legal skills certification is necessary. An interpreter can be deemed inappropriate by the deaf client, by the interpreter himself, or in certain circumstances by the hearing third party.

Frequently, people who receive Medicaid and who do not own a car are

How to Find Out Your and Your Deaf Child's Legal Rights

● ● ● ● ● ● ●

1. Read the book *Legal Rights: The Guide for Deaf and Hard of Hearing People* (the National Center for Law and Deafness, Gallaudet University Press, 1992).

2. Read the book *The ADA and You: A Guide for Deaf and Hard of Hearing People* (National Academy, Gallaudet University, 1992).

3. Contact the National Center for Law and Deafness, Gallaudet University, 800 Florida Ave., NE, Washington, DC 20002-3695.

4. Contact local advocacy groups for Deaf people in your area by looking in the phone book, a TTY directory, or by contacting the National Information Center on Deafness at Gallaudet University.

eligible for Medicaid transportation to and from medical appointments. Medicaid transportation can usually be used for appointments with pediatricians, audiologists, psychotherapists, and for special evaluations. Check with your local Medicaid/Welfare office to see if your family qualifies and if such a service is available in your area.

Social Security (SSI) benefits may be available to your child and this possibility should be explored through your local Social Security Administration office. When your child is of working age, has been employed for one year, and is out of work, he may be eligible for Social Security Disability Income (SSDI) benefits.

CHAPTER

3

Setting Limits and Avoiding Power Struggles

● ● ● ●

A large part of parenting is knowing how to respond to unacceptable behavior in a constructive fashion. Setting limits is the practice of consistently, yet lovingly, establishing understandable rules and directions for acceptable behavior and the consequences for misbehavior.

When parents define the line between right and wrong or safe and unsafe behavior, they increase their child's sense of predictability and security and make the child's world safer to explore. To that end, this chapter is devoted to a discussion of setting limits on your child's behaviors and experiments without engaging in power struggles.

We designed the parenting methods with two principles in mind: (1) misbehavior in children is a normal episodic event of childhood; and (2) discipline means instruction rather than punishment. Misbehavior does not automatically mean a child is bad. On the contrary, we believe that a child's misbehaviors frequently have a necessary and positive function.

For example, when seven-year-old Tanya resists her parents by refusing to brush her teeth for three days, she is exerting independence, albeit with bad breath. There is no doubt that Tanya is misbehaving and pushing her parents to the limit. However, this mild form of mutiny represents a normal maturational process of childhood. Tanya needs to test her skills in making decisions. Inasmuch as her parents dislike her behavior or disagree with her, Tanya can choose to go against their authority in order to exercise her independence and build her self-confidence. There is no better environment for a child to take risks and test out different ways of behaving than within the safety and unconditional love of her family.

Bear in mind that just as adults and children have different perspectives, so do hearing people and deaf people. A parent's priority might be to straighten the house before guests arrive, while a child is single-mindedly focused upon finding a lost toy car, even if it means tearing apart every closet in the house. Additionally, a deaf child may intensify a struggle if she feels she has little or no power in family discussions or decisions due to communication barriers.

Often parents lock horns with a child over messy rooms, taking out the trash, or doing homework. These time-consuming and energy-wasting struggles often result in tears, anger, and unmade beds. When a child spends most of her time struggling with you, she learns ways of controlling you rather than controlling her behavior (or her emotions). The purpose of avoiding battles with your child is to cause your child to grapple with the real problem.

If boundaries of behavior are defined by clear and predictable consequences, your child will make good behavioral choices more easily. She will test the limits, but in this way she learns and develops independence. When establishing rules and setting limits, take into consideration your child's age, communication needs, and developmental capabilities. A preschooler will have more difficulty managing the urge to have a tantrum than will a seven-year-old.

A child will be more invested in upholding limits and rules if she participates in creating those limits and rules. The hope is that gradually your child will integrate rules for acceptable behavior into her personal thinking, thus moving the locus of control from external rules to internal values.

As noted earlier, we believe the deaf child needs everything the hearing child needs with an additional strong and consistent emphasis on communication. For this reason, many of the parenting techniques defined here continually stress checking for comprehension, offering explanations, using clear and visual structures, and providing consistent and accessible communication. Clarity is essential when the parent is setting rules, teaching consequences, and disciplining.

By our definition, discipline does not mean yelling, demeaning, or (physically or verbally) intimidating a child. Rather, discipline should be viewed as a planned response to a child's behavior for the purpose of instruction. Clear communication will make this a smoother process. Words, concepts, and predictable structures can replace yelling, hitting, and harsh punishments.

Discipline should teach the child self-control, self-respect, and trust. The deaf child who learns and understands rules, consequences, goals, rewards, and how to manage and control her own behaviors is prepared to face all the exciting and difficult challenges of her world.

We have tried to explain each limit-setting technique in a straightforward and easy-to-follow manner. Obviously, no single technique or resource is effective in all cases; therefore, we suggest that you familiarize yourself with a number of parenting methods described in chapters 2–4 so you have a large repertoire to choose from.

Included in the descriptions of parenting methods, we offer specific ways to use and explain them to your deaf child. We have taken into consideration that any parenting techniques (especially limit-setting ones) will not be helpful to you unless they are modified to meet the specific communication needs of families with a deaf child. Our goal is to offer you many different ways to approach parenting your deaf child, while maintaining the priority of clear communication. We hope that some of our ideas can help you prevent difficulties and solve problems with your child in a home atmosphere where good communication prevails, power struggles decrease, and limits provide security.

THE THREE C'S FOR SETTING LIMITS

The three C's for setting limits are calm and clear correction, cooperation, and consistency. These can help you establish limits and avoid a struggle with your child. Although a productive process, making rules involves some level of conflict ("rules are meant to be broken"). But the conflict should not overshadow the provision of safety and structure for the child.

The three C's for limit-setting represent an easy-to-remember system for correcting your child's undesired behavior while reinforcing positive expectations. Each "C" word follows a step-by-step process of approaching your child and clarifying rules, limits, and expectations (calm and clear correction); enlisting your child's help in correcting the behavior (cooperation); and following through on your mutually agreed-upon behavior plans (consistency). By memorizing the three "C" words, you can establish a routine that encourages positive behaviors from your child.

How to Use the Three C's

Calm and Clear Correction
When pointing out an inappropriate behavior to your child, calmly focus on the behavior (not the child) as being unacceptable. Say "I did not like your screaming at the bank" instead of "You were a very, very bad girl at the bank". This approach can reduce a child's defensiveness and make her more open to redirection. You also reduce the chance of undermining her self-esteem.

Communication between hearing parents and a deaf child might result in the parent expressing that something is wrong in order to be expedient. The child may interpret that much more broadly to mean that she, the child, is bad if you don't make the distinction between the behavior and the child for her.

When correcting a child, make sure you are thoroughly understood. In order to ensure understanding, maintain eye contact with your child and use her most comfortable means of communicating. Incorporate communication techniques such as visual aids, planful playing, and nonverbal expressions. After delivering your message, check for comprehension by having her repeat what you stated.

Cooperation

Cooperation means interacting with your child to help her follow the rules and change negative behaviors into positive ones. Help your child become part of the process by pointing out previous evidence of her cooperation skills and past accomplishments in following rules. Ask your child to share feelings and thoughts about her misbehavior and difficulties she may have staying within your limits.

Some rules will be flexible and some will not. For those that are, allow your child to negotiate an arrangement where both of you get something out of the deal. For example, enlist her cooperation in working toward a compromise about bedtime. A compromise might look something like this: You let her go to bed at 8:30 instead of 8:00 if she doesn't put up a fight and hops right into bed and turns off the light. You can send the message that you mean business about the rules and still avoid a power struggle by showing your child that you take her opinions seriously.

You should not change the rules if you and your child have agreed upon a plan that has rewards built in. For example, if you both have agreed that 8:00 is the desired bedtime and you have a plan that rewards this, do not negotiate a later time with your child nightly.

Consistency

Your child can only follow rules and limits if you, yourself, follow them. You need to be consistent. She will find that when she tests the limits and rules, the consequences will always be the same. Children welcome consistency since it makes their world more predictable and putting up a struggle less desirable. We asked one child we know why she stopped badgering her mother with a particular request. She stated, "I know my mom won't give in, so it's not worth it."

The three "C" rule-making process is easy to follow and remember. Once you get the hang of it you can use this technique to state your expectations

Examples of the Three "C's"

• • • • • • •

A child was screaming to her parent in a restaurant. Watch how the parent uses the three "C" process to address this unacceptable behavior.

Parent: "I did not like your screaming behavior at the restaurant today. People don't want to listen to children screaming in restaurants. From now on I will not allow anyone in this family to scream in restaurants or other public places. If you cannot follow this rule, you will not come with me. Please tell me what I said about screaming." (Calm and Clear Correction)

Child: "You didn't like it when I was screaming in the restaurant and I can't come with you again if I'm going to scream."

Parent: "Right. You are a very good listener! I remember a few days ago when we went to the store and I never heard you scream once. I know you can do this when you try. Also, you may have been trying to tell us something with your screaming but you can tell us in other ways, don't you think?" (Cooperation)

Child: "OK—but sometimes I scream and I don't know I'm screaming. And sometimes you don't listen to me so I have to scream. What if I scream by accident? Can I still go to the restaurant?"

Parent: "Hmmmmm. You are saying that because you are deaf you cannot hear how loud your voice is sometimes. And other times you know that you are frustrated and demanding with your voice. How about this: when you start screaming, I'll let you know. If you continue to scream then I will follow the rule that you can't come with me until you have better control over your screaming. And if you are frustrated you need to say that to us without screaming. OK?" (Cooperation.)

Child: "OK."

This parent should then follow-up with this rule for all members of the family who scream at restaurants or public places. The parent should always handle the screaming with the responses she outlined. (Consistency.)

and establish rules both as prevention and after an undesirable behavior happens. You can create a solid parenting plan to deal with most of your child's misbehaviors by using this technique and other limit-setting methods described in this section (natural and logical consequences; the think chair; and plan, prepare, and prevent).

IGNORING AND DISTRACTION

Use ignoring and distraction when you don't want to draw attention to a particular behavior. Ignoring, by definition, means deliberately withholding attention from a child or situation. Distraction is a method of diverting your misbehaving child's attention to a more acceptable alternative. Both techniques work best with behaviors that have not been strongly established, such as sibling squabbles, temper tantrums, and annoying habits.

If you consistently ignore your child's temper outburst, she will quickly realize that there is no point in hysterically throwing herself on the floor. Ignoring means you ignore the unacceptable behavior, not the feeling or the situation that caused it. If the child is trying to communicate displeasure, frustration, or anger, she must be taught to express that in another manner. Consider whether your child has enough methods and arenas to express feelings and to assert herself. If she doesn't, use the activities in this book that focus on feelings expression, impulse control, assertion, and self-calming.

Distraction is an age-old tool for getting children to redirect their focus from the negative conditions that they may be experiencing to more enjoyable things. An example is when you tell your screaming child to look at the pretty picture on the doctor's wall while being stuck with a needle.

How Parents Can Use Ignoring and Distraction

To ignore unwanted behaviors, you should turn away, you should not respond either verbally or nonverbally, and you should stay in control. Give your child the impression that the magazine article is far more interesting than getting involved in "Mommy, tell Mr. Stupid to leave me alone!" Behavior that may be dangerous to your child or others should not be ignored. Turning your back on physically aggressive acts is not recommended.

To use distraction, first identify in your mind which of your child's behaviors cue you to her deterioration, such as crankiness. Secondly, step in when necessary to interrupt the child's pending loss of control and refocus her attention toward more productive behaviors. You can accomplish this by offering her something she finds pleasant and interesting to do. This means that you should have a "back up" list of activities to use in persuading

Examples of How to Use Ignoring and Distraction

• • • • • • •

1. You are waiting at the doctor's office with an impatient child: "Oh, look! We brought that neat book you like so much, let's read it together."

2. Adam is teasing Tessa: "Tessa, help me make dinner.—we can make the soup you like."

3. Annie is misbehaving as you're trying to get ready to leave your home: "Annie, you always seem to be able to find missing shoes around here. Do you think you can use your secret powers and locate your brother's shoes?"

your child to take her mind off the situation which is causing weakening behavior control.

NATURAL AND LOGICAL CONSEQUENCES

This technique is a sensible way to respond to undesirable behaviors. An example of a natural consequence is when a child leaves a bicycle in the driveway and it gets hit by the car—not purposely, of course. A logical consequence is when you restrict your child from using the bike for a period of time. These consequences teach your child the relationship between her behavior and the resulting outcome. The value of natural or logical consequences is that your child learns self-discipline through personal experience rather than because of your demands. She learns that her decisions and choices will shape her future.

In order to teach children responsibility, we must hold them accountable for their actions. Take the time to make sure your child understands her responsibility for her actions so that you do not fall into the trap of assuming she didn't know what she was doing. Make lists of standard rules with words and pictures, brief your child on your expectations early in the day or right before an activity, have your child repeat the guidelines and consequences for positive or negative behavior, and be consistent so your child can count on rules to stay the same. Investing time early on can save hours of crisis, yelling, and punishment.

How to Apply Natural and Logical Consequences

To use this technique follow this basic rule: when your child misbehaves, you provide an undesirable consequence that logically or naturally fits the misbehavior. The consequence replaces any type of punishment. For example, if your child fails to turn in her homework on time, the natural consequence would be a lower grade and the logical consequence would be to schedule more homework time. When her grades improve, schedule less homework time and more play time. This approach holds her responsible for her behavior and decisions.

If a young child has a tantrum in the supermarket, then tell her, "Everyone is staring at you!" (natural consequence). Or tell her, "If you continue this, I will not be able to take you with me the next time" (logical consequence). This doesn't force your child into submission but instead encourages her to make a responsible decision.

Be consistent and follow through with the consequences you provide. Follow these five guidelines for using logical and natural consequences:

1. Be sure that your deaf child understands what kind of behavior you expect in any given situation—use specific examples to teach this.

2. When a problem behavior occurs, apply a logical or natural consequence that fits that specific misbehavior.

3. Try to inform your child of the consequence of her misbehavior without being angry or smug.

4. While delivering the consequence, reassure your child that she will have an opportunity to try again.

Examples of How to Apply Natural and Logical Consequences

● ● ● ● ● ● ●

1. "The consequence for breaking your sister's toy will be to replace it by using money out of your allowance."

2. "Because the dishes were done poorly, you will need to do them again."

3. "If you don't clean your fish tank, the dirty water will kill the fish." (natural consequence)

5. If the behavior is repeated, apply the same consequence or come up with another that naturally or logically fits.

Throughout this process, try not to get into a struggle over the consequence. This defeats the purpose of letting your child wrestle with her own dilemma. Be patient! It takes time for a child to understand and experience the effects that the consequences have upon her.

PLAN, PREPARE, AND PREVENT

Just as a skilled business manager makes lists, writes appointments in a calendar, and predicts possible problems in completing her duties, so a good family manager needs to do the same. By planning your and your child's day and preparing her to handle stressful or difficult events, you can prevent a disaster. Parents and children have different perceptions of how their day should unfold. They have different agendas, priorities, and criteria for getting things done.

These differences make it difficult to navigate a busy Saturday of food shopping, housecleaning, and quality play time. By designing structured activities, daily rituals, and organized routines, you can eliminate some of life's recurring problems. Planning your day does not mean that you eliminate spontaneity or march your child through a set of tasks and retire at exactly "eleven-hundred hours."

All children need a sense of stability and clear expectations. Often the deaf child is unaware of plans, transitions, or unexpected changes. This makes it difficult for the child to regulate her emotions and she may become anxious or resistant, or have a constant sense that things over which she has no control happen "to" her. The child will find comfort in routines and predictable activities because this outlines for her what to anticipate and when to expect it.

How to Plan, Prepare, and Prevent

You can prevent many behavior problems by creating family rituals and efficient routines. Try structuring your sixteen hour day in manageable units of time. Think about possible trouble spots, such as periods of the day during which you cannot be flexible and times which you anticipate will be demanding and stressful for you or your child. When you organize your day in advance, even a busy day will feel more manageable.

For example, if you know that your child tends to be irritable or impatient at the end of her school day then don't arrange for an afterschool snack with Aunt Pearl who talks 400 words a minute and with a cigarette flopping in her mouth. Arrange that block of time instead to be calm and pleasurable for her. Similarly, if your young child's mood and tolerance for adult-oriented activities seems greater in the morning, then plan your outings to the store or cleaners for morning times.

Prepare your child for the day's happenings by explaining what she can expect to encounter in the next six hours—"First, we will go to the bank, then the supermarket, and, finally, we will visit your friends at the playground." You may even specifically describe each activity. For example, "When we are at the bank we will have to stand in line quietly. . . ." This can greatly reduce the problem behaviors related to unexpected changes or transitions from one event to another. Daily or weekly family rituals, such as bedtime routines and Friday dinner at Gina's Pizza, provide expected and familiar opportunities for your child to plan actions, prepare for changes, and behave well.

The plan, prepare, and prevent technique is vital for a deaf child who has problems with attention, impulse control, learning, or hyperactivity. For this child you may want to use charts, schedules, and the clock to help contain her energy and anxiousness.

Examples of Plan, Prepare, and Prevent
•••••••

1. "First we are going to the bank, then to the supermarket, and finally to the park."

2. "What can we bring to keep you busy while we visit Uncle Nicholas?"

3. "Let's list our schedule for the day together and at the end we'll write 'special treat'."

4. "OK, let's write down today's schedule—at nine we will wake, have breakfast and clean up; at ten we will visit Aunt Natalie, help with her lawn, and have lunch there; next, we will stop for gas and then return home; between two and four you have play time; at four, we can take a long walk, come back to prepare dinner, and follow our usual evening schedule. Be sure to wear your watch and you tell me when it's time for each activity. If there are any changes, I will tell you, OK?"

YOUR CHOICE

This technique offers a child options rather than directing her to do something. Due to communication obstacles, hearing parents are more inclined to give directives rather than explanations to the deaf child. If this is the habit, the child might obey or disobey without ever understanding all that is going on. Or she may chronically disobey in a misguided attempt at asserting her independence. The net result is the same—the child learns very little about self-control and responsibility.

When you allow your child to make real choices, you foster your child's self-confidence and sense of control. Giving choices actively promotes your child's skills in making critical decisions, evaluating options, predicting outcomes, and taking responsibility for the choices she makes. For example, a parent might say, "Your choice is one, to stay home and continue fighting with each other until you miss the beginning of the movie, or two, end this argument and go to the movies on time. Your choice!"

When you offer your child reasonable options and outcomes, it is easier for her to stop and think about solving a problem and making a good decision. Also, your child can better understand the cause and effect relationship between her behaviors and the resulting consequences. By providing your child with an opportunity for control, you are saying, "I respect your ability to make good choices."

How Parents Can Use Your Choice

Here follow some important things to keep in mind when using this technique:

1. We suggest that you designate fingers on your hand to represent the number of choices. Two fingers mean two choices and so on. Name and number each choice, while pointing to a finger—"No, you cannot stay home alone. Your choices are: number one, you can stay here with a sitter; two, you can visit with Aunt Joanie; or three, you can come with me." This structure helps to visually outline and clarify what your child's options are.

2. Don't offer a choice you may regret or cannot honor.

3. Be sure to accept your child's decision and refrain from influencing her to make the "right" choice.

4. When laying out the choices and their possible outcomes, focus on how your child will be affected rather than how you will be affected—make

---

Examples of How to Use Your Choice
● ● ● ● ● ● ●

1. To a child refusing to get dressed: "Would you like to wear the yellow shirt or the purple one with these pants?"

2. To a child refusing to eat: "What would you like to eat for dinner tomorrow? Help me decide."

3. "Swinging a bat in the house is dangerous, you can (pointing to each finger) give it to me, put it in the toy room, go outside with it, or, if you continue to play with it, I will put it away for a week — your choice."

---

this concise to keep your child from getting lost in a long explanation. In this way, your child can view the decision as her own. A consequence given for a choice must logically relate to the behavior you are trying to correct. (See logical and natural consequences above.)

5. If your child refuses to participate, inform her that she made the decision to have you take control.

When your child is involved in decision-making around simple issues like going to bed, doing her homework, and being on time for dinner, she gains invaluable practice. When confronted with making difficult choices with her peers (such as joining a group of kids who plan to skip school), she will have some knowledge of how to explore her options. And don't forget, giving choices keeps your child struggling with the problem rather than with you.

STAR

STAR (Stop, Think, and Act Right) is a "self-talk" technique that teaches a child to think before acting. This fun and easy-to-remember acronym can teach your child to slow down, review behavior, and consider her next step. A child can learn to follow internal cues in order to control impulsivity, outbursts, and habitual responses. Often, parents of a deaf child know the behaviors they want to see from their child but are at a loss for how to teach her the steps to get there.

Examples of How to Use STAR
● ● ● ● ● ● ●

1. "Whoa—hit the brakes! Let's slow things down and think about the right way to act at the library."

2. "Now that you have stopped to think about your next move, what do you think is the best thing to do, Ray?"

3. "You took control and stopped yourself before throwing that at your brother. What a STAR!"

4. "RATS! You lost control. Remember everyone makes mistakes, you can try again. What would you do if you could do that again differently?"

How Parents Can Use STAR

STAR teaches children a simple process of self-control: stopping, thinking, and acting right or responsibly. First, help your child stop all activity (turn off those arms and legs). Second, help her to think (turn on her brain) about her options, to consider the results of her behavior, and to make a decision about her course of action. Third, encourage her to test out the results of her decisions.

Suppose that your child has a difficult time controlling her anger and occasionally hits others. Once your child has learned how to use this technique, you can ask her to be a "STAR" and stop and think before she strikes out. This word then becomes a fun reminder of a better course of action for your child.

You can also use this technique to encourage your child to evaluate a situation in which she misbehaved. STAR spelled backwards is RATS—Review Actions and Try Some more. You can use this catchy and lighthearted expression to provide a simple structure for reflecting back on a problem that occurred. People often find it difficult to take a critical look at themselves. Saying, "RATS!" to your child might help break the tension and the resistance to reviewing actions and exploring alternative ways she might have acted.

TAP: A TECHNIQUE FOR PARENTS ONLY

TAP (Think and Prevent) is a self-talk method to assist parents in managing feelings of anger. A parent can use TAP (Think and Prevent) to stop negative events from spiraling out of control and to create an opportunity for herself to have an "internal conversation" about alternative ways of expressing angry thoughts and feelings.

All parents are entitled to feel anger and need opportunities to express and release tension. However, this should never happen at the expense of a child's well-being. A child's annoying behaviors can really challenge us emotionally. In order to control an angry response, parents must literally turn themselves off so that they have a moment to think about how to better handle the situation.

Try giving yourself a light tap on the leg to remind you to turn off, like a light switch, highly emotional responses. You must break the cycle of events that usually follows when you lose control and become punitive (experiencing guilt afterward). TAP helps you give yourself the chance you need to take a moment to think about alternative ways of expressing your feelings and coping with your child's behavior constructively.

How Parents Can Use TAP

If you tap yourself on the leg or arm when you feel the first sign of angry feelings, you use a concrete reminder to prevent unplanned words and reactions from occurring. TAP into your knowledge bank of previously successful ways that you handled your anger well. Develop a vocabulary that you can rely upon to express angry feelings, instead of using explosive words that have no value or purpose.

Here are three simple steps for using TAP:

Examples of How to Use TAP
• • • • • • •

1. (Say to yourself while tapping yourself:) "He's really trying my patience and I'm losing control. I'd better walk away."

2. "Bobby, I'm very upset. Please start cleaning up this mess while I walk over here and take a deep breath."

3. Self-cues you can use: "Take a few deep breaths"; "Leave now and calm down"; "Anger and voice are up, time to calm down"; and, "This will pass."

4. Say to your child or family: "I am really angry right now and I am going to the think chair (see the following). Don't bother me until I say that I am ready."

---

1. When you feel the first signs of parental "melt down" give yourself a tap and disengage from the situation. If it works for you, use the "Think Chair" (see pg. 52) for an explanation, and model a family approach to handling difficult feelings.

2. Once you have unplugged from the challenge your child is presenting, plug into your "self-talk" to control your anger. Tell yourself, "I can be calm" or "Becoming really angry is a waste of my energy!"

3. Return to your child with a renewed sense of self-control and calmly express your feelings. Your child will benefit from observing you modeling calm and controlled behavior.

THE THINK CHAIR

The think chair is another name for a popular behavioral technique called "time out." We call it the "think chair" or "think space" because we want to give children the message that time spent in time out is a time to regain control and think about a better way to behave. The short-term goal of this technique is to interrupt a specific misbehavior; the long-term goal is to teach your child reflective and self-control skills.

If you interrupt, remove, and direct your child to sit in a previously chosen place to think about her actions, you break the pattern of misbehavior. The "think" part of this technique is most important. Frequently, a deaf child is removed from a situation due to her behavior only to return later and repeat the behavior. It is critical that you provide information and options in on-going discussions or by using techniques such as "Your Choice," "The Family Council," or "The Three C's," so that the child can think before acting. After much practice, she can learn the negative impact of a behavior and choose better options.

This technique has a dual benefit in that it gives your family a concrete procedure for dealing with escalating negative behaviors as well as an area to cool off and recover control. The think chair is most effective in correcting persistent behaviors which are impulsive, hostile, and highly emotional. When used by the whole family, it loses its punishing qualities and becomes a way to support the value of self-control. In dealing with difficult behaviors, the think space helps you and your child avoid useless power struggles and complete loss of control.

How Parents Can Use the Think Chair
Here are a few suggestions for how to use the think chair or think space.

1. Pick a quiet and boring place in your home to be the think space/chair. This area should not be visually stimulating and should be away from the TV or nearby toys.

2. When explaining the think chair to your child, be sure to note what behaviors will get her a front row seat. Remind all family members to go there when they are losing control.

3. When a person is in the think chair, she must take responsibility for her actions. Blaming and denying are two ways to be sure to stay longer.

4. When using the think chair, tell your child in twenty words or less and in less than ten seconds why she needs to go there and what to think about. Stay neutral in body posture, tone of voice, or gestures. Do not go on with lengthy descriptions. This invites a power struggle or an opportunity for your child to bargain instead of learning. If your child tends to close her eyes (not listen), plan for this by having one word or sign to connote "think chair." Also, note that not listening will only intensify the consequences (more time, loss of reward), while quick time in the think chair will allow for her to resume what she was doing.

5. Always indicate how long she must stay in the think chair. (A good rule of thumb is a minute for each year in age, e.g., four years old equals four minutes.)

6. If your child is able, ask her to fill out a form while in the think chair. The form would have the problem behavior, what the child was feeling when she did it, and what she thinks is a more appropriate way to get what she needs. Drawing pictures is an excellent way to do this.

7. Use a timer with visible numbers to eliminate both having your child ask you if her time is up and your need to attend to her. You will help her gain control over the situation by putting her in charge of the timer. You can end her time in the think chair once your child has acceptably filled out her form.

8. If the child gets up before you feel she is ready, let her know that she needs to return or her time will start from the beginning. Physically guide her back if necessary. Remind her that she will be allowed to get up sooner if she focuses. Be consistent in your expectations or the Jack-in-the-box child will become a habit. Also, be sure to assess whether the amount of time or structure that you give the child is sufficient. A hyperactive child may need more support and structure.

9. When the timer reaches the designated number or when she has completed her form, ask your child to explain her thoughts. If she expresses adequate understanding of her misbehavior and better alternatives for future situations, she can leave the think chair; if not, she may need to sit

---

Examples of How to Use the Think Chair

• • • • • • •

1. "You are really having a hard time listening. I think you need to spend two minutes in the think chair."

2. "Hitting is not OK in this family. I've warned you two times, now you've earned five minutes in the think chair."

3. "You spent five whole minutes in the think chair. Now that you're calm, can you tell me why you had to sit here?"

4. "You are finished with your form and you look calmer—now let's talk about why you sat in the think chair and how you could do things differently next time."

5. "You scribbled on this form and are still blaming others. Think some more about your actions and responsibility in the situation."

---

through another session of thinking. If she has filled out a form, have her explain her answers to you.

10. Don't speak to or lecture your child while she is in the think chair. She needs time to think without you giving her attention for unacceptable behavior.

11. After you have used the think chair for awhile, allow your child to independently determine when she is finished. She may even become capable of going to the chair and stating her problems and how to avoid them. You can judge if and when your child can do this by her personality, development, and progress in correctly utilizing the chair. Some children need consistent external reminders over a long period of time, while others internalize controls more rapidly.

CHARTS, CONTRACTS, AND REWARDS

Many of the activities in this book include the use of charts, rewards, and behavior management (shaping behavior through positive and negative consequences). The use of rewards to change children's behavior has been practiced for decades. Some parents view rewards (material objects, gifts, special outings) as a form of bribery. But there is a big difference between giving treats to get a child to do what you want and using a systematic reward system to teach your child responsible behaviors. Giving a child rewards and privileges for improved behaviors is analogous to an adult receiving a paycheck for working. Problem-solving is hard work for children and deserves compensation or recognition.

Most children are not always motivated simply by the good feelings that come from accomplishing a task or from reaching a goal. They often need a tangible, external motivator such as a desired object, an outing, or a special privilege. When you reward desirable behavior, you reinforce your child's positive actions and encourage her to repeat them.

The end purpose in using external motivators is to help your child move from feeling good about getting a reward for hard work to feeling good about reaching her goal. At first a child relies on external motivators (rewards) and over time, through the use of reward-based systems, internal motivators (self-praise and self-confidence) will suffice.

Finally, contracts are used in real life to solidify deals between two or more people. Wouldn't it be nice if the courts could ensure that a contract signed by your daughter to clean her room would be followed? If she did not follow through, the presiding judge could dictate, "she is banned from watching television for one week!!"—SLAM goes the gavel! Oh, if parenting were that simple!

Even without a stern judge, contracts help a child follow through on a commitment because she promised and signed her name. Also, many good contracts include incentives that help keep the child interested.

We will describe five different types of reward-based systems that can be used in succession to help your child move from external to internal motivations: the token program, contracts, the chart and reward program, the point and catalog program, and the level program. These systems involve visual representations of agreements, gains, and rewards. Because the tokens, charts, catalogs, and level system keep the deaf child aware of the process, she will remain a more interested participant. The visual representations also take the onus off of you—when the child is improving on attaining her goals, you can point to her wonderful efforts for her to see. When she is not succeeding, you can discuss roadblocks and remind her of her responsibilities in making changes or asking for help.

How Parents Can Use Charts, Contracts, and Rewards

To begin with, you may need some help to discover what motivates your child. We've included a model assessment to help you investigate your child's wishes and motivators for changing negative behaviors into positive ones. The "My Wishes and Wants Test" (Appendix A) can be given verbally to a young child or photocopied for an older child to complete on her own. You can glean some good reward and motivator ideas from the "201 Rewards Children Love to Work for" (see Appendix B).

Next, choose from the chart and reward systems described on the following pages the system that best suits your child and family style. Consider your child's age, developmental abilities, and maturity level. For each reward program, the following guidelines should be considered to ensure success.

1. Have a family council to start planning your program.

2. Choose the task(s) you wish to accomplish.

3. Choose your reward(s) for successful efforts or accomplishments.

4. Always deliver the reward or privilege promised. Never make promises you can't keep.

5. Give your child plenty of time and always approach a reward program with a "try, try again" attitude.

6. Rewards should never be given before the desired behavior is displayed or the reward will simply become a bribe.

7. Never withhold or revoke an earned reward. ("If you don't do what I say, I will not give you the . . .")

The Token Program

The token program uses immediate rewards to reinforce desired behaviors and is best used with preschool children and those who cannot delay receiving a reward. As soon as your child displays the desired positive behavior, you give her a small reward or token (food, sticker, or a penny). For example, four-year-old Alex would get a sticker on his chart each time he asked for something instead of grabbing it. When he is immediately rewarded, the positive behavior is reinforced.

To use tokens, first select a target behavior such as a child asking to use things that don't belong to her. Next, select a reward (e.g., stickers) for exhibiting this positive behavior. Every time your child displays the target behavior, you instantly give her the reward. Using the chart in Appendix C, sit down with your child and explain to her how she can get her stickers.

Over time, your child will realize which behaviors bring her special attention. Most likely, as she grows, she will need more incentives to reinforce other, more complicated behaviors (Chart and Reward Program).

Contracts

Written contracts are useful for establishing concrete mutually agreed-upon guidelines and goals. By writing a contract you make an agreement with your child to perform duties, resolve conflicts, or behave in a particular manner.

Include parental responsibilities on a contract to highlight the team approach to problem-solving. For example, you might add, "Mom will remind Timmy when he is poking people" or "Dad will listen to Timmy when Timmy talks instead of hitting to express his anger." Examine the contracts in Appendix D to get ideas for your own contracts.

The Chart and Reward Program

With this program you use a chart of checks or points to record your child's progress. This eventually leads to a reward at the end of the day, week, or month. The charts can be custom-made to reflect particular problems, the child's developmental ability, and the family style. For example, a younger child might use chart "A," which has simple directives and daily rewards; an older or more developmentally capable child might use chart "B," which requires that she accumulate points throughout the week (or month) in order to earn her reward (see Appendix E).

For an effective chart and reward program,

1. Select behaviors you wish to reinforce.

2. Make a chart with your child that is visually appealing and developmentally appropriate.

3. Allow your child to choose an appropriate reward that motivates her.

4. Select the number of points needed to earn the reward.

5. Always give the reward if your child accumulates the points needed.

6. Change the chart or points needed if you feel it is too simple or too demanding. The charts in Appendix E will help you design a point and reward program of your own.

The Point and Catalog Program

In the point and catalog program, your child earns points (recorded on charts) which she can use to buy an item from a catalog of your design that displays the rewards. You and your child can make the catalog by drawing or cutting out pictures from magazines of desired rewards, activities, and privileges. Under each picture in the catalog write the number of points needed to earn that reward. Include rewards that are easy for your child to buy (ice cream cone equals ten points) as well as others that take more time and commitment (soccer shoes equals two hundred points).

If your child always has a messy bedroom, she could earn points during the week for keeping her room clean (see chart "B" on pg. 351). She can then choose a reward from the catalog after she has added up her points. Once she spends her points, she must earn more to continue purchasing items from the reward catalog. Put a tally sheet in the catalog to keep track of points earned daily or weekly and points spent.

You can also make a reward catalog that your entire family can use for reaching goals. Choose rewards that all members would enjoy. Or make a special parent catalog of rewards like a morning to yourself or a night out with your partner. Give yourself points for reaching goals, supporting your child's efforts, or successfully putting your child in the think chair. Let your child watch you pick out a reward from your catalog and give it to yourself!

The Level Program

This program is based on hierarchically organizing desired behaviors (charted by points) with corresponding levels. At each level, a child earns privileges. This program differs from the others in that the focus is not on earning rewards but on earning privileges. You will notice that the example in Appendix F is designed for your child to collect a specific number of points in order to graduate from one level and move up to the next. A child must maintain a certain number of points weekly to maintain her standing at that level or she moves down.

The program begins at level one, which includes basic responsibilities and related privileges and continues through to level four, the highest level of responsibilities and most desirable privileges. Use the examples in Appendix F to make a level program with your child. Involve your child in developing the responsibilities and privileges associated with each level. Come up with a developmentally appropriate number of points she must earn to move up to the next level or maintain each week to stay at her current level. As she reaches each level, she should start with no points and collect points again from scratch to reach the next level.

Bear in mind that your child's success must be measured by her ability to reach a level that matches her developmental capability rather than her making it to the highest level. Focus on your child's achievements within each level and the positive changes she makes in the process.

4

Techniques that Foster Changes in Behavior

● ● ● ●

Parenting is much fuller and richer than simply setting rules, limits, and guidelines. Love, nurturance, affection, physical contact, and humor are a few aspects of life that help us feel secure and happy. These demonstrations of love make up a family's heart and spirit. By giving genuine and caring responses to your child, you can reshape negative moments into positive ones and build your child's self-esteem and confidence so that he is able to make necessary changes. Without self-esteem and confidence, the ability to take on daily challenges is severely hampered.

We would like to stress that loving and nurturing your child should never be used as a method to get your child to do something; these emotions should be unconditional! It is unnecessary and potentially destructive to withhold these emotions even if you are doing it in the name of discipline.

Showing your love through your body language, playfulness, and expression gives a deaf child vital cues to support your words/signs. These expressions of unconditional love will strengthen the connections between you and your child.

Further, when he knows he is loved no matter what, your deaf child's self-confidence, self-respect, and belief in himself grow.

ENCOURAGEMENT AND POSITIVE REFRAMING

Encouragement and positive reframing focus on a child's strengths and positive intentions. By demonstrating an unconditional belief in your child, you lay the foundation for an "I can do!" attitude (confidence) and enthusiasm for personal growth.

You offer encouragement by words, actions, and feelings. Your child might need a hug after falling off a swing and some prodding to get back on. Or perhaps he might need you to be lovingly firm through all of the tears before his dance class (which, of course, he enjoys once there).

Positive reframing requires that you point out the silver lining to every cloud. When a negative or potentially negative situation occurs, you redefine (reframe) it in such a way that makes the child hopeful and motivated towards healthy outcomes. For example, "You tried so hard to help Daddy by carrying a big, full shopping bag. Next time we'll have you carry a smaller one and maybe we can avoid having the bag rip."

In order to work toward behavioral change, children must feel internal motivation. This is learned when parents identify and encourage any degree of progress toward a goal. Encouragement and positive reframing are especially useful in promoting a child's capacity for self-appraisal.

These techniques not only highlight the positives for your child, but remind you of what makes your child special. While it is easy to give encouragement when your child is doing well, it is difficult to be positive when he is not at his best. However, this is when it is needed most.

How Parents Can Use Encouragement and Positive Reframing

These two closely related techniques are often used together. You use them whenever you accurately paint a positive picture of your child's efforts and abilities. With practice, you can identify and underscore positive elements for your child in any situation, no matter how bleak it appears. Choose comments and questions that help your child assess and praise himself, such as, "Aren't you proud of yourself for studying for that test?" Make encouraging comments, such as, "You sure did make the dishes sparkle!" Reframe discouraging situations; for example, "Yes, you got a D, but it is an honest D—you studied, you really tried and you didn't cheat. I am proud of you." Boosting your child's self-confidence helps him have faith in his ability to confront everyday challenges and to create positive outcomes.

Some children find it hard to directly accept encouraging comments but can benefit from overhearing/over"seeing" your praise. For example, when Emily is present ask a third party, "Did you know that Emily swam the length of the pool today?"

Another helpful method for interrupting undesirable behaviors and extricating your child from negative situations is to review positive moments, "I remember when you . . ." In this way you help your child remember past successes, renewing his faith in his own ability as well as the bright side of life.

Examples of How to Use Encouragement and Positive Reframing

• • • • • • •

1. Whenever you feel the impulse, tell your child, "You are truly a terrific kid!"

2. After your child gets a good grade on a homework assignment, tell him, "You must be proud of yourself. Nice job!"

3. To a child picking up and handling a breakable vase: "Thank you for handling that vase so gently!"

4. To your partner or child's grandparent: "Guess what? Rick didn't suck his thumb for four hours straight!"

5. To a child who is often physically aggressive toward siblings: "Yes, you said that you would like to punch your sister, but what I am happy about is that you said it and did not do it—that is a big improvement."

MUTUAL RESPECT AND EMPATHY

Mutual respect builds your child's self-esteem and sensitivity to others. Empathy, the ability to understand another's point of view, is a necessary skill for building healthy relationships. Parents can best teach their child about mutual respect and empathy by demonstrating respect and understanding for him, for his feelings, thoughts, and experiences.

Though this sounds simple, accepting a deaf child fully means accepting the child's deafness. If parents are shocked, saddened, confused or angry about their child's condition, then the parents should seek help to cope with these feelings. In addition, the hearing family must learn to accommodate the deaf child's communication needs, which does not happen overnight. Therefore, a parent might have gaps in understanding how his child thinks and feels about things. This doesn't indicate the absence of mutual respect, it indicates a communication problem that will require more patience and time to resolve. The results are worth the investment of time and patience.

Families that base their relationships on mutual respect and empathy have an easier time living together, cooperating, and learning from one another. Without this base, parents and children fail to listen to each others' feelings and consequently fail to solve problems together.

How Parents Can Build Respect with and Have Empathy for Their Child

You convey respect (or lack of it) for your deaf child by many of your daily actions. You fail to respect your child when you talk down to him; purposely embarrass him; laugh at his efforts; exclude him from family communication; or look through his private belongings without asking permission. You convey respect by soliciting and listening to your child's opinion, by allowing him the latitude to negotiate his communication needs, express clothing preferences, choose friends, and pursue hobbies. You want to send the message that you value his taste and individuality. You demonstrate your respect for him through a myriad of subtle actions. By not rushing to your deaf child's rescue when he is trying to solve a math problem, repair a broken toy, or construct a Lego ™ skyscraper, you show respect for (and confidence in) his independent efforts and accomplishments.

Empathy, like respect, is best taught by demonstration. A parent who empathizes shows his understanding, compassion, and sensitivity for his deaf child's perspective. In order to do this, a parent must first imagine himself in his child's place or predicament and then share his perceptions with his child. The parent thus assists the child in exploring his emotions and behaviors and gradually teaches him how empathy contributes to the child's ability to have healthy relationships with others.

Show your child that you respect him as a total person, regardless of his hearing and vocal abilities. This is vital in shaping his capacity for respecting and liking himself. He is not a lesser person just because he does not fit into society's view of normal. Acknowledge and respect your child's unique abilities to communicate. Show empathy (understanding), not sympathy (pity), for challenges and obstacles that come his way due to his deafness or hearing loss.

HUMOR AND AFFECTION

Find ways to laugh, love, and, in short, enjoy your child. All of the parental worrying, drudgeries, schedules, and heartaches should be balanced by laughter, affection, excitement, and joy! There are no rules that say parents must always be serious. Allow your child to rekindle your playfulness—tickle, giggle, joke, go sledding, hug, love, and be downright goofy whenever you get the chance.

How Parents Can Use Humor and Affection

Love, cherish, and accept your child simply because he is himself. Your child needs to know that even when he misbehaves you still love him. This gives

---

Examples of How to Respect and Have Empathy for Your Child

• • • • • • •

1. Discussing where the child would like to go to camp for the summer: "I'm wondering what you would like to do this summer. Why don't you give me a few suggestions?"

2. "How do you want to have your hair cut this time?"

3. "What do you think?"

4. After a child describes a nightmare: "I can see why you were so scared."

5. "You had to ask us three times to repeat what we were saying. That's good that you kept asking. Was that frustrating for you?"

---

him the message that you may not love some of his behaviors, but you will always love him. This enables your child to take risks, practice problem-solving skills, and examine his behavior, without worrying whether his efforts will affect your show of affection.

Physical and emotional affection are key components of parenting. Verbal and nonverbal expressions of your feelings show your child that your support and love are everlasting. Such actions as saying "I love you," hugging, kissing, or affectionately playing with your child's hair (especially when he is not expecting it) tell him just how special and important he is to you.

Never overlook the value of humor. Like planful playing (pgs. 24–25), laughter, joking, and daily silliness greatly restore perspective. When parents defuse tension by seeing the lighter side of a problem, children feel less threatened and take more risks in examining their difficulties. Never make a joke out of your child—it is not funny to be "sacrificed" for the sake of a good laugh. This is especially important to keep in mind if your deaf child must work extra hard at understanding all family members (nuclear and extended). Do not allow him to become the brunt of a joke because of his efforts to keep up with the conversation. If he does not have all of the information or nuances, and feels left out, a minor tease can make him extremely upset. No joke made at his expense is benign.

Make sure your humor matches that of your child's. Help him to find the silliness in a situation as a way to accept human errors and imperfections. You may not think it's funny that your child has not cleaned his room for ages

---

Examples of Using Humor and Affection
● ● ● ● ● ● ●

1. "I love every inch of you . . . This little toe . . . This little finger . . ."

2. "Time for a family hug . . . Let's huddle."

3. "Uh, oh. Here comes the tickle monster."

4. "Whew . . . What a tough day we had. You're still my special little boy, Anthony, no matter what you do."

5. "Hey, let's get a bulldozer to help you make a path to your bed, huh? Come on, jump on my back and I'll be the bulldozer."

(as evidenced by a misplaced grape turning into a raisin). With a twist of humor, your child's messy room and fermenting grape can bring you laughter and a "scrapbook" memory for years to come, not to mention a possible commitment from him to keep his room a bit cleaner.

Even though your child is deaf, he will probably be able to laugh about deaf/hearing mishaps from time to time during his life. Humor helps us deal with difficult and frustrating situations. But the key to successful humor in these situations is that the humor is shared by and not directed at deaf people. Find humor in your own actions as a hearing parent. For example, you might tell your child, "Silly me, I was trying to call you from another room. That was smart, huh?"

TRY, TRY AGAIN

A try, try again philosophy gives family members permission to use mistakes to learn. By stating, "It's ok, try again!", you tell your child that it's normal to "mess up" sometimes and you appreciate his positive efforts. Giving your child a "learner's leeway," and the opportunity to make mistakes, allows him to try out new behaviors.

A deaf child in particular needs to know that mistakes are not failures, nor are they "bad." The child needs to separate the deed from the doer and feel supported by his parents regardless of failed attempts at improving his behavior. Problem-solving is a process of trial and error (two steps forward, one step back) that enables us to develop an accurate sense of right and wrong, mature thinking, and good judgement.

How Parents Can Use Try, Try Again

Keep expectations and goals for your child reasonable and developmentally appropriate so that he will more likely attain his goals. Express your satisfaction with his efforts to change negative behaviors instead of focusing on whether he reached his goals.

Try, try again informs your child that it is improvement, not perfection, that you appreciate. Your child will feel far more motivated if he understands that you recognize his efforts as his real success.

Don't be too demanding and unrealistic in your expectations of your child when he is attempting to make behavioral changes. Closely monitor your child to prevent him from spending too much time in the try, try again mode without achieving palpable successes. If you notice that your child constantly struggles with the same issue, behavioral problem, or communication style, assess whether your expectations (or his) are unrealistic. Constant failure teaches the deaf child that try, try again means failure, which is the opposite message from what this technique is designed to convey.

SPECIAL RESOURCES: BOOKS AND PLAY ITEMS

In this book, we often talk about interpersonal techniques and parenting skills. You will find it much easier to use these techniques and skills when you have concrete tools. By this we mean children's books, parenting books, toys, and games. Think of yourself as a handyperson—you could accomplish many things with a hammer, but you could accomplish so much more if you

---

Examples of Try, Try Again
● ● ● ● ● ● ●

1. "Maybe you can do it if you try it again."

2. "Oh well—I know you wanted to finish first. But you sure looked great out there."

3. "That's OK Adam, we all make mistakes—no one's perfect."

4. "You have been struggling for weeks to keep up in that class. What do you think would help make this easier for you?"

5. "This is the third time you had to ask us to include you in a conversation. I admire your efforts and we need to make some changes."

had a wrench, screwdriver, pliers, and a saw. In parenting, the more playful tools you have, the more you can create and repair.

Books

Parenting Books

At the end of this book you will find recommended readings relating to the specific problems and issues raised in each chapter. Some of the books are exclusively designed for deaf children and/or their parents, while others are more general parenting and children's books that may help give you a more in-depth understanding of an issue.

Children's Books

Reading is a wonderful activity and an excellent tool for sharing time, information, and non-threatening advice with your child. At the same time, reading provides an opportunity to safely explore a problem from another person's point of view. Many books focus on specific issues in order to give children opportunities to experience their problems from a variety of perspectives. Some books help children work through a particular problem by allowing them to follow a storybook character through the steps of problem-solving. Look at the end of this book for a listing of children's book titles you can use as resources for handling behavioral problems. In compiling this list we have taken into account the deaf child's need for visually stimulating materials.

How to Use Books with Your Deaf Child for Solving Problems

How can you help your child examine his own problems through a storybook character and hopefully come up with his own solution? Read on.

We advise that you read the book to yourself first and decide on a suitable method for presenting the book to your deaf child. For children age six or less, you may want to tell the story in your own words using the pictures as a visual focus. In this way you can concentrate on the child instead of moving your gaze and attention from picture to child to written word. As your child's attention span and reading skills grow, you may read portions from the book verbatim, take turns with the child in reading, or read the entire book with your child following along. Continually monitor your child's attention level and adapt your style to keep him involved.

When reading a book with your child, discuss the character's problems. Talk about each character's perspective and whether the characters view a problem in the same way or differently. You can also use a book to address a problem your child has by highlighting the character's positive behaviors.

As you read the book, encourage your child to point out the character's special skills, unique traits, and abilities that help him solve the problem. Try deciding together what the character's goals should be. Read the book(s) with your child and use the story to help you solve problems together. When you complete the book discuss together whether you think the problem was solved. How was it solved or not solved? Did the character solve the problem and reach his goals by using any particular skills? Ask your child if he has any suggestions for the character.

Play Items—Toys and Board Games

Toys and games help children manage difficult issues. Think of the amount of time your child puts into playing with dolls, board games, or puzzles. These play items provide hours of learning, amusement, and excitement to him. They also create opportunities for him to explore difficulties in a non-threatening and experiential way. For example, by simply bathing, soothing, and dressing a doll, a child practices using compassion and patience, and developing caretaking skills. You can modify this same play experience slightly to help a child adjust to the birth of a new sibling.

How to Find Special Play Items for Your Child

The following are catalogs of quality toys, play supplies, board games, and videos that can assist you in building your child's problem-solving skills.

> Childswork Childsplay
> Center For Applied Psychology, Inc.
> PO Box 1586
> King of Prussia, PA 19406
> (1-800-962-1141)
>
> *This catalog includes everything from a special "time-out" timer and goody jars filled with grab-size rewards to board games such as The Anger Control Game and The Divorce Game, as well as hundreds of problem-solving books for children and parents. All of the books and games are invented and used by play therapists, which speaks to their quality.*
>
> Constructive Playthings
> 1227 East 119th Street
> Grandview, MO 64030
> 1-800-255-6124
>
> Childcraft
> PO Box 29149
> Mission, Kansas 66201-9149
> 1-800-367-3255
>
> Discovery Toys, Inc.
> Martinez, CA 94553
> 1-800-426-4777

The Great Kids Company
PO Box 609
Lewisville, NC 27023–0609
1–800–533–2166

Troll Learn and Play
100 Corporate Drive
Mahwah, New Jersey 07430
1–800–247–6106

Sensational Beginnings
300 Detroit Ave #E
PO Box 2009
Monroe, MI 48161
1–800–444–2147

Hearth Song
6519 N. Galena Road
Peoria, IL 61614–3125
1–800–325–2502

Hand in Hand
Route 26
RR 1, Box 1425
Oxford, ME 04270
1–800–872–9745

PlayFair Inc.
1690 28th St.
Boulder, CO 80302
1–800–824–7255

This catalog of toys and games focuses on nonviolent, noncompetitive educational toys.

Uniquity
PO Box 6
Galt, CA 95632
1–800–521–7771

The items in this catalog, widely used by play therapists, focus on personal growth.

Animal Town
PO Box 485
Healdsburg, CA 95448
1–800–445–8642

This catalog focuses on cooperative learning.

Chinaberry Book Service
2780 Via Orange Way, Suite B
Spring Valley, CA 91978
1–800–776–2242

This service specializes in books that provide positive messages and good role models; stories are nonsexist and nonviolent.

The following are school supply catalogs that have great play items and educational materials, such as board games for teaching academics as well as poster kits that reinforce body care.

Lakeshore Learning Materials
2695 E. Dominguez
PO Box 6261
Carson, CA 90749
1-800-421-5354

Up With Learning
Catalog Division
19 Ridge Street
Pawtucket, RI 02860
1-401-726-5093

Chasell, Inc.
9645 Gerwig Lane
Columbia, MD 21046
1-800-242-7355

Educational Insights
19560 S. Rancho Way
Dominguez Hills, CA 90220
1-800-933-3277

Developing Communication in the Family

• • • • • • • • • • •

Mervin D. Garretson

As an individual who has been totally deaf for more than half a century, I believe communication to be what deafness is all about. Being deaf is not simply the inability to hear. Hearing loss may be the disability but lack of communication certainly could be considered the handicap.

So if there is successful early communication with the deaf child, the greatest hurdle has been overcome. Communication is not language, although language may be one of the vehicles toward effective communication. Gestures, fingerspelling, sign language, speech and speechreading, and body language are all modes of communication. Most people need more than one mode in order to function comfortably in a variety of situations.

Also, communication choices may be highly idiosyncratic, depending on each person, on the skills of the receiver and sender, and on the situation, whether it be informal (one-to-one) or formal (one-to-many, as in a classroom or at a lecture).

Practically every human being wants to and needs to communicate in order to touch as many lives as he can. In my book, communication means participation. That is, one does not communicate to; one communicates with, and in any way that will effect understanding and empathy.

Mervin D. Garretson, now retired, was a teacher and administrator in schools for deaf children and special assistant to four different Gallaudet University presidents.

Let me share some personal experiences with you. First, a little background on my own deafness. At the age of five I became totally, irreversibly deaf from spinal meningitis. We were living on a ranch in Wyoming, and later in a house in a small village near our ranch. My parents had normal hearing, as did my five brothers and five sisters. My mother had been a "little red schoolhouse" teacher and was easy to speechread, but I couldn't speechread my father at all, so he used a kind of two-handed finger alphabet and later on wrote with me. Two of my siblings learned to fingerspell and knew a few signs. Communication in this large, hearing family was not the best, but we got along.

During the school year I attended the Colorado School for the Deaf, some 800 miles away from home, so I was not with my family except at Christmas time and during the summer. Nevertheless we were a close family and Mother wrote me weekly letters and sent lots of packages with cookies and other goodies. I was encouraged to invite deaf friends to visit us at the ranch during the summers as the family realized a deaf kid could be quite lonely without free and easy communication.

After completing eleven years of schooling in Colorado, I went on to Gallaudet University for my baccalaureate, and later to the University of Wyoming for my MA, followed by doctoral studies at the University of Maryland when we moved East.

My wife, Carol, is hard of hearing, which at the beginning was not without its problems in our family of five hearing daughters. The girls tended to talk to their mother and sign to me, but at first they would all talk animatedly at the dinner table, which meant I was left out of the conversation. Carol finally laid down the law—when Daddy is around, always sign as you talk so that he is a part of the circle. That worked very well and the girls grew up to be good communicators, not only with me, but also with our deaf friends.

We had a very intelligent cocker spaniel, Penney, who understood immediately that I was deaf and practically became a "hearing ear" dog, although they were not training such animals during those days! Penney was so sensitive that when she observed the girls talking to me without voice, but with voice to their mother, she followed suit! She would get my attention and bark at me without voice, but always used her voice with the others! How's that for communication empathy? That's what I call conservation of energy—why use voice with someone who can't hear it anyway? Which is probably why many deaf people don't use their voice among themselves but will turn it on when with hearing people.

I've always felt that when communicating with each other, people should be aware of everyone within earshot or "eyeshot." Should a deaf person be present when hearing people are conversing, they should begin signing or at least making sure the deaf person is not ignored and left standing around feeling like a piece of furniture. The same goes for deaf people signing in the presence of a hearing person—they should use their voices, or at least make sure the hearing person is included in the conversation in some way.

Some years ago, I developed a paper on what I called "the unwritten curriculum." After teaching some twenty years, I became interested in knowing how much of and what part of the 365 days in the year were spent in a classroom. In taking account of all the time spent out of the classroom: walking down the halls; during recess; in the bathroom; during the lunch break; during after school hours; counting the time spent out of school for Thanksgiving, Easter, Christmas, and other holidays, and the long summer vacation; the actual time spent in the classroom for the average child, whether deaf or hearing, came to just eight percent of the total year. This means that 92 percent of their learning is taking place through communication outside of the classroom.

All of this incidental learning, which I call the unwritten curriculum, is communication-based. For the hearing child, it means effortless assimilation with their peers, neighbors, at home, at the marketplace, the shopping malls, through radio and television, in the offices of doctors and dentists, practically everywhere. What does this mean for the deaf child? If there's no visual communication, he's going to fall far, far behind his hearing peers.

Families need to ensure that clear, complete communication is going on in the home, that the deaf child is included in group and other conversations, and that real understanding occurs.

CHAPTER

5

Communication

• • • •

Developing a consistent family communication method makes an unbeliev-able difference in the overall functioning of your deaf child and family. A con-sistent home communication method will greatly influence your deaf child's development, social awareness, and self-concept. Without clear communica-tion, behavioral problems and discipline become dreadfully complicated.

In light of this challenge to deaf/hearing families, we suggest the following problem-solving activities to help your family learn about the value of good communication, closely examine the communication methods available to deaf individuals, and finally come together in making a communication com-mitment. Communication should always benefit the deaf family member(s) while ultimately facilitating family functioning.

COMMUNICATION

Communication relates to every area of a deaf child's development—social, academic, and emotional. Her self-concept, impulse control, behaviors, safety, cleanliness, and strengths will be affected by her ability to have opportunities to communicate.

If a deaf child is constantly misunderstanding, she will be less obedient, open, assertive, and attentive. Good communication is an acquired skill and is interactive, requiring a constant give and take between individuals. Current research shows that from birth, infants pick up many receptive language skills and structures. The eye gaze appears to be an important factor to the deaf infant—she moves from gazing at an object that catches her interest to watch-ing the parent for facial cues. You can use your gaze to guide the child's

The problems may look like this:
● ● ● ● ● ● ●

- Everyone nods their heads and no one knows what anyone else is talking about.

- One family member who has difficulty communicating with the deaf child always turns to another family member to facilitate communication.

- The deaf child is easily frustrated.

- The deaf child is left out of conversations.

- The hearing family members don't know how to converse with the deaf child.

- Hearing family members often say, "she (the deaf child) knows exactly what I am saying and is just pretending not to hear."

- People do not ask others to repeat themselves.

- Everyone communicates differently.

- One family member serves as an interpreter.

- The deaf child ignores communication.

- The deaf child often seems surprised.

- The deaf child shows behavioral problems such as throwing tantrums, defiance, destruction, and lying.

attention, commenting as you do on an object of interest that the child sees. Teach your child to take turns by waiting until the child faces you again. With a toddler, you can put yourself in the line of her gaze to make comments and physically show the child a sign/word you are using. For example, you can point to the door when you want a child to close it and move towards a chair when you want her to sit.

From infancy on, you can enhance your child's communicative strengths and create more successful interactions by thinking and using visual, tactile (touch), and kinesthetic (movement) means. Use mime and gestures to create visual contexts for communication; vary facial expressions to match the communicated content; and point when you are referring to an object, place, or person.

Consider usin̦   ̣trategies when communicating with your child:

1. Be sure to face th̦ deaf child when communicating.

2. Clear the visual path of all distractions (do not cover your mouth or sign around an object).

3. Remember to consistently use enhanced body language and nonverbal cues. However, do not over-emphasize speech or expressions since this makes signs and speechreading more difficult to follow.

4. Maintain constant eye contact.

5. Let one person speak at a time.

6. Pay close attention when the deaf child is communicating and, likewise, make sure she pays attention to you.

7. Be aware of light sources. When communicating with your deaf child, do not position yourself in front of a window or a lamp. This creates added eye strain and puts you in a shadow.

8. Use a soft ball or rolled up sock during family meetings to ensure that one person talks at a time. If someone wants to speak, she must have the ball.

9. Use an extra-large rearview mirror and bring a hand held mirror in your car. This makes talking to a deaf person sitting in the back seat easier. Always make sure your inside car light is working and bring a flashlight as well so that during nighttime travel everyone can be seen.

10. In a communication pinch, use the deaf child's TTY to communicate back and forth. You can only do this, of course, if the child is comfortable with her written English skills. Doing this also helps the child to get used to the TTY keys, abbreviations, and etiquette.

11. Getting a deaf person's attention can be done in many different ways. The following methods are used by many Deaf adults and children and are not considered offensive or impolite: flicking lights on and off; stamping on the floor or pounding on a table; tapping on the arm; waving your hands near the deaf person (but not right in her face); and for those who have some residual hearing, a quick, loud yell using a vowel ("AAAA" or "UUUU") or the person's name.

Share with your deaf child these communication aids. Encourage her to assert her communication needs whenever necessary and to remind others of the ways they can contribute to smooth communication.

You can expand your child's communication skills by using "wh" questions (who, what, when, where, why). "Yes/No" questions limit the deaf child's understanding, decrease the colorful nature of a story, minimize the child's analytical thinking ability, and shorten the degree and amount of interaction.

Teach your child to think for herself by offering her frequent choices. Use comparisons, asking which one the child chooses, likes, or prefers. For example, offer food choices, e.g., "You can have the sandwich with or without lettuce, which do you choose?" Or allow the child to decide how she wishes to budget her time, e.g., "You can do your homework now or do it later instead of TV time, which do you choose?"

While it is ideal for all family members to have the ability to communicate equally, it is common in a hearing family with one deaf child to find one person in the role of the "family interpreter." This person, often the mother or a sensitive sibling, facilitates communication between the deaf child and other family members. Although we understand the reasons why this might initially occur (mother was home more, a sibling was resentful, father worked late, grandmother was not good with languages), we cannot recommend this solution to family communication difficulties. The long-term results are detrimental—the interpreting member becomes stressed, the deaf child becomes more isolated and dependent, communication is indirect and incorrect, and the deaf child becomes fearful of dealing with the larger hearing public.

Always attempt to empower your child in a communication exchange. Allow responses to originate from her, pay attention to her interests and her initiations of conversation, take the time to validate what she has communicated, ask for clarification if there was a misunderstanding, and establish predictable family habits of checking to make sure that everything was understood.

Sometimes a deaf child does not know and is not able to express all of her communicative needs. Likewise, hearing parents use an auditory means of communicating and have been taught (through their parents) how to parent that way. Create opportunities for yourself to discuss issues of communication with deaf adults and/or deaf parents who can better articulate communicative needs than can a child. This certainly does not mean that a hearing parent should expect to communicate like a deaf parent—this is unreasonable and, of course, impossible. Examine successful models of communication by Deaf adults and then adapt these to meet the needs of your child and family.

Activities

[Note: For best results do these activities in succession since they build upon each other.]

. . . .

Activity #1: 101 Ways to Communicate

Materials: markers, poster paper
Age: 5–12
Vocabulary/Concepts: communication, list, easy, difficult

. . . .

This activity will give your family a multitude of ideas about the many ways to communicate. Begin by reminding family members that communication includes more than just "talking." For example, you can tell someone you are happy by smiling at them, drawing a happy picture, or skipping instead of walking. Dogs communicate happiness by wagging their tails. Next, take turns coming up with as many ways communication takes place as you can until you reach 101 ways to communicate (use a much lower number for young children) and write or draw pictures of as many ways as possible. Try acting out each suggestion.

When you've reached your target number, review the list and identify those ways that your family already uses. Then choose a few types of communication that your family does not use and agree to use each type for a half an hour at a time. For example, if drawing pictures is one method on your list then for the next thirty minutes have everyone in your family communicate only by drawing. You can do this with as many methods as you choose. At the end of this activity ask each family member what they learned. Encourage your family to note which kinds of communication they found easy and which they found difficult. Note when someone feels "left out" of a communication style as a way to encourage empathy and discourage blaming. When the deaf child is encouraged to identify her communicative needs, the whole family learns to accommodate differences instead of assuming a majority-rules posture.

. . . .

Activity #2: No Talking Aloud!

Materials: a meal
Age: 6–12
Vocabulary/Concepts: VOICE-OFF, no talking, communication,
COMMUNICATION BREAKDOWN

. . . .

This activity takes place during a meal and will help your entire family understand the efforts required for good communication. (The dinner table is often a place where the deaf child feels left out of the hearing members' communication.) Have your family prepare, eat, and clean up a meal without talking. No verbal, signed, or written language allowed. Before putting the "no talking" rule into effect, tell your family that during the meal everyone must also share what they did today and what they plan on doing tomorrow. For older children, do not decide ahead of time what you will be making for the meal or who is in charge of the various tasks. This will add to the challenge of the "no talking" period. If all of you maintain your sense of humor throughout this experience you will probably find this exercise very amusing. After completing the meal, ask each family member to describe how they felt while unable to communicate and understand each other clearly. You will all recognize how frustrating it would be to have to deal with this type of situation every day.

Activity #3: My Communication Book

Materials: notebooks or folded paper, stapler
Age: 5–12
Vocabulary/Concepts: brochure, book, PREFERENCE-MINE

Have each member of your family make a small booklet or brochure that explains to other people the best way to communicate with them. Children who are not able to write can draw pictures with your help. Explain to the children that this book/brochure will inform others about the appropriate ways to talk to them, get their attention, express thoughts and feelings to them, and develop a relationship. If you did the two previous activities, encourage each person to select communication techniques that they discovered worked best for them in their book/brochure. You can, and should, utilize the communication strategies mentioned earlier in this chapter. When everyone finishes their book, take turns reading and comparing each other's book or brochure. Ask what each person learned about the others and about herself.

If you have access to a video recorder, consider taping your family's instructions about how they like to communicate and watching the tapes together or showing them to extended family members and school personnel. You may even want to do this exercise annually as a way to check whether anybody's preferences in communication have changed, which often occurs when deaf children get more practice and exposure to various communication methods.

. . . .

Activity #4: The Six O'Clock News Special Report

Materials: pair of glasses, hat, pen, paper, clipboard
Age: 6–12
Vocabulary/Concepts: news, interview, reporter, communication,
   different situations, best, understand, OVER-MY-HEAD

. . . .

Tell your child that you are going to pretend to interview her for the "Six O'Clock News." Tell her this is a "Special Report" about communication with deaf people. You will ask many questions and she should answer them honestly and say what comes to her mind since many deaf children will be watching. If you like you could videotape this.

Now, don the hat and glasses and make a grand introduction. "Here from Pittsburgh, Pennsylvania, is Dominic . . ." With lots of animation and interest, probe your child for ways to describe when communication works and when it does not. Pay attention to your child's most spontaneous answers. Try to act neutrally towards any criticism, comment, or praise and continue to coax out more information. Keep the interview exciting and interesting as you try to get the most out of it. Here are some ideas for questions:

- In what way do you usually communicate?

- Do you like that way?

- How do you communicate with your friends? family? in school? extended family? stores? over the telephone?

- Do you communicate in more than one way?

- Which way do you like the best?

- When do you find it easiest to be understood?

- When is it the hardest?

- Which person (teacher, family, friend) is the hardest to understand? Who is the easiest?

- Everyone feels like giving up when they are frustrated—when have you felt like giving up?

- If you could change some things about the way people communicated with you, what would you change?

Use the information that you gather from this interview to discuss strong feelings that were described, new information you learned, and any changes that can be made. Have some of the children in the audience (you can switch roles or use other family members or friends) ask questions: "Dominic, I get frustrated because I don't like the way my teacher communicates with me. Do you have any suggestions?" Hearing family members might play the role of deaf children in the studio audience, asking questions of the deaf child being interviewed.

. . . .

Activity #5: The Good Communication Committee
Materials: poster board or large paper, markers, or crayon
Age: 3–12
Vocabulary/Concepts: committee, communication, list, understand

. . . .

Explain to your family that you are starting a committee in your home that promotes good communication and everyone is now on the committee. Together, make a list of all the important factors in good communication. Use the booklets, information, and lists from the previous activities to help you come up with your factors. Decide together which are the most important factors in good communication and write them boldly on the poster board. Encourage your child(ren) to draw pictures of each factor next to the statement for increased comprehension. Remember to consider the strategies on page 75. Make up a title for your poster board list and post it on a wall for all to see. On a regular basis, review these factors—note the difficulties that may arise, share ideas as to how to support and remind one another, and revise this list as your family becomes more aware of the intricacies of communication.

. . . .

Activity #6: Catch 'Em Communicating
Materials: dominoes or pieces of paper numbered one to six, two
    chairs, an egg timer or watch with second hand, poster paper
    with six good communication guidelines
Age: 7–12
Vocabulary/Concepts: good communication, understand, role-play, NEXT
    (meaning next person's turn), notice, catch (communication)

. . . .

This activity gives your family a way to observe and practice good communication skills. You can use some of the ideas presented in the beginning section of this chapter or from the previous activity to create a list of communication guidelines. (An example of a guideline would be "taking turns when communicating.") This activity requires that all participants pay attention to each other and ask for clarification when they don't understand one another. Post the communication guidelines for everyone to see.

Have two members of your family sit in the chairs—they are the role players. Instruct them to have a conversation about anything for up to three minutes. In that time, the rest of the family will watch and note which rules the two members followed. At the end of the three minutes, each member of the audience holds up a domino or piece of paper indicating the number of rules (between none and six) that were followed by each role player and explains what they saw.

To avoid making this into a competitive game, try the following: have each participant receive an immediate six if she listens and accepts feedback without arguing or becoming defensive (though anyone can disagree and state their point of view); the family can collectively work toward a total number of points (for example, thirty), and give yourselves a treat for reaching your goal; or during the role-plays, the audience can stop the timer and remind the role players which rules they did not use yet, then start the timer again. Invite extended family members, friends, or neighbors to join in.

. . . .

Activity #7: Interpret and Repeat

Materials: poster board or large paper, markers, flat disks or stones
Age: 7–12
Vocabulary/Concepts: interpret, ask again, repeat, not understand,
COMMUNICATION BREAKDOWN, OVERWHELMED, OVER-MY-HEAD, FINALLY-
UNDERSTAND

. . . .

This activity helps family members pay careful attention to communication; adapt their communication when needed; ask for clarification; observe that all members (deaf and hearing) sometimes have communication misunderstandings; note the patience required between deaf/hearing members; and, finally, note the difficulty that comes when one member is assigned the role of being the family interpreter. For this activity, you will need to have at least three participants.

Make a grid of lines on the poster board with a marker, dividing the paper into nine or twelve blocks. In the blocks, write any words that correspond to your family's life or habits—such as "school," "ice cream," "vacation," or "chores." You can use pictures from magazines, photos, or family photos for younger children. One person (person #1) tosses the marker onto the paper and then she must say something about the item on which the marker lands, such as, "my favorite ice cream is chocolate and I like to eat it in the summer." However, the trick is that she must tell only person #2, who will act as an interpreter. While person #1 gives her message to person #2, person #3 covers her ears and eyes. Then person #2 must accurately relate to person #3 what person #1 said. If the interpreter did not understand person #1, then she must ask for the explanation again. If person #1 was unclear, she must try another way to get her point across. After the interpreter relays the information, person #1 notes whether the interpreter got it right—if she didn't, the process begins again.

Communication clarification can be a tedious process, but often children will put more energy into the process when it is structured in the form of a game. You can also put specific topics into the grid that your family particularly wants to discuss. A variation on this game might include putting feeling words or pictures into the grid and having the children describe what makes them feel that way. At the end of the game, point out to all players the energy required to achieve clear communication. Highlight techniques people used, like miming, slowing down, or asking questions. Also, discuss how people felt about the process of using an interpreter. Talk about actual instances when family members were put in that position and how that made them feel.

COMMUNICATION COMMITMENT WITHIN THE FAMILY

The deaf child can only participate fully in the family if she has access to communication. This means that the family must adapt its style of communicating to accommodate the needs of the deaf child. Information exchanged in the family must be exchanged equally.

Young children learn new languages easier than older children and adults. Linguists have traditionally considered the time before the age of three to be the optimal time for a child to learn a language (though current research is indicating an even younger maximum age). This does not mean that a child cannot learn at a later age, but that it will be more difficult. The earlier you can make a communication commitment that matches your deaf child's needs, the better.

While exploring different choices in communication you will undoubtedly encounter the strong opinions of others. You may naturally gravitate towards people who share your ideas. Take time to listen to different points of view. Gather information from other parents of deaf children, from schools, from other deaf children, and most importantly, from empathetic Deaf adults.

Seek out and maintain contact with people who will not only give you information, but who will listen to your fears, questions, goals, and wishes for your child. Your feelings have merit. If you are feeling sad, angry, tired, frustrated, guilty, fearful, or confused—you are not unusual. Get support from your family, partner, friends, other parents or trusted professionals. Express your feelings and deal with them.

If your child senses that you prefer a particular communication choice, she may try to accommodate you at the expense of her own communicative needs. In short, she doesn't want to be disloyal to your feelings. If you are having difficulty accepting your child's deafness, she will clumsily act hearing; if you are embarrassed to sign in public, your deaf child will be embarrassed as well. You are not to blame for your feelings, but if you don't deal with them, they will have a strong impact on your child's ability to tell you directly what works for her. In addition, you may have to attend to a hearing sibling's strong feelings about having a deaf sister or brother. Feelings of frustration, anger, and jealousy in a hearing sibling can lead to resistance to a communication commitment.

In order to make a commitment, families must understand the various communication choices available. The descriptions below are derived primarily from the NICD (National Information Center on Deafness) Deafness Fact Sheet (1984, 1987, 1989).

American Sign Language: This is the language of the Deaf community, the language that Deaf people use among themselves. It is only in the past few decades that ASL has become recognized as a bona fide language, with a different grammar, syntax, vocabulary, and structure than English. Because ASL is a visual-gestural language, it appeals to a Deaf person's strengths and is, therefore, easiest for most Deaf people to learn.

Fingerspelling: This utilizes a handshape for every letter of the English alphabet. Most of the time, fingerspelling is used by deaf people when there is no sign for a word (such as "Toyota™"). The method of using spoken English with constant fingerspelling is called the Rochester Method.

Manual English: This is a form of signing that follows English word order and uses signs and nonmanual signals from American Sign Language. It is often called contact signing since the form is neither ASL nor English, but a mixture of the two.

Manually Coded English: This is a signing system developed to teach English to young deaf children. Words are signed in English word order and the system includes invented signs that connote English grammar—suffixes and verb tenses, for example.

Oral Communication: This form uses residual hearing, speechreading, and speech. This requires specific training in the use of (usually amplified) residual hearing.

Speechreading: This is a method which relies on the deaf person watching the speaker's lips, face, and gestures. Because only thirty percent of English words are available on the lips, and because many words look alike, this method requires a greater degree of attention and guesswork.

Cued Speech: By using eight handshapes in four positions, this method attempts to show different speech sounds (vowels, diphthongs, and consonants). For example, an open palm faced in would go to the side of the mouth when using the vowel sound *ur* (h*er*) and at the throat when using the vowel sound *oo* (b*oo*k).

Simultaneous Communication: This method uses speech, signs, and fingerspelling simultaneously.

Total Communication: This is not necessarily a method but rather a philosophy of trying any method (or language) and any combination of methods and languages to meet the individual needs of the particular deaf child.

The following activities will help your family explore communication choices for deaf individuals and encourage you to make a commitment to one specific communication method. If, after exploring the issue with your deaf child and family, it appears that you initially chose a method that does not meet your needs, bear in mind that it is never too late to change your family communication method. Keep an open mind to the thoughts, feelings, and concerns each person expresses daily regarding your family communication method. However, always remember that the deaf child must be an active participant in the family communication or "family" communication is not truly happening.

Activities
• •
Activity #1: The Family Communication Detective Agency
Materials: notebook, pen or pencil, list of sets of questions, Deaf
      adults, poster paper, markers, small index or business cards,
      poster board
Age: 6–12
Vocabulary/Concepts: detective, best communication, English, ASL,
      speak, sign language, speechread, cued speech, interview, ASK
      (CONTINUOUSLY), COMMUNICATION-DIFFERENT-DIFFERENT-DIFFERENT
• •

This activity offers a fun way to learn about different communication methods that work for deaf individuals and to help your family make choices. Before you do this activity, we suggest that you do the following activities (described above): "My Communication Brochure" and "The Six O'Clock News Special Report" (see pgs. 78–80). This allows your deaf child to define personal communication needs and preferences.

Pretend that your family members are starting up a language detective agency to help families with deaf members discover which communication method to use in their home. Suggest that by learning about the different communication methods available to Deaf people (oral, cued speech, American Sign Language, contact signing/Pidgin Signed English, manually coded English, etc.), your family can consciously decide on a communication plan that best suits the deaf family member. Consider reading (and reviewing) books that talk about different communication systems, such as, *Can't Your Child Hear?* (Roger D. Freeman, Clifton F. Carbin, and Robert J. Boese, PRO-ED, 1981) and *Choices in Deafness: A Parent's Guide* (Sue Schwartz, Woodbine House, 1987).

You may even want to visit schools in your area where you can view different systems in practice. Encourage your children to interview deaf individuals who use each method of communication and see how they feel about it. If you don't know many deaf adults, you may be able to meet some by contacting school programs servicing deaf children, state agencies for the deaf, and Independent Living Skills centers for the deaf in your area. If you have a hard time locating these, consider contacting the National Information Center on Deafness in Washington, D.C., for listings of local resources in your area.

You will need to come up with a detective interview form, and we list some sample questions to include on it below. The first set of questions gives a sense of who the person is that you are interviewing. This is important because your deaf child will be comparing herself to these people. For example, if your child was born deaf, she will likely have a more difficult time learning to speak English than a person who became deaf as an adult and had heard English spoken since childhood.

Set One

- When did you become deaf?

- Can you hear speech with hearing aids? How much?

- Do you call yourself deaf or hard of hearing?

- Do you have a deaf family or a hearing family?

- Do you have deaf or hearing friends?

Set Two

- What method of communication do you use?

- What is the best part of communicating this way?

- What is the worst part?

● Is it easy to do?

● Is it hard to learn?

● Are you comfortable with your form of communication?

Once your family has gathered enough information to understand the communication methods available to deaf people, you are ready to open your business. You might even have fun putting up a sign stating the name of your detective agency. Have your children design business cards. Make your family your first customers. Take turns being the detective who interviews each family member, either using the detective form or making up new questions. At the end of your interviews, have a company meeting to discuss your results. You can guide this discussion into a more serious analysis of the best communication mode for your family given the detective work completed. Any final decisions must take into full account the deaf child's preferences and needs to be a contributing member of the family. Consider opening your agency up to other families who need your services!

. . . .

Activity #2: Bell v. Gallaudet
Materials: library books or resource books on Edward Miner Gallaudet
 and Alexander Graham Bell, paper, markers, good actors
Age: 8–12
Vocabulary/Concepts: Edward Miner Gallaudet, Alexander Graham Bell
 (AGB), debate, agree, disagree, point of view, oral, sign language,
 communication, DIFFERENT POINTS OF VIEW, DISAGREE STRONGLY

. . . .

Another way your family can learn about the different communication methods available to deaf people and the history behind them is to hold a mock debate between the nineteenth-century American oral method supporter, Alexander Graham Bell, and his main opponent, a leading supporter of using sign language, Edward Miner Gallaudet. Read about these two men before the debate and take turns being on each side of the argument. (We recommend that you read, *Never the Twain Shall Meet: Bell, Gallaudet, and the Communications Debate* by Richard Winefield (Gallaudet University Press, 1987). (Because this book is written for adults, you should read through it and pick out the information pertinent to this activity.) Make a list of pros and cons for each communication method supported in the debate and discuss them later. This activity will help put your family situation into historical perspective while at the same time encouraging all family members, particularly your deaf child, to assert their points of view regarding family communication systems.

. . . .

Activity #3: The Communication Commitment Contract

Materials: *notebook paper, pencil or pen*

Age: *3–12*

Vocabulary/Concepts: *contract, agreement, promise, left out, respect,*
communication, ISOLATED/BY MYSELF

. . . .

After your family decides the best method of communication to be used in your home, bring all members together to sign a contract that pledges a team commitment. Make sure everyone understands how important it is to stick to the commitment once the contract is signed. Be as specific as possible about what to do when the deaf child is not in the room or when she steps into a room. Often, hearing people step into conversations and overhear or hear from another room, so you may want to include in your contract ways for the deaf family member to immediately become a part of a conversation (for example, briefly recapping what was just said when the deaf child joins the discussion). Figure out a way to designate a private conversation so the deaf child does not have to guess whether a conversation is private or if she is simply being left out. This can be done by closing doors; using "private-do not disturb" signs; moving a conversation to another room or behind a wall; or telling a child directly, "this is private and we don't want to share what we are discussing."

. . . .

Activity #4: Communication Commitment Club

Materials: *meeting place*

Age: *6–12*

Vocabulary/Concepts: *communication, commitment, club, meetings*
complaints, PRAISE, AGREEMENT

. . . .

Take the previous activity one step further by organizing a club that provides support and guidance to club members. Have regular club meetings to discuss family members' appreciations and grievances regarding the communication commitment. Make a list of club member requirements, such as learning five new signs a week or using the chosen method of communication at all meals. Appoint a communication spy for the week who eavesdrops on family members and reports back about whether or not family members have stuck to their commitments. Give praise and acknowledgement when the spy reports back efforts that are made. Make club membership exciting by throwing a party once in a while to celebrate hard work.

Activity #5: Communication Chips
Materials: *poker chips*
Age: 3–12
Vocabulary/Concepts: communication, chips, family, HIT-GOAL

Using poker chips, give family members a chip every time they make an effort to use your family communication method. Take turns being the "giver of the chips." Decide on a reward to give to family members who have accumulated a certain number of chips.

Activity #6: Learning Sign Language Together
Materials: *see activity for details*
Age: *all ages*
Vocabulary/Concepts: American Sign Language, words, TOGETHER

The following activities can help develop stronger vocabularies and a greater sense of comfort in using sign language.

Family Videotape: Using a video camera, make a training tape of signs. Your entire family can take turns as the teacher on the tape. Categorize lessons by subject matter, such as numbers, weather, school, or food. Make a video library of the signs and be sure to loan them to relatives.

Sign Pin-up for the Month: Buy an additional sign language book that you truly like. Photocopy and cut out the sign language pictures and tape the correct sign on all the objects in your home for up to a month. Be creative and silly and put the sign pictures on food in the refrigerator or on toilet paper. At the end of the month, when everyone can remember the signs, put them on index cards for later use. Do this as often as you like.

Sign Language Party: Have a party for adults and children where everyone must only use sign language to communicate. Assign family members as "sign coaches" to help people learn signs. Decorate the house with sign pictures drawn by your children. You may want to do the previous activity (Sign Pin-up) for a month and then leave the signs on the objects to help guests in your home. Play sign language games using hand shapes. You can order sign language activity books and games from catalogs listed below. Invite Deaf adults into your home to teach these games. Give out prizes for those who learned the most signs, signed the fastest, slowest, or the goofiest.

Signing Fun: Some vendors specialize in selling all kinds of objects with signs on them, such as t-shirts, necklaces, mugs, and other gift items. Reinforce your love for this language by purchasing a few such items for your home. See the resource list in chapter 2 for information about where you can purchase these items.

. . . .

Activity #7: TV Story Time

Materials: a closed captioned video with a story to interest your child, VCR, activities in communication commitment section
Age: 3–12
Vocabulary/Concepts: closed captions, story, not understand, pause, beginning, end, repeat, HOLD (one-handed sign), WAIT

. . . .

This is a simple activity you can use to encourage your child to ask for help, note misunderstandings, seek clarification, and become accustomed to using closed captioning. Watch a closed captioned video with your child and check for comprehension by asking questions, interpreting words which cannot be read, stopping the film to explain, and summarizing. Before attempting this activity you will have had to have arrived at a communication commitment in your family that uses the preferred communication method of your child. That method is what you practice in this activity.

Rent a cartoon your child would enjoy. For the younger child who cannot read, you will serve as a storyteller. Point to the TV screen to emphasize a message, highlight a word your child might know by sight, mimic the characters, and indicate a popcorn break. For the older child, watch a film and note that you will help when she does not understand a word or perhaps the words move too fast. Pause the film occasionally to answer any questions or clear up any confusions. Notice when the film captions might be moving too fast for your child; clarify English idioms; and take a break now and then so you can converse with your child about the film to see how much your child understands. For this activity to be successful and fun, you will have to set aside more time than the actual running time of the film.

Growing Up in a Bicultural Environment

• • • • • • • • • • •

Rosalyn L. Gannon and Jack R. Gannon

*M*ost deaf people, whether they admit it or not, live in two different worlds—deaf and hearing—and they do so because of the communication gap between those two worlds. As long as deaf people live in a sound-oriented world and must rely on a visual form of communication, there will be a bicultural environment.

Like a large majority of deaf offspring, we have hearing parents. We grew up and lived in two worlds. Now, as the parents of two hearing children, we continue the bicultural family cycle.

When we were growing up, school options for deaf children were basically oral versus manual. Deciding on the type of schooling was the first and most important decision our parents had to make after they had come to terms with our deafness. This was a decision that had the greatest impact on our lives and was, no doubt, our introduction to deaf culture. This was probably where our "differences" were most noted because, instead of attending the local public school where our brothers and sisters went, we attended a special school away from home.

Rosalyn L. Gannon is a sign language teacher at Gallaudet University. Jack R. Gannon is Special Assistant to the President of Gallaudet University. Both are Gallaudet graduates and former teachers of deaf children. They have two hearing children.

This introduction is adapted from "Between Two Worlds," which appeared in the Fall 1990 issue of *Gallaudet Today* (pp. 12–16). Reprinted by permission of *Gallaudet Today*.

Both of us are glad that our parents made those sacrifices. Attending a school whose mission is to work with deaf students provided us with opportunities to get a sound education, develop confidence and a healthy self-respect, and acquire social, leadership, and communication skills. Our schools are—and were—rich in deaf history. There are buildings, organizations, memorials to deaf people—the roots of our deaf culture. Under such circumstances, we could never use deafness as an excuse not to excel.

At school we were exposed to some of the best teachers in the nation. Many were deaf like us and individuals we came to admire, love, and respect. Most of them left a profound impact on our lives. We believe this experience contributed to our self-confidence and made us more well-rounded deaf people and more tolerant of the hearing world.

Our parents were discouraged from learning sign language because they were told that it would interfere with our speech development. This was the earliest futile attempt to get us away from the deaf world and make us members of the hearing world. As a result of this oral-only indoctrination, we often missed out on much of the family conversation when we were at home. In Rosalyn's family, where her sisters signed, she was more a part of the family. In Jack's family, where all conversation was oral, he was frequently the odd man out except when a family member would take the time to repeat what was being discussed. This feeling of exclusion was felt by almost all of our deaf friends who were the offspring of hearing parents, and the isolation was generally accepted as a way of life.

During our youth, terms such as deaf culture, deaf heritage, deaf pride, and American Sign Language were unheard of. Growing up deaf in a hearing family with limited communication is probably more "normal" than most people realize. It involves a lot of coping, especially for the deaf person. Much of that coping—for example, having to ask a family member to repeat what someone is saying—would not be necessary if the whole family could sign. When deaf members are not involved in family plans from the outset, they feel very left out and deprived of the opportunity to contribute ideas. The deaf member has the same right and need as other family members to be part of family discussions and to know about family crises, financial issues, and daily chitchat. Families also should have the same expectations for deaf and hearing siblings. When good communication is lacking, these needs are not met.

The greatest difficulty parents have is accepting the fact that their child is deaf and, in most cases, will be deaf the rest of his or her life. That is a normal reaction. Yet, the key to a deaf individual's success may well be the degree of the parents' acceptance of the child's deafness.

An important decision that parents must face is the kind of communication that will be used within the family. A free, comfortable communication environment is so important to the healthy development of any child. It is even more important to a deaf child and determines the extent of the child's involvement in the family. Each family member is confronted with the ongoing challenge and responsibility of involving the deaf member. Sadly, in most families that do not sign, this too often does not happen.

The difficulty in family communication is a reason most deaf members prefer to bypass large family gatherings and reunions. In these situations, they either feel like pests when they have to ask someone to repeat what is being said or are bored to death if they don't. So it is not really surprising that sometimes deaf members of a hearing family look at an all-deaf family, where communication is not an issue, and wonder about all the things they are missing.

Deaf children love their parents just as much as other children do. The fact that their parents can hear makes little difference to them when they are young. But those parents who cannot effectively communicate with their children will realize that the inability to communicate will take its toll as the children grow older. If deaf children cannot be involved members of their families, they tend to develop independently, often distancing themselves from non-signing members of their families as they become older. When and if their deaf child marries—most likely to another deaf person—the hearing parents' inability to communicate well with a deaf person will really hit home, but by then it is usually too late.

Deaf people, by nature of their deafness, will always live in two worlds. Hearing people have more of a choice. They can become part of the deaf world or they can ignore it. For deaf people, the choice to be a full, participating member of the hearing world is not as easy. It is up to parents to take the first step into the deaf child's world.

One of our friends advises parents of deaf children to "seek professional help to understand the child's deafness; learn how to communicate with the child and don't underestimate the importance and usefulness of using sign language; and give the child all the love and support he or she needs, and watch the child bloom!"

For new parents of deaf children, there is more information and help available today than ever before. Society in general is slowly moving toward accepting Americans who have disabilities and who are members of different cultures. It won't happen overnight; it will take years and years, but we are making progress. The best place to begin to encourage such changes is within the family. Parents can help by accepting deaf children as the individuals they are, and not by trying to mold them into someone else.

Our advice to parents is this: Learn to communicate with your deaf child as well as you communicate with other offspring in the family. Give the deaf child every opportunity and the responsibility to be a fully participating member of the family. Encourage pride and self-esteem. Get to know deaf adults. This experience will broaden your own horizons and help you understand and appreciate the impact of deafness on an individual's life. As your deaf child grows, make sure she is aware of all the opportunities available, and encourage and challenge your child to pursue those areas that are of interest and are appropriate. Become a champion of deaf people and their rights.

Today's deaf children have many educational options. When they leave school, they will enter a world that is much more aware of and sensitive to deafness and deaf people than when we graduated from high school. There are more programs, services, and opportunities available to them than ever before. Those who have been exposed to deaf culture have grown up with a sense of pride in themselves and their deafness and have not been tarnished by the negative stigma attached to deafness that plagued previous generations.

As deaf people gain access to a communication process they can understand and benefit from, as they become more fully participating members of society, and as more hearing people become interested in learning sign language, the differences between the deaf and hearing cultures will begin to shrink. Until then, most deaf people will continue to live in two worlds and attempt to enjoy the best of both.

CHAPTER

6

Cultural Diversity in the Family

• • • •

In the following activities we aim to encourage your deaf child to learn more about his own family history and relationships. Secondly, we hope the activities allow for your family to better understand and respect Deaf people and their culture.

The Deaf community supports deaf children in having a sense of Deaf history and cultural identity. Having a sense of belonging to a group of people who have similar experiences enriches one's self-concept and generally promotes a purposeful and fulfilling outlook on life.

FAMILY CULTURE

Deaf children sometimes spend years living with daily misunderstandings or lack of knowledge about their families. Detail your family history with your child to clarify family relationships and put these into some kind of time frame.

Take the time to explain the significance of religious ceremonies and the basis for ethnic values. Many deaf children identify strongly with their family heritage, e.g., Latinos, African-Americans. But specific explanations from you of the expectations, behaviors, and rituals unique to the child's ethnic heritage allows the child to identify in a more deliberate way.

Provide the child with an interpreter for all family rituals (weddings, funerals, graduations, bar mitzvahs) to ensure that your deaf child comprehends and fully shares in all family life-cycle events.

The problems may look like this:
● ● ● ● ● ● ●

- The deaf child often feels left out.

- The family feels sorry for the deaf child.

- The deaf child's facial expressions are full and dramatic compared to the more controlled faces of the hearing family members.

- Hearing family members frequently shout to get the deaf child's attention.

- Family members feel embarrassed by the deaf child.

- The family and deaf child pretend the child is hearing.

- The deaf child believes that deafness is a bad thing.

- The deaf child avoids any and all deaf people.

- Neighborhood children exclude the deaf child.

- Neighborhood adults and businesses treat the deaf child as impaired, infantilize him, give him special favors, and don't apply the same rules of behavior to him.

- The child with residual hearing (hard of hearing) seems awkward and does not fit in with either deaf or hearing groups.

- The hard of hearing child pretends to fit in with deaf and hearing groups, often missing many communicative and social cues.

Activities

Activity #1: Our Family History
Materials: books about family trees, butcher paper, markers or
    crayons, family photographs
Age: 6–12
Vocabulary/Concepts: family, mother, father, grandmother,
    grandfather, aunt, uncle, cousin, daughter, son, LONG AGO,
    generations, born, died, country names, FAMILY TREE (2-handed sign)

Learn more about your family ancestry together by making a family tree. The generational outline of parents, grandparents, and great-grandparents gives children a clearer concept of their roots. We recommend the book, *Do People Grow On Trees: Genealogy for Kids and Other Beginners* (Ira Wolfman, Workman Publishing, 1991) to help you design your own family tree. Include the name of a relative as well as the place they were born. Make a large table-top or life-sized tree out of butcher paper and crayons or markers, which are more visually dramatic. Go back as far as possible in your family history. Family photos may help to explain some difficult concepts. Often young children have a hard time grasping that parents or grandparents were once children. Help your children imagine their ancestors in another place and time by showing them pictures of the dress and environments of the other relevant eras and countries.

• •

Activity #2: The Family Book
Materials: pens, crayons, markers, magazines, scissors, paper, family
    photographs (copies or xeroxed copies)
Age: 6–12
Vocabulary/Concepts: see above activity

• •

Make a family book about the story of your family beginning three to four generations ago. Work together to find out your family history and include stories of older relatives and important cultural happenings. Have your children draw pictures or use photos. Cut out pictures of your ancestors' country of origin from magazines and history books. Bring your book to family gatherings and have your children read the book with other relatives.

• •

Activity #3: Family Interviews
Materials: family tree or family book (see above two activities), pencil,
    paper, TTY
Age: 7–12
Vocabulary/Concepts: see above two activities

• •

In order to elicit questions from and stimulate the curiosity of your child, do this activity following one of the previous two. At any family gathering, encourage your child to interview older relatives for information about their culture and history. Talk to your relatives in advance and prompt them to think of some stories that would appeal to children. Help your child by suggesting interview questions. Of course, the crux of this activity is comfortable communication. If the elders in the deaf child's family are unable to communicate effectively with the child, consider using the two previous activities to set up concrete and visual starting places for stories. In this way, both the child and elder can point to various pictures, backgrounds or clothes by way of explanation. To aid in communication, consider using a pen and paper, TTY, or, in this special instance, have immediate family members act as interpreters to clarify communication with extended family members. These interpreters might sign or repeat what was said if other methods of communication prove unsuccessful.

· ·

Activity #4: Cultural Celebrations
Materials: knowledge of your family's ethnic/cultural rituals
Age: all ages
Vocabulary/Concepts: family, culture, celebrate, party

· ·

Choose a day every year to celebrate your family's heritage. Invite family and friends to a day of food, dancing, music, folk tales, and games from your ethnic and national heritage. For example, if your family is of Italian extraction, organize an annual celebration with Italian food, music, and traditional dances. Also, your family can learn more about diversity within the Deaf community by contacting various schools for the deaf around the country, by learning more about regional signs, and by finding out how deaf people are treated across the nation or in the countries of your family's origin.

WHAT IS DEAF CULTURE?

For many years, deaf individuals have strongly relied on their language (American Sign Language or ASL) and the Deaf community. Following the research on ASL and the civil rights movements of the 1960s, the term American Deaf Culture was coined to describe the values and beliefs supported by its members. Deaf culture is something that Deaf people speak of with pride, knowledge, and love.

The Deaf community has been likened to other minority groups and is often referred to as a "linguistic minority." History shows that the majority culture (in this case hearing) often makes assumptions and decisions for the minority culture (in this case Deaf). Countless stories and policies reveal insensitivity toward and oppression of deaf individuals. Astonishingly, Gallaudet University (the only liberal arts university established specifically for deaf people) had never had a deaf president until 1988. Deaf individuals were first accepted into Gallaudet's graduate programs in the 1960s.

From the point of view of Deaf culture, deafness has little to do with the actual medical condition of not being able to hear. Rather, the Deaf culture stresses pride in American Sign Language, in the stories and performances communicated in ASL, and in the community and values of Deaf people. It does not matter whether one is audiologically classified as deaf or hard of hearing—anyone with a hearing loss who follows the norms of the culture is considered, with pride, "Deaf."

American Deaf Culture (like all other sub-cultures and communities) has a particular set of beliefs and acceptable behaviors. Examples of these include use of American Sign Language; strong and consistent eye contact; codes for personal space and touch; different use of facial expressions and taking turns than in English; matter-of-factly speaking about what one observes; and using flashing lights, foot-stamping, or pounding on a table to catch another's attention.

Deaf children develop a more positive self-concept and feel less isolated when they have a connection with other deaf people who share their needs. A deaf child of deaf parent(s) is most likely born into Deaf culture, identifies with that culture, participates in the community's activities, and learns ASL as a first language. A deaf child of hearing parents (and this constitutes approximately ninety percent of the deaf population) finds himself in a set of circumstances in which he must seek out deaf peers and adults and learn through them the ways of the community and the language. Historically, deaf children of deaf parents have taught the community's mores to the newcomers (deaf children of hearing parents).

Residential schools for the Deaf have traditionally been where deaf children (from hearing families) learn and live the Deaf cultural values. Because of the current trend of mainstreaming/inclusion in public schools, many deaf children are missing out on learning these cultural values. From a cultural point of view, the Deaf community sees this as a loss.

Regardless of the school they attended, communication style, or degree of hearing loss, many Deaf and hard of hearing adults seek out people like themselves and, therefore, become a part of the Deaf community. In fact, a high percentage of deaf individuals marry others in the Deaf community.

Many diverse groups of Deaf people live in different geographical areas and many cities have their own Deaf community, though there is but one American Deaf culture. In addition, Deaf communities are sometimes divided by race. Due to a long history of segregation, especially in the South, there is a strong African-American Deaf community that often uses a different variety of American Sign Language.

Among the growing numbers of immigrant and ethnic deaf individuals, many identify with their cultural or racial heritage before identifying with Deaf culture. In fact, one can think of these individuals as being multi-lingual and multi-cultural.

Activities

....

Activity #1: Deaf Like Me
Materials: soft and safe ear plugs (optional), paper, markers
Age: 6–12
Vocabulary/Concepts: feelings, VOICE-OFF, POSITIVE/NEGATIVE, OPPOSITE
POINTS OF VIEW
....

One can begin to understand the culture of Deaf people by getting a feeling for what it is like to be deaf. Choose a day when your family becomes deaf. If the situations that you are establishing feel safe, the hearing members can use ear plugs to eliminate some sound. The sounds should be turned off on the television, stereo, and door bell. TTYs and the relay service should replace the telephones. Hearing family members should pretend they are deaf. Shut off your voice and do not answer people when you cannot see them. If you can, take your deaf family out to shop, eat in a restaurant, or play at the park. Observe how others treat you. At the end of the day, reflect on what you have learned. Make a list of both the pleasant things and the challenges you experienced.

....

Activity #2: Deaf Heritage
Materials: *Deaf Heritage: A Narrative History of Deaf America.* (Jack
Gannon, National Association of the Deaf, 1981) props and
clothes for skit
Age: 7–12
Vocabulary/Concepts: Deaf history, perform, LONG, LONG AGO
....

Jack Gannon has written a book entitled, ***Deaf Heritage: A Narrative History of Deaf America*** that should be a part of your library. Read this book and choose stories and historical facts on Deaf heritage and culture to relate to and dramatize with your children in the form of family puppet shows, skits, or role plays. Actively teach your child about Deaf culture in the same way that you teach him about his religion or ethnic heritage.

Activity #3: Deaf Heritage II

Materials: paper, markers, crayons, cardboard for book sleeves, cloth
or construction paper to cover sleeves
Age: 8–12
Vocabulary/Concepts: see above activity

Make your own book together about Deaf heritage to be read by other children. Summarize interesting points in the history of Deaf people and have your children make illustrations and write or dictate the narrative. If your family prefers live action rather than drawing and writing, make a home video of the history of Deaf people, complete with costumes and props.

Activity #4: The Deaf Library

Materials: blank area on a shelf, books, magazines, newspapers related
to Deaf people and issues
Age: all ages
Vocabulary/Concepts: library, magazines, books, newspapers

In addition to encouraging learning, books confirm in a child's mind that a topic deserves attention. By collecting books about deafness and Deaf people, you make a statement to your family about the importance of the topic. Imagine how your child feels when he sees an entire book shelf in your home devoted to deaf-related books. A number of presses send out listings of both new books and all-time favorites. The Gallaudet University Press, the Gallaudet University Bookstore, and the National Association for the Deaf are great resources. See the resource lists in chapter 2 for more information. In their catalogs, you can find books your children can read independently or with your assistance. Collect and read sign language books, historical and cultural books, autobiographies, parenting books, textbooks, or magazines such as the *Deaf American*. You may find invaluable information in these resources. Collect children's books that appeal to your child's age and language capabilities. When you read adult books about deafness, share what you learn with your child at whatever level he will understand. For example, "I have to tell you what I read about Laurent Clerc today."

HOW TO INTEGRATE DEAF CULTURE IN YOUR FAMILY

Hearing parents of deaf children and adults in the Deaf community often do not have opportunities to become acquainted with each other. Hearing parents usually remain unaware of Deaf culture and community events, and Deaf adults do not have a pressing need to include hearing parents in Deaf community activities. An unfortunate result of such a division is that both hearing parents and Deaf adults do not understand or learn from one another, and the deaf child must navigate between them.

Your entire family can become comfortable with the idea of a Deaf community and can benefit from attending local Deaf events. When you meet welcoming Deaf adults, make sure to maintain contact with them. Ask them to let you know about Deaf community events. Work at building friendships with Deaf adults and subsequently invite them to your home.

When a deaf child of hearing parents begins to assimilate more Deaf cultural values, he may find conflicts between Deaf and hearing ways. This is not a bad thing. Your child has to begin somewhere in working out how he will handle his bicultural existence. If the deaf child becomes familiar with the values and behaviors of both Deaf and hearing culture, he will gradually learn to make adaptations when moving back and forth between the two.

At some point in your child's development, especially in pre-adolescence and adolescence, he may become a militant supporter of Deaf cultural values. If he has not already done so, he may at this time realize that many of his frustrations arise not because there is something wrong with him, but as a result of hearing people not understanding his needs. Always listen to your child's point of view and let him teach you what he is learning about himself.

Hearing parents often fear that they will lose their deaf child to Deaf culture. This is an understandable feeling since Deaf and hearing cultures are distinctly separate. However, you will never stop being your child's parents. The more you learn and stay interested in Deaf culture, the more you can participate in all aspects of your child's life.

Many states have parenting organizations that serve parents of deaf and hard of hearing children. In addition to giving support and guidance, these groups can introduce the Deaf culture to your family. We suggest that you contact one of these parenting organizations. You may decide to join one of them and if so you could establish a "subcommittee" that focuses on integrating Deaf culture into hearing families with a deaf family member. Call it the Culture Club if you like.

Your Culture Club could organize monthly activities at which Deaf adults tell stories to the children, talk about Deaf culture, and encourage children to feel pride in being Deaf. Celebrate together notable days in Deaf history, such as Laurent Clerc's birthday or I. King Jordon's selection as Gallaudet University's first Deaf president. Organize special trips together to visit colleges for the Deaf, Deaf clubs in your area, and special events in the Deaf community.

Consider holding a fundraiser to make money for the Culture Club or other special organizations of and for deaf people. Make the fundraiser an event related to Deaf culture by having games and events which teach about Deaf history. Sell t-shirts with sign language insignia or write and act in a play that teaches other children about Deaf culture. The show might include only deaf students or both deaf children and their hearing siblings. Your entire family can participate in Culture Club events.

Activities

. . . .

Activity #1: Write a Hero
Materials: paper, pen
Age: 5–12
Vocabulary/Concepts: hero, letter, send, LOOK-UP-TO

. . . .

The whole family can participate in this activity. Research current events and select a "deaf hero" to whom you would like to write. You might choose a sports star, such as Kenny Walker; an actress, like Marlee Matlin or Linda Bove (from "Sesame Street"); or a Deaf adult in your community who has done something to spark your child's interest. Write to several people if you like and be sure to encourage your child to note his pride in the hero's achievements as a Deaf person.

. . . .

Activity #2: The "Big D"
Materials: colorful poster paper or old, light-colored cotton sheet or
    material
Age: 6–12
Vocabulary/Concepts: big D, positive pride, INCREASE SELF-ESTEEM

. . . .

In Deaf culture, it is common to capitalize the "D" in Deaf when writing the word. This means that you are referring to all of the positive cultural aspects of being Deaf and not just defining deaf to mean "nonhearing." Explain this to your child and inspire him to take pride in his deafness by making a big "D" wall hanging. Cut a large (perhaps two feet by three feet) "D" out of light-colored material. Have your child write all the special things he can do on the "D." Refer to his being deaf as a special difference and encourage him to write out his special differences on his "D." Hang his big "D" on the wall in his room.

••

Activity #3: The Deaf Introduction

Age: 4–12

Vocabulary/Concepts: introduction, first and last name, city, state, school, MOTHER-FATHER DEAF?

••

When hearing people introduce themselves, they tend to shake hands and tell their name. Deaf individuals usually give more information to help "strangers" note vital information about the people and places they may have in common. This maintains ties and preserves the community. Deaf people usually tell their first and last names, their name sign, and where they currently work or go to school. Then they will mention the city and state in which they were born, and the schools they have attended. Practice this with your deaf child and teach each family member this special introduction.

••

Activity #4: The Deaf Pride March

Materials: old cloth for a banner, paint, poster board, pamphlets about Deaf issues/people

Age: all ages

Vocabulary/Concepts: Deaf pride, march, teach, DEAF AWARENESS (WEEK or MONTH)

••

What better way to show the world your pride than to march with a group of like-minded individuals? On a small scale, your family and interested neighbors can create banners and signs related to deafness and march in your neighborhood. Consider taking this idea one step further and organizing deaf peers and their families to march in a central location in your community. Contact a large agency servicing deaf people or a Deaf club in your area and inquire whether they do anything of this type on a regular basis. These days many states have a designated "Deaf Awareness Week." If your local agencies have no plans for a Deaf awareness event then suggest that it occur. Your family can offer to help plan it. Distribute literature to onlookers to raise their awareness. Literature might include: famous Facts about Deaf People (e.g., the invention of the football huddle is attributed to a Deaf person); how to Respond to a Deaf Person; Deaf Pride statements such as Deaf people can do everything hearing people can, and also some things hearing people can't do; and ASL Facts and Pictures. Have a lunch, dinner, or picnic to wrap up the parade.

● ●

Activity #5: Deaf Newspapers

Materials: membership in NAD and local Deaf organizations
Age: 4–12
Vocabulary/Concepts: newspaper, organizations, member, send

● ●

As members of local and national Deaf organizations, your family can receive a monthly newsletter or newspaper. These periodicals can keep you updated on Deaf social events and meetings, as well as major concerns in the Deaf community. Join the National Association of the Deaf (NAD), which sends out a regular publication. If your child is young or cannot manage reading the material, share the knowledge you learned with him. Encourage an older deaf child by having the membership in his name so that the publications arrive addressed to him.

● ●

Activity #6: Deaf and Hearing—The Bicultural Family

Materials: paper, pencil
Age: 5–12
Vocabulary/Concepts: culture, bicultural, behaviors, DEAF TENDENCY,
    HEARING TENDENCY (sign expressions indicating deaf or hearing
    ways), value

● ●

This activity elucidates the differences in values and behaviors between Deaf and hearing cultures. Begin by reading about Deaf culture. You can find books in the library or through catalogs mentioned previously in the Deaf Library activity. Identify specific values and behaviors supported by Deaf culture (such as, use of consistent eye contact or sitting in a circle when having a group conversation). List these on a piece of paper, and on another piece of paper list the hearing counterpart (such as, it is impolite to stare or people sit wherever they like during a group conversation). When you learn a new behavior, discuss it with your family. In Deaf culture, for example, numerous sounds are not considered rude because Deaf people cannot hear them. For example, a burp among Deaf people would not warrant an "excuse me" because no one would know what you are talking about! Yet, in hearing culture, it would be rude not to say "excuse me."

Solicit aid from any Deaf adults you know. Find out how things work in the Deaf community by asking many "what if" questions. After you've made a long list comparing the two cultures, try role-playing the behaviors, pretending that your whole family is either Deaf or hearing for a period of time (we suggest a half an hour). Afterward talk about what people learned. For example, have everyone "turn their voice off" and keep constant eye contact with each other while trying to communicate through signs and, if need be, gestures. It becomes clear instantly that eye contact is natural and necessary to someone who is using only visual cues.

THE INSENSITIVE HEARING PUBLIC

The deaf child faces daily challenges. Depending on the hearing people he deals with, those challenges might be enriching, frightening, infantilizing, or neutral.

Understanding extended family members who give support when needed and follow the family's communication decisions are like gold. However, this is not always the case for families of deaf children. Sometimes the extended family neither participates nor supports the communication mode or the child-rearing style of your nuclear family.

Teachers and administrators have a profound impact on your child. Teachers have daily contact with the child and are intimately involved in the development of the child's academic life, linguistic ability, and social self-esteem. Administrators set the tone of a program with policy-making and financial backing. A supportive teacher will attend to both your child's specific academic and communication needs. Many public school teachers have not had much contact with deaf children and need information about how to interact with your child (see chapter 13 on School Problems). Teachers of the deaf will have more specific training for working with deaf children; however, they may vary greatly in their communication skills, communication philosophy, and teaching approaches. Meet with teachers and administrators before your child begins classes.

Neighborhood children might form friendships with your child; however, over time, and as cliques develop, the deaf child is more likely to be ostracized. If your child has a particular talent, such as being a good athlete, his peers may seek him out as a friend because of that talent. If your child has other difficulties (hyperactivity or learning problems, for example) or is perceived as different by his peers, he may have trouble building friendships.

Neighborhood adults can play a vital role in setting the tone for interaction among children. Let trusted adults know how to communicate with your child. In fact, include these people as an integral part of your family's activities if possible. Invite them to join you in activities mentioned in this book (especially those that highlight and teach about the positive aspects of deafness).

Local businesses can serve as your child's practice ground for interacting with the public. Educate local merchants about how to handle your child. Let the salespeople know how to communicate with your child; inform them that you will often let your child handle interactions; and, above all, encourage them to treat your child as they would any other child.

Some deaf children become accustomed to being given things for free. Store owners or other hearing people in the community, such as school bus drivers or neighbors, like to give small gifts to a deaf child. We have heard stories about store owners giving deaf children drastically reduced prices on certain fixed price items, such as notebooks, toys, and health supplies. These gifts are often given with good intentions and take the place of real communication. Unfortunately, some hearing adults do this out of pity for the deaf child or to seek the child's affection. In all cases, the child begins to expect and feel entitled to receive something for nothing. Discourage such gift-giving and explain your concerns to these well-meaning adults. If they feel compelled to give gifts to your child, then suggest that they do so at appropriate times, such as holidays and birthdays.

Most deaf children could tell you a multitude of stories about their school bus drivers. Some bus drivers go out of their way to make the child feel safe and secure, while others actually yell and curse. Some drivers treat the deaf child with kid gloves, while others give special gifts and treats to the child. The drivers who frighten the child do so out of their own discomfort, lack of good boundaries, or inability to sense what is appropriate behavior. Many drivers form healthy friendships with the child while many others overstep their bounds. The school, the teachers, and you should take a lead role in educating the bus drivers in handling deaf children.

The general public briefly glimpses your child. Depending on the circumstances and the individuals you come into contact with, you may cause questioning looks, looks of curiosity, confused responses, genuine interest, or cruel mocking. In the past, deaf children have suffered many negative experiences at the hands of the ignorant hearing public. Movies, TV commercials, special reports, news, and weekly series have all begun to show deafness and American Sign Language in a positive light. This has fortunately altered the way the people view Deaf individuals. However, many people remain ignorant or insensitive about deafness. Your child must learn, over time, how to deal with the various reactions he receives in safe ways that maintain his self-integrity.

Activities

· ·

Activity #1: Deaf and Proud Brochure

Materials: sturdy paper, pen
Age: 6–12
Vocabulary/Concepts: brochure, teach, Deaf culture, history, ASL,
insults, myths, HEARING, MAKE-UP STORY

· ·

Together with your child, create a brochure teaching others about Deaf culture. Use part of it to teach some history, part to teach about myths or insults ("deaf and dumb," "deaf-mute"), and part to teach how to communicate with a deaf person (see chapter 5 for tips on communication). Have your child design this and pass it out to people. We suggest you try this out on respectful adults first.

· ·

Activity #2: Deaf Awareness Day

Age: all ages
Vocabulary/Concepts: honor, Deaf awareness

· ·

Our country has used designated days, weeks, or months to have citizens recognize various people, professions, and groups (Veteran's Day, Labor Day, Black History Month). Make a Deaf Awareness Day at your house and invite local friends, business people, and other adults. Use previous activities to teach Deaf culture, create deaf-related information pamphlets, show a video (home-made or borrowed) about Deaf culture or a related topic, have the TV with closed captioning on, invite a Deaf adult to tell stories, and have a professional interpreter on hand to demonstrate. Make the event fun and informative.

· ·

Activity #3: Community Communication Class

Age: all ages
Vocabulary/Concepts: ASL, class, community, learn, communicate

· ·

If your child communicates through American Sign Language, consider having a community communication class. Invite a Deaf person to tutor this class in your home for a period of at least eight weeks. Invite extended family, children, parents, and even community service providers, such as police, to join. Do this as an annual event and expand the group each time. Have parties, picnics, or get-togethers throughout the year to practice together.

. . . .

Activity #4: My Rights

Materials: paper, pencil, *Legal Rights: The Guide for Deaf and Hard of Hearing People* (National Center for Law and Deafness, Gallaudet University Press, 1992)

Age: 7–12

Vocabulary/Concepts: right, safe, respect, struggle, democratic, interpreter, equal access, complaint, discriminate, grievance, court, REBEL, DEAF-RIGHTS, STRUGGLE (ongoing)

. . . .

Teach your child what a "right" means in a democratic society. In simple terms, each person has the right to safety, respect, and equal treatment. Explain to your child how our country has had to learn this through trial and error (civil rights, women's rights, and the consistent use of the courts). Teach your child some of the rights which Deaf people have fought for—the right to have a job, to have an interpreter when necessary, to attend a good school, to have clear communication at school, to be treated equal to hearing people (without discrimination), and to file complaints when these rights are violated.

Have him post these rights on his bedroom door and/or request they be posted at school. Teach him to speak up when he finds communication unclear in any environment and encourage him to correct people when they treat him like he cannot do something he knows he *can* do.

If the child is older (ten to twelve), have him write a report for school. Purchase or borrow the book, *Legal Rights: The Guide for Deaf and Hard of Hearing People*. This book contains information your child would find valuable for such a report and, in addition, is a great resource for parents. You should have it in your library.

. . . .

Activity #5: Take It to the Highest Court

Age: 6–12

Vocabulary/Concepts: (same as previous activity), judge, restitution, FAIR, ALL-SAME

. . . .

By using the Family Council Meeting and the "Day in Court" format (see pgs. 19-21 and 339-340), you can begin to introduce the concept of rights and grievances. Use family meetings to teach your family about basic rights (safety, respect, equality) and specific deaf-related rights (access to communication, no discrimination). You may want to make a "Bill of Rights" for your family that encompasses all of these things.

When people in the family do not respect these rights, a grievance should be filed. You can design a paper that states "Grievance" on the top, and then asks what right was broken. Use the Family Council (with judge presiding, of course) to figure out a resolution for this grievance. If it is a matter of oversight, then reminders and perhaps an activity (we suggest many in this book) related to the issue will suffice. If it is a blatant act (someone purposely harming another person), restitution might be required. If it is a family problem (communication confusion for the deaf child), the terms of the family communication contract may need to be clarified or revised and ideas for solutions raised.

HELPING THE HARD OF HEARING CHILD TO FIT IN

The hard of hearing child often straddles two worlds and two identities at all times. On the positive side of this, he can move between Deaf and hearing cultures. The negative aspects result from the child not knowing quite where he belongs.

Swinging between different cultures, the hard of hearing child may be constantly questioned or distrusted by members of the Deaf and hearing community alike. The Deaf community may view the hard of hearing person's use of speech as "trying to act hearing"; while the hearing majority may view the hard of hearing person's use of ASL as silly because they perceive him to be like them.

What a child calls himself has repercussions—in the Deaf community, a child who calls himself "hard of hearing" may be seen as "putting on airs." "Hard of hearing" is a much more acceptable phrase in the hearing community—it implies hearing but with a slight problem.

A child who has a hearing loss in early childhood, for example, after age two or three, or who has a progressive hearing loss, will have to adapt to experiencing the world in a different sensory manner. Sometimes this changes daily. If this child had a particular fondness for auditory stimuli (chattered a lot, listened to music, liked to sing, or made constant sounds), he may find it hard to begin to rely more on his visual strengths and will need help to deal with ambiguity and his losses.

The hard of hearing individual may feel a more intense pressure to belong somewhere. He may think he has to "choose." One hard of hearing child said that sometimes he wished he were more deaf so that his family would respect his communication needs and other times he wished he didn't have to explain why he enjoyed speech to his deaf friends.

The hard of hearing child may, at times, enjoy the ability to speak and to be accepted by hearing people. In addition, he may receive praise from family and others about this, like "My gosh, his speech is so good you would not know he has a problem." While the child may perceive this as a compliment, at other times it may be a cross to bear. People may believe that the hard of hearing child's speech means that he understands as a hearing person would and thus they do not make any special efforts to communicate with him effectively.

Activities

. . . .

Activity #1: Deaf and Hearing: The Bicultural Person

Materials: "Deaf and Hearing: The Bicultural Family" activity (see pgs. 104–105)

Age: 6–12

Vocabulary/Concepts: culture, bicultural, hearing, skills, mix, identity, confusion, pressure, belong, DEAF, ON-THE-FENCE, DEAF TENDENCY, HEARING TENDENCY, BI–BI

. . . .

This activity is an extension of an earlier activity, "Deaf and Hearing: The Bicultural Family," but with a more individual twist. After doing the family activity, have a discussion about your child's view of himself. We suggest you carry on the discussion with your child in a one-to-one setting and later open it up for a Family Council Meeting.

Explain to your child that you realize that he has skills and traits that make him able to fit in either hearing or deaf groups. Ask your child what he likes about being a part of both cultures and what he finds difficult or confusing. Ask him when his "Deaf culture" skills are useful and when his "hearing culture" skills are a benefit. Ask him how he defines himself—Deaf, hearing, a mix. Question him about when he might feel pressure from others to conform and find out when he feels others make false assumptions about him, for example, when hearing relatives assume he can speechread all conversations.

This is not a one-time conversation but rather a discussion that will span many years of your child's development. The child will have to deal with these issues on and off for his whole life, and having practiced with loving family members while growing up will serve him well later on.

. . . .

Activity #2: All of Me

Materials: scrapbook, child's memorabilia

Age: 6–12

Vocabulary/Concepts: scrapbook, album, pictures, letters, awards, memories, skills, traits

. . . .

Together with your child, make a scrapbook with pictures (of both deaf friends and hearing friends), letters, and school awards. Have him write or dictate captions for the pictures that identify what part of himself is represented. Caption examples would be, "Here I am getting an award for my Deaf Awareness essay," "Here are my hearing friends from karate class," "This is my niece—I teach her sign language," or "This is my favorite music group—I listen to them all the time."

From time to time ask your child if you can look through his scrapbook with him. You may even want to create and share one of your own. Subtly, point out all the different aspects your child shows. Use the questions in the previous activity to explore your child's feelings about himself. If your child likes, you can add your comments (verbally or written on the bottom of the pictures) to help him discriminate different skills and traits. Your comments may concurrently emphasize your pride in him: "Here is Raymond receiving an award for writing about famous Deaf people"; "Here he is with all of his hearing friends, he tries very hard to communicate with them"; "I am proud that Raymond is teaching Natasha to sign because he says it is important to him"; and, "I am happy Raymond enjoys music."

Family Unity: Bringing Deaf and Hearing Family Members Together

• • • • • • • • • • • •

John Adams

W hat is meant by the term *unity?* Unity implies harmony among parts to form a whole—the condition of many, becoming one. Family unity requires that each member of the family contribute to the family whole. Parents, as the heads of the family, are indeed important in the development of the family unit. However, each family member is key in maintaining the unit's harmony. Each child contributes his/her personality, wishes and desires to add structure to the family unit just as a variety of colors, textures, and forms harmonize and provide structure to a beautiful landscape painting.

Parents of deaf and hard of hearing children encounter a unique challenge to family unity. Since most parents of deaf and hard of hearing children are themselves hearing, they experience the feeling of being "different" from their child. Some parents have stated that the child who was expected to be very much like them, after diagnosis of deafness, became a stranger with whom they had little in common. The deafness affecting their child was a real difference that seemed to set them apart. Their deaf or hard of hearing child became the focus of the family unit rather than an active member of it. The fact that hearing parents and deaf children do not experience the world in the same way demands adjustment in the family system.

John Adams, Ph.D., is a psychologist at St. Mary's School for the Deaf in Buffalo, New York.

Conditions affecting family members influence family unity in different ways. Deafness is a condition that has an impact on the family's overall communication process and the entire communication system within the home. The single largest issue facing parents in maintaining family harmony is the task of involving all family members in home communication. For parents who are hearing, a main source of stress is the need to communicate with their deaf child in a different manner than they do with their hearing child. (Greenberg, 1993). Research has shown that deaf children with deaf parents who share a common language have an advantage when attempting a variety of life's tasks. Communication within the family creates the bond that supports the structure of the family unit. Hence, communication is the backbone of a strong family structure. When there is inadequate communication, the outlets for venting frustration and working through difficult situations as well as celebrating happy moments or subtle enjoyments are often limited. All family interactions, both healthy and not so healthy, are forms of communication.

If you think back on some of your most enjoyable moments as a child, you may remember a trip to Grandma and Grandpa's house where you listened to them describe their past life experiences. Or, you may remember sitting around your own family dinner table where, during a meal, you discussed important things that happened to you on a particular school day. Or, finally, you might recall Sunday trips by car to the local ice cream parlor where you anticipated telling your parents your favorite flavor of the day. Each one of these scenarios involves family conversation, an important part of the family communication system. Family conversation represents an important vehicle for developing intellectual and social skills, and for developing a sense of belonging. Only when the deaf child is accepted as an *equal* participant in the family system, will the family be able to provide the full range of support that the child needs.

Early communication difficulties between hearing parents and their deaf children may disrupt the process of conversation and future interaction. If deaf children have limited participation in their families' interaction, their access to family life is restricted. A deaf or hard of hearing child is an important part of the family structure; if the child is separated, left out, or ignored while the family communicates—isolation occurs.

Parents may act differently with their deaf child than they do with their other children, altering family functioning, and, in turn, affecting future interactions.

One deaf professional tells a story of how early family interactions affected his life. One day while having lunch, the deaf man ate quickly, looking up on only one occasion. His friend asked if he were eating quickly so he would have time to relax and chat after lunch. The deaf man commented that when he was a boy growing up, dinner time was not important. He explained that his family carried on verbal conversations in which he could not participate. And, although he tried to become a part of these conversations by visually attending and speechreading, he still could not follow the interaction. After a while, he learned to withdraw from interactions that did not include him. Eating his meals quickly helped him to avoid frustration.

As this story indicates, the man's early interactions taught him that family dinner was not a time for dialogue and the exchange of information, but a time of confusion and exclusion. Unfortunately, this deaf man's experience is typical of what is experienced by many deaf and hard of hearing children brought up in families with hearing members. Dinner time should be an opportunity for family conversation, which plays a significant role in establishing family unity.

Besides interactive conversation, it is important for parents to provide activities in the home in which all members can participate and contribute — making a family meal, developing a family scrapbook, watching closed captioned television together, etc. All children need to be included in family activities on a daily basis to experience a sense of belonging, love, security, and family unity.

The following example illustrates how one family has dealt with these issues.

> Jacob is a six-year-old deaf child. His three-year-old brother, Jason, and his parents are hearing. In their household, a weekly family meeting is held to talk about the decisions to be made concerning the needs of the family. For example, each family member gets to help plan the menu for dinner every week. During a specific week, Jacob chooses macaroni and cheese as his favorite dinner choice, and helps to make his special dinner. Also, during this particular week, the family decides where they will go on their summer vacation. Jacob helps map the course for their trip. Jacob and Jason are active participants in family communication and therefore they contribute to family unity.

Today, the constellation of families is ever-changing. Some of these changes are evidenced by divorce, single-parent households, and by dual-career families. Even though families may be separated by divorce or by other means, there is a need for a family unit in which both deaf and hearing children can function. Each family has a structure that makes it unique. Each member *must* contribute his or her own unique qualities for the structure to become a family unit. As the number of families experiencing separation increases, so does the importance of communication between family members. The increased level of separation among family members underscores the importance of "together time" (for example, conversation at dinner). Deaf children may experience the feelings of separation and isolation even more acutely when they are not included in the everyday activities of family life.

Children need stability within their lives. The family unit, no matter the make-up, provides for that stability. Stability is necessary for family unity to continue and thrive. All members of the family must believe each is an important part of family functioning and each contributes to the stability of the family unit. Any change in the unit must be discussed openly and honestly with each of its members. Each change in the life of the family creates a time of challenge and an opportunity to grow. The family that faces the challenges together offers stability and unity to meet future challenges and changes.

Like a treasured painting in which each color is essential to the image and each brush stroke provides a unique texture to develop visual harmony, so a family is celebrated by all members. Each is essential to its stability, harmony, and unity.

CHAPTER

7

Family Unity

● ● ● ●

Attempting to teach children rules of living without a family atmosphere of guidance, support, and values is like trying to cook without a kitchen. The activities in this chapter are dedicated to improving family unity as well as to inviting children to think and make decisions for themselves, participate in family planning, and learn to share responsibilities. The activities help build connections by celebrating likenesses and identifying differences. This chapter also focuses on familiar circumstances (sibling fighting) and changes or variations in the family unit (divorce).

FAMILY UNITY

Our society encourages individual needs over group needs. In addition, economics can necessitate that both parents or the primary parent (in a single-parent household) work. Family time often becomes rushed, and accomplishing daily living tasks efficiently can be difficult. Some resulting family problems are:

1. a lack of a sense of belonging and usefulness to the family

2. a sense of isolation

3. strained, underdeveloped, or dysfunctional communication patterns

4. a diminished sense of cultural, religious, and racial heritage

5. inadequate opportunities to practice problem-solving, negotiation, compromising, and empathy

The problems may look like this:

●●●●●●●

- There are little or no family activities or responsibilities.

- Family members bicker often.

- Family members have very separate schedules.

- The deaf child spends considerable time at others' homes.

- Family members engage in name-calling.

- There is much tearfulness, anger, oppositional behavior, blaming, and fear related to divorce.

- One parent carries the majority of responsibility for the family.

- One parent complains about the other parent to the deaf child.

- Siblings constantly complain, fight, and compare.

- Parents play referee and constantly break up fights.

- Older sibling(s) show severe jealousy and anger over a new sibling.

In addition to dealing with finances, chores, and schedules, families with a deaf child have unique additional challenges to family unity. Often the deaf child starts school at a very early age, has long distances to travel to and from school causing limited daily family time, may attend a residential facility that reserves family time for the weekends, and usually has both "Deaf" and "hearing" cultures to contend with.

When all family members are relatively similar, coalescing around religious, racial, cultural, or ethnic heritages is easier. When a member or members differ from the family in some significant way, adjustments must be made.

All children need to feel they belong and can contribute to a special group. When you identify each family member's special talents and integrate them into the functioning of the family, you raise the self-esteem of everyone in the family. Thus, it is important to see your deaf child as a child who "can do." Notice how often you say, "Oh, she can't because she is deaf," and think of ways that she can contribute to the family life in her own way, however different from the hearing individuals in the family. Recognize how differences can add to rather than detract from the family personality.

Your deaf child will likely feel sensitive to being left out of communication and even what appear to you to be minor decisions. Being left out causes the child to believe that her point of view is not good enough, or that she is not important or not smart enough. Help your child see that her contributions (household responsibilities and participation in family decisions) are an integral component of the family's success and happiness.

A family that includes both deaf parent(s) and deaf children does not face this particular issue. The deaf parent naturally knows what it is like to be deaf; she may even have anticipated deafness in her child; and she can teach what she has learned to her child. While hearing parents can learn and employ important lessons from deaf parents of a deaf child, they cannot expect to create the same family atmosphere.

Negotiating differences in a family (such as having a deaf child in a hearing family) does not mean creating a perfect "Brady Bunch" family. It is not some imagined end result but rather the daily give-and-take from which respect and problem-solving skills will grow.

Support each family member's interests, no matter how divergent. Try out one another's hobbies and sports and attend events, games, shows, and concerts together. When feasible, have interpreters available for spoken events (plays, graduations, and award dinners).

Rally the entire family to lend support when a family member has a problem rather than labeling the individual as a problem to the family. This is critical since deaf children can feel blamed by hearing members for being deaf (labeling it as a problem). Likewise, hearing siblings may at times feel that the deaf child is the cause of all the family's problems and need assistance in distinguishing the various sources of family problems that compose the reality of the situation. Recognize individual and family accomplishments and create family ceremonies to celebrate successes.

Being a parent is quite a task and it is even more challenging when you are a single parent. Seek and maintain adult support networks, especially connections with other single parents and with parents of deaf children. Do not consider this a luxury, but a necessity. At minimum, have regular phone contact with other adults who share your situation.

Families come in all shapes and sizes—some families include trusted neighbors, parents living apart, step parents, two mothers or fathers, foster families, and several extended family members. Teach your deaf child about the different types of families that exist.

Activities

. . . .

Activity #1: The United States of the Jones Family
Materials: large poster board, map, markers, crayons
Age: 8–12
Vocabulary/Concepts: map, country, state, different, same, language

. . . .

Depending upon your child's knowledge of geography, you may want to begin this activity by explaining the definitions of a country and a state and how they look on a map. In this activity you can teach your child(ren) how everyone is a part of the family, while still being different. Pretend that your family is like a country. Invent a name for your family country and make a large drawing of what it might look like. Establish your country's language, style of clothing, culture, and special foods on the drawing. These should be realistic.

Next, divide your country into states and give each state to a different family member. Have each family member design her own state giving it a realistic name, language, special food, clothing, and special sites. For example, your deaf child should make her state's language the one she uses (or in cases where she is using different modes, the language she prefers). Special sites should reflect the things she likes to do, such as a lake for swimming. When you are finished designing the states and country, visit one another's states to learn about them. Talk about the differences of the individual states (people) as well as what binds your country (family) together.

. . . .

Activity #2: The Family Sign

. . . .

Whether you sign in your family or not, make a sign with your hands that can be used to identify your family's last name. Use this as a symbol of pride — take pictures using the sign at a family gathering, copy the sign on a T-shirt, or make a letterhead for family stationery.

. . . .

Activity#3: Family Rituals
Age: all ages
Vocabulary/Concepts: family, ritual, daily, weekly, monthly, annually, tradition, EVERY DAY, EVERY WEEK, EVERY MONTH, or EVERY YEAR

. . . .

In this activity you will invent a "family ritual" that can range from doing something special together once a week to an unusual family story told every

Christmas. A family ritual establishes a daily, weekly, or annual activity that is distinctively yours and fosters a special bond for the family. Your deaf child will enjoy these predictable themes if she attends a residential facility or has a long commute to and from her day program, which is often the case. Since the rituals should reflect your family's style, everyone should be involved in planning them. Here are several ideas:

1. Choose a special weekly family activity—a night at Joe's Pizza, a movie every Saturday, or regularly scheduled mystery trips to new places.

2. Invent a secret handshake, hand signal, or family talent that only your immediate family participates in doing.

3. Create a secret family recipe for a main dish or dessert to be made for parties, holidays, dinners, and picnics.

4. Make a family album that recognizes special events, school achievements, vacations, birthdays, and the changing looks of family members. Bring out the album once a month to add new information and to reminisce.

5. Take an annual trip or vacation that is planned and organized by the whole family.

6. Make a family time capsule for which you annually collect items to signify the year's events and achievements. Place your collection in a box to be opened years or decades later. You can seal one capsule and make a new one every few years.

7. Create special birthday rituals, such as having the whole family cook a birthday dinner.

8. Choose a time during the year for the family to work together on holiday or celebration gifts. Make candles, jewelry, preserves, cards, soap, sauces or candy. Package and store these for use during the holidays or for special occasions.

9. Create a family garden and allow for all family members to contribute to the design, cultivation, and harvesting.

· ·

Activity #4: Family Reunion

Materials: heavy-weight paper, special food, activity plans, camera, scrapbook, family T-shirts, the book *Do People Grow on Trees: Genealogy for Kids and Other Beginners*, (Ira Wolfman, Workman Publishing, 1991.)

Age: 5–12

Vocabulary/Concepts: family, reunion, annual, invitations, family tree, family relationship names, COME-TOGETHER AGAIN

· ·

Family reunions bring generations of relatives together, provide your child with the chance to get to know her extended family, and allow family members to update each other as well as feel a part of a community. Children should be involved in the entire process—making and sending invitations, planning activities, and cooking the meal. For the deaf child, learning about the planning process from beginning to end teaches her how to approach a task step by step. These are the kinds of incidental learning opportunities that deaf children often miss out on.

Have your child become familiar with her extended family. Use a family tree or the book *Do People Grow on Trees: Genealogy for Kids and Other Beginners* to explain how everyone is related. Your child can help you send out invitations and make phone calls to relatives (a good time to practice TTY, telephone, or relay operator skills). Have her think of fun games that will help people mingle and in which she can fully participate. Perhaps arrange for an interpreter for a portion of the reunion. Take plenty of pictures of the event. You can add to the fun by having T-shirts made with the family name or picture on it. Encourage family members to consider making this an annual event. You may suggest to your child that she keep the family spirit alive by writing a newsletter for her relatives, including pictures and an account of the family reunion. Perhaps she might send the newsletter quarterly to relatives, providing family news, stories, and information about upcoming events.

· ·

Activity #5: Phone Message

Materials: voice and TTY answering machines

Age: all ages

Vocabulary/Concepts: message, answering machine, TTY

· ·

Invent a message for your family answering machine that includes all the members in your family. Have each member, even house pets, take part in the recording. Make both the voice and TTY machine give the same message. You may want to overlap this activity with others outlined in this book. For example, you might add "Did you know?" trivia related to your ethnic heritage or to famous Deaf Americans (Chapter 6) to your message. Every time someone calls, your family answering machine message will greet them. You may want to make up various messages, monthly announcements, or unique family sayings for the machine.

PROBLEMS RELATED TO PARENTAL SEPARATION AND DIVORCE

At the time of this writing, divorce occurs in over one third of American families. Some of the negative aspects of divorce include erosion of the family structure and connections among family members, an adversarial legal process, and children dealing with split loyalties.

Statistics do not reveal that divorce and separation occur any more often in hearing families with deaf children. However, if incompatible parents have numerous disagreements about how to raise their deaf child, they may attribute their divorce to this.

Children often feel somehow responsible for a divorce. The younger the child, the more likely she might be to interpret her behavior as having caused the divorce. This may be intensified for a deaf child if her parents had difficulties coming to terms with the child's deafness. Remind your child that she is not responsible for her parents' decision to separate and that her wishes, behaviors, or deafness did not cause the divorce. As a parent, take care not to pin your feelings onto any one thing, particularly if it is related to your child.

Unfortunately, as parents attempt to improve an intolerable situation by separating the family, children often lose their sense of security and unity. In a deaf/hearing family, a deaf child may rely on one parent as her primary interpreter. Depending on how custody unfolds, the deaf child may fear losing her primary communication link (usually the mother) or losing all connections with the other parent (usually the father).

Children rarely choose not to have contact with both parents, even when one parent has been unkind. Allow your child to have access to your ex-partner as much as possible. Encourage letters, phone calls, and visits. Purchase a second TTY for the spouse who moves from the child's home. Anticipate communication problems that may arise. Be aware of the fact that the child may expect the parents to continue in the same communication roles (interpreter, for example) to which the child has grown accustomed.

A deaf child may have been less aware of discord between her parents as evidenced by (vocal) parental arguments. She may not understand the reasons for the separation. Encourage your child to ask questions. If your child has difficulty formulating questions, prompt a discussion by asking questions of your own. Focus on what the deaf child may have missed, e.g., "Did you know Mommy and Daddy were not getting along?"

Take the time to discuss with your child her ongoing concerns and feelings stemming from the divorce or separation. Expect sadness, anger, confusion, and, at times, misbehavior from her. Do not complain to your child about all the bad things your ex-partner has done. Likewise, do not protect your child from your ex-partner's irresponsibility or problems if they affect the child. For example, be frank about the ex-partner missing a visit: "Mommy didn't come when she promised and I am sorry that makes you sad"; or an ex-partner having a chronic problem: "Daddy has a drinking problem and he has to get help."

Be as clear and honest with the deaf child as you possibly can. Fantasy, ambiguity, and confusion will be much more difficult for her to assimilate than the truth. Let the child know in clear terms if you make the decision not to reunite. Let her know where she will live. Give her the means and the opportunity to contact the other parent. This may be an extremely emotional time for the parents, which makes explaining very difficult. Do not hesitate to explain to a deaf child in any words, signs, or pictures you have available. Use books, examples of other families, and TV to demonstrate the normality of the situation. Answer all questions honestly and on the child's level. Consider having teachers and other deaf adults help in clarifying and normalizing the divorce.

Activities

● ●

Activity #1: The Divorce Workbook
Materials: *The Divorce Workbook*, (Sally Blakeslee, Michelle Lash, David Fassler, Waterfront Books, 1985), paper, pencil
Age: 5–12
Vocabulary/Concepts: divorce, book, write, draw, many families
● ●

Make a divorce book with your child to help her understand the processes, feelings, and changes in your family caused by the divorce. You can use a book called, *The Divorce Workbook: A Guide for Kids and Families.* This is a "write-in" workbook that encourages children to write and draw pictures of what they are thinking and feeling about the divorce.

Activity #2: Family Calendar
Materials: twelve (enlarged) photos of your family, large construction
    paper, ruler, pen, markers
Age: 4–12
Vocabulary/Concepts: family, schedule, visits, mom, dad

Use twelve photos to represent your family, such as a picture of each family member, where each parent lives, or a picture of activities or events done with each parent. Make a pictorial calendar by enlarging each of the twelve pictures and using these pictures as the "photo" for each month. Use the calendar to indicate days a child spends with either parent. Mark down where she is spending holidays, what special events she will be attending, and general information that may help her sort out her schedule throughout the year. This activity provides your deaf child with a visual representation of the year and creates a sense of predictability in a confusing family structure. Explain that although the divorce changes some things, it doesn't change your love for the child and your attention to her needs goes on all through the year.

Activity #3: Who or What Is Responsible?
Materials: colored construction paper, pens, scissors
Age: 7–12
Vocabulary/Concepts: responsible, anger, promise, FEELING HOLD-IN,
    EXPRESS

Divorces often bring out the ways in which one parent has compensated for the other's weaknesses. After a divorce, the deaf child may become acutely aware of the lack of one parent's involvement in school functions, sports events, and communication. In addition, one parent may be less reliable. This may result in the child feeling angry and turning that anger inward ("I'm bad, that's why Daddy doesn't call") or outward towards the parent who is available.

To help focus a child's feelings, consider playing a game of "who or what is responsible?" Make a deck of cards by cutting up colored paper and writing on the paper various tasks, chores, and situations related to the family. These should include funny or mundane examples, as well as more serious ones:

- "Who is responsible for petting the cat every day?"

- "Who is supposed to burn the toast in the morning?"

- "Who decides to get a divorce?"

- "What makes people divorce?"

Your child may only tolerate a small number of divorce-related cards, so take it slow or the game will end in minutes. The goal is to precipitate a discussion about responsibility. Relate to your child some instances in which you did not do something you had responsibility for and explain how that affected other people. Then you might explain to your child that adults are responsible for the love and care of children and sometimes that doesn't happen, in which case kids can get mad. Talk about times that your child may have felt upset by promises broken.

Activity #4: The Family Quilt

Materials: scraps of old clothing, sewing tools, family photographs, glue, poster board
Age: 3–12
Vocabulary/Concepts: quilt, collage, separate, together

Using scraps of old clothing from each family member (including grand-parents, relatives, and/or new family members, such as step-parents or step-siblings) make a family quilt with your child. While cutting and sewing the pieces together, talk about how the separated pieces of cloth represent each person and that although you may be separate, you still have common threads that bind you together. You can also create a paper quilt or collage using the same principles and using photos and drawings.

Activity #5: One Home, Two Homes

Materials: two playhouses, two boxes, or two lists representing the parents' homes
Age: 3–12
Vocabulary/Concepts: home, different, same, like, dislike, miss, MOTHER HOME, FATHER HOME, COMMUTE

This activity will visually and actively help children recognize and express feelings about the differences between her parents and their homes. Invari-ably, children will mention the differences in homes, food, communication, toys, rules, and playmates. This is the start of a healthy understanding and should be encouraged.

One or both parents can explain to the child that you are aware of the differences between parents and that you want to help her understand these. Make this activity playful by stating, "Let's see what you remember about both homes." Using two models to represent each of the parent's homes (two pictures, drawings, playhouses, or medium-sized boxes), have the child explain the differences between these. With an older child, make two lists; with a younger child, ask her to draw the differences or show them to you using a playhouse. If necessary, use a home-made playhouse, furnished with bottle caps, spools, and boxes.

You can help identify some concrete differences (bedroom arrangement) and some interpersonal ones (the way Daddy wakes you up). Here is a list of suggested topics to cover:

- bed and bedroom
- house decorations
- bed and waking-time rituals
- kitchen privileges
- favorite foods
- meal habits
- TV privileges and rituals
- captioning decoder on the TV
- assistive devices (TTY, vibrating alarms, flashing lights for doorbell or telephone)
- communication system used
- members of the household
- the neighborhood
- favorite activities
- cars
- household rules and chores
- toys available
- goofy habits
- favorite places in each house
- pets

Once you have a firm sense of your child's point of view, you can respond with explanations ("Well, Daddy and Mommy like to eat at different times"); questions ("Do you like the new friends at Mommy's house?") and perhaps new plans ("Well, maybe I can get a decoder so you can watch movies when you visit"). You can later refer to this activity when the child complains or compares you to her other parent. For example, if your child says, "Daddy makes better pizza," you can reply with, "Yep, that's another difference you noticed. You like his pizza better? What does he do that makes it so good?" Don't go on the defensive when your child speaks like this. If the child notices that you become angry or hurt, then she may use these complaints to indirectly express feelings of anger or clam up for fear of hurting your feelings.

Sibling Conflict

Sibling conflict, evidenced by disagreements and arguments, is a natural component of social development. Conflict resolution skills must be learned both in school and at home, where adults can help children by modeling respectful communication and compromising.

Sibling disagreements give children the opportunity to practice conflict resolution skills. This is not to say that any sane parent should live in a war zone. Conflict resolution skills which rely on discussion, respectful listening, and compromise can make your home more peaceful, help children to value and enjoy each other, and help the deaf child prepare for future challenges.

Birth order and family role definition (e.g., the brains in the family, the athlete, the deaf child) can establish identities that create situations of conflict. Individuals often validate themselves through dominance (first over second born) and definition of self (I'm smarter than you). Children will notice the differences between themselves and how that affects the attention you give them. With deaf/hearing sibling groups, deafness can become a focus. "Just because she is deaf, she gets to stay up with you!"

Parents often experience their firstborn with questioning anxiety. As parents gain more experience they become less anxious and have more knowledge of child-rearing issues. When the deaf child is the firstborn, the parents must learn about general child development as well as how to raise a deaf child.

If your new baby is hearing and you have an older deaf child, make sure the older child understands that the sibling will benefit from using the older child's preferred communication mode as early as possible. This makes the older child a natural leader and introduces the hearing infant to the deaf child's communication.

If a newborn sibling is deaf, gauge your emotions and energy. If you are feeling depressed, guilty, or confused, you will be less available to your hearing child and she will sense this. Praise your hearing child for showing good behavior during a confusing time; however, be aware that she will need some time to process her own feelings.

As a result of having a deaf brother or sister, hearing siblings may develop special roles and characteristics. Parents may view the hearing child as the "saving grace" or the "normal" child. Also, the sibling may serve as a "parent helper" or act as "interpreter" for the deaf child. Through taking on these roles, the sibling may gain special skills (being responsible, sensitive, reliable, and bilingual) and/or have negative feelings (jealousy, shame, anger, and frustration).

Some hearing siblings, sensitive to adult needs, will sacrifice their own feelings to protect the parents. This may be especially true if there is a single parent or if the parents are having difficulty coping with their new child's deafness. An accommodating child will need help expressing any discomforts related to having a deaf sibling, "You know, I've been spending a lot of time at your sister's school and you've been doing such good work, too. Do you think I've forgotten about you?"

This kind of questioning gives permission for siblings to express unpleasant feelings about one another. Ignoring negative feelings intensifies them, while the expression of these feelings keeps children from acting them out. Be prepared for some graphic statements, such as, "I hate her and I wish she would die!" Rephrase this for your child in the form of a feeling statement, "You are very angry." If the child has been holding feelings in for a long time, you may need to be patient. Don't try to convince the child to change her point of view. Use art, writing, role-playing, talking, and doll play to allow for such expression to run its course.

Sometimes a sibling's harsh feelings have nothing to do with deaf/hearing issues. At other times the children will focus on this. The deaf child may have strong feelings about the hearing sibling who goes to the local school, doesn't need a hearing aid, talks on the phone, and may be allowed to venture out more in the community. The hearing sibling may have equally strong feelings about the deaf child needing a particular kind of communication, school, and involvement from the parents.

When a family becomes highly involved in the issue of deafness, a hearing child may interpret this effort to include the deaf child as excluding her (the hearing child's) needs. Decide which aspects of deafness are most important in your family (such as a communication commitment or attending the deaf child's performances) and which are optional (going to a Deaf community event). Give the hearing sibling some choices. Be sure that some events match the hearing child's interests (bowling, baseball, or captioned movies).

Sibling conflict is often caused by children's desires to get as much parental attention as possible. Therefore, it makes sense that if you are busy with the deaf child then the hearing child may express her frustration by fighting with her deaf sibling. If you find yourself constantly in a crisis mode with your deaf child, then ask yourself if that is necessary. If it's not, then slow down and spend more time with your hearing child. If it is necessary then seek additional support from family, friends, or professionals.

Excessive competition for a parent's attention and the "Mommy- or Daddy-likes-me-better" game often result from comparisons made by parents. Avoid comparisons between your children, whether good or bad. Don't teach sensitivity to deafness by comparison—"Your sister is doing fine in reading and she is deaf—you should be glad you're not deaf!" Instead, highlight each child's unique self: "You are a good speller, I bet you will do fine on that test."

In order to avoid the difficult bind of feeling like you must treat your children in exactly equal ways, focus on giving equal amounts of love and time according to each child's individual needs and personality. Your hearing child may deem anything that you do related to your deaf child as exclusively "for her." Be sure that special attention to the deaf child is not confused with family values. A family communication commitment is not exclusively for the deaf child, but rather supports a value that everyone must understand and agree to.

If your children are in the midst of a petty argument, do your best to ignore it. Let your children have practice in working out their own conflicts. If you are more skilled at communicating with the deaf child than are her siblings then you will likely serve as a go-between—this makes you a vital part of every minor argument and may make you appear to support one child over the other. Early in their relationship, insist that your children learn to communicate with one another. If you fail to do this then the hearing child may refuse to communicate with her deaf sibling out of spite or the deaf child may seek protection in lieu of asserting and taking responsibility for herself.

If a fight persists and adult intervention is needed, avoid taking sides. Effectively listen to each child's point of view, acknowledge feelings, and describe the problem as each child sees it. Use "I" messages to share your feelings regarding the problem and express your belief in your children's ability to arrive at a solution on their own.

Even with the best-laid plans, arguments will occur. Try to ignore the verbally or physically aggressive child—give attention to the one who was hurt. For example, if Carol hits her brother, the parents would go to their son and comfort him while completely ignoring Carol and what she did. If the fighting becomes dangerous, immediately separate the children and use the Think Chair (one for each child). Give them time to cool down and think through their feelings before requiring them to find a solution to the problem.

If one of your children "tattles" or reports on the other's misdeeds, validate the tattler's feelings, ("Well, it's obvious that you are mad at your sister") and then help the child come up with ideas on how to solve the difficulty ("Maybe you can write a letter telling your sister how angry you are, or perhaps you can rip up paper to let your anger out.") Remember that your children may seek you out for attention and to ease any communication frustrations they have among themselves.

Activities

• •
Activity #1: The Sibling Seminar
Materials: prepared lecture, an interpreter if presented to a group
Age: 8–12
Vocabulary/Concepts: brother, sister, teach
• •

In this activity, you will ask your children to work together to come up with a short lecture or seminar on interesting aspects of deafness. Consider offering your seminar to other children at school, in after school clubs, or at the public library. Help your children decide what important information to present, including a history of Deaf people, notable Deaf individuals, and communication methods. Help them to make it fun and interesting. The hearing sibling might do a portion of the seminar on how hearing people should behave with deaf people or perhaps she could research relatives of famous Deaf individuals. If this seminar is presented to a group of hearing children, have an interpreter available for your deaf child.

• •
Activity #2: The Friday Fights or Nightlife Negotiations
Materials: agenda board
Ages: 5–12
Vocabulary/Concepts: discussion, disagreement, negotiate, FAIR
• •

Conflict is healthy and normal; therefore, permission to "argue" in families should be established. However, families need to fight fairly. With this activity we hope to teach your children how to interrupt an angry conflict and put it aside for future resolution. This reinforces the STAR technique since it encourages children to stop and think before acting. Children need help channeling their anger and frustrations into problem-solving discussions.

With this in mind, designate Friday afternoons as the time when family "fighting" (family disagreement and negotiation) is allowed. Pop some popcorn and make a family event out of it. Every time your children begin to go at each other, remind them about the Friday Family Fight rule. On Friday afternoon, set aside time to give your whole family permission to talk about disagreements and problems that surfaced during the week. At the Friday Fight Night, encourage appropriate problem-solving behaviors.

Activity #3: Deaf and Hearing Sibling Celebrations
Age: all ages
Vocabulary/Concepts: brother, sister, same, different, celebrate

Make an annual event out of getting together with other families that include both deaf and hearing siblings. Make the event something worth looking forward to: go to a water park, have a cook-out with dozens of fun games, videotape a sibling amateur hour, have a sibling masquerade party at which siblings from the same family dress thematically, make a yearbook to which all siblings contribute and have it photocopied for a later mailing, and have siblings make T-shirts for the event. As you can see, the list could be endless. The goal of this activity is to provide a way for deaf/hearing siblings to celebrate their relationship and to meet other children in the same situation.

Activity #4: My True Feelings Book
Materials: paper, pens, markers
Age: 8–12
Vocabulary/Concepts: true feelings, like, dislike, bother

Make a workbook for your hearing child called, "My True Feelings about My Family Book." Introduce the book as a way for your hearing child to privately express all of the positive and negative feelings that she might have about her family. Tell her that you understand that she might have some very strong feelings and that is OK, but that she can put those feelings in a book and talk with you about them instead of getting into fights or perhaps ignoring her deaf sibling.

In the book, make a dozen or more pages with an opening question or phrase on top. Explore general family questions, positive and negative feelings, and devote some pages to ideas about what to do with these feelings.

Here are some examples of headings for workbook pages:

● Draw a picture of your family.

● Draw a picture of doing something fun with each person in your family.

● What drives you crazy about family members?

● What do you like about your family?

● Draw or write about fights you have in your family. Who do you fight with?

● What do you like about having a deaf sister?

● What don't you like about having a deaf sister?

● What would you change in your family?

● What are some things your parents don't know about your feelings?

As you can see, the questions focus on family. If your child has conflicting feelings about her deaf sibling, this activity may allow her to begin to express them. Ask your child if she would like to share any part of her workbook with you. If she does, be prepared for some honest and angry descriptions; for example, "I hate my sister—I don't know why you brought her home!" Validate her feelings associated with this entry ("you sound mad") and do not squelch this expression. Remember, if a child can express feelings in a safe way, most likely she won't have to punch, call names, and badger to let off steam. Do not do this activity if you feel tentative about allowing these feelings out of the box just yet. This activity asks for honesty, which is not always sweet. You might also do this activity with your deaf child to explore her feelings. Give your child the choice of keeping the book in a private place, throwing it away after writing in it, or finding acceptable ways to manage and solve some of the problems that may have surfaced in her workbook.

. . . .

Activity #5: All Tied Up for the Moment
Materials: three bandanas or string
Age: 8–12
Vocabulary/Concepts: discuss, teamwork, LOOK-AT-EACH-OTHER
. . . .

This activity helps teach your children to work together closely on a task among themselves—literally! Have two children stand side-by-side and tie them together at the ankle and the knee of one leg and at the elbow. (Remind signing siblings to be patient since they will have to sign with one hand!) Give each child separate tasks to do, such as watering the plants and collecting all the pillows in the house. Without any guidance, let your children attempt to do these tasks and work out this funny situation. Dilemmas are "bound" to happen (such as who moves first) and will offer opportunities for the children to practice negotiation and compromising skills. If your children experience communication difficulties, this will become immediately apparent.

If you have access to a video recorder, try taping this event for future viewing. Not only will your kids get a good laugh watching themselves stumbling around, but they will be able to evaluate their skills in working together. You may want to join the activity and tie yourself up with either your child or mate. This will give you the opportunity to model for your children how to get tasks done through cooperation.

● ●

Activity #6: Famous Siblings

Materials: library research, paper, pencil, roll of butcher paper
Age: 8–12
Vocabulary/Concepts: brother, sister, famous, past, future, SHOOT-UP
FAMOUS

● ●

This activity is intended to encourage your children to develop respect for their sibling relationship. Have your children research famous siblings. The Wright Brothers are a wonderful example: you might take the family to the airport for an air show as a reminder of what two brothers accomplished together. Point out the skills of famous siblings and compare them to your children's. Suggest that your children research famous deaf/hearing sibling pairs.

Next, have your children write an article together and date it twenty years into the future. This article should describe some great future events that your children will have accomplished together. They are famous siblings of our future! Come up with possible news headlines. Use positive reframing and encouragement after doing this activity when you see your children do something cooperatively; for instance, "Wow, you guys did that just like the Wright Brothers!"

● ●

Activity #7: "Can I Have Your Attention Please?"

Materials: manila envelope, slips of paper, pencil
Age: 7–12
Vocabulary/Concepts: attention, please, message

● ●

During the hustle and bustle of the day, adults can often overlook a child's hidden messages of feeling left out and wanting attention. Make these hidden messages more obvious with a "Can I have your attention please?" envelope. Explain to your children that at times you may not realize that someone is feeling left out. Tape a large manila envelope to your bedroom door and put the words "Attention Please" on the front. When any family member needs special attention or feels left out, she can leave you a message in the envelope. Check your envelope on a regular basis and respond quickly to requests by giving the children what they need immediately or setting up a time when you can do this.

. . . .

Activity #8: Red Tag/Green Tag Game

Materials: red and green construction paper, scissors, pens, empty
box

Age: 4–12

Vocabulary/Concepts: red, green, cooperate, GET ALONG, fight, control,
your choice, THINK-SELF, GROUP COOPERATE

. . . .

This family activity uses previously mentioned tactics of ignoring, distraction, positive reframing, your choice, and natural and logical consequences. When playing this game you ignore petty arguments, redirect your children to focus on positive aspects of their relationship, and give them the power to choose the outcome. The goal is to "catch" your family members being cooperative and good to each other. You will need an empty box and small pieces of red and green construction paper.

We suggest you play the game for one week. All members need to agree on a family reward for being successful at this game. The green tags represent times that family members get along (avoid fighting) and the red tags represent times that family members fight. Put these tags into a box each time an interaction is observed and at the end of the week, if there are more green than red tags, your family can receive its reward—if not, your family can "try, try again" the following week. Green tags can be given when your children play nicely together, avoid fighting, stop a fight in progress, and/or simply sit nicely on the couch together. Children should know that their parents do not need to witness the positive behavior to qualify for a green tag. They can tell their parents about the positive situation and still receive the tag.

The Parents' Role in Helping a Child Develop a Positive Body Image

• • • • • • • • • • •

Max Fitz-Gerald and Della R. Fitz-Gerald

*C*hildren are our greatest resource. Parents have a key opportunity and the primary responsibility of guiding their deaf children's development of self-esteem, values, and responsible health habits. Most parents want to do a "good job" in rearing their children. From our work with parents, we have observed that information, in combination with practice and comfort, can go a long way in helping parents with this challenging opportunity.

One key area of information needed by parents is an understanding of the natural physical and psychological development of children. One common thread that runs through this development for children of all ages is curiosity. Children are naturally curious and seek information about themselves and others. Infants and toddlers continually explore the world around them. As language forms, the young deaf child frequently gestures to communicate "why?" "where?" or "how come?" It seems children's curiosity is like a sponge absorbing moisture nearby. It is from curiosity that children learn about themselves and their world.

Just as with hearing children, deaf children's curiosity will range from

Max Fitz-Gerald, Ph.D. and Della R. Fitz-Gerald, Ph.D., are clinical sexologists in private practice in Florida. For more than 20 years, they have been conducting sexuality education workshops for parents and professionals involved in the education of deaf and hard of hearing children.

questions like "why does it rain?" to "why does the penis get hard?" Younger children freely approach parents, as they look up to their parents for information and acceptance. Sometimes children's natural freedom may catch parents off guard. Parents may overreact or not respond at all. Children quickly absorb this and may begin to think they have made a mistake. Often children will begin to view their parents as unapproachable and some questions as not askable.

Keeping the word "natural" in mind, parents can begin to explore becoming more comfortable with themselves and more approachable to their children. All thoughts, actions, or questions have answers from a factual base and/or a value base. When one of those fearful situations occurs, parents might count to ten to collect their thoughts and then respond honestly.

Parents need to try to respond to their children's questions. Parents of deaf children can answer using drawings, pictures, gestures, role-play, and other forms of communication. If parents do not like how they responded, they can go over the communication again! Parents who model honesty in feelings and thoughts can build positive self-esteem, trust, and acceptance.

Cracks in the foundation of self may leave deaf children vulnerable to a variety of body-related issues. These cracks are usually formed very early by unanswered questions about self. This may lead to a great deal of confusion and misinformation or even fear about their bodies and how their bodies work. Approachable parents can provide valuable information to answer their children's natural curiosity.

Children absorb information about their world through three major sources: direct learning, indirect learning, and observation. Direct learning occurs through personal experiences, while indirect learning occurs through reading and talking. Listening to and watching others form the observation source. The avenues of reading, talking, and listening are affected in varying degrees by a hearing loss. Thus, deaf children may depend more heavily upon personal experiences and watching.

The fact that deaf children depend heavily upon personal experiences has led some to believe that these children are "overly" interested in their bodies and sex. This belief is not true. Deaf children are simply learning through the method most available to them, their experiences.

From birth, children begin the journey of combining their sexual biology, sexual identity, sexual roles, and sexual orientation into what will form their psychological identity. The first six years of children's lives have been called the "Golden Years." During these most important years, children are continually absorbing everything their immediate environment has to offer. While in the cradle, comfort or discomfort begin to form regarding trust, self-esteem, and body function. The way parents hold, touch, play, gesture, speak, and respond to their children's natural exploration of self and the world around them provides the foundation for the development of either positive or negative self-esteem.

Deaf children follow a similar path or self-development found in hearing children. However, there may be a one- or two-year delay, which may parallel the deaf children's delay in language development. A study conducted by the authors found that a sample of deaf adults had less accurate sexual information than their hearing peers, and they depended upon peers for information about sex three times more than hearing peers. The extent to which deaf people receive accurate information about sex seems to depend on their age, education level, access to mainstream culture, and overall communication skills. These results may reflect how important it is for parents to become involved in their deaf children's education regarding sex.

Parents need good information about how to help their children build positive self-esteem. With good information about natural development, parents can more positively guide their children. The different stages of development are outlined by ages below.

The ages of three to twelve are filled with opportunities for parents to guide healthy self-development. Sometimes it is helpful to recall your own childhood curiosity, to read material on child development, and to talk with other parents. Since three-to-twelve is a very productive and challenging time for children, there are some key points parents should keep in mind about these years of development.

Between three and four years of age, children are still learning trust, acceptance of self, and how the body functions. Emotional safety (being loved and knowing parents can be counted on) is just as important as personal safety. Verbal and nonverbal recognition and acknowledgment by parents of a child's mastery of tasks goes a long way toward building positive self-esteem. Reinforcing a child's male or female identity and helping the child realize the differences between sexes is important. It is equally important to realize that the mastery of body function goes beyond potty training, as children naturally touch their own genitals and may compare themselves to their playmates.

From five to seven years of age, recognition of mastery of "big girl" and "big boy" tasks reinforces positive self-esteem. Childhood sex games such as "doctor/nurse" and "show-me-yours-and-I'll-show-you-mine" are very common among peers at this age. These comparison games are very natural for children and demonstrate their curiosity. It is most important for parents not to over-react or punish their children for these activities. These games represent an excellent opportunity for parents to provide information to their children.

During these years, building friendships allows children to further learn how to trust themselves and others. At this age, children are usually involved in role-playing and daydreaming, which helps them define their sexual identity and sex role. Pleasing parents is generally important during this stage.

For many deaf children, as with hearing children, between eight and twelve years of age, the peer group begins to become more important than parents. Peer group comparison and acceptance become the by-words for children at this age. As children separate from parents, they begin to make independent decisions. If there are disagreements with parents, secretive behaviors often emerge.

Some children may experience puberty as early as age eight or nine, while most begin body changes at eleven or twelve. Others will begin puberty even later. Puberty is often a challenging and sometimes frightening time for both children and parents. It is a time when parents need a lot of patience and understanding. Remembering what puberty was like for parents themselves can often help parents relate better to their children's experiences.

By twelve, most girls will have begun pubic hair growth, menstruation, and breast development; while most boys will have begun voice changes, pubic hair growth, and the capacity for wet dreams. As these biological changes occur, more curiosity about sex naturally develops. This is a good time for parents to be more actively engaged in providing information to their children about the natural changes in their bodies and emotions.

During this age, masturbation and sexual fantasy may increase in frequency. Mutual sexual exploration usually increases as well. The body changes or the lack of body changes can create awkwardness and modesty. Sexual orientation is fairly well-formed and adherence to rigid sex role models is common at this age. For some children at this stage, having a sweetheart is important. Comparison of self to others, as well as images of "body beautiful" and "super jock," generally add more stress to an already stressful stage.

The more parents understand about their children's development, the more information and support they can offer. The approachable parent can initiate discussions and interactions with their children at all ages by

- Recalling their own natural childhood curiosity,

- Giving verbal and nonverbal assurance that their child is "normal,"

- Role-playing/discussing family or neighborhood events,

- Sharing values and why they are important,

- Listening to and drawing from children,

- Exploring plots in television programs and movies, and

- Providing and using helpful books and films.

CHAPTER

8

Body-Related Issues

● ● ● ●

This chapter addresses issues and problems related to poor body image, over- or under-eating, wetting and soiling, hygiene, sexuality, and privacy. By learning to understand, respect, and like his body, a child can become more comfortable in overcoming any difficulties related to his physical development.

Children often attempt to gain control of parents or situations through non-control of their bodies (elimination, hygiene, and eating). In addition, each of these problems can evidence psychological unrest which may be related to low self-esteem, poor body perception, environmental stresses, or lack of education.

The fun activities in this chapter will visually stimulate and educate your child about nutrition, hygiene, privacy, and sexuality, while providing a refreshing approach to handling the overwhelming strain that these types of problems or issues cause. Each activity focuses on your child's abilities and the positive feelings that come with learning about, respecting, and being in control of one's body.

We urge you to talk to a physician if you identify a potentially serious overeating, undereating, or elimination problem. Inquire about developing a serious plan, monitored by a doctor, for weight loss, weight gain, or toileting practices. If you wish to seek mental health services as well and would like some information of what to look for and what to expect see pages 31–35 for a more detailed description of this support service.

The problems may look like this:
● ● ● ● ● ● ●

● The child complains about disliking various body parts.

● A child often says he is ugly or looks funny.

● Family members tease each other about features.

● A child eats continually or right after a meal.

● A child will eat only junk food and you're worried.

● A child eats exclusively from one food group (for example, carbohydrates).

● A child is inactive.

● A child often has unwashed hair, unbrushed teeth, body odor.

● A child age four or older nightly wets the bed.

● A child age four or older frequently soils.

● A child touches private belongings of others.

● A child does not respect private rooms.

● A child touches private parts of others.

● A child explores his sexuality in a public space or shared areas of the home.

● A child begins exploring his sexuality with younger peers.

● A child voices myths or misunderstandings about body parts, procreation, or relationships.

POOR BODY IMAGE

A child learns about his body by watching you in yours, by your response to him, and by age appropriate facts that you teach him. Deaf children learn much with their eyes; therefore, modeling is of great importance.

Your child may respond to his body out of mere habit, in which case a change would include a change of pattern. Your child may respond to his body out of emotional need, in which case a change would include finding ways for the child to express and solve fears, concerns, and misunderstandings.

Problems with the body (eating problems, soiling and wetting, inappropriate sexual exploration, poor hygiene, and lack of exercise) occur naturally in a child's development. If problems persist for an extended period of time or intensify, have your child examined by a medical professional. Seek professionals familiar with deafness who can communicate with your child or, at minimum, are willing to learn about deafness.

Maintain an open dialogue with your child to explore his view of himself and any problems he presents. If you cannot alleviate the symptoms, consider consulting a mental health professional who works with deaf people. A qualified professional may determine that your child has concerns you may need help handling.

Pay attention to how you and your child define his being deaf. If you teach your deaf child that there is something wrong with him then he is likely to feel somehow damaged. Teaching a deaf child about his deafness as a difference to manage and feel proud of helps to create confidence and integrity.

While children need to learn about their differences, no child benefits from simply being defined by one of his traits. Avoid reinforcing bad habits by pigeonholing your child in a role such as "the chubby one," "the baby," or "the deaf child who needs extra protection."

While a child learns much from his immediate environment, exposure to television, magazines, and advertisements can become a very strong form of education. The visual images provided by the media can be potent and confusing to the deaf child without explanations from his parents. Outline TV times and approved shows. Frequently, take the time to watch the programs your child watches to get a sense of the content and of his perceptions of what is going on.

Consistent and clear communication about good nutrition, sexual urges, privacy, and exercise can give your child an opportunity to ask questions and straighten out misunderstandings. Exposure to deaf adults shows the child that he can grow up healthy and well-adjusted. In addition, he may have questions that only a deaf adult can answer.

Activities

. . . .

Activity #1: The Golden Eyes Award

> Materials: paper, pencil, gold metallic wrapping paper, old plastic
> children's sunglasses, certificate
> Age: 6–12
> Vocabulary/Concepts: strengths, capable, award, CAN!, EYES STRONG

. . . .

Many deaf children benefit from drawing attention to the natural strength of their eyes. By concentrating on their visual acuity, deaf children realize they are as capable as hearing individuals. This activity stresses this point as well as suggesting some reasons why deafness is an asset. Explain to your child that you plan to have a small family party during which he will receive a "Golden Eyes Award." At this event, family members will honor his visual acuity.

Prior to the event, make a list with your family of all of the things that the deaf child can do because of his deafness—communicate in sign language, exhibit and read body language, and have terrific facial expressions. Then make a list of all of the distracting and loud noises that the deaf child fortunately doesn't hear—Aunt Lily's terrible singing, Dad's old static-filled radio. Make this list fun and light-hearted. Have a nice family dinner and present the deaf child with his Golden Eyes Award. (You can make this award by wrapping gold metallic paper around plastic sunglasses and sticking them on a certificate. Use a certificate from an office supply store or make one of your own.) Family members can read off the list of assets when presenting the award. Allow your child the opportunity to give an acceptance speech.

. . . .

Activity #2: Body Bothers
Materials: paper, pencils
Age: 5–12
Vocabulary/Concepts: body, bother, dislike, wish
. . . .

Have everyone in your family make a list of all the things they wish they could change about their bodies. Identify these wishes as normal—everyone has a few bothersome things they would change. Whether a birthmark, big feet, ears that hear differently or not at all, or poor eyesight, every person finds fault in themselves. Discuss the fact that although there may be an aspect to your body that you do not like, it doesn't mean that you are unlikable. Also identify all the nice things about yours and others' bodies that you like. Encourage family members to do the same. Don't encourage the idea that deafness is a deficit or a problem; yet, concurrently, allow your child to voice any complaints about being deaf or about how people respond to this. The important thing is that you accept any "bothers" as valid and offer opportunities for your child to express his feelings about this.

. . . .

Activity #3: Body Bothers Puzzle
Materials: old magazines, scissors (adult and child), paper
Age: 5–12
Vocabulary/Concepts: body, bothers, puzzle, wish, trade, give, names of
    body parts
. . . .

This activity makes light of body bothers and focuses on how our body parts go together. Find as many different body types as possible pictured in magazines. Each person should have the same number of "body" pictures. Cut these pictures out and then dissect the pictures into body parts like a puzzle. When you have done this to several pictures, you can begin the trading game. Each person should have their original picture(s) cut up as they consider what part of the pictured person's body they do not care for.

Then each person in turn will ask the other "Can I have a nose from your pictures?" or maybe, "I don't like the legs on my picture, want to swap?" This trade goes on until each of you creates a totally new body!! Of course, you can imagine the results—disorganized, disproportionate, and funny bodies. Use this exercise as a springboard to discuss how there may be things that we don't like about our bodies but that sometimes it would be even more ridiculous if we could "borrow" a part of someone else's body that we liked. Discuss how hair, skin, body size, and shapes come as a unit.

. . . .

Activity #4: "Because I Am Deaf I Can . . ." Storybook
Materials: paper, pencil, markers, crayons, paint
Age: 7–12
Vocabulary/Concepts: can, book, special, skills, CANI, SKILLED
. . . .

Make a long list of things your child does well because he is deaf. Include in this list signing skills, patience in speechreading, use of the TTY, and use of an interpreter. With this information, write a story called "Because I Am Deaf I Can . . ." and make your child the star. Include in the story instances of how his unique skills helped another person or "how he saved the day." Emphasize that if it were not for these special talents, the ending of the story would not be so sweet. Have your child draw pictures for the story and share it with others.

EATING PROBLEMS: OVEREATING/UNDEREATING/ JUNK FOOD EATING

Poor eating habits and weight gain often result from a lack of education about nutritious foods and exercise. Involve the deaf child in making shopping lists, in comparison shopping at the market, or in making nutritious meals and snacks. Try eating meals in new and adventurous settings (in your child's tree house, fort, next to a camp fire, or in your backyard). Concepts about good food are better learned through visual and tactile examples and your child will more likely eat the food if it is visually appealing, fun, and tasty.

Deaf children are often astute observers and learn by observing family members, friends, residential school staff, and the media. Monitor yourself, your cupboards, and what your child sees on TV. If your child is a residential student, stay in close contact with the staff at the school to explore how your child can learn and practice making smart food choices.

Every child has normal, age-related food dislikes, peculiarities, and tastes. In a young child, refusal to eat certain foods or even entire meals may be an attempt to assert independence or gain control, or simply a message that he is not hungry. While reflecting on your child's resistance to eating, ask yourself if your child has ample ways to state his opinions, take responsibility, act autonomously, and contribute to the workings of the family.

If you have failed to include the child in daily family discussions, negotiations, and problem-solving, then he will seek other arenas to gain control (such as food intake). Over time, overeating, refusal to eat, or poor eating habits may be used by the child to gain attention and engage parents in power struggles. Refrain from struggling with your child over food (by either forcing consumption in a light or junk-food eater or by restricting a child who is overweight). Save your energy for more productive problem-solving tasks (see Ignoring and Distraction, pgs. 43–44), such as working on family communication or making sure that the child has sufficient arenas to appropriately gain attention and assert himself.

For the deaf child, dinner-time can be very stressful (mouths full, heads turned, hands busy, and a lot of background noise). If the child feels left out of daily meal rituals, he may displace his frustration onto food by refusing to eat, eating rapidly, or taking his meal into another room.

Eating problems may serve as a smoke screen by calling attention away from other emotional or behavioral problems. This is not necessarily an intentional act nor is it done only by children. Many adults suffer from eating disorders when they cannot express themselves or are not ready to address their emotional difficulties.

Some children have strong negative reactions to the texture of certain foods. If your child seems to do this consistently and also shows a preference for particular cuts and textures in clothing and nightwear, these could be signs of sensory difficulties. The etiology of your child's deafness (Rh factor, prematurity, and maternal rubella) may contribute to central nervous system or sensory difficulties. Occupational therapists trained in evaluating sensory defensiveness could determine if your child is more than just a picky eater.

Eating often provides people with temporary comfort or relief from boredom, loneliness, or emotional upset. In many families, deaf children do not have deaf peers in the neighborhood, which can result in more computer/TV time or more stress on the parents to provide entertainment. Help your child become involved in socially and emotionally rewarding groups that combat boredom and loneliness. It may be a challenge to find Boy/Girl Scouts, sports teams, or after school and summer activities for your child. Networking and car-pooling with other parents, other deaf schools, and your child's school is vital. Sports events specifically for deaf children are extremely rewarding activities. Most schools have teams and events that bring a broad group of children together.

Activities

••

Activity #1: The Greenlight/Redlight Diet

Materials: red, green, and yellow stickers

Age: 5–12

Vocabulary/Concepts: red, green, yellow, healthy food, vitamins, minerals

••

We learned about this fun, kid-friendly diet from Dr. Lauren Solitar Gansler, a friend and colleague who specializes in eating disorders. Later, through our research, we discovered a book written about this special diet called, *The Stop Light Diet for Children* (Leonard H. Epstein and Sally Squires, Little, Brown & Company, 1988).

This diet program is designed to change your entire family's eating habits. It involves the whole family working as a team, thus removing blame from the overweight child and making it more appealing to him. Also, importantly, it gives your deaf child strong visual reminders for dieting and eating healthful foods. Whether you use the Stop Light Diet or another type of program, the color-coded food categories are the pertinent feature of this diet when working with children.

The diet is simple and easy to understand. All foods are divided into three groups: red, yellow, and green, like the signals on a traffic light. Green foods are very low in calories and fat content and high in vitamins, minerals, and fiber (e.g., fresh green vegetables, fresh fruit, whole grains). Yellow foods are the proteins, milk products, some carbohydrates, and some fruits and vegetables. These foods are the mainstay of a healthy diet, but are also higher in calories than green foods. Red foods have little nutritional value and are high in calories and fats (e.g., potato chips, soda, candy).

In order to code your food, you will need to purchase green, yellow, and red stickers. With your child, go through your kitchen and mark foods by category. Put red, yellow, and green tags on food in the refrigerator, in cabinets, and on shelves. Next, have your family plan meals that include appropriate amounts of foods from each color category. The program will establish a language that your family can use; for example, "You get to choose two yellow foods and as many green foods as you like." Model good eating habits: "I'm going to eat only one red food today." Encourage your child when he chooses to eat a limited amount of yellow or red foods by saying, "You chose a green food instead of a red food—that's great!" Try using STAR to help your child stop and think before eating a red food. Remember to consult your doctor before setting up any diet plan you may use with your child.

• •

Activity #2: The Greenlight/Redlight Diet Reminder

Materials: pocket-sized notebook(s) with red, yellow, and green
    dividers; camera; food magazines such as *Gourmet, Bon Appetit*
    or *Good Housekeeping* to cut out pictures of food; weekly school
    lunch menus; pen

Age: 5–12

Vocabulary/Concepts: see above activity

• •

This is a handy, "on-the-go" reminder to help the deaf child make good food decisions in the lunchroom cafeteria or at a residential school. When your family has become familiar and comfortable with the Greenlight/Redlight Diet, have all members carry a small notebook with red, yellow, and green dividers. Use Family Council Meetings to describe meals eaten at work or school and decide whether the food is a red, green, or yellow item. Use weekly menus to review upcoming meals. Write the foods in the various color-coded notebook sections or use magazine pictures/photos for the child who cannot read.

Family members can carry their book with them to look up food. If a child does not know how to categorize a food, have him write it in the back of the notebook and identify the category in a family meeting or at a later time. In family discussions, model confusion, temptation, and choosing. Do not call foods "bad" or become punitive if a person chooses to eat junk, rather note how that choice affects the body and one's health. Point out that food in moderation (a red food to three green) makes the most sense.

• •

Activity #3: My Healthy Body

Materials: large roll of paper, markers, old magazines and newspapers,
    STAR technique (see pgs. 49–50)

Age: 6–10

Vocabulary/Concepts: healthy, unhealthy, fatty, junk

• •

This visual activity shows your child that the foods he eats "stick" to his body and can make his body healthy or unhealthy. You will need a piece of paper large enough to accommodate a tracing of your child's body. First, have your child lay down flat on his back on the paper and trace an outline of his body from head to foot. Cut out the picture of your child and give him some markers and crayons to fill in facial features and clothing. Turn the picture over and draw the other side. Next, search through old magazines and newspapers and cut out pictures of food items that are healthful and unhealthful. Work together to identify fattening, high-cholesterol, and sugar-loaded food items. At the same time, look for healthy foods such as grains, low-fat dairy products, fruits, vegetables, and low-fat proteins.

Once you have collected pictures of these food items, paste the healthy food items on one side of the drawing of your child's body and the unhealthful food items on the other side. Discuss with your child how eating unhealthful foods may make a person gain weight and feel tired or sluggish. Explain that if he eats nutritious foods, he will have more energy and feel better (natural consequences).

Try taking this exercise one step further to reinforce diet and food restrictions. Display your child's body collage on the wall. Explain that every time he chooses to eat a food from the healthful side of his body he will receive a point. If he chooses a food from the unhealthful side, he will not get a point. Decide upon a certain amount of points needed to receive a reward. Use the "STAR" technique to build his self-control as he stops and thinks before eating the wrong foods. You must model good eating habits. You may want to participate in this activity by making your own body collage and choosing from the healthful food pictures.

. . . .

Activity #4: Placemat Messages
 Materials: single-colored placemats or contact paper, heavyweight
  construction paper, permanent markers or oil-based paints
 Age: 5–10
 Vocabulary/Concepts: healthy, unhealthy, choices, goals, results
. . . .

Using a single-colored plastic placemat, have your child use permanent markers or oil-based paint to paint messages, pictures, and sayings that will remind him of his eating goals. Encourage his sense of humor and help him to design the placemat to meet his individual needs. You can also cut out pictures of healthful food items from a magazine and press them between two pieces of waxed paper. Or cover a drawing or collage with clear contact paper. We also suggest that you have your child put representations of healthful and unhealthful foods on his placemat and see if he can list what everyone else at the table is eating. Use the placemat for all his meals. Parents can make their own placemats to show that everyone has important things to remember when it comes to eating. As your child becomes more aware, he may point out unhealthful eating habits of other family members. Encourage this since good health should be a family goal.

Activity #5: Restaurant Menu and Family Dining
Materials: 11″ × 17″ paper, markers, computer, magazines
Age: 6–12
Vocabulary/Concepts: healthy, menu, choose, restaurant

Using a computer, hand-lettering, or pictures, have your child design a restaurant menu for breakfast, lunch, and dinner. Talk with your child about what you've eaten at different restaurants and then make up a healthy food menu for home. The family can choose the week's meals from the menu. A few nights a week, plan and cook healthful meals together and serve them as if you are in a fancy restaurant. Use candles, nice tablecloths, and perhaps even a server (who gets tips, of course)!

Activity #6: The Weekend Shopper/The Weekday Student
Materials: shopping lists, pencils, special care packages
Age: 8–12
Vocabulary/Concepts: healthy, plan, shop

This activity is especially important for the child who attends a residential school for deaf children. It will help to reinforce your child's good eating habits. First, read and do some of the previous activities that offer ways to teach children about healthy and unhealthy food. Next, take your child shopping and ask him to compare two items—"Do you think potatoes or potato chips are better for your health?" Have him choose a weekend meal with two or three healthful components and one unhealthful one (showing him that moderation is the key to healthy and happy eating).

On your shopping trips, allow your child to pick two healthful snacks for the weekend (e.g., raisins, peanut butter) and two for school. Wrap up one surprise for school that he can take with him or that can be sent later. Include dried fruits, juices, nuts, popcorn, and any choice of the many cookies and cakes now made with natural, low-fat, and unrefined ingredients.

Find out what kind of food the school cafeteria serves and seek ways to encourage healthful additions. Consider using or forming a parent's organization to accomplish this.

HYGIENE PROBLEMS

A child with poor self-image may make no effort to improve his hygiene due to his belief that it will not improve his social circumstances with his peers. Often, deaf children are isolated from other deaf peers; and hearing peers in the neighborhood may choose to ignore the child or, in the worst case scenario, taunt or bully him.

Make sure your child has several sets of friends (school, neighborhood, activity-related friends). Having many friends provides a compelling motivator for your child to take care of himself. Expanding your child's social network may require that you drive your child to a local class (art, aerobics, karate); encourage sleep-overs and invitations to dinner, and socialize with other families that include deaf members.

Some childhood fears related to hygiene are directly related to experience. Young children commonly have a fear of water or being bathed (getting their face wet, getting cold, or getting soap in their eyes). This may later become an obstacle to forming good hygiene habits. Explore possible fears related to any hygiene activities, such as showering (fearful of getting his face wet), teeth-brushing (gagging), or shampooing (soap in his eyes). A deaf child with sensory integration problems may find certain types of hygiene activities extremely aversive in that they put his body "on alert."

It is important that parents encourage self-hygiene skills when age-appropriate and when the child is physically able to accomplish them. If parents do too much for the child, dependent hygiene behavior can become a rigid habit. For example, you may find yourself dressing a child who is already in elementary school. If this sort of thing is done on a regular basis, the child misses the opportunity to feel a sense of accomplishment.

Teach your child about proper and effective hygiene practices. Make this fun and interesting, not just another lecture. Plan an outing together with your child to purchase all the necessary tools and products for good hygiene. Let your child know that you associate good hygiene with maturity and the right to privileges.

Activities

. . . .

Activity #1: Hygiene Kit
Materials: colorful bucket or travel case, toothbrush, face soap,
    sponges, shampoo, powder, lotion, oil, comb, brush, carved soap,
    and craft paint (for toothbrush)
Age: 3–10
Vocabulary/Concepts: clean, body, hygiene, bucket or case, hygiene
    items

. . . .

The hygiene kit can be used at home or can be a loving reminder for the child who is attending a residential school. It can be modified to appeal to younger or older children. Purchase an attractive container (a bucket for younger children and travel case for older ones) and fill it with a toothbrush, sponges, soap, shampoo, powder, lotion, and a hairbrush. Personalize the kit by writing or painting your child's name on the container or on the various items. Put in special goodies, such as a designer toothbrush and fancy soaps. The toothbrush can be personalized by using a water-resistant craft paint—designate a brush for each of the days of the week or simply paint one in a special manner. For younger children, design and cut sponges into the shape of hands, feet, face, and other parts of the body to visually remind the child of body parts that need washing.

Activity #2: Poster Child Clean

Materials: camera, blown up pictures
Age: 3–10
Vocabulary/Concepts: clean, compare, better, THUMBS-UP

Have your child clean and beautify himself to his heart's desire. Take a picture of him looking his best and have it blown up to poster size. Put the picture in his room as a daily reminder of how great he looks when he is clean. Just for fun, have your child take a picture of himself when he is very dirty. Now you have before and after shots to hang side-by-side.

Activity #3: Clean and Happy Potato-Head

Use those famous Mr. Potato-Heads made by Playskool™ to remind your preschool child of each part of his body that needs to be cleaned. Every morning or evening, go through the process of sticking on each part of Mr. Potato-Head's body to indicate what part of your child's body has been cleaned.

Activity #4: It's a Deaf, Wet World

Materials: light cotton gloves, rubber mat, scissors, permanent marker
Age: 3–5
Vocabulary/Concepts: body part names

Purchase a pair of thick cotton gloves that you or your (younger) child can wear to wash and fingerspell body parts or the steps to a bathing routine. After teaching names and spellings or signs of body parts, stand behind the shower curtain and give your child a cue for the next body part to be washed. Peek out to see if your child understood. Cut out pieces of a rubber tub mat and decorate them with the "I Love You" insignia using permanent markers. Stick these on the tub sides and shower walls.

WETTING AND SOILING

Wetting and soiling by a child four or older may be the result of underdeveloped muscle control due to medical factors or inactive use. Nocturnal bedwetting can be caused by a small bladder or other physical conditions.

For some children, wetting and soiling are a behavioral expression of anger, frustration, or defiance. For others this is a response to emotional stress (new situations in which your child feels anxious or uncertain or new challenges, such as a new baby in the family).

Reflect on any worries or disappointments that your child may have. A deaf child with limited methods for emotional expression may resort to regression as a means of communication. First, attempt to understand the reasons for the child's anger and frustration. Next, make changes in the environment or teach the child more productive means for expression of feelings.

Wetting and soiling may be a result of developmental immaturity combined with maladaptive or inadequate toilet training practices. Pressure from you to achieve bowel and bladder control before the child is mature enough may create fear or anxiety. This, in turn, may cause any accomplishments to be temporary.

During toilet training you may want to show or lead the deaf child to practice these skills. Resist the temptation to become overly physical, such as carrying him to the toilet or holding him there. Consequently, he may identify physical intrusion or pressure with the process and resist for these reasons. The use of nonthreatening and nonpunitive methods will avert power struggles. Refrain from insisting on immediate gains.

Help your child recognize the physical sensation of needing to eliminate or "needing to go." Together, practice specific exercises to increase control of the sphincter muscle.

The child who has a tendency to become intensely involved in play may not want to stop to use the toilet. Whereas a hearing child might need and respond to a verbal reminder (parent calling to him in play), a deaf child would require a visual reminder from the parent. Unfortunately, the child may experience this type of reminder as intrusive.

Use motivational techniques and activities intended to emphasize your child's partnership with you in trying to accomplish this task. Help your child share control and responsibility by having him be a part of the learning process. He can help you wash his clothing, bed sheets, and any other soiled items. It is especially important to do this in a nonpunitive and matter-of-fact manner. Refrain from expressing your anger or embarrassing your child as a means of manipulating him into controlling his body functions.

· ·

Activity #1: Forests and Hockey Pucks

Materials: paper (especially yellow and blue), markers, scissors
Age: 3–6
Vocabulary/Concepts: dry, wet, soiled, forest, sun rays, rain, hockey
    puck, GOAL-APPROACH, YOU BIG (BOY or GIRL)

· ·

In this activity you chart your child's progress for seven days and reward him at the end of the week. It is most successful for children who do not need to be retrained or require medical supervision. Charts and reward systems work well for toileting problems and work best for children who need external motivation. In addition, the visual cues are engaging to the deaf child and place the problem not only "inside" his body but "outside" on an objective chart—the problem and solution can now be shared. For better results, combine this with other activities in this chapter, such as "The Instruction Manual."

For bed-wetting and daytime wetting: Draw a landscape of a forest. Next, draw and cut out a sun with seven removable rays of sunlight. Draw and cut out seven large rain drops. Now you are ready to chart your child's dry and wet days.

For children who soil themselves: Draw a picture of a hockey player and a goal and then make seven removable hockey pucks. This scene will help you chart your child's progress in ending his soiling problems. If you need assistance in designing these charts, use pictures of forests from a *National Geographic* or cut out hockey paraphernalia from a sports magazine and paste these onto a large sheet of paper.

Explain to your child that the rays of sunlight represent dry days, the raindrops depict wet days. Likewise, hockey pucks in the goal represent days on which he does not soil himself and pucks out of the goal show accidents or misses. Every day your child does not wet his bed or his pants, he gets a ray of sun; use pucks in the goal to represent days he makes a bowel movement in the toilet. Let your child control his chart by putting the rays, raindrops, and pucks on it. Give a reward for a desired number of rays of sunlight or pucks in the hockey net. Decide with your child how many successful days he will need and what the reward is for reaching his goal. Reward small gains initially so that he is quickly reinforced in his successes. As your child becomes more comfortable and capable you can increase the expectations.

. . . .

Activity #2: My Instruction Book

Materials: paper, crayons, markers, stapler or yarn, camera
Age: 3–6
Vocabulary/Concepts: toilet, teach, wet, soiled, feelings, STEP-BY-STEP,
 YOU BIG (BOY or GIRL), WOW!

. . . .

This activity makes relearning toileting a fun and understandable process.
You and your child will make an "instruction manual" on how to go to the
bathroom. By using a step-by-step process and pictures, you create for your
deaf child an accessible method to handle a touchy and confusing subject.

First, look closely at the problem and investigate the cause. Ask yourself
if the problem is medical (weak sphincter muscles, small bladder, or constipa-
tion); emotional (anxieties, fears, poor self-concept); developmental (immaturity, new baby in the home); oppositional behavior (to get back at a parent,
another way to say "no" or to assert himself); or simply a lack of education
(did not learn toileting procedures correctly). If your child is using toileting
as a way to assert himself, develop other ways for him to do this. Examine
your rules, restrictions and avenues for your child's self expression. This information will help you in writing your toileting instruction manual because it
clarifies the steps your child must take to correct the problem.

Next, explain to your child that you will help him reach his goal by making a special instruction manual for toileting. Show him a few examples of
how an instruction manual is written and drawn. (Make sure your example
has good pictures). Now you are ready to make your own manual.

Step A: Draw or take a picture of your child's body in a bathing suit and identify
body parts using language familiar to your child (e.g., pee-pee, bum, etc.). Introduce more clinical and generic terms and signs, too (e.g., vagina, penis).

Step B: Draw or take a picture of your child pretending to be wet or soiled and
ask him to draw how he feels next to the picture. On the following page, draw a
picture of your child dry and clean with corresponding feelings. Use this opportunity to explore his thoughts about either feeling dry or being wet or soiled.

Step C: Draw or take a picture of your toilet and bathroom at home complete
with toilet paper and toilet bowl.

Step D: Drawings or pictures in this step will differ for each child's unique
problem. Use information you have worked on earlier (causes), and draw a
few pictures showing your child struggling with the problem and then resolving it. For example, if your child's problem is caused by a lack of muscle
(sphincter) control, have your child draw a picture of himself practicing
sphincter exercises (see Retention Olympics pg. 154).

Step E: Draw a picture of your child looking as if he has the urge to go to the bathroom.

Step F: Draw a picture of your child sitting on the toilet, wiping, and flushing.

Step G: Draw a picture of your child content, happy, and feeling successful. (Note: If you take pictures of your child rather than using drawings to illustrate these steps, you will give your child playful practice doing each of the steps while modeling for the camera. However, if your child is at all embarrassed or reticent, use drawings.)

Activity #3: Retention Olympics

Make an olympic sport out of your child exercising and strengthening urethral sphincter muscle. Once your child has learned how to squeeze his sphincter muscle to control (stop and start) the flow of urine into the toilet, you can make an olympic event out of the number of times he stops the flow of urine into the toilet. Record his progress and encourage him to beat his latest record.

Activity #4: Designer Underwear
Materials: child's plain underpants, permanent marker
Age: 3–6
Vocabulary/Concepts: special underpants, wet, dry

Using fabric paint and a few pairs of new underwear, your child can create "designer underwear." Write "empty" or "dry" on the back of the underwear. Your child may not want to ruin his new underwear after putting so much energy into creating it. For nighttime wetting, have your child decorate his bed sheets.

LACK OF EXERCISE

In our fast-paced television-infected society, exercise can be last on the list of your child's activities. If your child has few friends in the neighborhood, you may find he seeks solace in sedentary activities.

Parents who model and promote physically active life styles are more likely to have physically active children. Involve your entire family in exercise on a regular basis. Vary the type of exercise to keep it entertaining and fun, and vary the location to keep it fresh and new.

Contact local Deaf organizations to find out if they have ongoing bowling, volleyball, or baseball games. Inquire if these activities cater to families and whether there are any "junior" Deaf leagues.

Inspire your child by educating him about deaf athletes. Though there are a few deaf players on professional hearing teams, many deaf athletes participate in the World Games for the Deaf, more commonly referred to as the Deaf Olympics. Perhaps your child will want to find out more about the olympic events, who is competing, and where the Deaf Olympics will happen. If you are fortunate enough to have financial resources and time, your child could attend this event.

Activities

....

Activity #1: The Family Activity
Materials: appropriate sports or activity gear
Age: all ages
Vocabulary/Concepts: activity, exercise, health, together
....

Choose a sport or physical activity in which the entire family can participate. Softball, skiing, tennis, roller skating and even dancing are terrific fitness activities that the whole family can enjoy. Although you want to avoid activities that rely on auditory sense, some deaf children find dancing delightful and will follow a strong rhythm or follow their own internal flow—of course others find it boring or become extremely self-conscious.

We suggest that you do the activity of your choice on a regular basis. Increase interest in the activity by taking lessons, subscribing to related magazines, and taking your kids to see the "experts" in the field. For example, if you choose tennis as your family sport, play tennis with your child, join a tennis club, buy tennis magazines, and go to or follow a few professional tennis tournaments. Encourage each member of your family to pick a favorite star athlete and follow his or her career. Your family activity doesn't have to be a traditional sport. Try tap dancing, jump roping, or scuba diving. Most importantly, do it often and do it together.

....

Activity #2: The Aerobic Video
Materials: video recorder, VCR, aerobic outfits, poster board markers
Age: 8–12
Vocabulary/Concepts: exercise, workout, warm-up, active, slow down
....

Move over Jane Fonda—we've got a video that will knock your gym socks off! Your family can make a workout or aerobic videotape to be used by your entire family on a once- or twice-a-week basis. Begin by choosing exercises your child enjoys doing. The exercise tape should include three parts: warm up, aerobics, cool down. Choose activities that fit into these three categories. You and your child may want to review exercise tapes currently available in video stores to get ideas and have a better understanding of how a "workout video" looks.

Design the video to suit your child's age and abilities (a three-year-old can tolerate about fifteen minutes of hopping and ball-bouncing, while an eleven-year-old can last thirty minutes to one hour). Include physical activities in the tape that highlight your child's talents such as jumping rope and dancing. Choose music with a strong beat that the deaf child can enjoy. You may want to brainstorm with your child about ways to make an exercise video more fun for deaf people. Consider inserting captions (on poster board) to indicate the next exercises, how to perform them, or how many repetitions will occur. You can also have the child sign directions and encouragements on the video. You can make your workout video by taping your family dancing, jumping, stretching, and skipping to a planned routine.

· ·

Activity #3: Deaf Sports Activities

Materials: access to organizations and schools for deaf people, *Deaf Sport: The Impact of Sports within the Deaf Community* (David A. Stewart, Gallaudet University Press, 1991)

Age: 6–12

Vocabulary/Concepts: sports, activity, TEAM-PLAY
· ·

It is important for deaf children to participate in sports. Natural benefits of sports involvement include regular exercise, a sense of self-confidence, and the opportunity to interact with other deaf peers. If your child is not attending a residential school, research and involve your child in a sport in your local Deaf community. Attend games at your child's school even if he is not participating. This may motivate your child to consider sports activities elsewhere. You can contact The American Athletic Association of the Deaf (1-800-393-8710, voice; 1-800-393-8710, TTY). A good book to read is *Deaf Sport*, which discusses how sports play a key role in maintaining a vibrant Deaf community.

SEXUAL DEVELOPMENT / PRIVACY

A deaf child's body and sexual development is affected by both social and communication factors. The child needs environments that make him a vital part of all interactions and that do not leave him with a pervading sense of being "separate" and "different." The more the child can communicate directly with his parents, the less anxious he will be about physical, social, and sexual development.

We must teach our deaf children to value themselves and their bodies and that there is acceptable and unacceptable behavior. Hearing parents may feel tempted to be too lenient with their child (allowing him to enter the bathroom without warning, permitting him to rummage through a parent's private closets or drawers). In these cases, the child develops a confusing sense of appropriate boundaries and privacy and his behaviors will reflect that. Conversely, parents may find they are unnecessarily strict or protective (not allowing the child to explore the immediate neighborhood, restricting dating until a late age). In these cases, the child has limited opportunities to venture, practice, and master social skills.

It is never too soon (or too late) to talk about sexual issues. Your discussions should relate to the child's behaviors, questions, and new exposures. Your communication should match the child's age and preferred communication mode. Some parents may feel uncomfortable either due to difficulty in communicating or due to the nature of the topic (sexuality). It becomes more difficult for these parents as their child enters early adolescence. In these cases, the schools "take over" the task and, unfortunately, the parent's wisdom, experience, and values are not adequately transmitted.

With clear communication, good assertion skills, and a strong sense about right and wrong, your deaf child need not be any more vulnerable to everyday dangers than the hearing child. However, the deaf child will be at greater risk if he habitually accepts unclear communication, if he "goes along with the crowd," or if he does not understand socially acceptable behaviors.

Unfortunately, issues such as sexual abuse, AIDS, and pregnancy are not confined to the hearing community and are issues that deaf children need to understand. Take the time to evaluate your own values and feelings related to these issues and prepare yourself to respond to questions. Teaching and problem-solving about privacy, ownership, asserting oneself, and self-care is an excellent and necessary foundation for ongoing discussions. If you "save" all of the education for adolescence, you will find you are overwhelmed and often your teenager is not as receptive to your input.

Teach your child about privacy and appropriate and inappropriate touch. There tends to be more touching among deaf people, yet within the Deaf community there are norms for this (see chapter 6). Hearing people may touch deaf children more often due to anxiousness about communication. Touching deaf children should never replace clear communication.

Teach your child about issues of privacy, ownership, and basic rights. Reinforce these with concrete examples in your household.

In a residential school for deaf children, privacy and public space presents a challenge. The children may have their own bedrooms and activity areas; however, the residential staff may need to constantly monitor the children for safety in a manner which might not occur at home, thus causing less opportunities for independent behavior and decision-making. Communicate closely with your child's residential staff to understand how they teach and honor privacy while maintaining a safe environment. In addition, get to know the children who live with your child to acquaint yourself with the influences his peers may have on him.

Activities

· ·
Activity #1: Private, Public, Personal
Materials: roll of butcher paper, markers (green, red, blue)
Age: 4–12
Vocabulary/Concepts: private, public, or NOT PRIVATE, personal or
      PREFERENCE, FORBIDDEN
· ·

The goal of this activity is to have deaf children learn about public and private space through visual representations and categorizing. Begin by explaining to your child what is meant by public areas of the body—note what people usually see every day (face, hands, arms, and legs) and how that changes through the seasons. Next, define private parts of the body as those parts that are covered by bathing suits and underwear (the genitals, buttocks, and breasts). Third, describe personal places on the body. These are places that a person does not expose or places he does not like to be touched. You might find it helpful to explain this by an example of your own, "Well, I know that hair is a public body part but it is very personal to me and I don't like anyone to touch my hair—I'm that way about my feet too!"

As in one of the previous exercises in this chapter, ask your child to lie down on a long piece of wrapping paper. (You can use old newspapers taped together, as well.) Draw an outline of the child's body. Have your child do a body drawing of you as well to facilitate discussion. Before doing the drawing, ask each other which body parts you prefer not to have touched, thereby modeling how to ask permission when touching someone closely.

Next, draw in the face and anything the child wishes (hair, pants, a button, rings). Tape the drawings to the wall and begin the categorizing game. Circle areas of the body that are public in green markers or crayons. Discuss how that changes depending on where you are. For example, at home you might walk around in bare feet but in school you do not. Or, wearing a bathing suit is OK at the beach, but is not acceptable in the supermarket—this can be a funny and light discussion.

Now, ask your child to circle areas of the body that are private in red—you can circle yours as well. It is not necessary at this point for your child to get it "right"—it is more important to get a sense of what he understands and believes in order to better teach safe and healthy concepts. Circle areas on your body drawing that are private and discuss what makes them private. Use the appropriate names and signs for private spots—penis, vagina, bum, and breasts. Note these areas on your drawing as "my" private areas and on the child's as "your" private areas. Define each person's private areas as belonging to them, and that means others cannot touch them there. Explain that there are times that others might need to touch private areas (the doctor might if the private area is hurt and Mom or Dad is there; or for the younger child, you should mention that Mom and Dad help him clean his private areas sometimes).

Circle personal areas on your drawing in blue and explain why certain areas of your body that might be considered public by other people are personal to you because you don't like people to look at or touch them. This is a great opportunity for deaf children to begin to assert their likes and dislikes about how others touch them—"I hate when the principal of our school pats me on the back from behind—it scares me!"

Use this activity as a reference for future discussions. Praise your child when he speaks up for himself regarding touch and his body.

● ●

Activity #2: Public, Private, Personal Places
Materials: Post-its™ (green, red, blue)
Age: 6–12
Vocabulary/Concepts: (see above activity), places, favorite things, like, dislike

● ●

This activity is an extension of the previous one and teaches your child places in your household that are public (shared spaces), private, or personal. You will need green, red, and blue post-its. The green represents public places; the red (or pink), private; and the blue, personal. Walk around your house and stick the post-its on areas that are deemed public (possibly the dining room table, the refrigerator, or the living room couch).

Next, identify private places (the toilet, each person's bed, the dog's bed, the cat's litter box, the shower, someone's diary). Discuss why these might be private—because you pee there, because only you sleep on your bed, because the dog has his own bed. Note the signals of privacy—when the bedroom door is shut; when the bathroom door is closed; when something is locked, like a diary; or when someone tells you "this is my private piggy bank—please don't touch it."

For the last, personal places category, use blue post-its. This category is the one that accounts for individual and family styles and personalities. For example, the TV may be a personal item in some households because the parents determine what is watched and for how long. Or there may be one chair in the house that is used only by Grandpa or the cat. Or maybe Dad is very particular about the kitchen when he cooks and does not like anyone to disturb him. Encourage the deaf child to identify his personal spaces—"This is my favorite cup. I got it from uncle Ted and I want people to ask me before they use it." Or "I don't like when people bother me when I am on the TTY."

You may be surprised that your deaf child has noticed things that you have never explained. On the other hand, it may be startling to discover what your child has been missing. Thus, this activity will serve as a way to clarify misunderstandings.

Activity #3: The Line Is Here!
Age: 5–12
Vocabulary/Concepts: BOUNDARIES, permission, touch, private

Teach your child the concept of boundaries by having him define progressive degrees of privacy. Begin with the boundaries of your property (it is not respectful for people to step on your lawn), the physical boundaries of your house (people who do not live here must ask permission to come inside), and your body (a person must have permission to touch another's body). See if your child can think of ten or twenty ways a person expresses his wish for privacy (or boundaries); for example, by closing a door, pulling the shades, or wearing particular clothing.

Activity #4: Off Limits

Make a list of things in the home or on a person's body that are "off limits." Tape little signs saying "off limits" (or use the international symbol of a prohibition, a circle with a line through it) on these things and/or on a person for a short period of time to reinforce the need to respect these private places or items.

. . . .

Activity #5: Good Hat/Bad Hat or the "No" Theatre of Touch

Materials: hats, magazines, stuffed animals, dolls, body drawings,
scissors, tape

Age: 8–12

Vocabulary/Concepts: good, bad, negative, positive, culture, permission,
no, stop, FINISH! (one-handed sign), POSITIVE / NEGATIVE

. . . .

Most deaf children are fascinated by drama, and love a chance to play charades or anything resembling it. In this activity, the goal is to highlight the different ways to touch and to encourage children to feel comfortable saying "No," and for them to learn when to do this. It is important to point out the differences between the ways that hearing culture and Deaf culture use touch (see chapter 6). However, in each of these cultures there are better and worse ways to touch. When in doubt, ask permission.

You will need a few hats, some magazines, and possibly some stuffed animals, dolls, or body drawings. Use the magazines to cut out hands, legs, lips, shoulders and whatever parts of the body one uses to touch another person. Tape these pictures all over the two hats, leaving room in the very front of each hat for a "smiley face" or a plus sign ("+") drawn on a small piece of paper to represent the good touch and on the other a frowning face or a subtraction sign ("−") for bad touch.

Now the show begins! Model wearing one of the hats and proceed to act out a good way to touch—you can use a doll, another family member (with permission), or a body drawing for your co-actor. It is most effective and useful to act out an everyday occurrence, such as getting another deaf person's attention. (A good way to do this would be to tap with the tips of the fingers lightly on the shoulder.)

Next, ask the deaf child to put on the "good" hat and show a good way to touch. Have the audience (other family members) wave their hands in applause for the "good" way. Next, use the "bad" hat and show a bad way to get a deaf person's attention, such as slapping the deaf person from behind, grabbing his arm, or grabbing his face and pulling it towards you. After the "bad hat" actor acts out his role, encourage the audience members to put on the "good" hat and tell the "bad" hat actor "No!! Stop That!!" and then show a good alternative to the bad action.

Everyone must have an opportunity to play each role; to be a co-actor; and to use dolls and body drawings if the actions are too rough or if the "bad hat" actor is acting out touching private areas. You can also put a smiley face or "+" or a frowning face or "−" on a doll and have the doll do some of the acting.

Activity #6: My Cherished Possessions

Materials: paper bag, small items (trucks, dolls, trinkets, books, balls, bubble gum), dolls, stuffed animals

Age: 5–10

Vocabulary/Concepts: private, special, CHERISHED, no, stop, FINISH (one-handed sign), SHARE

As described earlier, a deaf child may have difficulty with boundaries, privacy, and knowing what is valuable if he has experienced a chronic lack of communication. For example, he may have been permitted to invade others' privacy to get information (such as opening mail) in lieu of getting an explanation. Conversely, a parent might have done the same (rummage through a child's room) instead of struggling to communicate with the child. This activity helps break the cycle by teaching the child ownership and assertion skills.

You will need a medium-sized paper bag, random small items that fit into the bag (small dolls, trucks, trinkets, books, balls, pens, bubble gum), and dolls or stuffed animals. Explain to your child that you are going to pretend that these items are cherished items. Put all of the items in the bag and ask your child to hold it tightly—these are precious things.

Explain that you are going to use the dolls one at a time to ask for items from the child and each time the child can decide to give the doll an item from the bag or not. Stress that if the child does not want to give up a precious item, he should say "no" and that the child can become more insistent if necessary—"NO, NO, NO!"

Use the dolls or stuffed animals to ask for the items in a variety of manners. The doll might be rough—"Give me that truck!"; threatening—"If you don't give me that truck I'll get you in trouble"; pleading—"Please, please, please"; or manipulative—"If you give me that then I'll give you something next week." By using different personalities in acting this out you will see when your child gives in and relinquishes a precious item. Often a child will do this when the doll or animal asks nicely or offers a trade. This offers you an opportunity to point out to children that just because someone is nice to them does not mean that they have to give up a precious item. When the child refuses to give something up, ask for an explanation to help your child put language to his feelings and to further build his assertion skills.

This activity may appear to come in conflict with the concept of "sharing." In fact, it can be paired with sharing. When asking a child to share, it is not useful to teach him to loan and give up items all the time. If the child feels as if he has been coerced into "being nice" then he may find a way to retaliate. A discussion might clarify what things the child is willing to share and what things feel "precious" so that you can set up guidelines. Finally, if your child is very shy and can easily be taken advantage of, you should work at building his assertion skills. This would include encouraging him not to share so much and to say "no" more frequently, until this skill becomes more integrated.

● ●

Activity #7: The Private Box
Materials: small cardboard box or shoe box, diary
Age: 4–12
Vocabulary/Concepts: private, box, yours, diary, book, no peeking
● ●

Give a younger child a box and let him know that he can put all of his private items in it and you will not look inside. Give an older child a diary and promise to never read his private book. These promises must be kept or the point of the activity is certainly lost.

● ●

Activity #8: The Door Sign
Materials: paper, markers, string
Age: 5–12
Vocabulary/Concepts: privacy, welcome
● ●

With your child, make a door hanger (like the "Do Not Disturb" signs found in hotels) that states "Knock first—I want privacy" or with a profoundly deaf child "Flash light first—I want privacy" or "Wave paper first—I want privacy." The light can be flashed if the switch is on the outside of the child's room; a paper can be slipped beneath the door or put through the crack in the door to get his attention. The other side of the sign can say, "Come in—I want company."

● ●

Activity #9: Private Time
● ●

Set up a special time every day when all members of the family have a private time. Depending on your child's age, establish fifteen minutes to an hour a day when he either goes to his room, selects a private space to sit, or is given permission to take a walk on his own. Everyone in the family should participate in "private time."

Activity #10: My Private Body

Materials: books, especially *My Body is Private* (Linda Girard Walvoord,
    Albert Whitman and Company, 1984)
Age: 4–12
Vocabulary/Concepts: private, touch, want, don't want

Take the time to read books designed to teach children about unwanted
touch. A good book to read with your child regarding appropriate and inappropriate touch is called *My Body Is Private.*

Activity #11: So Let's Talk

Materials: on-going openness and discussions
Age: all ages
Vocabulary/Concepts: permission, clean, feelings, problem, stop, HOLD,
    right, wrong, choice, THINK-SELF, result/consequence, responsible,
    think-about, values, family, religion, sexuality, genitals, teenager,
    adult, SPEAK-UP, date, sex, pregnancy, birth control, disease, AIDS,
    safe sex, careful, condom, abortion, gender identity, gay, lesbian,
    MULL-OVER, ASSERT, FORBIDDEN

In this activity, we will define two frameworks for teaching your deaf child
about sexuality. One is used over a longer period of time and is the most
preferred; the other addresses specific issues, and often gets introduced to
the child by the phrase "we need to talk." We will focus mainly on the gradual
approach, since we do not advise "saving up" information for one big talk. By
gradually sharing information that suits the age, communication style, cogni-
tion, and personality of your child, you will make it easier for him to understand and digest. The "specific issue" talk happens if a child does something
which needs an immediate response (such as masturbating in the living room)
or is entering a new developmental phase and you need to update information
or provide more specifics (for example, if the child starts to menstruate or
begins dating).

Do not assume that your child's school is doing the job. Find out what
they teach at the school, create a parents' advisory group and contribute your
ideas to the curriculum, stay in touch with the teacher to learn the topics she
covers, and learn the vocabulary of the school curriculum.

The long-term teaching method at home should cover the following areas:

The Function of Body Parts: As early as preschool, you can start to teach about
bodily functions and body parts. Children ages three and four will have many

questions about everything, so you can begin to use this opportunity to teach them about their bodies. Use generic clinical terms and find out from a Deaf adult, or an ASL-fluent teacher, the signs for various body parts.

Privacy/Ownership: Refer to some of the activities in this section for guidance regarding the essence of privacy and boundaries. Once your child is out of diapers and attends school, he will encounter a whole new set of social expectations. Teach privacy, asking permission, and respecting others.

Self-Care/Hygiene: Promote understanding, responsibility, and pride about self-care and cleanliness. Describe the natural consequences of ignoring hygiene (teeth will get cavities, friends might tease, and rashes can develop). Try some activities in the Hygiene section of this chapter.

Feelings and Expression: Children who can identify, express, and handle feelings will be better able to control impulses and have empathy for others. Refer to Chapter 11 on moodiness for some ideas about helping your child develop these skills. Again, use language that your deaf child will feel comfortable using when he is upset, hurt, sad, or confused.

Problem Solving: The following is a rough outline of what deaf children need to know in order to master problem-solving skills at different ages. Each child will have his own time, order, and practice mode for these skills. The essence of our STAR program includes the following areas:

1. The child must learn to curb impulses.

2. He must be able to distinguish "right" behavior from "wrong" behavior.

3. He must realize that his behavior may have consequences.

4. He must think through choices and consequences before acting out.

5. He must realize that when making choices there may not be a clear "right" or "wrong" choice. Gray areas exist between right and wrong.

6. Your child must be aware of his responsibility in making choices.

7. The child should recognize the value in assessing, reviewing, and trying again if necessary.

Children who are in preschool and kindergarten can manage the first two skills; seven and eight year olds can begin to internalize consequences; and eight year olds through twelve year olds should be able to work on steps four through seven. Throughout your child's development, use terminology that refers to choice, responsibility, consequences, and reflection.

Values and Morals: These vary according to the beliefs of each family and community. Your child needs to understand that different families have different religions, beliefs, and values regarding work, money, marriage, etc. Let your child know when something is a family belief or value, "In our family we do not believe in eating meat."

Sexual Expression: This area relates to many of the above. Even young children have orgasms, masturbate, and have sexual feelings. Teach your child about sexual body parts, how to deal with sexual feelings, what your family values are in relationship to sex, how to keep genitals clean and safe from harm, and what is considered private.

Body Development: Notice changes in your child's body as he grows. Talk to him about how he is different from people of another gender and age. Discuss with your child natural body changes, such as menstruation, hair growth, emotional changes that indicate that the child is becoming a teenager and, later, an adult. Use activities from this chapter to assist you. Although you may have already taught your child at a younger age about a topic (e.g., puberty) you should update that information to match his age. Try to anticipate changes so that the child feels prepared.

Assertion Skills: Teach your child how to state his opinion, how to speak up for his rights, and how to ask for help when he needs it. See "My Rights" in chapter 6 and "My View, Your View" in chapter 11.

Relationships: Teach your child about the various types of relationships between people—friends, relatives, husband, wife, step-families, boyfriend, girlfriend, partner, etc. Explain how these relationships were formed (through direct bloodline, marriage, two people agreeing to have a relationship). Even if your child usually asks questions, check for understanding about various relationships and their contexts. Refer to chapters 6 and 7 for activities related to this topic.

Sexual Relationships/Procreation: This topic can be handled very simply when a child is young: "Sometimes people love each other and like to kiss and hug" or "When a man and a woman decide they want to have a baby together—the man puts sperm into the woman and that makes a baby." Second and third grade curriculums often include units on how the body works so you can borrow what they've learned in school to help you explain things. Between the ages of eight and twelve, you can start to introduce more complex concepts. Older children may want to read on their own, based on your recommendations.

Dating: You can introduce the concept of dating early on as a way to explain the progression of relationships. As your child gets older (ten to twelve), tell him what people do on dates and at what age he can expect to begin dating based on his desires as well as your family's rules and values. When your child begins to show interest in dating, you should let your child know the specific process you support (e.g., phone/TTY calls for a while; meeting the boy/girl; meeting the date's parents; dates at your home; dates in a group; dates with others; and then private dates). If your child is spending a substantial portion of time with another deaf or hard of hearing child, become acquainted with that child's communication style as well. Do not let communication struggles interfere with your finding out the most you can about your child's date.

Sexual Intercourse/Pregnancy/Birth Control: Sexual intercourse and pregnancy go hand-in-hand and are topics to be addressed as your eight to twelve child learns and understands how the body functions. When you explain to your child in more detail about how a body develops from a child's body to an adult's body you can include an explanation of why the changes occur (to equip adults to have children when they feel ready). Birth control is often a difficult subject for parents to introduce to their pre-adolescent or adolescent for fear that they may be construed as encouraging sexual relationships. Many parents would rather have their child be knowledgeable and thus, hopefully, safer no matter what. You can always teach the facts along with a strong dose of your own values. "Some people have sexual intercourse and use birth control. I would prefer that you tell me if you are considering having sex and we can discuss what to do." Or, "Some teens have sex and use birth control—we don't want you to have sex until you are older and married." Your child will most likely learn about birth control one way or another. If you do not discuss it with him then he might learn things that are incorrect and he will assuredly be without the benefit of your opinion.

Sexually Transmitted Diseases (STDs): Although it seems that addressing the topic of sexual diseases can wait until adolescence, your child will benefit from a gradual education. Explain that some infectious diseases are transmitted by very close contact or through blood. As your child learns and understands more about the body and sexual intercourse, you should introduce the concept of sexually transmitted diseases and describe what safe sex means. Every family has a different way of approaching this based on their beliefs. Distinguish facts from beliefs ("You can get AIDS from having sex with someone who has the HIV virus. They might not even know they have it. People can stay protected by using condoms or not having sex. In our family, we do not support people having sex until they are adults.") It is not ridiculous to teach children about STDs; adolescents are one of the fastest growing groups contracting AIDS and other STDs.

Abortion: Regardless of your moral beliefs on this issue, children (especially older children, who are reading) will come across this topic. When your child is old enough to understand (ages ten to twelve), you should explain what an abortion is, how they are obtained, the controversies surrounding abortion, and your stance on the matter.

Gender Identity/Orientation: Throughout your child's development, he may experiment with same and opposite gender behaviors, dress, and attractions. Help your child to express himself in a safe manner. Younger children are much less concerned with these issues, while children aged eight and older will become very rigid about traditional gender behavior. If your child likes to dress or act in a manner different from his peers (for example, a nine-year-old boy who wants to wear nail polish), help him to envision the response this may create from his peers and to avoid a situation that might cause him to be teased, bullied, or harmed.

. . . .

Activity #12: So Let's Talk II
Age: all ages
Vocabulary/Concepts: see previous activity

. . . .

In the previous activity we noted the "what" of sexual education. Here are some helpful "how" suggestions to communicate to your child about sexual development.

1. Use the language that your child is most comfortable with and understands best.

2. Use incidental learning experiences. "Well, those dogs are having sex and might make a puppy."

3. Practice using sexual signs and words on your own, in the mirror or with other adults first. Some people become embarrassed by sexual language and hearing individuals might blush at the graphic nature of sexual signs.

4. Talk with Deaf adults to develop your own comfort in using sexual signs.

5. Try to stay neutral and as matter-of-fact as you can so that the topics don't become "taboo" or "emotional."

6. Engage both parents in the process. In a single-parent household, enlist trusted relatives and neighbors to talk to your child, too. While having a parent or trusted adult who is the same gender as your child can be important for your child throughout his childhood, this becomes even more important when he is age nine or older. At that age, he may become shy and embarrassed to talk to an adult of a different gender.

7. Introduce books throughout the child's development that address the above topics. For younger children (three to seven), provide books with colorful pictures and animal characters. As the child grows older, books on the human body with more text are appropriate.

8. Make sure your child has contact with pregnant animals and women. Use these experiences to explain the process of gestation and birth. If possible, have your child be present when an animal gives birth.

9. You are not merely teaching your child about "sex." You are also teaching about development, body growth, privacy, safety, values, control, respect, relationships, assertion, sexual feelings, and self-expression. These issues surface every day and offer opportunities for learning.

10. Do not ignore questions or behaviors. If your child asks a question and you don't know how to answer, say so — "I will have to think on that one."

11. Be aware of what is on TV, what clothes are in style, what are new fads, and what the school notices about your child. The more you understand about your deaf child's developmental world, the more you can understand his point of view.

Tips for Understanding Your Child's Fears and Anxieties

● ● ● ● ● ● ● ● ● ● ●

Neil and Susan Burgess

When we were growing up our parents handled our fears and anxieties in a way that worked for us. They no doubt learned this from their parents, and then reapplied those memories and lessons to us when they themselves became parents. However, as hearing parents raising our deaf son, Adam, we quickly realized that many of the experiences that we had had growing up didn't prepare us with any firsthand knowledge of what it was/is like for our son. Many of his impressions, reactions, fears, and anxieties seemed to us to be unusual and in some instances unreasonable.

Our son Adam is a handsome nine-year-old boy with curly red hair and lots of great freckles. He loves to read, play video games, ride his bike, and play with his friends. He takes karate classes and exhibits a good deal of self-confidence. He is quite intellectual and has a great sense of humor. He is very comfortable carrying on conversations with adults. During the day, Adam hears fairly well while wearing his hearing aids. At night without them, and in the dark, our self-assured little man takes on quite a different persona, becoming a child reluctant to go to bed and to sleep because it means being alone.

Neil and Susan Burgess are the parents of Adam, who has a progressive hearing loss, and Mark, his younger brother. They live in the Boston area.

Hugs and kisses, then lights out! No big deal, right? Not! In darkness, he lies there unable to convince himself that we, his parents, are still in the house; so in he comes, "I just came in for a drink of water." Or "I just came in for a hug." Or "I think I heard a noise." Or "I had a bad dream, can I sleep in here with you?" This has been going on nightly for his whole life. Alone in his room, Adam experiences darkness, silence, and feelings of total isolation. Couple this with his very active imagination and voilà! No sleep! How about a night light? Scary shadows. How about a regular light? Too bright to get sleepy. He just doesn't want to be alone.

When he was younger, Adam spent most nights sleeping with us in our bed. No, he wouldn't start out there, but in the morning, there he was! As he grew older and larger, this arrangement, as you can imagine, became very uncomfortable.

Adam has an adorable younger brother named Mark. Mark, who is two-and-a-half years younger than Adam, idolizes him. As is the case with most younger siblings, Mark tends to drive his big brother crazy, always trying to get his attention and wanting to play with him. Adam, the typical older sibling, is more interested in his friends and preferred activities that rarely include Mark. However, Adam's tolerance level for Mark increases as bedtime approaches. By "lights out" time, they are the best of buddies and they have decided that Adam will sleep in Mark's room. So it goes. Sleepovers provide another way to solve Adam's nighttime problems. During weekends and vacations, Adam is always asking for someone to sleep over, or for permission to sleep over at someone else's house. (It is only recently that Adam has been able to sleep over at a friend's house. After several unsuccessful attempts, he has overcome those fears.)

There seem to be no clearcut solutions. A combination of flexibility and understanding on the part of all family members is required. Adam has gradually done better in this area. He is able to sleep alone now and does so with increasing regularity.

Emergencies and alarms also trigger extraordinary responses from Adam. Everyone is supposed to react to emergencies, right? React, yes, panic, no! A couple of incidents in particular stand out in our minds as examples of these extraordinary responses. As background to this first story: we have a wonderful respite worker who has been helping us with the kids for the past three years. She is fluent in ASL (American Sign Language) and gets along great with both boys. They love her and are very comfortable with her. They are very happy to have her taking care of them. One afternoon, they all decided it would be a nice idea to take in a movie together. All sounds harmless, right? Unfortunately, halfway through the movie, a fire alarm sounded and the building was promptly evacuated. To add to the confusion, it was pouring rain when everyone arrived outside the theatre. Our respite worker removed Adam's hearing aids so they would not be damaged by the downpour and then held both boys hands very tightly so they would not become separated in the large, confused crowd of people. As a result of these very appropriate and necessary precautions, you guessed it, she was unable to communicate with Adam to calm him and assuage his fears.

Scary nightmares followed this incident. Although Adam has worked very hard on various coping strategies, he still remains quite skittish whenever there is any loud noise. Alarms in particular cause him tremendous anxiety.

Subsequent to the movie theatre incident, Adam was in a medical facility for a routine evaluation when the fire alarm sounded (again). He panicked and "took off" away from Mom who, fortunately, caught up with him and proceeded to follow the emergency instructions. By the time they arrived in the lobby, Adam was in a complete state of panic. He was hyperventilating and seemed to be close to blacking out. He was so obviously distressed that two hospital staff members came rushing over to assist. The staff arranged for Adam and Mom to go across the parking lot to a different building where it was safe, and far away from the situation. As we were already tuned in to Adam's "alarmophobia" and had, along with his therapists, been working with him on coping strategies and various techniques he could use to calm down after a scare, such as this one, the incident had a happy ending. (For the record, there actually was a small fire on the third floor of the building in this case. It was quickly extinguished and all was back to normal very shortly thereafter! Phew!) Less scary and more predictable situations, such as fire drills at school, have also been a source of similar anxiety for Adam.

Fear of abandonment evokes some unusual responses from Adam. Although we are rarely late for anything, on one occasion we were five minutes late picking Adam up after a therapy appointment. Despite the fact that he was among friends and professionals in a facility where he has been comfortably going for many years, his condition upon our arrival would have to be described as highly anxious. Although we have seen many children exhibit similar reactions, it would seem that our son's fears of abandonment and his reactions have carried on to an age much older than might be considered normal. We have learned through this experience to remind him before leaving him anywhere that WE WILL DEFINITELY come back for him and that he should not worry or panic if we are a few minutes late.

Adam is a very bright and sensitive child. He has always cued in to concerns and fears of others, often without any of his own sensory input. When he was much younger, he was unusually preoccupied with the possibility of a "bad person" breaking into our home at night, especially when Mom and Dad had gone out for the night. Our neighbor across the street, and very close family friend, has done an excellent job watching the boys for years. Occasionally, while babysitting, the neighbor would react to the many normal noises of our one-hundred-twenty-year-old house with intense concern. This would scare the wits out of Adam to the extent that whenever anyone around Adam heard a noise, day or night, he would "fear the worst." Although he still suffers some anxiety, with help and support from his family and professionals, Adam's fears in this area have diminished to a great extent.

Adam is almost ten years old now, our family is thankfully very close. We all have been through a lot together. Whether it is a fun family day shared together at our favorite water park, or a more difficult time such as spending the afternoon helping Adam cope with a situation that was traumatic for him, every day provides us with an opportunity to learn more about what it is like to grow up deaf in a hearing family and a hearing world. Rearing a deaf child can, in some ways, be very different from rearing a hearing child. Even though some of these experiences seem very unusual to us, we know that what we have experienced is, for our family, quite normal. We intend to continue learning and to proceed with, what we feel are the key ingredients to success and happiness: communication, love, and support.

CHAPTER

9

Fears and Anxieties

• • • •

Whether of heights, doctors, water, dogs, getting lost, insects, monsters, or the dark, childhood fears and anxieties are often normal reactions to developmental challenges. These fears may result from or be aggravated by the deaf child's lack of information.

Some fears may become more pronounced at certain ages and stages of maturation; but, in time, most will diminish with the help of information, experimentation, and gentle encouragement. Some fears and habits that are not overcome during childhood may continue into adulthood (e.g., public speaking). If your child's normal and developmentally appropriate fears, anxieties, or nervous habits become irrational, persistent, overpowering, or result in a panic state, then you should seek professional help.

When guided to confront her fears and nervous habits, your child can develop skills and confidence to prevent her difficulties from becoming paralyzing obstacles to her enjoyment and further growth. The activities that we've developed and collected for this chapter are all geared towards this goal.

FEARS

Fears are necessary to human survival; they alert us to dangers and provide us with an internal early warning system for harmful situations. Many fears are normal and developmentally appropriate, such as stranger-anxiety in infants and fear of the dark in preschool children, and will diminish over time with encouragement, experimentation, and explanations.

Many types of fear are instinctual in nature, such as the movement we make in response to loud sounds, loss of balance, or sudden motion. The deaf child will more than likely need to see or feel an item to allay her fears or interrupt a startled response. For example, she may need to see a person before that person touches her, or she may need to visually investigate a perplexing noise.

Specific fears, such as fear of water or animals, often originate from upsetting, frightening, or misunderstood experiences. Distinguish between normal and necessary biological fears (early warning systems) and those that are limiting your child's experience.

Explain to your child that fears are a part of everyone's life and development and that some fears are good to have. Normalize her fears by reading her stories about people who have similar fears and anxieties. Give examples from your own childhood about how you overcame similar fears. Consider having a conversation with a deaf adult who can give examples of how a deaf person has managed and overcome certain fears.

Adults must remember that a child's vivid imagination can transform a small fear into a grandiose phobia. Children who are sensitive and generally anxious by nature may be prone to have more difficulty with fears. Additionally, a deaf child who experiences a deprivation of information in a hearing environment has only her thoughts and fantasies to draw upon for answers. The sooner the child's fantasies (especially fearful and emotionally-laden ones) are known and discussed, the better equipped she will be to handle new developmental challenges.

Encourage your child to share with you everything she knows about her fear. If you find it is based in misunderstanding or lack of information, try to clarify for her the reality of the situation without invalidating her fear. A child may hold strongly to her version of reality if she learned it from a trusted source—a friend ("Yep, your neighbor is a bad man and he has an axe"); a misguided relative or adult ("God will punish you and take all of your toys away if you lie"); or something shown on TV (dolls becoming monsters).

The problems may look like this:

● ● ● ● ● ● ●

- The child's eyes open wide, she shakes her head and backs away.
- The child spends a large amount of time "avoiding" a feared object.
- The child has chronic fears of monsters and bad guys that won't go away.
- The child has screaming fits at the doctor's office.

Adults can unintentionally instill fears in children to make them obey (for example, "the bogeyman will get you if you don't get in your bed"). Some adults may tease a fearful child as a joke or to "get them used to it." At such times, adults forget that the tease may feel traumatically real to the child. Therefore, never use feared objects as a disciplinary measure and never dismiss a fear your child has or tell her that she is a baby and should not be afraid.

Hearing parents of a deaf child may naturally feel compelled to protect her since they cannot imagine themselves feeling safe without hearing. Deaf children manage safety and fears just fine using their strengths and skills. Parents should avoid becoming over-involved in protecting the deaf child from her fears, otherwise the child's feelings of helplessness and weakness are deepened and reinforced. Support and soothe your child as needed, but always keep in mind that you want to teach her to shift from depending on others to feeling confident about depending on herself.

Fears can also be used by a child to manipulate her parents and to gain attention. Avoid becoming manipulated by your child or providing her a secondary means of getting increased attention because of her fears. In cases like these, think of the behavior of the deaf child as another effort at communicating—she may be trying to tell you she wants more attention or she may be avoiding accepting responsibility. Give the deaf child methods, language, and structures to assert feelings and needs.

Children are more prone to have difficulties with fears if they are living in a conflictual, unpredictable, or overly authoritative environment. This type of environment can promote feelings of insecurity and loss of self-confidence. Carefully consider your child's living circumstances and assess them for conflict and problems which might promote fears. Provide an anxious, fearful, or sensitive child a safe environment where she can freely explore, "play out," and conquer her fears or worries.

Activities

· ·

Activity #1: The Scarecrow
Materials: paper, markers, index cards, child's old clothing (pants, shirt, sneakers, socks, hat), pillow case, stuffing (newspaper works)
Age: 3–8
Vocabulary/Concepts: scarecrow, afraid, practice, fear, OVERCOME

· ·

Scarecrows are made to scare away intruders (crows) and to keep birds from eating the valued crops. This activity asks you to make a scarecrow with your child that is actually a replica of herself and that can help your child playfully "scare" away or better deal with fears. What better way to conquer a fear than to play with it?

First, make a long list of skills and talents your child has to combat her fear. For example, for a child who is fearful of dogs, list her skills in being with, caring for, and enjoying other animals—even a goldfish. Take your list and write the word for or draw a picture of each skill on separate three-by-five index cards. Additionally, come up with a half-dozen positive statements, such as, "I am strong" and "I can do it!" and "I am smart and courageous."

Next, stuff your child's shirt, pants, and socks and put a pair of old sneakers on the resulting figure. For the head of the scarecrow, use a pillow case. Stuff it and then draw your child's face on it. Top it off with her favorite hat. Next, take all the skill cards and tape them onto the scarecrow. Finally, dress your child as the feared object (throw a black piece of material on her and turn her into "the dark"; dress her as a dog, doctor, or snake). Notice how this activity allows your child to try on the role of the feared object or situation—a great way to reverse roles. If she feels unable to do this, model her role for her the first couple of times.

Have your child (who is pretending to be the feared object) try to scare the scarecrow and in response the scarecrow uses her skills, which are pasted all over her, to fight off the intruder. This dramatizes for your child how she can use her numerous skills to ward off her fears. Play out this scene as often as needed and keep your scarecrow around to remind your child of her skills and success in warding off her fear. Eventually you can take the skill cards off the scarecrow and carry them with you to use when encountering the fear. We suggest that you write the skills on a white baseball cap that is worn by the scarecrow. When the child's scarecrow does not need the hat anymore, your child can wear it herself. This play and rehearsal activity enables your child to feel more comfortable dealing with her fear in a safe environment.

● ●

Activity #2: Fear Week

Materials: read "Relaxation Center" activity (pgs. 263–265); books,
　　TV programs, magazines, and pictures of what child fears
Age: all ages
Vocabulary/Concepts: fear, STEP-BY-STEP, process, FEAR REDUCE

● ●

This activity, "Fear Week," is based on a behavioral technique called "desensitization." In this step-by-step process, a child is given opportunities to become accustomed to her fear—in small doses that gradually increase over a period of time.

Before beginning "Fear Week," teach your child ways she can counteract her fear, such as using the relaxation techniques taught in the "Relaxation Center" on pages 262–265. Have her use self-talk techniques, stated skills, and positive statements (see "Scarecrow" activity) when confronting her fear. Find substitutions or distractions, such as counting numbers, thinking of a special place, or repeating a phrase like "I can be calm"—whatever works to keep your child calm. Throughout the week of these "fear encounters," model calmness, confidence, and optimism. This encouragement is imperative. With each day of the week, her fear will be introduced to her in a small amount and paired with a fun activity or game to gradually counter-condition your child. Below we outline a "Fear Week" using the "Dreaded Dog" example.

The Week of the Dreaded Dog

Day 1: Read charming, illustrated dog books and stories. Study the books with your child and talk with her about the friendly, silly, and nonthreatening behavior dogs display in the books.

Day 2: Watch TV programs and movies about dogs. Select movies such as *101 Dalmations* that depict dogs as fun, harmless, and a "man's best friend."

Day 3: Read books and see movies that show real life pictures of dogs. Choose dog books with lots of puppy pictures as they are least threatening. If your child becomes fearful at any point, have her use relaxation, self-talk, and positive statement techniques discussed earlier.

Day 4: Observe dogs from a distance. Go to a dog show and sit a good distance away. Visit puppies at a local pet store. Watch a neighbor's dog from a car or fenced-in yard.

Day 5: Role-play and practice meeting a dog. Have your child ask a friend or relative that has a friendly dog to participate in "Fear Week." Double-check to make sure this dog is super-friendly, never bites, and is good with children! Using a picture of a dog, role-play and practice meeting the dog. Show your child how to interact with this friendly dog and explain how she can do this.

Day 6: Meet the dog on a leash. Keep the dog at a distance (about a yard or two away) and introduce your child to the dog.

Day 7: Play with the dog. Have your child meet and play with the same dog in whatever manner she is comfortable. Mission completed!

Activity #3: Monster Friends
Materials: paper, markers, clay, dolls, pictures, old clothes
Age: 4–7
Vocabulary/Concepts: monster, friend, friendly

Make a friendly monster with your child. You can make it doll-size or human-size. It doesn't matter if the monster looks frightening, just be sure to remind the child that the monster is helpful and will be a good friend. Encourage her to try to use this friendly monster to make friends with the monsters that are frightening to her.

Activity #4: Play in the Dark
Materials: flashlight(s), *Shadowgraphs* (Philalt Webb and Jane Corby, Running Press, 1991) book, glow-in-the-dark stickers, paper, pencil, markers, small objects to touch
Age: 4–10
Vocabulary/Concepts: fear, dark, guess, fun, games, ENJOY

Since your deaf child relies heavily upon her eyesight for navigating her world, darkness can create a virtual "blackout" of security. Without light, the child is less able to communicate and to know what is happening around her. By using different play techniques, you will introduce the dark as a potentially fun time. However, don't turn out the lights and immediately assume your child will be engaged in the play. Instead, use some desensitization principles (see "Fear Week" activity) by starting slowly with games that have human touch and light and then proceed to lights off when the child is comfortable.

Here are some fun games to play in the dark listed in an order that might make them more palatable to your child. The first four use light and human touch so that your child has some familiar supports; the latter activities rely on tolerating total darkness for a short (and fun) period of time. Initially, the games can be played during the day with shades drawn and lights out and later they can be played at night when the room can be completely darkened. Use your child's own bedroom since she needs to become accustomed to being in the dark there.

1. Bring several flashlights into your child's bedroom and perform a light show. See if you can catch each other's light. Try to find special dolls and toys with the lights. Dance on the ceiling. Use colored balloons or colored cellophane over the flashlight to create colorful spheres or streams of light.

2. Using the book, *Shadowgraphs,* learn about making hand shapes and shadows in the dark (with flashlights as the source of light). Make or create your own hand shadows by inventing new ones. Try to use sign language on the wall and see if others can guess what you are saying.

3. Turn off the lights and have your child touch your face and guess what kind of expression you are making. Sign into each other's hands and try to decipher simple messages ("I Love You" sign or fingerspelling "Hi" for example).

4. Place glow-in-the-dark stickers on the walls and ceiling of your child's bedroom. They make for wonderful fun in the dark.

5. Give a piece of paper to your child. Turn off the lights and ask her to draw pictures of a door, house, or person. Turn on the light after a few minutes and look at the silly picture. Extend the length of time the light is off by having her draw more complicated pictures.

6. Turn off the lights and have your child touch different objects. Have her guess what they are.

7. Turn off the light and make funny faces or body statues, then turn on the light to see what faces or body shapes others have created.

8. Have your child change something in the room, then turn on the light and guess what she has changed.

9. Extend some of this play outdoors to have some summer fun. See how many fireflies you can count starting at dusk. Or play a game of flashlight tag with family and friends. Each player has a flashlight and the person who is "it" tries to "tag" the other players with a beam of light. You can do several variations on this game by playing statues, release tag, or by playing in teams.

Activity #5: Water Play
Materials: see activity for ideas
Age: 3–8
Vocabulary/Concepts: water fun, play

Here are some fun ways to accustom your child to water. (For these activities, hearing aids must come off!)

1. Fill a child's wading pool with water and apples and have an old-fashioned apple dunk (bobbing for apples). Give the child prizes for successfully getting different parts of her face or body wet.

2. Purchase a "Water and Bubbles Activity Box" from Lakeshore Learning Materials (see address on page 69). This box is filled with hands-on waterplay items and scientific discovery activities.

3. Rainy Days: Put on your rain boots and leave the rain coats off during a warm summer rain. Take your child out in the rain to splash in the puddles, get her hair wet, and let the rain fall on her face. See who gets the wettest.

4. Sit in puddles, make dams to catch the rain, or tip your mouth up to the sky for a rain water drink.

Activity #6: Doctor Play

Materials: doctor kit, dolls, stuffed animals, white shirt, first aid
      supplies, small pad of paper, pencil, small vitamin bottles
Age: 4–7
Vocabulary/Concepts: doctor, help, sick, medicine, shot, scared, better

Using a child's doctor kit, dolls, and stuffed animals, play "going to the doctor." Using a white shirt, a home-made operating room cap, and a stethoscope, make your child an M.D. Bring several stuffed animals with various ailments to her hospital. Create a waiting room, an examination table, and pads for prescriptions. Expand the doctor kits to include real band-aids, wooden popsicle sticks for splints, gauze, medical tape, cotton, empty vitamin or pill bottles, empty hydrogen peroxide bottles, tongue depressors, and a board to act as a stretcher. Pretend to be an ambulance by taping an inflated red balloon to the end of a flashlight and twirling it in the air.

As you play with your child, have the animals show apprehension and allow your child to soothe them. Throughout the play, mention how good and brave the doll is while going to the doctor. Make sure the game ends with the doll feeling safe, happy, and "all better." Switch roles and allow your child to be the patient, the patient's parent, or a nurse.

Activity #7: My Helpful Interpreter

Materials: access to certified interpreters
Age: all ages
Vocabulary/Concepts: interpreter, talk, watch, ask, LISTEN WITH YOUR
      EYES

It is quite common and appropriate for a young deaf child to have her parents act as her primary support and to assist in her communication with the pediatrician. However, as the child's language becomes more sophisticated, consider accessing an interpreter for doctor visits. In this way, the child can begin to ask direct questions of the doctor and also receive information that can alleviate fears. Parents who act as interpreters may have difficulty explaining medical procedures, whereas an interpreter (signing or oral) is trained to make technical language accessible to deaf clients. Federal laws mandate that deaf individuals have equal access to clear communication, and facilities that receive any federal funds are required to pay for this service. Be sure that your child has some prior experience with using an interpreter in less feared settings to help her to become accustomed to the process.

ANXIETIES

While fear is a momentary reaction, anxiety represents a general feeling of impending doom. Anxieties can begin as specific fears that grow into general, all-encompassing feelings of apprehension and insecurity. For example, if a deaf child is not taught to interact with hearing store owners, cashiers, or waitpeople she may become very agitated in public and seek to literally hide behind her parents.

A child who is overanxious may withdraw from challenging activities because she feels incapable of dealing with real or perceived dangers which she associates with that activity. Anxious children usually worry more than others, lack confidence, and feel incompetent. A key difference between anxious deaf children and anxious hearing children is that deaf children receive fewer clarifying explanations, less information, and fewer reassurances. Even the smallest lack of information can contribute to a host of fears; therefore, teasing out the real from the perceived with the deaf child is vital.

Anxiety can also be learned, in part, from another person. If a parent is anxious, a child may copy this trait. Reflect on any concerns you may have that are specifically related to raising a deaf child and how these may be perceived by your child. No child likes to be defined as a "worry" to the parent. You may find yourself performing as the child's main advocate and feel responsible for negotiating for your child's needs and fighting for your child's rights at every turn. Try to relax; accept the fact that some things are fine the way they are. Talk with trustworthy professionals or other parents about your experience and make time to enjoy your child fully.

Encourage your child to fully communicate her worries to you. Ask about the first time she can remember feeling anxious about a particular circumstance and when she felt most able to handle her worries.

Empower your child by helping her come up with a plan to deal with the things that contribute to her anxiety. When experiencing the "can't" syn-

The problems may look like this:

● ● ● ● ● ● ●

● A child is afraid to try things on her own.

● A child withdraws from numerous activities and cannot give reasons.

● A child behaves in an infantile fashion after age four.

● A child chews her nails, sucks her thumb, and picks at skin.

drome, remind your child of all of her "cans." Highlight for her the special skills that help her feel in control and more capable of handling her worries, such as relaxation or problem-solving skills and successful past experiences.

Activities

Activity #1: Worry Warrior

Materials: cape, wand (or stick), simple face mask, cut-out of the letter "W," skill cards from "Scarecrow" activity, poster board, scissors

Age: 4–7

Vocabulary/Concepts: worry, warrior, shield, skills

Explain to your child that you are going to transform her into the "Worry Warrior—Conqueror of Fears and Foes!" With her help, create a costume that makes her look like a "super-hero." A cape, wand, mask, and shirt with a big "W" on it will do. The Worry Warrior needs a backpack to keep her "worry weapons" inside. (These weapons are three-by-five index cards with a word or picture of each of your child's skills as listed in the "Scarecrow" activity.) In other words, every possible skill your child has will become a weapon against her worries.

Put these "skill" index cards in her backpack. Once she has the Worry Warrior outfit and backpack filled with her skills she is ready to play. Pretend the Worry Warrior is confronted with worry after worry, that is, all her major fears and anxieties. Using her backpack of skills, have her pull out a weapon (skill) to fight off the worry. For example, if the worry is "afraid of getting lost," then the weapons could be"good at getting help," "knows her telephone number," and "doesn't wander away."

Write any new skills that surface during the game on the index cards and add them to the pack. Play this game as often as needed. Have her bring her "weapons" (skill cards) when she leaves home to remind her of her capabilities.

You can also make a cardboard or poster board Worry Warrior shield that has a handle on the back for the child to hold. On the front of the shield, tape or write all of the child's skills and have her use the shield in role-plays, illustrating for her how her strengths protect and shield her from being overcome by fear.

Now that your child is aware of her own power and skills, she is better prepared to deal with anxiety-producing situations. Older children can participate in this activity by drawing a cartoon of the Worry Warrior. Frame by frame, and following the same guidelines as described above, have your child draw herself as the Worry Warrior character in the cartoon. Encourage her to include how she deals with her fears by using her skills.

Activity #2: Merry Mantras
Age: 6–12
Vocabulary/Concepts: repeat, talk to yourself, reminders, THINK
POSITIVE

Whether or not we know it, we often use sayings, coined phrases, or self-talk to help us through difficult times. In a traffic jam, we might tell ourselves, "Take a deep breath"; when we feel frustrated or angry, we might use the reminder, "Count to ten . . ."; and when we have many bad things happen all at once and we feel overwhelmed we might repeat, "One day at a time." Alcoholics Anonymous is famous for using many phrases like—"Easy does it," "One day at a time," and the serenity prayer ("God grant me the serenity . . .").

You may have learned these or similar phrases from your parents, teachers, books, or TV. Many of these self-talk mantras have come to you naturally—you did not seek them. If the deaf child misses some incidental learning experiences, she needs to actively be taught these valuable tools. Make them "stick" by creating active and visual reminders.

Notice the different times that you use "self-talk" mantras. Mention to your child where you learned these and how they help you. Use them in a deliberate manner so that your child can see their purpose—"I'm going to count to ten since that car made me soooo mad!"

Try having your child look in the mirror every morning and say, "You are fine just the way you are." You can repeat three times together, "I can change and control myself," with more expression each time. You can recite a special phrase with your child nightly when you tuck her into bed, "You are a very special person, and people love you". You can remind your child to say to herself, when being teased, "I will ignore teasing" or "I will focus on myself."

If you notice that your child becomes attached to a special self-talk mantra, make a card with the mantra on it for a surprise. Suggest that the child make a poster for her room. Or make a bumper sticker to remind others of the same thing. If your child likes to read, ask her to look for little sayings on car bumper stickers or on billboards. Research some phrases that important Deaf people have said. Have older family members teach some new ones. Collect dozens and put them in a book to share with others or to save for an appropriate time.

Think of new phrases that might help your child manage a particular fear or developmental hurdle. Depending on your child's age, English skills, or choice in communication (for example, ASL), you may need to adjust the saying.

· ·

Activity #3: Worry Dolls

Materials: Guatemalan worry dolls, or, alternatively, other similarly small dolls

Age: 6–12

Vocabulary/Concepts: worry, share, forget, later

· ·

Sometimes a child cannot let go of a worry but can find relief in letting someone else (temporarily) take care of it. Sometimes a talk will reassure a child that a parent can take care of the worry and sometimes it is useful to have the child use something else. This simple activity allows your child to identify her feelings of concern; gives her a playful way to redirect these concerns; and allows her to learn how to let go of worries for the time being.

There are lovely tiny dolls from Guatemala called "worry" dolls that can be found in creative gift shops, especially those specializing in ethnic gifts. Natives of Guatemala advise removing a doll from the box for every worry that you have, allowing the doll to do the worrying for you. The doll can be kept under your pillow to whisk away worries while you sleep. Six worry dolls come in a set, which limits the number of worries a person can have. You can substitute other dolls or figures you have in the house if you do not own an original set of worry dolls. You may want to limit the worries to three at a time as a way to help your child prioritize and focus her concerns.

Explain to your child that the doll will share worries and help children so that they can sleep, play, and focus on other things. Mention that often when the doll helps, solutions to worries can be found later. You can keep the dolls in her bedroom, in yours, or in a common area—let your child decide since these are her worries. The child can use the dolls to notify you that she is concerned about something. When she goes to the worry dolls and takes one out, ask her what she is worried about.

Activity #4: Safety Video
Materials: video recorder, VCR
Age: 5–12
Vocabulary/Concepts: safety, afraid, help, careful

Children feel empowered and capable if they understand and can control their fears. By writing, directing, and acting in a safety video that examines her fears and anxieties, she can feel like she is an "expert" in handling those same fears and anxieties. In our experience, deaf children adore the chance to perform and get an enormous amount of satisfaction from this.

Subjects to consider exploring in video format might include water safety, strangers, animals, fire, body safety, and other life situations that may make your child fearful and anxious. Make sure she comes up with solutions for feeling safe in these situations. Once the video has been completed, encourage your child to show it to younger deaf children so that she can teach them important skills for safety.

Activity #5: The TTY Connection
Materials: TTY, written emergency procedures
Age: 7–12
Vocabulary/Concepts: safety, police, fire, help, call, CALL (TTY), TYPE

Anxiety is accentuated if a child does not know options for dealing with frightening situations. Emergency situations, such as fire, illness, or accidents are real concerns. What if your deaf child were in a fire? How would she know there was a fire? What if you were the only parent in the household and you became ill, requiring an ambulance?

Begin teaching your child from a very early age what she should do in each of these situations. You can lessen your whole family's fears by making sure that you have an operable fire alarm that flashes lights as well as sounding an alarm. Talk with your local fire department about having a special alarm installed that connects to the station. Put a tot finder sticker, available from the fire department, in the children's bedroom windows. A TTY is also a must.

Begin by teaching your child how to use a TTY and have her practice either by calling directly or by using a relay service available for those people who do not own a TTY. Next, visit your local fire station and police station and familiarize them with your family, introducing them to your child. Advocate for your local police and firefighters to own and use a TTY and offer to show them how it works. Tactfully educate them on your child's legal rights to have access to these public service departments. Familiarize them with the way that your child types by having them talk with your child on the TTY in the station or from home.

Establish an agreed upon emergency procedure that includes your child evacuating the house, seeking help from neighbors, dialing numbers listed clearly by the phone, and rehearsing a clear, quick message, such as, "Help! Me Tammy! Come now!" If your family, local police, or fire department is aware of this code, they can respond immediately.

Your child should be taught to leave the building if the fire alarm goes off or if something catches on fire. In your TTY connection plan, you should note such situations. A child rarely has to use such procedures, but that is what emergency safety plans are all about—the one-in-a-million situation. In addition, a feeling of well-being and safety may result for your child (and you) if she feels prepared.

An activity such as this serves many other functions: you alert the neighborhood and public service professionals to your deaf child and her needs; you allow your child to see police and firefighters as helpful and approachable; you model for your child how to advocate for her rights to access; you facilitate confidence in your child when using the TTY; you encourage family members to use the TTY and relay services; and, most of all, you teach your child that the world is not all that frightening and she is capable of functioning perfectly well in it.

FEARS AND ANXIETY RELATED TO SEPARATION

A deaf child who has grown accustomed to having her needs met with little or no effort on her part or by manipulating others may become overly dependent, making normal and necessary separations from parents traumatic and difficult. This child may not develop confidence in her ideas and instincts and may feel unequipped to make decisions or solve problems.

The problems may look like this:
● ● ● ● ● ● ●

- Your child holds onto your hand in most situations.
- Your child refuses to go to bed, take a bath, or stay in a room alone.
- You and your child have a daily struggle over going to school.
- Your child refuses to spend overnights even with trusted and familiar relatives.

A child who is constantly supervised and held to a strict rule-oriented structure may act obediently but become very dependent on others. She may not adequately develop her own internal controls and skills she will need to be more autonomous. Do not teach obedience at the expense of independent thinking. The situation might be different if your child is highly impulsive, has an attention disorder, or learning problems. This type of child needs consistency, structure, and reinforcements over a long period of time in order to gain internal controls.

Try to strike a delicate balance between protecting the deaf child from harm and allowing her to try things, fail, and try again. This does not mean that a parent should let her child stumble through tasks with no directives. Give enough instructions for your child to understand the task, set rules for safety, and allow your child to manage the rest. If she fails and is frustrated, then console her, give her feedback, and allow her to take a break if necessary. Emphasize your belief that she can do things on her own. Don't rush to your child's rescue if she has difficulty, and be tolerant of imperfect results.

Some situations are difficult for a parent to refrain from intervening in, however. It is very painful to watch a child ostracized, teased, and treated unfairly by the general hearing public. Seek out places where your child is warmly welcomed and teach her how to cope with ignorant behavior rather than isolating and over-protecting her.

Over-protection is an understandable response by (hearing) parents, but the results are costly to the child's self-esteem, independence, and development. Always ask yourself if you are "protecting" (keeping the child fundamentally safe) or "over-protecting" (keeping the child from learning to deal with day-to-day frustrations and challenges).

Children need to learn independence and the ability to separate from their parents in gradual steps, beginning in infancy. Show your child that she can depend on you to be available when she needs you. If your child gains attention for being baby-like and dependent, she will have a difficult time imagining her identity as anything different. Attaining any independent mastery would mean the loss of a previously reinforcing self-image.

Paradoxically, the more confident and connected a deaf child feels to her family, the easier it will be for her to gain a firm sense of independence. If she is always yearning to be a part of the family, she may avoid being separated. If the child is a part of the daily communication, shares in problem-solving, and feels respected for her differences, she will be better able to master developmental separation.

What looks like a problem with separation may stem from a misunderstanding. Be clear about transition times, and the beginnings and endings of events, appointments, holidays, playtime, TV time, homework, time outs, vacations, and the school day. When a deaf child is aware of the context of a situation (e.g., that she will come home every day after preschool), her fantasies can be put to rest.

Practice age-appropriate problem-solving with hypothetical ("what if") games and discussions. (Between the ages of three and six, children have difficulty hypothesizing.) Praise independent efforts and accomplishments and emphasize improvement and progress rather than results.

Utilize trusted baby-sitters and specialized respite services or trade off with other parents of deaf children in order to give yourself some adult time. You need to take breaks. This will also give your child opportunities to be on her own with other adults. Make sure baby-sitters can comfortably communicate with your child.

Activities

. . . .

Activity #1: "You Can Do It" Telegraph Signals
Materials: private supportive signal between parent and child
Age: 3–8
Vocabulary/Concepts: special, between us, support, YOU-AND-ME PRIVATE

. . . .

If your child has a hard time dislodging herself from you when going to day care or to a new place, teach her how to read secret messages sent through holding hands. Tell her you will gently squeeze her hand a certain number of times to mean something special—three squeezes means I-Love-You or four squeezes means You-can-do-it! Teach your child these telegraph signals prior to a separation to help her to feel more confident in letting go of your hand. You can also use standard signs or create your own to convey special meaning across a distance—the "I Love You" sign flashed through the car window, a wink as you are walking away to mean "you're the best," or a "thumbs up" to mean "way to go."

. . . .

Activity #2: The Chain Gang

Materials: construction paper, scissors, glue, pen or pencil
Age: 7–12
Vocabulary/Concepts: independent, connected, on my own, chain, separated, MYSELF!

. . . .

Remember those paper chains you made in grammar school out of construction paper? Get out your scissors, paste, and colored paper and put those dormant skills to use. Cut enough strips to make a six-foot to ten-foot chain. Next, make a list of all the independent, capable skills your child has for separating from you. Write or draw each of these skills on a strip of the paper.

Now stand next to your child, face-to-face, as close as possible. Take each strip of paper with the skills written or drawn upon them and read them out loud one at a time. Paste each of these paper links together to begin to make your chain. As you make several new links, have your child step back to make way for the growing chain of skills and independent abilities. Continue until the entire chain is made. Talk about the fact that she is very skilled ("Look at all these skills!") at being apart from you. Explain that just like the chain, when you are separated from each other, your thoughts and love make you very much connected.

Let your child take her chain with her when she goes to day care, school, or any other place as a reminder of her independent skills. Add links as you or your child notice new skills. Use an incentive program and reward your child (see pgs. 55–58) for accumulating a specific number of links. In all new situations, always plan and prevent a dependency "attack" by preparing your babysitter with a few distractions before you leave; these could be toys and games that your child enjoys. You can prepare your child for upcoming separations and new situations by visiting these places beforehand and discussing what's going to happen. Family good-bye kisses and hugs playfully prepare your child for the separation. Before leaving, always bring out the chain of skills to remind your child of her ability to be separated from you.

●●●

Activity #3: On-My-Own Kits

Materials: (depends on which "On-My-Own Kit" used) briefcase,
backpack or bag, family pictures, bedroom items, special
surprises, "I can do it" list, camera, list of important phone
numbers, first aid kit, *Playing It Smart* (Tova Navarra, Barrons,
1989), special activity game books, special videos
Age: 6–12
Vocabulary/Concepts: alone, independent, support, family, surprise,
separate, miss, capable, emergency, patience, YOURSELF BIG (OLDER)

●●●

The four kits described below are designed to help your child deal with various levels of separation from her parents. They are listed in order from short separations to lengthier ones:

The Independent Kit

Fill a bag with games, books, and toys that your child enjoys and can use on her own. Whenever your child separates from you (and needs support or distraction), suggest that she bring her Independent Kit and remind her of how great she is at doing things independently.

The Home Alone Kit

Older children may have a hard time coming home to an empty house or being left for a few hours while a parent runs errands. There are laws in each state which note the minimum age for leaving a child home alone. Please consult these when making a decision to leave your child alone. A child may better cope with being alone if you give her a kit (knapsack or briefcase) with items that can help her to feel safe as well as a list of fun activities to do while waiting for a parent to return. The kit should include a list of important numbers (see "The TTY Connection"); a first aid kit; a book on safety and independence such as, *Playing It Smart;* and special game books, videos, and/or a list of other activities that your child can do during this time. You may want to put a little snack in the kit or write a note indicating what goodies are in the refrigerator. Give your child something to look forward to by letting her know that there is something special waiting for her in the kit (a little note or a new gadget).

The Overnight Kit

It is natural for a child to feel insecure away from home; however, when that "insecurity" becomes an "inability," the child needs help gaining confidence to be apart from you. Enlist the help of a relative or good friend who is willing to provide the trial run sleepovers for your child. You will need an old brief-case or knapsack to hold the items for this kit. With your child, pack the briefcase with items such as a wallet containing pictures of the family, a famil-iar item from her bedroom (stuffed animals, toy, pillow case, pillow), a special surprise (bedtime snack, bedtime book), and an "I can do it" list. Make this list with your child and write down her independent skills as well as activities she likes to keep herself busy (books, games, and conversations). Role-play how she would take her "I can do it" list out of the kit and choose an activity when she feels lonely or misses you. Use encouragement and STAR to stop and think—"I am safe, I'm OK"—before giving up or crying for her parents. Provide an incentive by offering to take her out for brunch the next day for a successful sleepover.

The Residential School and Camp Kit

Because the deaf child's schools, services, and friends are often far from home, she may need special support to grow accustomed to these away-from-home adventures. Extended stays at residential schools and overnight camp or week-long visits to Grandma's or a friend who lives far away require a special homesickness prevention kit. Along with the regular kit items men-tioned in the overnight package, include these extra items:

1. A fun surprise that she can open on a specific night each week that she is away. For example, kiss a piece of paper and leave your lip marks for her; give her a small toy or game that she can play with her friends at camp; give her a joke book or a small box of snacks.

2. Include a small booklet of family photos to serve as visual reminders. Have her take a camera along to log the stay away and share experiences with you later. Encourage her to make an "away from home" booklet of photos of her and her friends at school or camp.

3. Make sure she has an extensive "I can do it" list of activities to last for the duration of her time away. While she is away, send new items (pictures, cards, stickers) for her to add to her kit.

4. Consider buying a compact TTY for your child. Give her instructions for using the TTY relay service to expand her repertoire of people she can contact. Pack any other items that have been helpful to her in the past (night light, small flashlight, card with important phone numbers on it, or a journal).

Prior to sending your child on her first experience away at school or at camp, have a few practice "camp nights" over at a friend's or relative's house. Re-member to give the child her kit during these practice nights.

●●

Activity #4: Transition Tools

Materials: family-related plans and schedules
Age: all ages
Vocabulary/Concepts: plans, now, next, schedule

●●

Pay attention to the transitions in your child's life. Major transitions are the daily school/home transition; the weekend school/home transition, if your child is a residential student; the vacation/school switch; and the time spent waking from sleep or preparing for bed.

Develop predictable tools to help during these times. Think of the tools as both predictable actions and emotional supports. For example, when a child comes home on the weekend from residential school, predictable actions might be for her to put her bags in her room, place her homework and books on the desk, and check her calendar for upcoming plans. Emotional supports might be a designated snack time with a parent during which the child fills the parent in on her week. This is a time for detailed questions about what the child's feelings and thoughts are in connection with friends, school, teachers, and studies. During the discussion, the parent might mention what has happened at home in the child's absence and also list any activities planned for the weekend, "As you know we are shopping on Saturday and visiting Grandma. Did you have any ideas for this weekend? Do you have homework you can show me so we can plan how much time it will take?" On Sundays, you might have a similar discussion which reviews the weekend, plans the week, and anticipates next weekend's plans.

Transition tools can be used to ease any change. Here are some ideas for action-oriented tools:

- schedules
- graphs
- cleaning up and putting away
- snacks
- marking on a calendar
- behavior charts
- using a journal and
- using a clock or timer.

Some emotional support transition tools are

- hugs
- special walks

- special stories

- discussions

- journal writing and reading together

- saying "hello" to people in the area

- feeding a pet

- having an age-appropriate transitional object

- small banners saying "welcome home" or "good luck in school"

- problem-solving discussion

- taking photographs and

- planning telephone calls.

Activity #5: Key Chain Finder
Materials: key chain with name tag and photo, recent family photo
Age: 4–7
Vocabulary/Concepts: lost, key chain, family, ask for help, REQUEST

In our work with young deaf children, we found that they often voiced the fear of being lost in a large store or mall. The child experiences true terror when she does not know how to tell someone hers or her parents' names or when she cannot communicate her needs. Help your child feel more capable of dealing with being lost by making a special key chain. Key chains sold at photography stores are made so that a picture can be inserted between two pieces of clear plastic. Make an identification tag insert that contains the name, address, phone number, and description of your child and put it into one of these key chains. Have your child help you write all this information on the tag. Next, select a recent picture of your family. Explain that this picture will make sure that whoever helps her find her parents will know what her parents look like. Clip this key chain to your child's belt loop, shoe, or other piece of clothing when you go out in public. When you go to the store, point out to your child the people who work at the store—behind the counter, near cash registers, or those people who wear name tags. Explain that these are the people she should go to when lost since they know just what to do to help find a child's parents. As a parent, you may have a bit more peace of mind knowing that your child would seek help from a safe and responsible adult.

Nightmares and Nighttime Fears

Sleeping well does not necessarily come naturally to all children. In fact, a third of all children experience sleep-related problems at some point in their lives. Sleep problems can be understandable reactions to a host of challenges children face. Problems can be related to negative associations with bedtime and sleep, specific fears, separation difficulties, loneliness, stress, unresolved conflicts, and overstimulation.

Become familiar with your child's sleep experiences and the negative or positive aspects she may associate with sleep. See that your child gets sufficient sleep, is on a regular sleep and nap schedule, and that her concerns are addressed during the day.

Specific fears that can interfere with sleep include: fear of the dark, of separation from parents, and of dying or not waking. As noted earlier in this book, a deaf child may feel particularly vulnerable in the dark since her key sense, eyesight, is diminished. Without light, she has less ability to communicate and know what is occurring around her. Shadows may seem particularly frightening to her and the light pattern in her bedroom (such as on the windowshades) may require adjustment.

Fear of the dark may increase in the elementary years as your child develops an awareness of potential dangers in the world. Reassure your child of her safety, practice sitting with her in the dark, and play games that accustom her to the dark during non-sleep times (see the "Play in the Dark" activity in this chapter).

For sleep a child must learn to separate from her parents without anxiety. If the child has no tools for self-soothing or skill at independence, she will feel terrified to be alone. Help your child to develop positive sleep associations and ways to soothe herself after you have said "good night" by using transitional objects such as pillows, blankets, dolls, stuffed animals, or special pajamas.

If a child's sleep environment feels secure, comfortable, and connected to

The problems may look like this:

• • • • • • •

- A child goes for the hundredth cup of water or thousandth toilet stop and "I love you" before bed.
- A child runs to your bed in the middle of the night.

the parent, she can then separate herself and sleep. She thus has internalized a feeling of safety sufficiently to enable her to go to bed on her own.

We all experience partial awakenings during the night. It is developmentally appropriate for children to have dramatic partial awakenings (moaning, thrashing, sleepwalking and night terrors) before age six. If a child learns to self-soothe, she will promptly return to sleep.

Some children become lonely in bed and crave the reassurance of their parent's company. This may be more pronounced in an only child since she goes to bed without the company of a brother or sister.

A child who worries excessively about problems and dangers may find lying alone in bed an uncomfortable and even frightening experience. Do not use the time just before bed to discuss the day's problems because your child may then dwell on these problems. Set aside other times during the day for your family to support the child and to "make peace" with her worries. Use bedtime as preparation for sleep.

Nightmares and restless sleep may be caused by unresolved internal conflicts or stressful events, such as a test, a fight with a friend, or parental divorce or discord. Conflicts repressed during waking hours can emerge as frightening dreams when your child's defenses are lowered during sleep. Seek to uncover the causes or themes of recurrent nightmares and fears. Help your child to face and reshape bad dreams and feared objects/events and imagine more positive resolutions. If problems persist, consider counseling as a tool to explore ways of dealing with these problems.

Allowing your child to sleep in your bed may seem like an easy answer to relieve her discomfort. However, over time you will notice this pattern does a disservice to everyone: the child learns to depend on her parent(s), she may feel shame from not keeping up with peers who sleep alone, she may feel that she is separating the parents (by sleeping between them) or that she is taking the place of a partner (in a single-parent home), she may find the proximity to adults in the bed at bedtime to be overstimulating, she may refuse to stay with sitters, and parents may begin to resent the child. If your child has difficulties sleeping, draft and carry out a plan that will support her in sleeping in her own bedroom.

Very young children as well as those who tend to easily become overstimulated have difficulty transitioning from waketime to bedtime activities, and do not know how to "wind down" or relax physically and mentally. Establish predictable bedtime routines that ease the transition from more to less activity, such as a story, special time with a parent, and a bedtime snack. Your child might watch TV at some point late in the evening, but the TV is no substitute for a good bedtime ritual since it is neither soothing nor interactional. You may want to write down your routine for everyone to remember. Always give your child plenty of advance notice that bedtime is approaching.

Sleep patterns vary from child to child and year to year—just when you think your child has reached a consistent pattern, it may change. Keep a mental or written chart of erratic changes. Consider how life events, stressors, and your child's development might affect your child's sleep patterns.

As your child grows older (ages nine through twelve), begin to teach her the concept of a biological clock. An adolescent may assert her independence by defying sleep, not realizing that her body has its own schedule, like it or not.

Activities

....

Activity #1: Nightlight-No Fright
Materials: nightlight, nonflammable/noncombustable paints, craft
    materials as needed
Age: all ages
Vocabulary/Concepts: nightlight, see, fear

....

Your child may view nightlights as babyish. If your child's fear of the dark is related to her inability to see and feel safe in her environment, then try putting a new twist on an old idea by creating a sophisticated nightlight. Your child can help you design a very special nightlight. Use a store-bought night light to create your own nightlight out of noncombustable plastic, paints, and craft materials. Perhaps you can have a stained-glass expert help you make an attractive outer shell for the light. Reassure your child that nightlights are not just for babies—many adults use nightlights to prevent them from becoming disoriented in the dark.

....

Activity #2: The Goodnight Door
Materials: paper, pencil, camera, independent skill list, *Goodnight
    Moon* (Margaret Wise Brown, Harper, 1947), flashlight
Age: 3–8
Vocabulary/Concepts: independent, goodnight, skills, flashlight, routine,
    wake, reminder

....

This activity is based on the same principle as the book *Goodnight Moon*, a must for parents of young children. In this story, a young rabbit comfortably goes to sleep in her own bed after saying "goodnight" to everything, including the moon. This routine allows the rabbit to fall peacefully asleep. You can establish a similar routine for your child that offers many visual supports to diminish her fear of darkness.

Begin by reading, or re-reading, the book *Goodnight Moon* with your child. Explain that she can do the same goodnight routine as the rabbit, but that she will be saying "goodnight" to real things in her life. Make a list of objects, people, and happy events in your child's life and then photograph these. Next, make a list of "independent skills" (going to school, going to a relative's alone, or playing a game on her own) and take a photograph of your child actually doing or re-enacting these for the purpose of taking the picture. Have your child decide whether to put these pictures on the inside of her bedroom door, the wall next to her bed, or ceiling of her bedroom.

Every night, right before she goes to bed, have your child say "goodnight" to all the people, objects and special things in the pictures on her door, wall, or ceiling. Following this, support her efforts to sleep through the night by showing her the pictures of skills and remind her to use these skills to securely make it through the night on her own. Try giving her a flashlight and instructing her to use it in the middle of the night should she awaken. She can shine it on the pictures on the door or ceiling as a reminder of all the people that make her feel safe and happy and on the skills that she has to help herself.

. . . .

Activity #3: No More Nightmares Book

Materials: crayons, markers, construction paper, magazine pictures,
    scissors, glue, stapler or yarn
Age: 4–8
Vocabulary/Concepts: bad dream, scary, no more, Whipped Cream
    Dreams (happy dreams), RESOLVE

. . . .

In this activity, you and your child will work together to write a children's book about her scary dreams and how she can cope with them. Lack of information and feeling disempowered are two deficits that a deaf child might experience if she has to navigate a hearing environment for a majority of her day. When she has nightmares, she often re-enacts these feelings. By making this special book, your child will have an opportunity to face up to and overcome the frightening aspects of her dreams. Once she feels in control of her fears, the activity will help her reshape the bad dreams into good ones.

You will need paper, crayons, markers and construction paper to make your child's special book. First, explain the activity to your child and express your commitment to helping her solve her nightmare problems. Next, encourage her to tell you about a few nightmares (most kids can remember the content in vivid detail) and select a few to be described in the *No More Nightmares Book*. Start the story by having your child draw pictures of herself in a few scary or anxiety-provoking situations that she has had during the day. You may discover the cause of your child's nightmares during this activity.

Now, have her draw pictures of the nightmare. Encourage as much detail as possible in this part of the book. This repetitive, story-telling experience greatly diminishes the impact of the nightmare, thereby giving your child more control over her feelings and mastery over the bad dreams. End the book with a story depicting your child overcoming a nightmare by using her skills and "Whipped Cream Dreams," which you define for her as comforting, safe dreams and nice dream-endings. Come up with at least a dozen Whipped Cream Dreams and/or nice endings. These specially designed dreams should be created by your child and be used in exchange for her nightmares.

In this way, your child uses her creativity and skills to "rewrite" and change the story line of her nightmares in a positive fashion. List and draw pictures of her Whipped Cream Dreams in the book. It is imperative that your child conquer her nightmare problem by the end of her book. Positively reframe efforts and encourage her to change the story line if she focuses on a negative ending.

Now you have a terrific book to read with her at night to help her vent her fears, face her nightmares, and resolve the problems presented in her nightmares, all prior to falling asleep. You may want to keep the book near her bed so that she can turn the light on and look up a few Whipped Cream Dreams to replace her nightmares or consciously end a nightmare in a more comforting way. Do not use the parenting technique of ignoring this problem as a way to solve it. This is a difficult problem for a child to deal with alone and she needs a lot of loving reassurance.

. . . .

Activity #4: Safe and Sound Book or Video
Materials: paper, markers, crayons, stapler or yarn, video recorder, VCR
Age: 3–10
Vocabulary/Concepts: safety, world, don't worry

. . . .

Have your child write a story about people, things, and happenings in her world that make her feel safe. The story should focus on how these safe things continue to be safe throughout the night. Encourage her to write down these things, like "parents are in the next room, we have fire detectors, I know how to call the numbers of the fire department and police station." Read the book together when your child needs reassurance about going to sleep. Put this book on a video and have your child watch it as a night-time activity prior to going to sleep.

. . . .

Activity #5: The Goodnight Pillow
> Materials: plain pillow case, fabric marker
> Age: 3–8
> Vocabulary/Concepts: goodnight, safe, I-LOVE-YOU

. . . .

Turn your child's pillow case into a "sleep security system." On a plain pillow case, draw with fabric pens a few pictures, words, phrases, or signs (such as the "I love you" hand shape) that will make your child feel safe and secure. This pillow case and pillow can become a permanent part of bed. Anytime the child needs a reminder of how safe and secure she is, she can turn on her flashlight and look at the "sleep security system pillow."

. . . .

Activity #6: The "Give It a Rest" Drawer or Box
> Materials: paper, pencil or markers, empty drawer or box
> Age: 3–10
> Vocabulary/Concepts: worry, drawer, box, safe, TAKE-CARE-OF

. . . .

Explain to your child that she can put her worries and concerns aside for the evening so that she can get a good night's sleep. During waking hours, write down or draw a picture of the worries and concerns she has had during that day and put them in a special drawer or box for safe-keeping. Help her to understand how important a good night's sleep is and that you can both attend to her worries the next day. You may want to keep this drawer or box in your room if the child voices any concerns that the bad thoughts will "escape." You can reassure the child that you will keep the bad thoughts or worries in the Give It a Rest Box. If the child becomes obsessed with worries right before sleep and you find that this activity does not soothe her, consider using bedtime to think of all of the good things that happened that day or to discuss Whipped Cream Dreams.

Teaching Responsibility

● ● ● ● ● ● ● ● ● ● ● ●

Ruthann and Michael Schlang

*L*et me introduce myself—I am a deaf mother and my husband and our two teenage children (Michael and Dana) are deaf. I was an only child of hearing parents and became deaf at the age of nine months due to a high fever.

Throughout my childhood, my parents exhibited constant patience, support, and care. Consistent communication was the norm in my home and my parents kept me informed about their own histories, their points of view, and, in short, their lives. Even though they did not sign, my parents always saw that I was included and that made me feel like an important member of the family.

My mother was especially sensitive to my needs and made sure that I understood what went on in our family life. Inevitably, every Thanksgiving, Easter, and Christmas, the family would be chatting and mingling and I would find myself bored since I was not an active part of the conversations.

While this could certainly be a frustrating situation for me, my mother devised a way to make sure that I was not left out of the family news. After everyone had gone home, she would sit down with me and catch me up on every detail she could remember—all of the incidental stories about the different family members.

Ruthann Schlang is a teacher's aide at the South Shore Educational Collaborative in Norwell, Massachusetts. Michael Schlang is a senior in the EDCO program at Newton North High School, Newton, Massachusetts.

Another example of my parents' sensitivity to keeping me informed was the way they watched TV with me. While I was growing up, we did not have closed captioning, yet my parents would always tell me in detail what was going on, even during the commercials. In my parents' actions I saw patience and care and, therefore, I believe that I became more patient growing up.

Open communication helped when I began to have questions about being deaf. When I was about six years old I was home for the summer from a residential school for the deaf. I asked my mother, "What is wrong with me anyway?" My mother replied, "Nothing is wrong with you, you are a healthy, beautiful, and mischievous tomboy." I said, "I think that it is more than that, Mom—is there something wrong with my ears?" My mother replied, "No, there is nothing wrong with your ears but your hearing. When you watch TV, you can't hear what they are saying, right?—that is your difficulty." I asked my mom if my ears were broken and my mother reassured me that they weren't. She drew me a picture of the ear and the severed nerve that had caused my hearing loss.

I realized then that I was deaf and began asking a litany of questions about who might be deaf in our family—"You? Daddy? Cousin Roy?" The only other deaf relative I had was my cousin Julie who also had cerebral palsy. When I questioned whether I, too, had cerebral palsy, my mother assured me that I didn't.

My daughter Dana also had questions about being deaf and how her deafness related to that of other family members. When she was two years old she would stare at Howie's hearing aid and say, "Daddy's hearing is broken, Mommy's hearing is broken, and my hearing is broken." While she started to identify with us, she noticed that her hearing grandparents had a different mode of communication (voice) than ours (signing). She would ask Nanna, "Why don't you sign?"

When she became three, I became pregnant again and she would sit in my lap and pat my belly and say, "Mommy, I want a sister." She was insistent about this and I pointed out to her that it would be nice to have either a brother or a sister. She said, "OK, Mommy, but he must be deaf!" I asked, "Why?" She replied, "I'm deaf, you're deaf, and Daddy is deaf—the baby has to be deaf, too." "Well, maybe the baby will be hearing but if he is we will teach him to sign."

So you see, we really had only a Deaf cultural environment at home—we were deaf parents with deaf children, and deaf friends. Even so, I felt it was my responsibility to teach the children about two cultures. Maybe I didn't teach them enough about relating to hearing people, because they are sometimes shocked when they go into hearing environments. I don't feel bad about that, but I do feel that they will need to learn how to deal with hearing people. Their grandparents are one thing . . . they know them closely. Relating to a hearing public is a really different experience.

When I was growing up I lived in two cultures, being proud of my own Deaf culture while still respecting my family's hearing culture. I have taught this to my children. In addition, my husband Howie and I have been committed to a structured home life. We have felt that it was important to have predictability in our children's lives and had expectable bed, meal, and play times, while also having rules to help guide our children.

Teaching respect for hearing culture, solving problems, and handling difficult feelings has not always been easy. When Michael was in a mainstream junior high classroom (after being in a deaf school), he had many difficulties with his hearing classmates.

He would come home daily and say, "I don't feel that the hearing students respect me. Mom, you taught me to respect hearing people and I tried very hard to do that, but why can't they respect me in return?" I would tell him, "You have to show them daily that you have courage and confidence. Show them with your body language and your actions." As time went on, Michael was better able to do that, but it was after much struggling on his part.

Michael tells the story like this:

> On the first day of seventh grade, I was ready. I was willing to extend full respect to my hearing peers. I went in and they were not nice to me so I reciprocated. I refused to be a coward. Of course, that meant I got into a lot of fights. But I really thought through my options and felt I had to stick up for myself many times. Once, a boy came up to me and pushed me without reason. I thought to myself I have three choices: (1) I can push him back, (2) I can go away, or (3) I can punch him.

Although I taught Michael to persist in finding nonviolent ways to make the other children respect him, he felt that fighting caused the hearing students to respect him. I warned him a few times that fighting is not a solution to a problem, but he disagreed with me.

Michael has always thought before he acts. I think he learned that from our giving him and Dana choices. I would always give them exercises in thinking. For example, I would ask them, "Which playground do you want to go to?" They had to think about this and come up with an answer. I would ask them to think about what shoes were appropriate for the playground. One might say, "I can't wear these because they are dangerous." And I'd continue to ask, "So what do you wear?" "Sneakers." "Fine!!"

When the children were young, they hated to go food shopping with me. So I would think about options I could offer them instead of commanding them: "Either you can come with me or stay with a babysitter." Most of the time they would choose the babysitter.

While I taught my children the freedom of choosing, I also gave them firm limits. For example, they knew that they could not have a cookie before breakfast. We offered choices when it was reasonable for the children to decide and always tried not to conflict with the existing rules.

My children learned to dress themselves by my giving parameters for choices. For example, I would say, "It is going to be a hot day out there today, do you want to wear a tank top or a short-sleeved shirt?—you make the decision." Dana chose her clothes when she was three, and would put her clothes on and ask my opinion. Michael did this when he was four. Their clothes did not always match but I accepted that. It felt like a small compromise on my part.

Every day I would carve out one-to-one time with each of my children. Since Michael was younger, I would first give him a bath, then play with him and read him a book. When he was ready to go to bed we'd play one game. Later, Dana and I played three games and that was the understood limit. Then I would read her a story and she'd go to sleep.

We had a lot of consistency in our home but we were also sure to have non-routine family activities. There was always something special that happened, such as going out for ice cream or going to the playground, and we would base these events on the mood of the kids.

I kept communication lines open with my children. If they had a bad dream in the middle of the night, we would talk about it. I was always ready to discuss things with them.

Michael has this to say on the matter:

> I think the best term for our family communication is "open." We always talked—we had continuous communication. Perhaps we didn't talk about everything, but at least ninety percent of things. We confronted feelings and created honesty and understanding. Honesty has always been important in our family.
>
> I remember one time when I was standing on the counter in the kitchen and my mother caught me. In the discussion that followed she asked what I was doing wrong. I replied that I should not stand on a counter in the kitchen and, secondly, that I should not do so with scissors in my hand. I explained that what I had done could be dangerous if I had fallen. In this way, I learned right and wrong, and if I made a mistake my parents always stressed that I should accept responsibility for it and then learn from it.
>
> It's funny, I have done the same thing in my summer job working with deaf children. Often, if I thought a child did something wrong I would hold off on punishment and leave it up to the child to admit responsibility.

Grounding was not a method I used in parenting Michael and Dana. I didn't feel that it taught them much of anything. I always used a "time out" approach and encouraged our children to think about their problem and how they could change or correct their errors the next time—my emphasis was on learning a lesson from mistakes.

I usually gave them ten or fifteen minutes to think about their mistakes. After the time was up, we had a discussion in which I insisted that they "think" and come up with ways to approach the same situation in the future. If they could do this, I was satisfied.

I do not believe that sending a child to a bedroom is a good method of punishment. I never felt that this would solve anything. Instead, I have felt discussions are the best method of resolving problems. When we discussed problems together, I always felt that my children were learning how to solve problems—a skill that they could use for the future.

I didn't punish my children much. I had confidence that they could resolve their problems on their own or between themselves if they were fighting. If they could not find a solution, I trusted that they would come up to me and ask for help—and for the most part they have, and still do.

CHAPTER

10

Irresponsibility

• • • •

The ability to take responsibility is necessary for independence and success. The activities in this chapter address procrastination, laziness, messiness, going to bed and waking on time, and oppositional behavior. The common goal of the activities is to improve your child's ability to take responsibility. This includes paying attention, organizing, following directions, completing tasks, and motivation. We wish to emphasize that the lack of clear communication will exacerbate these problems, while efforts to inform and include the deaf child in family communication will contribute to resolution. The deaf child is in danger of becoming more dependent than his hearing peers when he is not given the chance as they are to try, make mistakes, try again, and learn from the results.

GENERAL IRRESPONSIBILITY

Some children show indifference toward their obligations, successes, and mistakes. This behavior is often caused by one or more of the following: (1) an inadequate understanding of what is expected; (2) disorganization, resulting in the inability to begin a job and carry it through to completion; (3) lack of motivation; and (4) difficulty concentrating.

Your child will learn responsibility best through verbal directives, consistent cues, visual reminders, and expected rewards and consequences. Offer choices that help structure the beginning, middle, and completion of projects.

Instead of directing your child's behavior through punishment ("no," "go to your room") or excusing your child from seeing a task through correctly

The problems may look like this:
• • • • • • •

- The child stops a task midway through or does it haphazardly (greasy dishes, messy homework, only half the room cleaned).

- The child says "no" to everything.

- The child says he understands and then has a thousand questions later.

- The child watches the cars, the dog, the refrigerator, anything but you when communicating.

- The pitter-patter of little feet coming out of the bed for the hundredth time.

- The child has to have hearing aids and TTYs replaced constantly.

- The child has no sense of the value of money or how to save it.

- The child wakes up ready to play at a significantly earlier time than the rest of the family.

- The child says "later," "I will," and "wait" and waits until the last minute to tackle a task.

- The child jumps from one thing to the next without finishing any task.

- A trail of clothes, books, and toys leads to your child's room.

- The child's bedroom looks like a mountain of chaos.

("Well, if you don't do it right, I'll do it myself"), teach your child skills that foster self-discipline and independence. First and foremost, your child should understand the correlation between responsibility and privileges. Responsibility creates personal pride, decision-making privileges, increased respect, and autonomy. Show your child how his actions positively or negatively affect others. The more he takes responsibility himself, the more he will be trusted with freedoms and privileges.

Adults are naturally more capable of accomplishing tasks than children. However, an adult must allow the child to experience trials and errors. Problems with responsibility will decrease if parents instruct but do not preach, if they clarify consequences but don't take over the child's job.

Well-meaning parents often fear letting their deaf child practice simple tasks, such as paying for things in a store, sleeping at a trusted relative's, crossing the street alone, or riding a bike. When a parent overprotects a deaf child and does not teach him how to manage on his own, the child may feel that he can do "nothing" while the parent will do "everything."

Pay attention to the inner words and phrases you use and the internal conversations you have about your deaf child. Notice when you hear yourself say "can't," "poor child," "but he's deaf," "if only he were hearing," "he needs me," or anything that might contribute to your child learning to distrust his abilities. Rewrite these with "can," "he can learn," "he needs to grow," "he can use his eyes."

Some children refuse to accept responsibility in an attempt to express their independence and autonomy. If you give your child more chances to learn and practice real and gratifying independence, he won't need to fight for it in detrimental ways. If you fear that he will grow older and fail to face new challenges squarely, he may actually follow that path and, lacking confidence, unwittingly undermine his own gains.

Teach your child that the ability to take responsibility has nothing to do with the ability to hear. You must not excuse and ignore unacceptable behaviors and your child must not learn to use his deafness as an excuse.

Keep informed of what your child is doing at school, in social groups, at camp, or at temple or church. You may learn that, surprisingly, his actions differ vastly from what you see at home. In fact, it is common for a child to display more mature and socially conscious behaviors at school.

Adequately challenge your child, but don't overdo it by pressuring him to manage responsibilities beyond his developmental capacity. Repeated failures in attaining his goals will likely damage his self-confidence and decrease his motivation to continue trying. Consult with books, friends, and teachers to verify that your expectations match your child's skill level and developmental capabilities.

Activities

● ●

Activity #1: "I'm Responsible" Association

Materials: "Level Program" (see pg. 58), small card for license
Age: 6–12
Vocabulary/Concepts: license, responsible, privilege, ADVANCE-A-LEVEL

● ●

This activity encourages your child to take on more responsibility and, as a result, gain more personal power and practice decision-making skills. When we speak about personal power, we mean that a person is in charge of his actions and decisions and has the ultimate responsibility for the positive or negative outcomes (natural and logical consequences).

Driving a car, that is, having a driver's license, is an earned privilege. Describe to your deaf child how one earns a driver's license (studying, practicing, taking tests); how one keeps it (driving safely, following highway rules, having the car inspected, paying for a title); how a driver can get points marked against him due to unsafe driving habits; and, finally, how a driver's license can be revoked. You might note that a license only gives you the privilege to drive a car—to drive a commercial truck (which requires more skills and responsibility) more complex studying, practicing, and testing is required. Explain to your child that he can work towards the privilege of a "responsibility license" and a membership in the "I'm Responsible Association."

First, read about how to design "The Level Program" (see pg. 58). The chart in that program can be used as a model for this activity. Depending on your child's developmental ability and age, chart out responsibilities required and the resulting privileges. Each of the four levels progressively adds responsibilities that result in more privileges.

For example, at level one the responsibilities consist of making his bed and getting up on time in the morning. The privileges might include playing a board game with a parent and/or a later bedtime. Level four would require more demanding responsibilities, such as getting up independently (by using an alarm designed for deaf people). The privileges would correspondingly increase, like having the option of deciding on his own bedtime. As your child moves from level one to four in the Association he can receive his "responsibility license." If he maintains this level, celebrate by throwing a party.

Once he receives his license he will be allowed to stay on level four and slowly increase his privileges from week to week. Of course, if he is not successful at maintaining level four, his license is revoked. Use parenting techniques such as Your Choice; STAR; Try, Try Again; Logical Consequences; and Modeling. TAP yourself when you feel the urge to nag or yell at your child to do a job. Instead, let the chart and its privileges or denial of those privileges do it for you.

. . . .

Activity #2: No, No Beans

Materials: white lima beans
Age: 3–7
Vocabulary/Concepts: no, beans, RUN-OUT, reward, NO-NO

. . . .

Young children are often responsive to smiley and frowning faces as ways to connote yes/no, right/wrong, good/bad, and desirable/undesirable. Using white lima beans and a permanent marker, write the word "no" or draw an unhappy face on five beans. Tell your child that he may say "no," "you can't make me," and/or "I don't want to" only five times a day. Carry with you five "no, no beans." Each time your child says something oppositional, says "no," or refuses to do something, give him a "no, no bean." Let him know how many he has left before he runs out of "no, no beans." Remind your child that once the beans are gone, he can't receive his reward—he must have one remaining. If he makes it through the day with at least one bean left, give him a special reward.

Activity #3: Mime Time/Rhyme Time
Age: 6–12
Vocabulary/Concepts: your decision

If your child does not pay attention to you the first time, interrupt your frustration with a humorous mime (or rhyme if your child has enough residual hearing and enjoys vocal word games). Without using words, act out your request silently. Children get a kick out of this and it definitely breaks the tension. For the interested hard of hearing child (who understands the concept and enjoys rhyme) you can also try asking your child to answer you in a rhyme when you ask him to do something. This is also a good way to confirm that he is paying attention.

Activity #4: Bank On It
Materials: piggy bank, allowance, bank account in child's and parent's name, bank, calculator, times table chart, paper, pencil
Age: 8–12
Vocabulary/Concepts: bank, save, MONEY GROWS, interest, teller, deposit, withdrawal

American culture values having, managing, and spending money. Unfortunately, deaf children often do not have the opportunity to handle many of their own financial transactions (such as paying at a store). As they become young adults, they are oftentimes sheltered from paying their own bills, having a bank account, and developing a good sense of money management.

If your child is given an early chance to understand and control his own money, you will better prepare him to manage his finances upon becoming a young adult. Let your child pay for items in a store and count out change. Devise a way for your child to receive a small weekly allowance instead of buying the child something any time he asks. Give your child a piggy bank and help him save up for a very special thing that he may want. Show him how full the bank needs to be for him to afford the desired item.

Transfer the concept of the piggy bank to the concept of a savings bank. Explain that adults save large amounts of money for big things, like college tuition, cars, houses, and vacations. Open an account for your child and teach him to add to it regularly. Give him opportunities to communicate with the teller, check the addition in his bank book, and delight in his increasing savings.

Use incentives to encourage your child to save: match your child's deposits by putting in one dollar for every five dollars he saves or give him a bonus ten dollars to be spent in any way he chooses for each fifty or one hundred he saves. As he gets older (perhaps twelve), introduce him to the concepts of checks, working for a living, budgeting, and handling a checking account.

....

Activity #5: The Pet Project
Materials: "Chart and Reward Program" (see pgs. 57–58), books on
   chosen pet, space and accoutrements for pet [Note: Pets are
   living things requiring varying and often costly levels of care. Do
   not choose a pet that you cannot afford to care for properly.]
Age: 6–12
Vocabulary/Concepts: responsible, pet, care, duty, clean, feed
....

Children who are irresponsible and lack the motivation to take care of themselves often do a wonderful job caring for an animal. Teach your child to complete tasks and meet expectations to maintain an animal—feeding, cage-cleaning, exercising, and bathing the animal. Invite your child to help choose an age-appropriate animal—anything from a goldfish to a horse.

Start by introducing the idea of keeping a pet to your child. See how motivated the child is to care for a pet. Explain the responsibilities required to keep a pet. Next, set up a Chart and Reward or level system that will measure mastery of skills the child will need before you will consider getting him a pet. For example, doing household chores and attending to self-hygiene show that the child can clean up after the pet and keep the pet healthy.

Following that, read books on your child's chosen animal. Discuss the pet's needs and special responsibilities required in caring for this animal. Make sure your child understands the priorities (e.g., "If the cat box needs to be cleaned and you want to play ball, you will need to clean the box first"). When you feel your child understands and has committed to the basic responsibilities of pet care—it's time to welcome the new critter into your home. Keep in mind that earning the privilege to have the pet is only the beginning of learning responsibility. It's a process of trial and error that will show the importance of following through on responsibilities. (The natural consequence of not letting a dog out is that the child must clean up the "accident.") Your child's success at pet care will prove that your child is capable of being responsible for himself.

Caution: If your child is not successful with this activity, you may very likely end up with an extra responsibility of your own, so consider his choice of pet with this in mind.

Special Issues Related to Irresponsibility and Dependence in Deaf Children

Your child may have slipped into the habit of irresponsibility due to a number of factors: lack of knowledge on the child's part; lack of expectations on the part of adults in the child's world and/or the hearing public; lack of access to communication; and lack of appropriate devices, services, and resources. When your child is introduced to and learns how to use a TTY, alarms, relay operators, interpreters, hearing aids, and TV closed captioning then he minimizes his reliance on others for vital needs. Some Deaf people own hearing dogs; have visual alarms to alert them to important noises, such as their baby crying; and have houses designed with light switches in convenient locations, such as on the outside of rooms so that people can flick a light to get the attention of the deaf person inside the room. This takes the place of knocking on a door for deaf people.

However, having these items does not necessarily create "equal" access. A hearing aid simply helps with residual hearing—it does not turn the child into a hearing person. A closed-captioned TV helps only if the child is able to follow the written English. A TTY and relay operator require practice and some written language capabilities. An interpreter is useful in formal situations and must adequately match the child's communication system.

Hearing aids are often a point of struggle for children and parents. Talk with your child's audiologist to understand the type of hearing loss your child has and how the hearing aid might benefit him. Teach your child the advantages of wearing an aid, but do not force the child to do so. Often children go through stages: they may choose to wear an aid only in certain situations; they may actually like the aid if their friends wear theirs, much in the same way that braces on the teeth have become more acceptable; or they may find the aid uncomfortable due to a bad fit or the nature of the amplification. Listen to your child's point of view regarding this. Do not make a struggle out of it since this allows the child to displace other feelings and situations onto this struggle.

Get a TTY as early in your child's life as possible. Use it daily and teach your child how to use it. Encourage other important friends and family members to own one if possible. Use relay operator services when your child wants to contact a hearing person who does not have a TTY.

Get alarms for morning awakenings. The sooner your child can use his own alarm, the less he will depend on you. You will be grateful for this when your child is pre-adolescent and adolescent, and he will appreciate his independence.

All televisions thirteen inches or larger manufactured since July 1993 include a closed captioning decoder chip. Make sure you have an external closed captioning decoder if your television does not have one.

Use interpreting services when needed early in the child's life to ensure that vital information is transmitted (especially in large meetings, doctor's offices, and in legal situations). Many people hire interpreters for large family events, such as weddings and funerals. Teach your child that having access to communication is a right and not a privilege.

Hearing dogs are trained to respond to sounds to allow the deaf person independence and safety. These dogs will respond to an alarm clock, door-knocker or bell, a smoke alarm, telephone/TTY ring, baby crying, stove or microwave timer, and a person's name being called. In order to get a dog, the deaf person must contact a local training facility, go through an application procedure, spend time training with the dog, and pay an (expensive) fee for the dog. Often training facilities require the child be a certain age (at least twelve) or an adult who will be able to train and treat the dog well. If you are interested in researching this option for your child, you can receive a list of service-dog training programs in your area from Service Dog Center, P.O. Box 1080, Renton, WA, 98057-9906 or call 1-206-226-7357 Voice/TTY.

The sooner your child becomes used to using assistive devices, the better. The message these convey is that he is as capable as the rest of his family in all areas of daily living. Explore the options for fire alarms that have flashing lights or a very loud alarm.

Activities

· ·

Activity #1: TTY Fun and Safety
Materials: TTY, plastic TTY cover, permanent markers, lampshade,
        paper board, masking tape
Age: 6–12
Vocabulary/Concepts: TTY, CALL, careful, clean, cover, LIGHT FLASHING
· ·

Use the activities entitled "The TTY Connection" (pgs. 186–187) and "TTY Games" (pgs. 329–330) to teach your child fun and useful skills. Consider having your child draw on the plastic TTY cover or create a cover of his own. Have him write or draw TTY directions and care for the TTY above the device (ask the distributor to clarify these for you). For children aged three to seven, have a special light or lampshade on the lamp connected to the TTY for an added treat each time the phone rings. Get a TTY telephone book and make one of your own with all of your child's friends and contacts. Answer the phone by using the TTY first to model for your child. Of course, all frequent callers should know what a TTY sounds like and that your family will answer by voice or TTY.

• •

Activity #2: Care of the TTY

Materials: TTY, old computer keyboard or typewriter, safe place for TTY, TTY cover, paper, markers

Age: 5–12

Vocabulary/Concepts: see above activity

• •

While your child is learning and enjoying the TTY, he also needs to understand the responsibility involved. When you are teaching a younger child to use the TTY, remember that it may be difficult for him to be as gentle as you or as conscientious. One remedy for this is to give your child an old keyboard from a computer, an old typewriter, or an old telephone for the child to use when in play. In this way the younger child can experiment freely with finding the keys and having conversations.

Make the care of the TTY easy—have the TTY in a secure place away from heat and cold; allow the TTY to be easily accessed by the child without him dropping it, bumping into it, or needing to climb; the TTY should not be in a play or eating area; have a cover for the TTY that stays in place when it is not in use; make a sign with your child to put near the TTY that says, "I don't like to drink, I don't like dust, be gentle with me;" and model for your child handling the TTY with care.

Whenever you have guests, a party, holidays, or do any of the activity events described in this book ("Honor Your Child Dinner," "Let's Party," "The Community Communication Class," "Deaf Awareness Day"), have your child show guests how to use and care for the TTY. When anyone buys a new TTY (family members, police, fire station, a new friend), have your child show them his skills and knowledge. Perhaps you can even videotape him doing this and he can give a copy of the video to his school or he can present it to the local TTY distributor.

· ·
Activity #3: Deaf Adults as Role Models
Materials: deaf adult willing to open his home to you
Age: 5–12
Vocabulary/Concepts: capable, FLASHING-LIGHTS (for doorbell, telephone,
    alarms, and baby cries)
· ·

If you know any Deaf adults (teachers, aides, tutors), let them know that you would like your child to visit their home and see how a Deaf adult lives. If you don't know any Deaf adults try making some contacts through state schools for the deaf, local chapters of NAD (National Association for the Deaf), or by calling state rehabilitation agencies to see if they service a deaf clientele. Once you have befriended some Deaf adults and feel comfortable, propose your idea. Deaf children are often fascinated by seeing an environment that is designed by and for a Deaf adult.

· ·
Activity #4: "Deafinitely Yours" Poster
· ·

There is no better way to cut through resistance than through humor. A poster called "Play It By Ear" was created by Deafinitely Yours Studio, and it makes the concept of hearing aids fun. On the poster are drawings of dozens of different hearing aids personified with different personalities ("Stone Deaf," "Very Hard of Hearing"—with two aids in one ear, and "Deaf Impaired"—with no hearing aid). Consider purchasing this poster for your home or your child's school. You can get a copy by writing or calling Kenneth P. Glickman, 814 Thayer Ave., Silver Spring, MD, 20910, 1-301-588-0965 (TTY).

· ·
Activity #5: The Magic Hearing Aids
Materials: hearing aids
Age: 3–5
Vocabulary/Concepts: hearing aids, magic, pretend, fun
· ·

For a preschool child, use your imagination to make the hearing aids come alive. With the swoop of a magic wand, you can pretend with your child that the hearing aids have wings and can fly him over the living room. Perhaps they can grow and fill with air, much like a life jacket. Or maybe they can act like little hands and wave to bugs in the air. All of these are simple, fun scenarios to motivate your child to wear hearing aids.

. . . .
Activity #6: My Special Hearing Aid Box
Materials: jewelry or wooden box, stickers, rhinestones, pictures,
        paints, markers, small piece of velvet
Age: 5–10
Vocabulary/Concepts: hearing aids, box, beautiful, careful
. . . .

Things become special to some people when stored in something beautiful or especially attractive. Think of how many gifts, snacks, perfumes, or letters have seemed special to you because of the way that they were packaged.

Explain to your child that his hearing aid is a very special device that deserves a special box. Note that the aids are made just for him and show how they fit only his ear. Depending on your child's personality and your finances, consider shopping for this box or making one on your own. Use a medium-sized jewelry box or wooden box. Have your child decorate the outside of it with anything he likes—magazine pictures of his favorite stars or animals, rhinestones, drawings of dinosaurs, pictures of him wearing the hearing aids, decorative lettering that reads "my hearing aid" or a painting of his own. Line the inside of the box with velour or velvet. This will protect the aid if the box is dropped. Make one box for each hearing aid or use one box for both. Perhaps your child would like to make hearing aid boxes for his friends or teachers. Encourage him to have a box to take to school as well.

. . . .
Activity #7: Learning to Care for Hearing Aids
Materials: Ear Gear (Carole Bugosh Simko, Gallaudet University
        Press, 1986), poster board, markers, hearing aids
Age: 6–10
Vocabulary/Concepts: hearing aid, care, parts, clean, store, KEEP
. . . .

Ear Gear is a very informative book with ample pictures that explains what a hearing aid is, how it works, and how to care for it. It also discusses problems that arise with children related to hearing aid wear. Read this book with your child or pick particular chapters to help educate him on the care of his hearing aid.

If your child needs more visual reminders or needs to have reinforcement, you may consider making a "yes/no" chart for hearing aid care. (*Ear Gear* contains some useful suggestions for such a chart.)

Under the "no" column, put pictures or words of places your child should not wear the aid (bathing, swimming, sleeping, when sick, or when actively playing). Under this column also include the places the hearing aid should not be left (in a pocket, backpack, or lunchbox; near heat or cold, like a stove, near a window, or near a radiator; near water, like on a sink, a tub, or next to a pool; or in random places, like on the floor, kitchen table, a desk, or atop the TV). And, finally, note the "no" things that can ruin a hearing aid—dust, heat, pets, young children, dropping it, stomping on it, toothpicks, water, and sharp objects.

Under the "yes" column, note the times to wear the aid. These may vary with each child, so find out from the audiologist the times suggested for use of the hearing aid. Also take the time to understand your child's point of view on the matter. Draw or show a picture of your child's special hearing aid box under this column. Note the proper things to use to clean and care for the aid: soap and water for hook, tube, earmold, and jacket; a damp cloth to wipe hearing aid parts; a dry toothbrush to brush dirt from the earmold, microphone, and controls; a screwdriver to tighten loose screws; a battery tester; a wax remover; an air bulb to blow water out of the ear mold; and silica gel to dry water from inside the case or receiver.

Consider setting up a hearing aid care incentive program and checking off "yes" and "no" activities that pertain to your child. Reward your child based on a predominance of "yes" checkmarks. For visual fun, you can make a huge black-and-white drawing of a hearing aid and draw dividers (like a grid or like a puzzle) in the drawing. Color in each part daily when your child has a "yes" day. For a younger child you may want to keep the drawing to a maximum of five to seven portions. When the hearing aid is colored in fully, the child receives a reward.

• •

Activity #8: My Helpful Interpreter Request

Materials: "My Helpful Interpreter" activity (see pgs. 181–182), TTY
    activities (pgs. 186–187, 329–330), paper, pen, TTY, relay service
Age: 8–12
Vocabulary/Concepts: interpreter, request, need, comfortable, name,
    ASL, English, voice, time, date, who, what, when, where

• •

This activity builds upon the activity we call "My Helpful Interpreter," many of the activities in chapter 5, and the TTY skill-building activities (pgs. 186-187, 329-330). In this activity you teach your child the process of requesting an interpreter. Begin by explaining the role of an interpreter to your child (to make communication clear, to match the deaf person's needs, to maintain confidentiality). Use examples of any meetings, doctor appointments, TV programs, or performances he might have seen or participated in where an interpreter was present.

Next, ask your child to describe when he best understands—at school? home? with friends? Ask him when he feels most comfortable with communication. Recognize his communication preferences, "Oh, you like when Mr. Giamia uses ASL and uses pictures." Have him tell you as many details as possible to support what he liked about the "positive" communication experiences. Write these down.

Pretend that he is going to need an interpreter and together write your child's name, the pretend place and time for which the interpreter is needed, and your child's communication preferences. Next, practice typing these on the TTY. Use this process for actual appointments, meetings, and situations when you are requesting an interpreter. You can even create a standardized form to assist your child in organizing his thoughts.

GOING TO BED AND WAKING ON TIME

For most families, sleep time is an unrecognized sport. It's a battle of the wills and a game of winners and losers involving constant competition between what you want and what your child wants.

A child who wakes too early causes problems for his family. He tends to wake others, to get into mischief, and to become tired and irritable early in the day. If the child is used to having others around or relies on them to feel safe and calm, he will naturally seek others for company.

The early riser can benefit from a plan to gradually spend more time alone, having a list of "what-to-do-when-alone" options, and having a step-by-step process of what to do during the early morning time. Have him practice quiet, independent activities that are respectful to others and that might allow him to fall back to sleep (reading in bed, writing, telling a make-believe story to himself, and coloring). Encourage all of these activities to happen in bed.

Children who have difficulty waking up are often grouchy and combative, late, and rushing to do morning routines. Their behavior stresses the entire family, causing scheduling problems and a bad start to the day. Work together to develop a plan (use an alarm clock with flashing light or bed vibrator) that assists your child in assuming responsibility for waking on time. Remember, getting up on time needs to become your child's job, not yours. He needs to experience the natural consequences for failing to do this. The earlier you can teach this skill, the better. If you wait to teach this skill in adolescence, you are sure to have more struggles.

Deaf children can be very responsible about waking on time with the correct technology (bed vibrators, alarms with flashing lights). Light sleepers may easily be awakened by flashing lights while heavier sleepers may need a bed vibrator.

Remember that consistency will assist your child in developing good waking habits. Be consistent about bedtimes that honor the amount of sleep your child needs and be consistent about expecting your child to wake himself.

Activities

● ●

Activity #1: *Good Night/Good Morning Club*
Materials: "Chart and Reward Program" (see pgs. 57–58), paper,
 markers
Age: 5–9
Vocabulary/Concepts: good night, good morning, club, bedtime, IN BED,
 wake up, privileges, earn

● ●

The "Good Night/Good Morning Club" creates night and morning rituals that respect your family's sleep styles and teaches your child to take responsibility for his own sleep or morning difficulties. This activity uses a "Chart and Reward Program" (see pgs. 57–58) by asking your child to accumulate a desired number of points on a chart to earn club privileges. Give your child the choice of accomplishing his responsibilities and earning club advantages (rewards and positive logical consequences) or to ignore responsibilities and remain out of the club (less privileges).

Discuss the club idea with your child and create an enticing list of club privileges he can earn by being responsible at bed or waking times. Club privileges might include: later bedtime, new pajamas, sleepovers with friends, new bed toy, or new videotape to be watched in the morning.

Next, make a bed or morning time routine that is documented on a chart. Write down a step-by-step routine in which your child must accomplish specific tasks to reach his ultimate goal. For example, your child's routine may be: eat dinner, do homework, play, pajamas on, wash up, read a book, in bed at 8:30, light off at 8:45. For each task your child accomplishes, he receives a point. Decide upon the desired amount of points or checks needed to join the club. Remind your child of his independent skills (sports, hygiene, homework) and how to use these to be responsible and eventually make it into the club.

Design your child's chart to meet his needs, strengths, and developmental capabilities. If, after some use, the chart seems too difficult, then revise the chart to suit your child's abilities. The activities in this chapter (such as the "Bedtime Soap Opera") as well as in other chapters (the "Good Night Door" — see chapter 9) can be done in addition to this "Club" activity for extra support.

Always remember to give points and count them daily. If your child begins to resort to old, unwanted habits, remind him that it is his choice to earn "club privileges" and it is his personal success if he does so. Continue using this activity until the sleep or bedtime problems have been greatly decreased or are no longer a problem.

● ●

Activity #2: Wake Up and Smell the Coffee!
Materials: bed alarm attached to light or bed vibrator, "Chart and
 Reward" program (pgs. 57–58)
Age: 8–12
Vocabulary/Concepts: wake up, fun, ready, GROW-UP
● ●

This activity sets up a process for encouraging your deaf child to begin to take responsibility for waking. The goal is to introduce the concept for your eight- or nine-year-old and to aim for full proficiency by age ten or eleven. Self-waking is one of the most difficult things that children learn to do on their own and without the proper technology and training, deaf children may not accomplish this until late in their teens. Buy an alarm, attachment for a lamp, and a bed vibrator. Together with your child, show these (with pride) to family, friends, and neighbors. Receiving these items should feel like a rite of passage to the child. Support this notion with comments such as "Yes, Uncle Nicholas, he is getting so much older and responsible, now" or "This is just like the alarm your teacher Mrs. Tessa has—do you want to take in the box to show her and your classmates?"

Once your child has bought into the idea of using the alarm, most of the work is over. Help your child get used to using the alarm by doing the following:

1. Create a behavior plan that offers rewards for each morning he awakes on his own. Or make a chart and have a weekly Saturday morning breakfast reward for good efforts (see "Chart and Reward" pgs. 57-58).

2. Make the initial use of the alarm extremely rewarding—first use it every Saturday morning for waking in time to watch favorite cartoons; use it for special summer outings; or use it to wake your child so that he can have a favorite breakfast.

3. Create a system of writing a note to his teacher when he wakes on his own.

Remember to make the whole process fun and rewarding. Do it slowly and make the tougher waking days (Monday mornings, test days) the very last goal. You may need to create a waking plan that includes reminders initially and slowly reduces these.

. . . .

Activity #3: Bedtime Soap Opera
Materials: ongoing story from book or your own creation
Age: 4–10
Vocabulary/Concepts: continue, unfinished, STORY MORE TOMORROW, STORY
ADD TOMORROW

. . . .

Give your child a good reason to hop into bed. Make up a saga that continues each night. Make the characters people in the house, but change the names slightly to make it funny or make your child's name the same as the main character in a fictional story. Have the hero be a deaf person or create a land of deaf people. The story should be safe and silly. Always leave the end a mystery to be continued the next evening. If you have difficulty creating your own story, read a novel that appeals to your child.

. . . .

Activity #4: Wake Up Map
Materials: small labels
Age: 4–8
Vocabulary/Concepts: wake-up map, numbers, FINISH (two-handed sign),
next

. . . .

If you need a little sleep in the morning and your child wakes up with the roosters, plan and prevent by visually mapping out a routine the night before. Put numbers or labels on activities you want him to accomplish in succession. Show him the routine before he goes to bed. For example, put number one on his toothbrush and face cloth, number two on his clothes, number three on a cereal box and milk, number four on a morning video, and number five on a coloring book.

PROCRASTINATION

Procrastination may be your child's way of avoiding situations that create uncomfortable feelings or fears of failure. It is not uncommon for a deaf child to avoid homework that he does not understand or to avoid communication situations that have not been successful (such as going to the store).

Through discussion and observation, find out what your child finds most unpleasant about a task. Support him as soon as possible rather than allowing avoidance to take over. Give real life examples of how prevention helps stop problems from getting bigger.

Some children who procrastinate use time to wear a parent down. Since clarity in communicating directions and expectations may take more time in a family with hearing parents and deaf children, do not allow your haste to teach bad habits or to put you in the position of doing the child's responsibility.

A child with limited opportunity or skills to assert his opinion can use time as a weapon in power struggles with parents. Often, "not doing" is an indirect expression of disagreement or anger. Redirect this by encouraging your child to express disagreement actively through discussion and negotiation rather than passively through procrastination. Create ongoing, formal Family Council Meetings (pgs. 19–21) and informal methods (spur-of-the-moment discussions) for this to occur.

Procrastination can become a limiting pattern of behavior that is difficult to alter once learned. Address your child's problem with procrastination as soon as you notice it. The earlier you catch and attempt to change this behavior, the less it will become an ingrained method of dealing with daily demands.

Your child's perception of time-related responsibilities may be different from yours. Remember that the child has his own priorities and, therefore, chores, homework, catching the bus, and practicing multiplication tables may not be as important to him as they are to you.

Activities

. . . .
Activity #1: The What's Next Room Chart
Materials: white shelving paper or butcher paper, crayons, markers,
    dry-erase markers
Age: 6–12
Vocabulary/Concepts: next, responsible, day, night
. . . .

Take the guesswork out of tasks for your deaf child. Minimize the time you spend wondering if he understood what was expected of him. Make a full-length room border that covers the four corners of your child's room or make a chart out of a long sheet of contact paper and write on the border or chart with crayons or markers the hours of the day from morning to night. Try to divide the chart into half-hour segments.

Discuss the daily routine with your child from waking up to going to bed. Draw pictures of each activity, cut them out and paste them on the border in the order of the time of each event. Try to make a complete border of scheduled activities, including teeth-brushing, dressing, bus-catching, straight through to bedtime story and lights off.

This provides your child with a clear picture of what is next, what he is expected to do, and how much time he has to do it in. On days when your child's schedule changes, peel off the nonapplicable activity and replace it with the applicable one. Review the expectations and daily routine with your child the night before by "chanting" out each activity as it appears on the border. This is a playful way to remind your child to follow directions without telling him what to do next.

. . . .

Activity #2: The Appointment Book

Materials: pleasant-looking appointment book, pencils or pens
Age: 8–12
Vocabulary/Concepts: appointment, plan, hurry, your choice, TIME
APPROACH

. . . .

Children love to have adult-like things and your older child (age nine to twelve) will appreciate a mature approach. Buy an appointment book that your child likes. Each night, or on Sunday night, record your child's responsibilities for the day or week. Go through each day, stating the time to wake up, catch the bus, and play. Note project deadlines and help your child think of a plan to get these done on time. You may want to note times when you are available for helping with homework or with projects.

If your child does not follow through with his scheduled appointment time or responsibilities, let the natural consequences of this failure do the work for you. In other words, he will experience the effects of his laziness and procrastination (not doing a report on time results in a bad grade or a late night of cramming). Keep referring your child to his schedule and let him know it is his choice to put things off, but remind him that it will make it more difficult for him later. Use TAP (pgs. 50–51) to redirect your own actions; deny your urge to nag or yell when he does not follow through.

. . . .

Activity #3: Magic Memos
. . . .

Post reminders of things your child needs to do in funny places, using Post-it™ notes or sticky pads. Be creative and post reminders on his pillow, in his underwear drawer, inside a shoe, or directly on a misplaced object.

. . . .

Activity #4: Later, Early, and Now

Materials: three coffee cans or boxes, construction paper, scissors, markers

Age: 7–12

Vocabulary/Concepts: later, early, now, POSTPONE, ON-TIME, ready, consequence

. . . .

Helping your child to understand the dynamics of procrastination could make your child more receptive to change. You can teach your child that procrastination is one of many alternatives that a person can choose from.

Cover three boxes or coffee cans with paper and write on them "Later," "Early," "Now." In a Family Meeting, discuss how people can choose to do a task later (procrastinate), now (on time), or before a deadline (early). Discuss times when people should never procrastinate, such as in emergencies. Discuss consequences of the three ways of approaching a task. With each approach there are compromises, and being early or on time usually give better long-term results (better grades, job promotions, and acceptance on sports teams). Use your sense of humor; for example, ask your child to imagine what would have happened if Thomas Edison postponed going outside with his kite, "Nah, I don't want to today." What would life be like if the people who invented closed captioning had decided to sleep instead? What if a firefighter did not want to drive on the day when an alarm sounded? What if a football player decided he did not want to play on Super Bowl Sunday?

Have everyone in your family write a short note and drop it in a designated can every time a family member is early, on time (now), or late on a task. Help your child write a short note or draw a picture of something if he is unable to write. At the end of a week, have another Family Meeting and review the cards and the decisions people made. Model both "on time" and procrastinating behavior for your child to observe, "Oh no, I don't want to put gas in the car today and I am choosing not to do that!" and the result, "Oh, I don't have enough gas to go to the movies, darn!" You can set up a reward system that gives the family something fun to do together if there are more "now" and "early" situations than "later."

Refer back to these concepts, "I'm going to be early with paying my bills so that we can have time to go to the park together." Notice if your child needs to learn other skills in order to accomplish a task and seek out plans and activities to teach the necessary skills.

MESSINESS AND NOT PICKING UP AFTER HIMSELF

When parents come to the aid of their child who shows irresponsible behavior, they unknowingly reinforce this behavior and don't encourage the child to own his behavior and its consequences.

Messiness may be your child's expression of his personality and independence. Just take a look at any adult's desk, bedroom, or kitchen to get a flavor of the different tolerance people have for messiness.

To parents who are orderly and clean, a child's messiness may seem like utter defiance. In fact, messiness may be a result of poorly developed organization skills, concentration problems, or genuine oversight of details.

Consider your and your child's personality style; appreciate and find humor in the differences that exist between the two of you. Make expectations and tasks reasonable, clear, and understandable. Use many visual and graphic representations to serve as reminders and organizing tools. Help your child break down a project and structure it into more manageable steps. Look for improvement rather than perfection.

Activities

• •

Activity #1: The Doesn't Belong Box

Materials: medium-sized cardboard box
Age: 5–12
Vocabulary/Concepts: doesn't belong, auction, buy back, STAR

• •

For this activity you'll need a medium-sized cardboard box, some patience, and yourself as a role model. First, write on the cardboard box "Doesn't Belong Box." Next, sit down with your family and listen to each person's view on family responsibilities for cleanliness and picking up. Note when there is a "pick-up problem." Explain that after a family member uses or plays with something that needs to be put away, he can either put it in the proper place or put it in the "Doesn't Belong Box." If another family member sees an object that has not been put away, he can put it in the box. At the end of the day, family members are to look inside the box and put away their own belongings.

The logical consequence of not putting away your things at the end of the day is that they will be set aside for an "auction" at the end of the week. At the auction, the owner of the item must "buy back" his possession by offering services (doing extra chores, emptying the box by himself). Of course, school books and needed objects cannot be auctioned; just apply a logical consequence instead for these.

Support this activity by using parenting techniques such as "Your Choice" — "Either put it away now, put it in the 'Doesn't Belong Box' to put away later, or you'll lose it for a few days." Tell your child to use STAR to stop, think, and remember his belongings. Model putting things away and using the box. Have your child draw pictures on the box to help remind him of his responsibilities. Always keep your sense of humor while holding the "Auction." Act like a real auctioneer: "Going, going, gone to the kid with the baseball cap for his offer of cleaning the dishes tonight!" Keep your child's developmental age in mind when expecting him to remember his things or considering what he needs to do in order to "buy back" his item.

This activity playfully teaches responsibility and logical consequences. It makes cleaning up as easy as throwing something into a box. Over time, the "Doesn't Belong Box" will become less necessary. Your child will become accustomed to putting things away and will find that it is much easier to clean up immediately rather than risk losing the item.

Activity #2: The Team Chore Chart

Materials: poster board, markers
Age: 4–12
Vocabulary/Concepts: team, chores, responsibility, TAKE-TURNS

This activity will probably not be new for you. Making chore charts have long been a part of American family life. However, this chore chart has a slightly different twist. What makes it different is that the chart requires all family members to do chores as if they were players on a team. Without "team" members doing their share, the team will not win. If everyone does their team chore, then the entire family wins a mutually agreed upon reward, such as a trip to a favorite restaurant or the purchase of a new household item.

We believe that responsibilities and household chores bond a child to his family and home; a sort of membership in a club. Participating in washing the dishes, vacuuming, clearing the table, and making one's bed gives a child a sense of value, worth, and accomplishment. This ultimately builds self-esteem and self-reliance and prepares your child for more demanding future responsibilities.

The first thing to do is to make your "Team Chore Chart" by deciding on daily chores that need to be done. Depending on your child's age and developmental ability, choose between three and seven chores to be accomplished each day. Explain to your child that doing his chore for the day is the same as doing his part on a baseball, soccer or football team. Each member needs to do his chore to help the team win or, in this case, to win the reward.

Encourage your child to remind others to do their chores for the sake of the team. You may want to include a "personal chore" section in your chart that requires your child to do homework, make his bed, or practice basketball layups.

....

Activity #3: Get a Job!

Materials: paper, pencil, want-ad section of the newspaper
Age: 9–12
Vocabulary/Concepts: job, pay, work, check, duties

....

As much as you may balk at the thought of paying your child to be responsible, money is a strong motivator. Paying your child for accomplishing tasks can teach him some important lessons in life skills related to work, personal responsibility, and earning money. Show him how people look in the classified section of a newspaper to find a job. Tell your child that it is his responsibility to get his chores done, like a "job." In the form of a classified ad, write out special job descriptions, the amount to be paid (real or token money), and "advertise" for new jobs by posting them on your family bulletin board or refrigerator. At the end of the week, your child can get his "pay check" if the job is done properly.

Managing Moods and Valuing Feelings

• • • • • • • • • • •

Kim Kelly

*H*ave you ever awakened from a dream in which you were trying to escape someone or something frightening and your feet would not carry you to safety? Or, you were trying desperately to get help and found that you no longer had a voice? Attempting to reach a destination but unable to find your way? I would imagine that your relief has been as great as mine when, upon awakening, the realization has finally crept in that it was "only a dream."

What, you may ask, does all this have to do with moodiness in young children? First, I would like to ask that you keep in mind the feelings produced by the dream experience: the frustration, helplessness, fear, and vulnerability. We, as adults, can find relief in the discovery that these experiences were only dreams. But, for children, this experience is not just a dream but their day-to-day reality.

At no other time in one's life are needs so great and skills so few as in early childhood. Beginning in infancy, a child is entirely helpless and dependent upon the instincts of caretakers. We must guess, when an infant cries, just what the cry is communicating. Is it hunger, a need to be held, or a diaper in need of changing? Parents often breathe a sigh of relief when, finally,

Kim Kelly is a licensed independent clinical social worker who currently works as the Director of Deaf Services and the Resource Team at South Shore Mental Health in Quincy, Massachusetts. She is also in private practice in the Greater Boston area.

language arrives and a child is able to begin using words to name basic needs. However, the ability to identify a wish for juice long precedes a child's ability to talk about or even identify more complex feelings and needs. A three-year-old may be able to let an adult know of the desire to watch "Sesame Street." But that same child will be unable to use language to communicate the profound sense of loss experienced when a new sibling arrives, or the let-down associated with the end of a long-anticipated event.

How nice it would be if a four-year-old could say "Mom, do you have a few minutes . . . I really need to talk about something that has been bothering me?" Instead, Mom is likely dealing with the manifestation of these bothersome feelings in the form of moodiness, tantrums, defiance, or aggression. Clearly this is not a time when Mom or Dad is likely to be empathic and wanting to explore a child's inner experience. After all, these behaviors also tend to bring out similar feelings of frustration and helplessness in adults— many of whom were raised by a generation of parents who believed that children should be "seen and not heard," or that a crying child should be given "something to cry about."

Add to this already complex process a language difference between parent and child by virtue of a child's deafness. Before a parent can even arrive at the point of intervening with problem behaviors and attempting to understand their antecedents, a system of communication must be established. It is not uncommon for this difference between family members to be both the source of great frustration for the child and the greatest impediment to negotiating a mutually satisfying system of communication.

Teaching a child to manage moods and value feelings is to teach a child two of the most significant self-esteem builders. After all, we all feel better about ourselves when we "behave" and are pleasant. Likewise, self-esteem grows when a child learns that feelings are to be respected and listened to, not shamed and dismissed.

Our nerve-endings, when they properly develop, are our best protectors against serious injury. If we were to touch a hot stove, a quick message would be sent to our brain signaling pain and an equally quick response would cause us to remove our hand to prevent further injury. In the same way, feelings become our best protectors against harm of other sorts. A child who learns to respect inner feelings and instincts will know when a playground bully is out of line, will talk with adults about being bullied, and, ultimately, look for new playmates. A child whose feelings have not been nurtured may dismiss uncomfortable feelings and endure uncomfortable circumstances.

Similarly, our feelings teach us about that which feels good and rewarding. They become a "barometer" to be relied upon, ever informing us of our needs, likes, dislikes, dangers, and pleasures. The calibration of this fine tool begins in early childhood. It requires a delicate parental balance of empathy and limits; the willingness to "listen" to that which words cannot yet express; the creation of words and a common language; and, ultimately, teaching a child to use words as well as actions to explain feelings.

11

Moodiness

• • • •

This chapter groups behaviors related to feelings of anger, sadness, frustration, and irritability under the heading of moodiness. They can become problematic when a child is unable to control or appropriately express them. While emotions are a part of every child's developing personality, most young children do not know how to harmoniously integrate thoughts, feelings, and actions.

Sometimes deaf children have no way to name, categorize, or normalize the emotions they feel. They need an "emotional education" to learn what it is that they are feeling (feeling signal), words and names for those feelings, and appropriate actions for expressing them. We designed the activities in this chapter to increase your child's feeling-related vocabulary and to teach her playful ways to control and express her feelings.

POOR ABILITY TO IDENTIFY FEELING STATES

Feeling states are the internal sensation of emotions such as anger, sadness, happiness, and fear. If a deaf child is taught to categorize feelings by words/ signs, the feelings do not become overwhelming, frightening, and out of control. When able to identify and acknowledge what she is feeling, the child is more likely to get the support she needs.

Children need ongoing instruction and assistance to manage their feelings effectively. We recommend using the following three-step process:

1. Learning to recognize feeling signals by observing others and noticing how an emotion feels in her own body. Examples are tightening of the jaw, clenching the fist, a fluttering in the stomach, and a flush of heat to the head.

The problems may look like this:

• • • • • • •

- Child has tantrums, screaming, hitting, and breaking things.
- Child frequently cries or whines.
- Child has red face, bulging eyes, popping veins when angry.
- Child swears, is defiant, and refuses to discuss difficulties.
- Child always wants your attention.
- Child appears to best express only one emotion (such as anger).
- Escalating negative cycles of tantrums, crying, and moodiness are followed by punishment by the parent or caretaker.
- Child does not understand what caused her to have feelings or reactions.
- Child does not understand how actions affect feelings and visa versa.
- Child does not express feelings but rather lets them build up and then explodes all at once.
- Child becomes easily overwhelmed by feelings.
- Child blames feelings on others.
- Child brings up issues at times when you cannot attend to them.
- Child is unable to identify what is bothering her.

2. Identifying and naming a feeling. Ask your child what a particular feeling signal indicates. "You got all red in the face, were you mad? embarrassed?"

3. Learning what to do with a feeling. You can help your child identify how an expression of a feeling can have positive or negative results.

Your child may have a particular physical make-up that makes her sensitive to touch, foods, noises, lighting, or gravity. Because of the way your child's central nervous system reads stimulation, she may exhibit emotional expression in a manner that seems extreme (e.g., the child hits if her hair is played with). If you want to investigate this possibility further, contact an occupational therapist who specializes in sensory defensiveness and deafness.

Consider and rule out possible physical causes of your child's mood, such as fatigue, hunger, or over-stimulation. Plan ahead in order to avoid situations that may frustrate a tired or over-stimulated child.

Praise your child when she expresses herself appropriately. Be patient. As your child matures, so will her ability to identify, understand, and communicate her feelings. You can assist in this process by experimenting with physical and verbal outlets for expressing feelings appropriately. Keep in mind her developmental skills and limitations.

Your child's expressions may appear to be more graphic for a number of reasons: a) when signing, she probably will have stronger facial and bodily expressions; b) when learning to identify and express new feelings, the child might "overdo" it; and c) the child may feel an urgency to get her point across, especially if it is important to her. Once she feels more capable of communicating effectively, the latter two factors will recede. However, pronounced expressiveness is the norm in the Deaf community as well as for the deaf person who is not an active community member.

Observe direct examples of signs and expressions by watching and talking with deaf adults and teachers of deaf children. Have a sign book handy as a reference. To enhance your child's learning about feelings and their expression, use visual reminders—a feelings chart, feeling cards (see following activity), a feelings book, and a journal.

Create a supportive family environment in which feelings and their appropriate expression are unconditionally accepted. It is not the feeling but what a child does with it that is important. With support, a child can trust that expression of feelings will not lead to ridicule, criticism, or rejection.

Some feelings may be easy to express while others are not. This varies between individuals, families, genders, and cultures. In some families, anger is easy to express while intimacy is not; in some cultures humor is second-nature while seriousness is difficult; and for some individuals expression of sadness is a sign of weakness and anger is a sign of strength. Examine how each member of your family is affected by your family's style of expression. Try to become more accepting of the feelings that seem unnatural to you and your family—this will make the child's feeling education more inclusive and flexible.

Socially acceptable expression of feelings can be learned through parental modeling and practicing identifying and naming "feeling states." Model effective feeling expression through assertiveness rather than through aggression or unproductive complaining. When you make a mistake in your expression of feelings (losing control and yelling, for example), it is important that your child knows that. Teaching "perfection" is not a useful goal; teaching how to acknowledge problems and to attempt to change them is much more realistic and constructive.

Activities

∙∙

Activity #1: Feeling Cards
Materials: three-by-five index cards, pen, markers, crayons, one-step camera and film
Age: 4–12
Vocabulary/Concepts: (see list of feelings below), feeling games, match, right, wrong

∙∙

Children initially express feelings physically. Over time, words can take the place of this physical expression. For the deaf child, an early vocabulary of feeling states will better allow for the development of effective ways to express emotions other than through physical means.

Using the list of feelings below, write each of these feelings on a three-by-five index card with your child. On the back side of the card, draw or place a photograph of your child expressing that specific feeling. We recommend investing in a few rolls of film to take pictures. Your child will be more able to make a connection between the feeling word and the way it actually looks and feels when she is expressing it. You and your child can play to identify feelings with this deck of cards. Here follows a list of some of the most common feelings; but a toddler or preschooler will only need and understand the most basic emotions such as happy, sad, mad, scared, funny, hurt, and confused (don't understand).

mad	strange	embarrassed	calm
sad	funny	talkative	great
happy	cool	curious	cheerful
angry	beautiful	clever	fresh
frustrated	encouraged	loved	brave
warm	uncomfortable	unloved	gross
proud	excited	free	inferior
quiet	confused	sensitive	worthless
shy	weird	ugly	worthwhile
nervous	stupid	successful	depressed
scared	worried	disappointed	troubled
lucky	insecure	likable	hopeless
joyful	rotten	strong	skillful
small	selfish	left out	capable
safe	grouchy	energetic	confident
upset	put down	hateful	smart
silly	used	unimportant	accepting

alive	sick	important	jealous
hopeful	awkward	hurt	secretive
creative	furious	sorry	positive
stubborn	crazy	rejected	wonderful

We have designed some games you can play with your cards, but we encourage you to invent some of your own. To help your child integrate feelings when using these games, reinforce what the feeling is, what makes a person feel that way, and how to express that feeling appropriately. Use your feeling cards throughout the day. When your child becomes moody and doesn't identify or appropriately express her feeling, have her go through the deck and choose a card or two that indicate her emotions. Model for your child when you have a specific feeling by selecting a card yourself.

Try some of these feeling card games:

1. **Feeling Charades:** Have family members take turns picking a feeling card and acting out that feeling. Other family members can try to guess the feeling.

2. **Flash Card Feelings:** Use the deck of feeling cards like "flash cards." Go through all the feeling words and have your child try to guess the name of the feeling when you are showing the picture side or what the expression looks like if you are showing the word side.

3. **Feeling Mix and Match:** Duplicate your cards to play a mix-and-match game. Put both decks of cards on the floor with one deck showing the word side and one exposing the picture side. Try to match the expression with the word.

4. **Right and Wrong:** Select a card from the feeling deck and have family members take turns showing the right way and the wrong way to express that emotion.

....

Activity #2: The Feeling Box

Materials: large box or container, feeling cards (see previous
    activities), relaxation tools (see pgs. 263–265), hat, paper
    plates, popsicle sticks, tissue, mirror, puppets, dolls
Age: 5–12
Vocabulary/Concepts: feelings, magic wand, relaxation, I want
    attention, mirror, rip, talk, express, calm, help, skills, books,
    consequences, choices, CALM-DOWN, FEELING HOLD-IN, EXPRESS

....

This box contains an "Emotion Encyclopedia" that family members can use when dealing with feelings. Most importantly, this activity gives both parents and children acceptable ways to vent emotions while taking responsibility for and control of them.

A feeling box is a large container of games, activities, and tools to help identify and express feelings. Using the contents of this box, the family can find the necessary structure and guidance to express and manage anger, sadness, or general moodiness. To begin, write "Feeling Box" on your container and draw pictures of people who are mad, happy, or sad on the box. Next, fill it with these items:

- Feeling cards: described above.

- The Magic Wand: a stick covered with glitter.

- Relaxation tools: see activity "Relaxation Center" on pages 263–265. You can either put the tools in the box or make a list of what relaxation tools are and put that list in the box.

- "I-Want-Attention" Hat: a hat with a sign that has written on it, "I Want Attention."

- Feeling masks: on paper plates draw faces depicting various feelings, cut holes out for the eyes, and paste a popsicle stick to the underside. Make masks for all of the feelings your child can imagine expressing.

- A mirror, tissues, a few puppets and dolls, and skill cards: see "My Skill Sack" (pgs. 308–309).

- Books that show children having difficult feelings and learning how to manage them. *The Living Skills Series* (Joy Berry, Grolier Enterprises, Inc., 1987) has a number of books with engaging pictures.

- Telephone books and newspapers to shred, stomp, or write on.

- A wise old stuffed doll or animal who listens very well.

- Markers and paper.

- A plastic telephone, broken telephone, and/or a cardboard box drawn in the shape of a TTY.

- Blanket for soothing and holding.

- Dominoes.

Put the feeling box in an accessible area in your home. When your child becomes agitated, whines, or is angry, direct her to the box to help her playfully label and express feelings. Here are examples of how each item can be used.

Magic Wand: Use the Magic Wand to help your child deal with disappointments; tell her to make a wish and wave the wand to express how she wishes things could have been.

I-Want-Attention Hat: When your child tries to gain your attention with negative behavior (tantrums, whining, crying), teach her to use the, "I-Want-Attention Hat." Tell your child to put on the hat when she needs attention. When your child puts on the hat, immediately praise her and either give her attention at that moment or at a mutually agreed upon time.

Puppets, Dolls, and Feeling Masks: Use these for expressing and play-acting feelings. Role-play real life situations to help the child figure out ways she can handle emotional challenges. Use these items with plan, prepare, and prevent techniques (see pgs. 46–47) to prepare your child for distressing or problematic events (such as going to a toy store and not being able to buy what she wants).

Feeling Cards: Direct your child to the cards when she is feeling "moody" and needs guidance to define the feeling.

Mirror: Have your child look in the mirror and describe what she sees, (angry face, sad face, happy face).

Skill Cards: If your child has inappropriately expressed a feeling, ask her to look through her "skill cards" and pick out a few skills that could help her express feelings more appropriately the next time ("Try, Try again").

Tissues: The tissue is there for crying—an acceptable way to express feelings.

Relaxation Center: Let your child know that it is much easier to express feelings when she is relaxed and in control. (See pgs. 263–265 for relaxation tools that are very useful for calming an anxious, over-stimulated, or agitated child.)

Books: Your child may find particular stories and pictures to validate her experience. In addition, for many children books are like old, reliable friends.

Old Telephone Books and Newspapers: Your child can rip, shred, poke, and push paper to her heart's delight to vent anger. The act of shredding teaches an aggressive child a new physical action. Do not encourage punching or kicking since these actions can translate easily to hurting people and can potentially make trouble some day.

A Wise Old Stuffed Doll or Animal: Sometimes an inanimate object with an understanding face allows children to express their feelings. A doll like this is the ultimate listener.

Markers and Paper or Newspaper: With these, a child can draw her feelings, draw what happened, or draw what she wishes had happened. Or perhaps she can draw as a way to refocus her energy. The child can use the newspaper as large drawing paper and draw the person with whom she is angry, upset, or disappointed. She can tape the paper on the wall and tell that person just what she thinks and feels about the situation. Steer her away from threats and revenge ("I'll hurt you when I see you!") and toward owning a feeling ("I am sooooo mad because you kicked me and I don't want you to be my friend anymore").

A Plastic Telephone, Broken Telephone, and/or a Cardboard Box Drawn in the Shape of a TTY: These can be used for a child to practice assertion skills by pretending to call someone and telling them just how she feels. She can let her imagination run wild—perhaps she would like to call the President and report that her teacher was mean, or call a deceased relative or pet to tell them that she misses them.

Blanket: This can be the "safe blanket" or the "make-you-feel-better blanket" or the "I-need-to-cry blanket." Sometimes a child needs to be held and comforted and this is a way for her to give that feeling to herself. Wrapped tightly around her, the blanket also helps to calm a child who is experiencing a sensory overload.

Dominoes: These can be used as described in the activity "The Domino Effect" (pgs. 245–246) to help understand how situations, feelings, and behaviors connect.

Whenever your child begins to inappropriately express an emotion, give her the choice of using the feeling box or expecting you to mete out a consequence. Initially, join her when she goes to the box, encourage appropriate use of items, and model positive ways to express feelings. When the child knows how to use the box correctly, she can choose to use it alone or with an adult.

· ·

Activity #3: Mime Your Moods

Materials: clown or regular make-up

Age: 5–12

Vocabulary/Concepts: act, VOICE-OFF, feelings

· ·

Using clown make-up or face paint, transform your child into a mime. For fun, we suggest that you also become a mime. Have a mirror handy and practice making all types of emotional expressions. Notice how different your face looks when you are angry from when you are happy. Put on small plays using different feelings for the "theme" of each show.

. . . .

Activity #4: Feelings Chart

Materials: store-bought feelings chart, markers, felt pieces, velcro,
glue
Age: 5–10
Vocabulary/Concepts: feeling, today, now, feelings together, all the
feeling words on the chart, mixed-up feelings
. . . .

Make or purchase a feelings chart for your child that includes simple facial expressions with the name of the feeling beneath each face. (You can order a feelings chart from the *ChildsWork, ChildsPlay Catalog*—see pg. 67). Make faces with different feeling expressions out of felt and attach velcro to the back. Write on a large piece of white felt "Today I Feel" and hang it on your child's door. Every morning, afternoon, or evening, or whenever useful, have your child choose the facial expression that indicates how she feels at that moment and stick it on the chart.

. . . .

Activity #5: Feelings Journal

Materials: diary, blank book, or spiral notebook; pencil or pen
Age: 8–12
Vocabulary/Concepts: private, EXPRESS, write, share
. . . .

Older children enjoy writing their feelings in a diary or journal. Buy a special book for your child to note her daily emotions. Help by keeping your own journal and showing her how to write feelings and thoughts on paper. Make this book private and on no occasion should you look through it without your child's permission. If your child asks you to look through her book, comment positively. Also, ask if there was something particular she wanted to tell you by showing you her journal.

A few pre-packaged "feeling journals" you can purchase that not only give spaces for children to write or draw their feelings, but guide them through some feeling explorations are: "*I am Special and Marvelous Me*" Workbooks (Linda Schwartz, The Learning Works, 1978-9); "*Feeling Good about Your-*

self" (Debbie Pincus, Good Apple Inc., 1990): and *My Life* (Delia Ephron, Running Press, 1991).

● ●

Activity #6: Happy, Mad, Sad Whipped Cream Faces

Materials: can of whipped cream, paper, markers, books or magazines
　　　with pictures, blackboard, chalk, play clothes
Age: 3–5
Vocabulary/Concepts: happy, mad, sad, feel, any other feeling words
　　　child knows or is learning

● ●

For the deaf toddler, preschooler, and most kindergarten children, you will need feeling education activities that are not reading-based. This activity gives a hands-on approach to understanding basic feelings (happy, mad, sad), how they vary in intensity, and how the feelings are expressed.

First, talk about the feelings "happy," "mad," and "sad" with your child while drawing faces to represent them. Next, look through books or magazines with the child and ask the child what the person or animal is feeling—happy, sad, or mad. Once your child has a basic sense of what these faces represent, you can move on to some creamy fun.

Clear a kitchen table or a play table and cover it with a vinyl tablecloth. Wear play clothes for this activity! Next draw on a blackboard or on a piece of paper three feeling faces—mad, happy, sad. Now, ask your child how a person might feel in various situations, e.g., how would she feel if she were kicked? Or role-play a situation, asking your child how she would feel. If she says "sad," take a can of whipped cream and draw a sad face in front of her on the table. She can put her hands into the face and do whatever she pleases with it. Continue asking questions and highlight her responses by making a whipped cream face—do this for as long as she remains interested.

You can ask your child, "Is that just a little mad or really big mad?" If she said "big mad," you can make the face big with huge, gritting teeth. Ask her to show you how she would play with the whipped cream if she were happy (smiling and tossing it), sad (sad face and less energy), and mad (squeezing the whipped cream tightly with a grimace). Have her draw faces in the cream with her finger. Use some other feeling faces for scared, confused, and silly.

Because this activity is tactile, the child will stay engaged. Create some ideas of your own—make stories on the table with drawings that show feeling responses. Play with some small, sturdy, washable dolls in the cream.

. . . .

Activity #7: My View, Your View

Materials: chairs

Age: 8–12

Vocabulary/Concepts: MY VIEW, DIFFERENT POINTS-OF-VIEW, reason, opinion, like, dislike, agree, disagree

. . . .

One of the best ways for a child to avoid inappropriate expression of feelings is to have reasonable assertion skills. And one of the fundamental building blocks of assertion skills is being able to figure out and express a point of view. This activity affords your child an opportunity to practice just that.

A deaf child may surmise from experience that her teachers, parents, and the hearing public are more powerful than she. She may fantasize about growing up and gaining that power or may fight to show her independence, "No, I won't!" It is valuable over the long-term for her to understand that her point of view is just as important as any adult's or hearing person's, that she can agree or disagree and not be punished, and that the power that adults have is the power to set rules and teach for health, safety, and security.

Now for the activity. This activity requires participation by at least three people. If you can enlist all your family members, that would be great!

Tell your family members that you are going to play a game in which they each have to state their point of view on a subject. When each person states their point of view, they start off by saying, "My point of view is," (There is a wonderful ASL sign for "my point of view.") Start off with an easy topic, like marshmallows. The first person says, "My point of view is that I hate marshmallows"; the next, "My point of view is that I love marshmallows in cocoa"; and the last, "I don't know, I have never eaten marshmallows."

Ask members to provide reasons for their view, such as, "I never eat marshmallows because they stick to my braces." Next, ask participants to state their opinion and then say so if they agree or disagree with someone else. ("I agree with Anthony. I dislike marshmallows, too. They are too sweet and feel funny in my mouth.") Insulting disagreements, such as "You are wrong!" or "How stupid," are not acceptable.

Move on to more varied topics, such as sports teams, school work, clothing styles, and current events. Encourage your child to say more than just "I like" or "I dislike" by modeling alternatives, e.g., "I was so upset when I found out about the earthquake on the news."

As a team, you can try to earn points—one point for every opinion stated and one for saying "I agree" or "disagree" in a respectful way. Set a goal and celebrate when you earn enough points to achieve it.

TANTRUMS

Tantrums and emotional outbursts are developmentally appropriate in children between the ages of two and six. They occur as a result of a child not having the capability and control necessary for expressing feelings verbally. Angry feelings can at times become so intense that your child's thinking becomes disorganized and confused.

For your deaf child, the reverse may also be the case—her confusion and disorganization may be so great that she becomes furious. Often the child's confusion stems from inadequate communication—she may feel left out, different, and one or several steps behind in family happenings.

Anger and frustration create emotional and physical tension that needs to be released or defused. Without the linguistic means to express anger, frustration, and dissatisfaction, the deaf child opts for more physical expressions (tantrums, aggression, impulsive behavior, or even headaches). By being able to organize powerful feelings through language, structured options, and by depending upon consistent parental responses, the child can learn the foundation of understanding and expressing feelings.

If a deaf child does not have adequate formal language to understand her own feelings and a communication environment that allows her to express these, her ability to understand others' feelings (empathy) and how she affects them will naturally be impaired.

Limited communication may lead parents to rigid discipline or physical punishment, and to bodily remove children from a difficult situation. This type of disciplining teaches the deaf child to avoid or leave a problem situation and reinforces the belief that problems are resolved through aggression. Verbal explanations, whether spoken or signed, and a gradation of privileges, on the other hand, teach responsibility, consequences, and problem-solving skills.

The context of comings and goings must be explained to your child. We have heard countless stories from deaf adults and children about not knowing where they were going, why, for how long, and when and if they would return. A child may have a tantrum if you take her out of school early for no apparent reason. A happy event such as a holiday can become disastrous if the deaf child does not know when the festivities are supposed to end. A parent interrupting a TV program can seem purely malicious if the child is not warned to anticipate bedtime.

In addition to communication factors, if your child frequently has tantrums, she may have a particularly low tolerance for frustration, changes, over-stimulation, or simply being told "no." Or perhaps tantrums or violent outbursts of anger could be your child's attempts to solve a problem by having an adult give in to her desires. Do not let your child's tantrum turn a "no" into a "yes." Doing this teaches her that tantrums get results and lessens her desire to learn more acceptable methods of negotiation.

Do your best to ignore or distract your child rather than give her attention for inappropriate behavior. Keep your angry feelings under control so that both of you are not having a tantrum at the same time. Model ways to express angry feelings, recommend the Think Chair to your child and to all family members—make calming down a family expectation and not just an expectation for the child.

Activities

. . . .

Activity #1: The TNT (Tantrum 'n' Tirades) Corner—A Family Affair

Materials: designated corner or place in house, STAR technique
Age: 3–8
Vocabulary/Concepts: lose control, express, calm, your choice, BLOW-UP

. . . .

Tantrums are normal in children aged two through six and usually decrease with age. However, sometimes they continue or increase if a child doesn't discover useful ways to express her anger, disagreement, or individuality. In this activity, you can structure your response, teach acceptable ways for stating opinions, and nurture her independence and your sanity.

The TNT Corner is an area of your home, or a place outside of your home, where your child may have a tantrum. Think of this as a sort of "hotel" for tantrums. Actually, this is a creative adaptation of the "Think Chair" by another name. Let your child know that she has your permission to have a tantrum, but only in the designated area. Show her where the TNT corner is located and consider having a sign indicating "Tantrums Only!"

When your child begins a tantrum, suggest that she go to the TNT corner or guide her there. While in the tantrum corner, she can let it rip! Ignore her while she is in the tantrum corner. TAP yourself for an extra boost of support to keep you from getting sucked in. As with the Think Chair, if she refuses to go, give a natural or logical consequence until she gets herself there. Carry her there if need be. Once she is finished, she can leave. Ask her how she got there, how she could have prevented the tantrum, and what other ways she can think of to express her strong feelings. Give her suggestions for these alternatives, such as using STAR; saying how she feels with words like, "I'm really, really mad!"; and using relaxation techniques (see pgs. 263-265).

Combine this activity with other activities to help your child think of specific methods for dealing with strong feelings other than using the TNT corner. Reward and praise your child when she goes to the TNT corner on her own or solves her problem without using the TNT corner. Also, use distraction—nothing squelches a tantrum better than giving your child something better to do! You can use the TNT corner when you lose your temper. Model how you sort out your own feelings, calm yourself down, and successfully cope with obstructions in your path.

Bring your TNT corner with you when you travel and remember to plan well and prepare for or prevent any vulnerable situations you might anticipate for your child. (For example, over-tired and over-stimulated children obviously do not fare well at a supermarket.)

. . . .

Activity #2: Volcanoes and Sodas

Materials: can or bottle of soda
Age: 8–12
Vocabulary/Concepts: HOLD-IN, BUILD-UP, EXPLODE, express, little by little

. . . .

In our experience, deaf children delight and benefit from seeing visual metaphors for problem behaviors. Show your child what happens to angry feelings when you store them up inside and don't express them appropriately. Shake a soda can while naming situations and occasions during the day that might make a person angry. Take the top off (outdoors, of course) to show how a person explodes over little things because of all the anger and "shaking" she has felt all day. Explain how to let out anger in small controlled steps instead of all at once.

You can also do this activity by pretending that you are a volcano. You might even want to order a "Build Your Own Volcano" kit from *Educational Insights'* catalog (see pg. 69). Show your child how a volcano begins to rumble, shake, and spurt out lava before it explodes. Explain that these are warning signs that the volcano will soon erupt. Throughout your child's day, notice when she is becoming agitated, and suggest that she is rumbling or beginning to shake and may need to express herself little by little rather than holding things in and exploding later.

. . . .

Activity #3: Slow Motion

Age: 3–7
Vocabulary/Concepts: slow down, think

. . . .

When you can see your child coming close to throwing a tantrum and she needs the opportunity to stop and think about how she is feeling, suggest that she tell you in slow motion. You can practice this technique and model for your child how to express anger by telling your feelings in slow motion. For example, "I am - very, very - angry - that you - did not - pick up - your toys." The entire family can benefit from the practice of taking control of emotions and slowing down to say things with thought.

· ·

Activity #4: The Domino Effect

Materials: dominoes, long sheet of paper, markers
Age: 8–12
Vocabulary/Concepts: dominoes, cause and effect, INFLUENCE,
     alternatives, changes, behavior, feeling

· ·

The concept of cause and effect is sometimes difficult for a young child to understand. She will often realize that something made her angry or upset but she will not see it in the context of a long chain of events. In this activity, we hope to create a visual chain of cause and effect by simply using dominoes.

Do not be tempted into teaching the "cause and effect" concept when emotions are intense because the child will become defensive: "I told you not to take the dog into the yard and now look at what happened." Set aside a calm time to teach the principles of this activity. This activity might provide a good follow-up to a tantrum, but be sure you are emotionally settled before embarking if you want to have a truly fruitful discussion.

Using a box of dominoes, first set one domino on its short edge. Remind your child that the domino stands alone but feelings and people are not like that—they influence each other. Put a second domino next to the first, then a third, and so on. Ask your child to tap the one on the end to see what happens. Explain that all of the dominoes react to each other. This is the way situations, people, and feelings interact.

Set up a domino and call it "ice cream." Ask your child what feeling that creates in her—probably "happy." Call the next domino "happy." Tap "ice cream" and watch it influence "happy." As your child catches on, add more dominoes to represent a chain of events, feelings, and the effects on other people.

Suppose a neighbor child stole your child's favorite baseball glove and your child was upset. Set up a domino for the neighbor stealing the bat; one for your child's angry and upset feelings; one for the behavior she displayed (cried and punched the door); one for your reaction of scolding her for punching the door; one for her increased crying; and finally, one for her being told to go to the "Think Chair." You can even spread the dominoes on a piece of paper and write or draw what your child reports next to each one.

Line them up and tap—they're all related! Now show your child how to make an adjustment by changing one of the dominoes. Ask your child which domino she might change to avoid becoming so upset and punching something. Make suggestions if she cannot come up with ideas. Then line up a different row of dominoes from that point, showing the child that there could have been a whole different string of events as a result of changing only one event.

For example, if the "punching the door" domino was changed to running inside and telling Dad about the baseball glove, what would have happened? After you have used this procedure for a number of times, create a sign or a cue to represent the concept. (A finger making a tapping motion as if hitting a domino would do.) Then, at future times, you can ask, while using the cue, "What influenced that behavior? What did you feel right after that happened?"

Note: If you give your child practice with a feeling vocabulary then this activity will be more fruitful. Take the time to point out to your child how feelings influence behaviors and how behaviors influence feelings in others.

WHINING, OVER-SENSITIVITY, EXCESSIVE CRYING, COMPLAINING

Parents of hearing children might imagine that a deaf child does not whine because she doesn't use her voice much to express herself. But, oh yes, deaf children can whine. They whine with every inch of their bodies. Parents might surrender to the wishes of their child to avoid having to witness further whining. Soon, whining children discover that tears and a high-pitched voice help them to get their own way and to be excused from dealing with responsibilities.

As with tantrums and emotional outbursts, whining, excessive crying, and complaining are often a result of one or any combination of the following:

1. A deaf child may have limited practice in using language to effectively express her feelings. Whines, sobs, or incessant complaining become "catch-all" responses to a host of feelings and situations. To teach the child how to express feelings and problem-solving, you must help her learn how to identify specific difficulties that she experiences.

2. Poor frustration tolerance or an inability to delay gratification will cause a child to dissolve on the spot. The child feels like the world is "too much" for her to handle and this chips away at her self-confidence. Teach this type of child to gradually tolerate waiting and delaying gratification.

3. A child may have problems with attention, learning disabilities, or prob-

lems with sensory integration and may display a "melt down" behavior. This child may complain because she cannot pull herself back together. In essence, she is on overload and needs to regroup. Observe when your child breaks down and try to develop predictable and non-punishing strategies to cue, calm, and reorganize her. Consult with knowledgeable professionals (teachers, neuropsychologists, occupational therapists, learning disability specialists, and pediatricians) for suggestions and advice.

4. A child may have learned that by wearing down her parents, she gets what she wants. Note that we use the word "wants" not "needs." Once this pattern becomes established, your child will often ask for and receive more but never feel satisfied. The child's original intent may have been to have her needs met. For example, if a child has no deaf friends in the neighborhood and is picked on by other children she may "need" support, new friends, and help to feel good about herself. If she was not able to communicate her problem and did not find a way to feel better, she may have become possessive of the TV, crying each time the channel was changed. She displaces bad feelings onto this other situation. If parents give in to her demands regarding the TV, a negative pattern is created and she still feels badly about herself and has no friends to boot.

5. A child may not understand the steps that lead to emotional overload due to her limited ability to identify, differentiate, and express feelings as they are experienced.

While a deaf child may vocalize when whining or complaining, she is more likely to exhibit strong and pleading facial expressions; she may become physically intrusive by pulling on your shirt or standing in front of you; or she may use repetitive and insistent chanting, signs, or physical movements. If you decide to give in to your child's demand, do so immediately so that your child's perception of success (getting what she wants) is not strongly associated with mood persistence (continued whining).

Some deaf children find themselves picked on incessantly by peers, siblings, and neighborhood children. As a result, they might either become aggressive or withdraw in response. Often, a child who internalizes the jeers and bullying will look sad, complain, and hide from social interactions. This child needs to learn assertion skills (see "My View, Your View"; "Catch 'Em Communicating"; and many of the feeling activities in this chapter).

When you teach your child to speak her point of view, teach her also that her posture affects her message. Point out to her if her shoulders are slumped, her signing or voice is weak, her eyes are darting here and there, or she is pulling away. Encourage her to look at people directly, to sit or stand straight, to use strong signing or a strong voice, and to stay physically involved in communication.

Activities
. . . .
Activity #1: Say It Again, and I Will Listen
Materials: feelings education activities
Age: 5–12
Vocabulary/Concepts: repeat, LISTEN (with your eyes), HOLD (one-handed sign), right way
. . . .

When a child has developed a pattern of incessant complaining, she needs to learn a new method for expressing herself. An adult can help her to break the cycle. Practice the feelings education activities outlined earlier in this chapter to be sure that your child knows her options for how to identify and express what is on her mind.

Each time your child begins her cycle of weeping, whining, or complaining, ask her to explain herself in another way. You may want to develop a few reminder lines or cues, such as, "I want to listen but ask me another way" or "Say that again a different way" or simply "Hold" or "Say it again." If you are signing, you may want to do so without eye contact for a five- or ten-second interval while she is using a less-desired method of expression.

When you sense she has "paused," give her eye contact again and ask, "Now, what were you saying?" If you are speaking, deliver the cue and then look away momentarily. With this small intervention, you begin a new cycle of reinforcement—you attend when she uses new skills. By redirecting the child, you give the message that you are willing to listen to what she needs, but only in a useful and productive manner. In short, she knows you still care.

If she does not take the cue, walk away and indicate you will talk when she is ready. Do all of this in a neutral and terse manner and, by all means, be consistent. If you give her attention one day when she complains and not the next, she will keep using the undesired behavior.

. . . .
Activity #2: Best Time, Best Place to Talk
Materials: poster board, camera, markers, pencil, appointment-card-sized paper
Age: 5–12
Vocabulary/Concepts: best time, best place, later, busy, give attention, HOLD (one-handed sign), ONE-TO-ONE, SIT TOGETHER
. . . .

Sometimes a child may get into a cycle of complaining simply because she has tried to attract parental attention or support consistently during the "wrong" time or at the "wrong" place. If the child repeatedly interrupts a parent while the parent is on the phone, cooking dinner, or attending to another child, she may start to believe that the only way to get anything is to demand it.

For this activity use a camera that produces immediate pictures (a regular camera will do but is not preferable). Have your child take pictures of you doing a task from which you cannot be interrupted (cooking, on the phone, at the check-out stand in the store). Just for fun, put on an exasperated expression for the photo.

Next, take a few pictures of places where you find it difficult to have a conversation (in a public place, while still in bed, or in the bathroom). When you have your top five "no" places and situations, take pictures of your "yes" times and places. You may want to combine time and place by including a clock or a clock drawing in the photo to represent the time. Together with your child, make a poster entitled "Best Time, Best Place to Talk"—with a "yes" column of pictures and a "no" column.

For extra fun, you may want to make appointment cards and keep them (with a pencil) in a pouch beneath the poster. When your child asks to talk at a "no" time, pull out a card and write a better time to talk with a special message on that says "I love to talk to you" or "my special kid." If you are a two-parent household, take turns responding so that one parent doesn't become the sole problem-solver.

. . . .

Activity #3: A Sensitive Heart and Thicker Skin

Materials: tissues or paper towels, glass of water, (thick paper, paper bag, or piece of a plastic bag)

Age: 8–12

Vocabulary/Concepts: sensitive heart, sensitive, thick-skinned, PROTECT SELF, energy, accept, insult, tease, ignore, talk to self, ASSERT, SPEAK-UP, save energy

. . . .

Often when a deaf child can see a physical representation for a problem she finds it easier to understand, the child does not feel blamed, and, of course, it can be playful. When you have an over-sensitive child constantly picked on by peers, who doesn't know how to stand up for herself, and who becomes more sensitive as a result, it can be hard to give feedback without adding to the problem.

In this activity you will show your child what happens when she consistently absorbs insults, takes teasing to heart, and can't handle everyday confrontations. Begin by telling her that you have noticed that she has a "very sensitive heart" or perhaps a "very big heart" that makes her feel things strongly. Let her know that you love her for her big heart, but that you don't want to see her continue to suffer because she can't screen out things that don't belong in her heart, like insults or rejections.

Next, take a tissue or a paper towel and flatten it out. Let this represent her and all of the energy that she has in a day. Ask her to state something that she is sensitive about or offer your own example: "You complain that kids at school tease you—OK, pretend that this is Joe calling you a bad name." Pour a little water in the middle of the tissue and watch it spread. Compare this to the way one comment spreads and influences her. Give a second example and pour more water. By this time the tissue should be pretty soaked.

Ask her to explain what she sees. Point out that the nasty comments have absorbed all of her energy and made her full of negative thoughts. Ask her what she might do if she is filled up with negative thoughts and needs to go take a test, go to the lunch room, or stand in front of her class to give a report. Surely, feeling bad about herself will make all of these things difficult. She may even try to avoid them by saying she isn't hungry or by pretending that she is sick.

Now, how to show your big-hearted girl how to change all this? Get a thick piece of construction paper, a paper bag, or a piece of a plastic bag— anything that is somewhat water-repellent will do. Put this item over the tissue and talk about helping your child develop a "thicker skin" so that she can save her energy for better things. Use the same examples as before only this time pour the water on the water-repellent item instead of the tissue. Have her feel the tissue. Show her that the tissue is much drier. Explain to her that if she doesn't take teasing to heart then she will have much more energy and sensitivity left for the positive things that she chooses and her energy will not be based on what others do or say to her.

Ask your child to brainstorm with you ways that she might develop a thicker skin. Here are a few of our suggestions:

Ignore: A child can do this by turning her head; moving her chair; turning her chair; walking away; putting up her hand or book to cut out the stimuli; or telling someone, "I am not listening to you" and cutting off a conversation.

Self-Talk: A child can practice a few cues that help her redirect herself to other things. She can tell herself "They are trying to make me upset—Ignore them"; "I can control my energy"; "Count to ten"; "Focus on myself"; or "I can stay calm." Any mantra will work as long as it helps your child to keep from absorbing negative comments thrown at her.

Assertion: Have your child practice stating her opinion. (See the "My View, Your View" activity in this chapter.) Help her find one or two sentences she can say when someone is bothering her—"I don't like that so I am leaving."

Energy Conservation: Help your child to admit that something she has tried again and again to change will not change and that sometimes you just have to let things go (for example, a friendship that won't work out). Help her find other options to revert to; for example, making new friends, starting a hobby, getting involved in a new activity to meet other children; or seeking out people who accept her better.

And, while you are teaching your child smart ways for her to address taunting and teasing, you should also encourage her to tell you, her teachers, and other adults in authority about such incidents. It will then be time to teach her peers to respect differences.

The Many Manifestations of Hyperactivity

• • • • • • • • • • • •

Terrell Clark

Flitting . . . like a mosquito without a purpose. Picking up a toy truck, playing with it briefly, discarding the truck for a magazine, glancing at a picture, dropping the magazine, spinning briefly, pulling open a drawer, fiddling with the contents in the bureau, then turning to dart across the room. Making eye contact for half a sentence—rarely for a full comment or question. Never sitting through a full half-hour television show, even when keenly interested in the action. Sam was a slim boy of six with seemingly inexhaustible energy and with whom it was exhausting to live.

At ten, Jon was miserable in school. He was constantly being scolded. He just could not keep his hands to himself. He squirmed in his seat, fidgeted with pencils, tore through paper when he tried to erase mistakes. He argued with other children. He complained to teachers. He received occasional detention sessions and endless threats of loss of privileges. He would always start lessons and assignments with a dismissive shrug and could never seem to finish them.

Melissa, also ten, was fairly smart and liked books. Reading provided vivid adventure for her. She loved discussing stories and characters from books with the instructional aide in her class. Even when engrossed in such discussions,

Terrell Clark, Ph.D., is a licensed psychologist specializing in the development of deaf and hard of hearing children. She is director of an interdisciplinary clinical and research team at the Children's Hospital in Boston, Massachusetts.

the shadow of a fly on the windowsill could divert and momentarily capture her attention. She was the first to notice footsteps approaching in the hallway. In reading group, she never seemed as interested in what the teacher and her classmates were sharing as in what they were wearing. She was the only one to notice and comment on an unbuttoned shirt cuff. She was constantly interrupting the flow of the lesson in group time. Even though she did not always appear to be paying attention, she still seemed to learn everything . . . and showed that to the aide when they had one-to-one time together.

Three children—Sam, Jon, and Melissa—each deaf. One is overtly hyperactive. All three are inattentive in some way—easily distracted (and sometimes attracted to small and relatively inconsequential details of sights and events surrounding them), fidgeting (squirming, fiddling, or doodling), not focusing on the task at hand, impetuous seemingly without regard for potential consequences. The traits of inattention and distractibility, impulsivity, and hyperactivity contribute to their shared diagnosis of ADHD or Attention Deficit Hyperactivity Disorder. ADHD appears to be more prevalent among boys than girls—or at least more males are diagnosed than are females. In the general population, approximately three percent to five percent of school-aged children present with ADHD. No comprehensive study has been undertaken to determine the prevalence of ADHD in deaf children.

The attention deficits of children with ADHD vary. Some children exhibit difficulty "tuning in." Their attention may wander from the teacher in a class lesson, they may have trouble getting started on assignments and projects, ending one activity and shifting to a new one may prove problematic. Some children exhibit difficulty with sustaining attention. Once started, they do not persist with what they think of as "work." They have trouble completing assignments and projects. Some of these same children are able to play for relatively long periods of time when engaged in activities of their own choosing and yet do not persist with and complete tasks that others have directed them towards. Some children have trouble maintaining their focus of attention. They may appear restless, seem to *need* to move around, and tend to move from one thing to another. These children are the most likely to be seen as "hyperactive."

Regardless of the communication method (signed language, spoken language, written language, or a combination), considerable concentration and attention are necessary on the part of the child to access language and information. Problems with sitting still, concentrating, accomplishing transitions, and completing tasks therefore may have more serious implications for youngsters who are deaf than for other school children. Attentional difficulties can be most disruptive to the deaf child's basic communication.

At four years of age, Marcus had not yet acquired much language. Even if explanations were offered, he could not understand the "why" of consequences. He asserted himself through negative, even combative, actions. Nobody could seem to communicate with Marcus, and he could not explain himself. Running a toy firetruck along a ledge of the building outdoors at recess, he might suddenly find himself scooped up, the firetruck plucked from his grasp, and his arms pinned to his sides as people scolded him about the dangerousness of his activity. While he does not understand their words, he can read their expressions. The faces are not pleasant. He feels enraged. He kicks and tries to squirm free of the hands that hold him. He turns his face away and buries his eyes in his own shoulder. He is not a happy, playful preschooler. Big people here never smile at him, and he hates this place.

The inability to attend to language may so severely interfere with effective communication that a significant delay in language acquisition can occur with the ADHD deaf child. It is extraordinarily difficult to intercede with children who have limited language skills. With language, deaf children can accept explanations, negotiate behaviors and contingencies, express preferences, and comply with requests. Using language to explain rules and expectations is one powerful method adults use for teaching children how to conform socially. Without an understanding of the "rules" of socially acceptable behavior, children appear wild, disrespectful, even dangerous. While underlying ADHD may not account for all language acquisition problems, inattention and distractibility certainly can contribute to many difficulties with communication and behavior in deaf children.

How do parents determine whether a child has ADHD? Many preschool-aged children exhibit a high activity level, fairly short attention span, and impulsive behavior. In the context of appropriate expectations under certain circumstances—such as around the table at a family gathering or for a short lesson presented to a small group of children—most preschool youngsters can sit quietly and restrain themselves briefly. Exaggerated and repetitive patterns of overactivity, impulsivity, and inattentiveness distinguish ADHD in very young children.

When a repeated cycle of reprimand and correction becomes evident, parents may seek help in understanding their child's behavior and their own responses to the behavior. Sometimes, complaints about a child's "never sitting still" or being "oblivious to risks" or "not obeying rules" will lead a family physician or school teacher to question whether these behaviors stem from ADHD.

A diagnosis of ADHD is not made simply on impressions of overactivity, impulsivity, and inattention. Since ADHD is essentially a medical diagnosis of a neurodevelopmental or biological disorder, a physician is an essential player in the determination of this condition. Diagnosis is best handled by a team of specialists who have experience working with children who are deaf.

The evaluation process may require the involvement of a child psychiatrist, physician, pediatric neurologist, psychologist, and educational personnel. The diagnostic team should work in coordination with parents and teachers who have known the child in a variety of settings and for a long time. Evaluation components typically include a) conducting interviews and making direct observations; b) obtaining assessments of cognitive abilities, of psycho-social function, and of achievement; and c) conducting a physical and neurologic examination of the child. Through questionnaires and by observing the child, attentional qualities may be measured. The child's medical, educational, family, and developmental history is considered. This information may be gathered from written records as well as interviews with the parents, school personnel, and with child care providers. A vision screening is often advised. Psychological and educational tests may be indicated—including measures of intellectual functioning, visual-perceptual-motor abilities, academic achievement, adaptive behavior, and social-emotional adjustment. Since attentional difficulties, restlessness, and high activity patterns may accompany other medical and psychosocial conditions, the diagnosis of ADHD can be made only after ruling out other possibilities.

Though their impulsivity, insistent demands, difficulties concentrating, carelessness, and short fuses may make for exasperating times in the family, children with ADHD do not set out to purposefully misbehave. Making an accurate diagnosis is essential to implementing appropriate interventions. Understanding the diagnosis often helps parents cope and de-fuse previously volatile patterns of interaction. Understanding what behaviors the child cannot control will assist in developing a plan for behavior management. Psychoactive medication is often prescribed for children with ADHD. Medication in conjunction with behavior management techniques can have powerfully positive results.

One avenue of intervention is that of building skills and clearly conveying expectations to the child with ADHD. For the child's sake, adults need to make efforts to break the cycle of scolding, of dissatisfied looks and comments, of punishment—and to replace that cycle with genuine opportunities for the child to practice appropriate behaviors and build competencies. Make "rules" or expectations explicit (through charts and pictures if necessary) and reinforce the child's compliance through praise, smiles, check marks, star charts, and other positive incentives.

Break down tasks into smaller and more manageable steps so the child feels less overwhelmed. Simplify directions and assign short tasks that can be completed successfully. See the child through the steps of completing the task or project. Within the routines of the home and with the child's daily schedule, vary tasks frequently and expect only short periods of concentrated effort and "work." Some parents find that more eventually gets accomplished when they permit homework time to be interspersed with a chore, a shared activity, a video game, or setting out clothes for the next day.

Since the child may find comfort in predictability, use consistent schedules, rules, and routines. Anticipate changes in the usual schedule in advance—like upcoming holidays or vacations, an evening when there will be a babysitter, or visits by relatives. Some families find that using a calendar and communicating two or three times about the same anticipated change helps prepare their children for such occasions.

Many children with ADHD are overactive. A dilemma for parents of these children is whether to allow the child to run around to let off steam or to corral the child. These children have difficulty moving from undirected activities to structured tasks (such as coming in from playing outdoors and being asked to settle in to do homework). After school, many parents find that their children respond well to getting focused structured work done first and then unwinding with recreational activities afterward. So long as the child is engaged purposefully on a task or in an activity, adults may need to permit some movement and tolerate fidgitiness from a child with ADHD. Behavior that becomes frenzied or "out-of-control" will require adult intervention.

Sometimes, the child with ADHD is literally flooded with too much happening all at once. At such times the parent might try reducing the potential distractions and minimizing the confusion. Remove the child to a more contained and quiet location. Cut down on the number of people with whom the child must interact. Fewer demands can mean better compliance with those demands/requests that need to be made upon the child.

"Time out" can be used successfully as an intervention for deliberate non-compliance with a clearly stated "rule." The consequence of "time out" must, however, be applied with fairness and without passion or anger. The "rules" or expectations for appropriate behavior need to be clearly conveyed. Ask the child to restate the rules as a way to demonstrate true comprehension. Once assured that the child understands the rules, if the consequence for deliberate transgression is to be "time out," then the consequence needs to be consistently applied. "Time out" needs to be brief and the child then needs to return to the situation where the problem behavior arose and be given another chance to attempt compliance.

Whether following a schedule, marking off a check list of accomplishments, settling down when provided a quiet spot in which to do so, or complying with expectations after a "time out," interactions with children need to end positively. Nagging, punishment, and anger do not shape more competent, compliant, contained behaviors.

That Tina was deaf did not surprise her parents. Her older brother was also deaf. So was one of their uncles. Tina's brother, already in junior high, had also been diagnosed with ADHD and stimulant medication had been prescribed for him when he was eight years old. He had done well on the medication. Both his parents and his teachers noticed he was less "hyper" and less demanding. He accomplished more in school and he enjoyed being included in a circle of friends he had made at school. When relatives noticed and commented that Tina also seemed distractible and impulsive like her brother, her parents were not surprised. They had noticed too. Further, they had been told that symptoms of ADHD often appear in more than one family member. That Tina might also benefit from stimulant medication had not occurred to her parents because she was not intolerably overactive. One day, she was particularly excited about showing her father a ribbon she had won. Going from the living room to her bedroom to get the ribbon of which she was so proud, her parents counted nine detours Tina had taken. She had been attracted to or distracted by nine things that competed with her focusing on the source of her pride and exuberance. It was on that day that they decided to discuss with their physician the advisability of medication for Tina. Perhaps that intervention would also prove helpful to her.

Many different types of medications are prescribed for children with ADHD. Use of medication needs to be monitored. Often, physicians will use a questionnaire or rating scale to help quantify observations and monitor changes in behavioral patterns. Parents and teachers may be asked to report about the child's behavior, academic performance, and attentiveness, as well as about interactions with parents, siblings, teachers, and peers or classmates.

A combination of factors offers the best possible outcome for children who are deaf and who have ADHD. These include accurate description and diagnosis of ADHD (involving thorough evaluation by specialists experienced in working with deaf children), explanations and counseling offered to parents, implementation of behavior management strategies, conscientious efforts towards assuring positive interactions with the child and within the family, provision of effective and appropriate educational intervention, and, possibly, use of psychoactive medication.

RECOMMENDED READING

Carrillo, J. M. & Kim, M. M., (1992, May). *A Guide for Parents of Children with Attentional Difficulties.* (Available from Children's Hospital, 300 Longwood Ave., Boston, MA 02115.)

Goldstein, S. & Goldstein, M., (1990). *Managing Attention Disorders in Children.* New York, John Wiley & Sons, Inc.

Parker, H. C., (1992, May). *Children with Attention Deficit Disorders: ADD Fact Sheet.* (Available from Children With Attention Deficit Disorders (CHADD), 499 Northwest 70th Ave., Suite 308, Plantation, FL 33317.)

Parker, H. C., Storm, G., Petti, T. A., Anthony, V. Q., (1991, Fall/Winter). Medical Management of Children with Attention Deficit Disorders: Commonly Asked Questions. *Chadder,* (Available from Children With Attention Deficit Disorders (CHADD), 499 Northwest 70th Ave., Suite 308, Plantation, FL 33317.)

CHAPTER

Overactivity, Attention, and Impulse Problems

• • • •

If your child seems unusually active; has a hard time paying attention; and/or is sudden and impulsive in his behavior, this chapter is for you. The activities in this chapter have been designed to help parents and children learn to manage highly active and physically intrusive behaviors, impulsivity, short attention span, distractibility, and impatience. We encourage you to continually question whether your child is understanding and whether his excessive moving and impulsivity is his best attempt to understand and control his environment.

Unfortunately, children who tend to be impulsive, unresponsive to direction, and heedless of danger cause parents and teachers great worry and exhaustion. They also receive more than the average amount of negative feedback. This becomes an unfortunate pattern that reinforces diminishing self-worth and escalating behavior problems.

Paradoxically, the active and alert child can be very bright, full of fun, charismatic, observant, and truly enjoyable to know. But these attributes and skills are often overshadowed by a few disheartening and negative behaviors.

The activities we offer will not only be helpful for children who have been diagnosed with Attention Deficit Disorder (with or without hyperactivity) but for children who keep going and going and going—even they outlast the "Energizer." The activities aim to teach children how to recognize overactive behavior, stop and think, monitor their activity level, take control of their actions, and calm themselves down.

GENERAL OVERACTIVITY AND INATTENTION

A deaf child who shows attention problems or hyperactivity may be doing so due to neurobiological, communicative, health-related, or psychological reasons. Observe your child over time and in varying situations to get a better handle on the context of his behaviors.

ADHD (Attention Deficit/Hyperactivity Disorder) is defined as a neurobiological problem characterized by excessive and undirected motor activity, inattention, and underdeveloped impulse control. It is a diagnosis that should be made by a physician with critical input from those people who are close to the child, especially family and school. Often this child has the greatest difficulty with school demands

At times a child with ADHD may have significant problems with attention but does not appear to be hyperactive. This child may present symptoms of being "spacey," "disorganized," "forgetful," or "careless with tasks."

Findings show that heredity may play an important role in ADHD (it runs in families). It can also be associated with prenatal and perinatal problems (mother's health and habits during pregnancy, toxemia, long labor, and fetal distress).

A deaf child may exhibit overactive behaviors and a habit of physically exploring his environment because information has not been clear, not within eyesight, or not delivered in the most accessible manner. In short, he may be constantly searching for visual information to understand his world. We

The problems may look like this:

• • • • • • •

- The child acts like he had ten cups of coffee.
- The child moves from one item or task to the next in a matter of minutes.
- The child has difficulty in school.
- The child has difficulty with even short waiting periods.
- The child seems to enjoy struggling with a parent.
- The child is punished often.
- The child is labeled as "bad."
- The child often appears spacey and appears to tune out of conversations.

recommend that you consult professionals knowledgeable in deaf issues and ADHD who can help determine whether your child's behaviors are a result of ADHD, communication problems, and/or other factors.

A hyperactive deaf child, just like any other child, will generally respond well to clear and consistent communication. If communication issues are primarily responsible for the child's inattention, disobedience (not "listening"), impulsivity, or excessive activity, interventions should help the school and family become more attentive to his needs. While working with the school to intervene, you can use ideas described in this section and in the following activities with your child if he is not diagnosed as having ADHD.

A deaf child's vision maps what is happening around him. He may have a barrage of visual distractions, such as an ever-running TV, people and pets in motion, and glaring or dim light sources. Be sensitive to your child's visual environment and find ways to make it easier for your child to attend.

The inattentive and overactive child has difficulty concentrating on one task, sustaining attention over time, moving between tasks, and screening out peripheral or unrelated stimuli. A child can be easily distracted without being overactive.

An overactive or easily distractible child can, at times, be very attentive to certain situations or particular tasks. He tends to like new and stimulating material but within a predictable structure. People working with this child should keep this in mind. If your child's school does not employ organized and sensitive strategies in handling your child, then question whether they know what to do with such a child and encourage your child's teachers to seek additional consultation if you feel it is necessary.

The overactive and inattentive child is often impulsive as well. He does not stop to consider consequences—his behavior often appears to be rude and inconsiderate. Teach your child words and concepts to explain and categorize his behavior (attention difficulties, overactive, must keep busy) and avoid labeling him as "bad." Take full advantage of "windows of opportunity" by focusing on your child when he is being attentive.

Explain to the child that his behavior, and not he, is a problem. Point out to him cues that can indicate to him that he is becoming distracted (e.g., looking around, shaking a leg, breathing faster). Explore ways to help him start, maintain, and finish a task (problem-solving strategies, self-talking methods, reviewing cause and effect, and creating a predictable structure). Ultimately, the child can learn to monitor himself.

Help your child tune into his energy and attention level throughout the day, before and following specific activities and during transitional periods. Refer to activities in this chapter such as "Movement Metaphors" and "The Control Panel." Use fun, visual measurement indicators for this, such as clock

---

Tips for Tired Parents
● ● ● ● ● ● ●

● Having a child who is constantly on-the-go, needs non-stop reinforcements, and can step into dangerous situations at any time, can be tiring, to say the least. Here are some reminders to help you along the way:

1. Make things simple: Give simple directives, one step at a time. Furnish your child's room in a simple, pleasant manner with things to help with daily tasks (calendars, schedules, and certificates for good behavior). Make your expectations fit your observations of your child; prioritize what is important and try not to worry about the rest. Simplify stressful times (holidays, birthdays, vacations) so that you are not overwhelmed and left with no energy.

2. Reward with what is handy, not what you can buy: You have a smile, a hug, a wink, and kind words—use these as your child's rewards. Next, use items already in the house as rewards, such as TV, computer, swing, park, or skateboard time. Your child can earn

---

faces, timers, colorful calendars, eye-catching schedules, and playful metaphors.

An overactive and inattentive child has difficulty delaying gratification, finds waiting boring, and wants what he wants NOW! The parent is often put in the position of grabbing his hands, saying "no," and punishing the child. As a child gradually learns to use "waiting skills" such as relaxation techniques, imagery, pacing, and distraction, he will begin to feel better about himself.

Your child may frequently intrude into others' personal space. Children must learn to recognize the need for privacy (see chapters 6 and 8). Your child may use his hand to get attention (waving, tapping a shoulder or knee); however, if he pokes, slaps, tugs at clothes, or touches your face, you will need to redirect him. Be sure all family members respect agreed upon codes.

For some children, overactive or inattentive behavior may mask avoidance. If a child repeatedly experiences failure, he may have no incentive to finish a task. This, unfortunately, reinforces feelings of inadequacy. See that your child knows how to break a task down into manageable parts when

time for any of these pursuits based on behavior. You don't have to spend money rewarding good behavior or producing new thrills when your child becomes bored.

3. Make rewards quick and repeated.

4. Change rewards often (to keep ahead of your child's need for novelty) and make the rewards match your child's personality.

5. Find places and activities that offer your child the opportunity to excel and feel good about himself.

6. Make tasks active and make waiting fun.

7. Give yourself a break—you have earned it.

8. Do not get caught in a constant struggle with your child; don't struggle; do not struggle! This type of child will seek out a struggle because it is more stimulating than chores or homework. Walk away, laugh, tell a joke, count to ten, but avoid the struggle!

necessary so that he can experience success (completion) at frequent and regular intervals during the process. Search out tasks, skills, and hobbies that your child can master.

Many children show inattentive or hyperactive behavior when they are having emotional difficulties. Reflect on past and present stressors on your child. Consider having your child evaluated by a physician and mental health professional if you have questions about the cause of your child's behavior.

Harness your child's boundless energy and redirect it into productive activities, such as sports, hobbies, and even housecleaning. Provide structures that help organize him while affording him an opportunity for positive accomplishments and praise. Teach your child how to physically relax (using relaxation techniques) and to control his actions through "self-talk." Provide a calm, structured, and familiar atmosphere that he can depend on.

If your child is diagnosed with ADHD (showing inattentiveness, hyperactivity, or both), he may need to try a medication in addition to behavior modification, more structure, and learning how to handle his condition.

Activities

∙∙

Activity #1: The Relaxation Center

Materials: designated area of your home, bubbles, child's sunglasses, crepe paper, pinwheel, soothing pictures

Age: 6–12

Vocabulary/Concepts: relaxation center, breathe deeply, EXHALE-INHALE, peaceful

∙∙

When you say "relax" or "take it easy," your child may not know how to do that and may interpret that to mean "stop what you are doing." You can teach your child how to physically relax and mentally control impulsive actions. The techniques we describe aim at helping your child take control of his body and calm himself down. Once relaxed and in control, he is in a much better place to think through his actions and monitor his activity level. Create a special Relaxation Center for your child that includes a soft mat to lay on and the following "relaxation tools."

Breathing Tools

Simply telling your child to take a deep breath and calm down doesn't sound like fun. Grab his attention by playing breathing games:

1. Have your child take deep breaths and slowly blow into a bubble wand. Instruct him to make as big a bubble as possible until he makes a record-breaking bubble.

2. Using child-sized sunglasses, tape a piece of crepe paper or soft flexible paper of four inches in length onto the nose or bridge of the glasses. The piece of paper should be directly in front of his nose and fall down to his chin. Have your child put on the glasses, take a deep breath, and try to keep the paper off his face for five seconds. Make a game out of increasing the amount of time he must try to keep the paper afloat. Make sure he takes deep, long breaths and blows out the air as slowly as possible in order to keep the paper off his face.

3. Using a pinwheel, instruct the child to hold it at arm's length and see how long he can blow to keep the pinwheel going. You might put small stickers on the pinwheel when the child does well or write messages on small blank stickers such as "I can stay calm."

Picture Tools

Teach your child how to soothe himself through visualization and fantasy. First, look through magazines and picture books for peaceful environments and photos. Second, use these environments (like the ocean, the sky, or a meadow full of flowers) as the scenery for a visualization. Third, make up a story that places your child in that peaceful place.

My Own Tools
Discuss with your child at what times he feels relaxed and what causes this to happen. Encourage your child to come up with personal ways to calm down, such as reading a book, doing slow push-ups, or listening to music (if your child finds pleasure in this). Add calming tools to your Relaxation Center and praise your child when he offers a new suggestion.

You may want to design a "relaxing" area that resembles the "Cool, Calm, and in Control Corner." When your child begins to become overstimulated and frenzied, instruct him to go to the Relaxation Center and choose an activity that will help him calm down. Praise him for using the Center without being told. Model how to use the Center: listen to a relaxation tape, use the breathing exercises, or lay on a mat and close your eyes. Take relaxation tools with you when the family is away from home to avert overactive behavior.

• •

Activity #2: The Car Wash, The Bear Hug, or the Jelly Roll
Materials: soft blanket, soft cloth
Age: 3–12
Vocabulary/Concepts: feels good, like, dislike, bear hug, light touch, enough, FINISH! (one-handed sign), PREFERENCE MINE

• •

These techniques can relax and calm your child through light touch ("The Car Wash"), heavy muscle pressure ("The Bear Hug"), or close containment ("The Jelly Roll"). Based on your observations and discussions with your child, choose one of the three relaxing mechanisms. To make an appropriate choice you will need to know if your child has any averse reactions to light touch or close containment. If your child has sensory problems, then light touch might send him through the roof.

However, if your child doesn't mind light touch then try the "Car Wash" option. Have your child lay on his back, close his eyes, and give you his arm. Pretend to put his arm through a car wash. First the rinse—lightly run your fingers down his arm; then the wash—lightly massage his arm; then the rag wash—tickle his arm with a soft rag or cloth; then the rinse again—lightly run your fingers up and down his arm; and, finally, the blow-drying—blow on his arm lightly. Depending on your child's interest, age, and ability to sit through the Car Wash, the entire activity should take between one minute and a half-hour to complete. Remember to respect your child's right to refuse to be touched and make sure this relaxation activity is done upon his request.

If your child prefers firm pressure, then use the "Bear Hug" or the "Jelly Roll." Often children who like heavy pressure will seek out those people who hug solidly. Take a few minutes to give your child a firm, encompassing hug. Let him determine the amount of time this should take. Also, you may want him to tell you how to do it—"Should I wrap you with both arms, or one?"; "Do you want to sit in my lap or stand?"; "Would you prefer that I put both hands on your shoulders and press?"

If your child would like a variation on the above theme, have him pick a big blanket with a texture he likes. Ask him to lay straight in it and roll the edges tightly around him. Hold him in this position for as long as he likes and have a cue designed that tells you he has had enough. You may want to have a designated process you go through, such as counting to ten, or saying, "jelly roll, jelly roll, to gain control, to gain control" while you wrap him. Sometimes children like to roll themselves up and this, of course, should be encouraged as a self-control mechanism.

. . . .

Activity #3: The Control Panel
Materials: cardboard, markers, buttons, gadgets, string, paper
Age: 5–10
Vocabulary/Concepts: control panel, brain controls body, remote-
      control car, STAR button, distractor, you're great, fast, slow,
      practice, different situations, self-control (CONTROL INSIDE)
. . . .

This activity can help your child tune into his energy and make choices about what to do with it. Begin by telling your child that you believe deep within his mind and body he has the ability to control his behavior. This ability is sort of like a "Control Panel." You can use the example of a radio-powered car or airplane to explain to your child how a control panel actually works. He must turn on the control panel in order to control the speed and direction of his body. You may want to draw or find a simple illustration depicting how the brain controls the body's functions just as a control panel controls a remote-control car.

Make a control panel with your child by using a piece of cardboard, markers, string, paper, levers made out of paper, buttons, and lots of creativity. It must have a lever that controls speed, a start and stop button, and an emergency brake. Additional "options" include a "STAR button"; "distractor reactor" (a button to help him focus and pay attention); and a "you're great button" to put instant self-praise at your child's fingertips. You can make levers and buttons color-coded or make shapes very distinct so that your child has ways to visually discriminate between the various controls.

When the control panel is finished, plug it in. Use a piece of string to connect the control panel to your child. Have him respond as if the panel controls his movements. Turn the panel toward your child so that he can see what buttons and levers you are using. Playfully test the panel by holding it in your hands and turning it on and off, moving it fast and slow, and using the emergency button to stop action immediately. Pretend you are at the restaurant, playground, classroom, doctor's office, and maneuver your child through each of these situations. Press the "you're great" button each time your child responds by controlling his behavior.

Model control by connecting yourself to the panel and having your child maneuver you through some situations. Have him hold the panel and take control of his own body. Have your child practice how he would control his behavior in a variety of situations. Explain that the panel may be made out of cardboard but it really exists within him. Show him how he can mentally use the panel to interrupt behavior, control actions, slow down, and think before he acts. You can encourage your child to use his panel by making statements such as, "press your STAR button" or "quick, press the emergency stop button" or "pull down the lever and slow it down."

. . . .

Activity #4: Movement Metaphors
Age: 4–10
Vocabulary/Concepts: animals, slow, fast, normal, activity level, animal
        match situation
. . . .

This activity will help your child to: 1) identify when his activity level is calm, normal, or highly active; 2) understand the appropriate activity level for a specific situation; and 3) use methods to focus his attention and take control of his behavior. Metaphors can help children notice when they start to lose control and assist them in visualizing how to monitor their behavior.

Using your child's favorite animals, pick out ones that are fast (a rabbit, a jaguar, or a lizard), normal (a dog on a leash or a young pony) and slow-paced (a turtle, a prowling cat, or an elephant). Explain that you are going to teach your child how he can feel himself becoming "wild" and how he can slow his actions down by pretending to be these animals. Play act the selected animals and depending on the "style" of the animal, make slow, normal, or fast movements.

Have your child move to the pace of each of the selected animals. Ask your child how it feels inside when he is wild, normal, or calm. Play a game in which he must look carefully at you and guess the animal you are imitating. Once he has a good sense of these slow, normal, or fast animal behavior cues, praise his ability to control his speed. Practice using different animal speeds in a variety of situations.

Now you have a reference by which your child can measure his pace.

Plan, prepare, and prevent your child from becoming out of control by alerting him to the certain situations that require calm and normally active behavior. Prior to going to the supermarket, tell him the animal's activity level that you require. Combine this activity with the STAR technique and just before he loses control suggest he "think about" which animal pace he should be doing with his body. Playfully indicate to your child that he is becoming too active by pretending to be the animal that moves at that pace.

You can use the movement metaphors with a reward system. Your child can earn a sticker on a chart each time he follows cues (independently or with your help) and chooses the appropriate speed level. Decide upon the number of stickers needed to obtain a reward. Give small animal surprises (a coloring book on elephants or a small toy turtle) for good efforts at self-control.

● ●

Activity #5: The Cool, Calm, and in Control Corner

Materials: designated area of home, table, chair, crafts that help your
     child concentrate and focus, construction paper, crayons,
     coloring books, origami, music and tape player, relaxation tools
     (see pgs. 263–265), STAR worksheet
Age: 5–12
Vocabulary/Concepts: CALM, control, break, HYPER (jumpy)
● ●

Explain to your child that, together, you will be making a special place for him to practice and use skills for controlling over-active behavior. Acknowledge that you understand how very difficult it is for him to slow down and listen to directions. Therefore, this special corner of the house (family room, bedroom, or living room) will become the "Cool, Calm, and in Control Corner" (CCC Corner).

Here are several suggestions for setting up the CCC Corner:

● Choose an area of a room where your child will not become distracted. An actual "corner" of a room might help to limit your child's visual field. Try placing a small table and chair facing a wall.

● Put books, games, and crafts in the CCC Corner that support controlled and quiet concentration skills. Identify activities that your child finds interesting but that require him to sit at a table, such as playing cards, doing crossword puzzles, coloring with crayons or markers, doing origami (paper folding), knitting, doing needlepoint, and fitting together puzzles. Include well-tested activities that tend to focus your child for a period of time.

● If your child hears well enough to enjoy music, place a tape recorder on the table with tapes that tend to focus your child.

- Have relaxation tools available to him (see activity "The Relaxation Center" on pgs. 263–265)

- Decorate the wall with pictures that your child feels are calming and comforting.

- Put a big star on his wall to remind him to stop and think before he loses control.

- Place a timer on the table. Decide which overactive behavior he needs to gain control of. Anytime your child becomes over-stimulated or out of control, direct him to the corner and set the timer for the amount of minutes he needs to regain control. Consider setting up a reward system to reinforce his use of the corner (see "Chart and Reward" Program pgs. 57–58 and Appendix B).

Model using the corner to calm down when you become over-active. We do not suggest using the corner punitively. Children should identify this space as a positive place where they can go to calm down. It should be enjoyable and have firm "play" guidelines. Pack up a few activities from the corner and make a cool, calm, and control bag "to go."

Activity #6: Put on Your Shades

Maintaining eye contact can be difficult for an over-active child. And with a deaf child, this poses a drastic obstacle to a parent's ability to guide, warn, cue, and divert a child from danger. Teach your child more sustained eye contact by using imaginary glasses that help him pay attention and look at you without becoming distracted. When your child is able to look at you *without* his "glasses," note how terrific his eyes have become and how his glasses must be correcting the problem.

Activity #7: The Sign
Age: 5–12
Vocabulary/Concepts: time, time left, clock, HOLD (one-handed sign),
WAIT

Have your family decide upon a simple sign to do with your hands, such as an index finger or a "hold" ASL sign, to indicate that a family member is being demanding or interrupting someone and needs to wait. Use this sign to help your child recognize when he is interrupting. Give him a time limit within which you will respond to him (e.g., one minute later, in five minutes).

Sometimes pointing to the clock hands or writing down at what time you will talk to him allows your child to keep checking on his own until the promised time. Respond at the time you had stated you would or give a good reason to postpone. Don't use "in five minutes" as a catch-all phrase that really means anywhere from five to thirty minutes. This makes waiting highly unpredictable for your child. In addition, he will bug you every minute to know if it is time yet. Encourage your child to count the number of seconds he needs to wait (distraction) before you will respond to him.

IMPULSIVE ACTION OR REACTING WITHOUT THINKING

An impulsive child has an action plan that usually includes two steps. For example, see/do, want/grab, feeling/discharge. The primary missing link between the two steps is pausing to think.

The deaf child in a hearing family may have learned some of these habits as a result of being a voracious explorer in a hearing environment. The child should be encouraged to explore, wonder, and question but should also be taught restraint.

Many children take action before considering how their choices of behavior may affect them later. If a deaf child shows impulsive behavior, then pay close attention to communication issues. You can help this child by intervening with clear language and cues.

It may be the breaks in communication rather than his inability to hear that contribute to impulse control problems. Communication and language are significant variables in impulse control since language naturally curbs action. With a young, deaf toddler "no" begins to mean "halt." However, as the child gets older, language must serve as an explanation, a redirection, and a method of expression. If a deaf child is taught and understands communica-

---

The problems may look like this:

● ● ● ● ● ● ●

- The child touches things immediately—no restraint.
- The child is out the door, in the treetop, and in the street without a worry.
- The child repeats an action for which he was just punished.
- The parents feel that they are always reacting to behavior.

tion and cues, he can use self-talk ("Mommy said no"), he can express himself instead of acting ("Dad, I want the other color!"), and he can negotiate ("Please, I want to go now").

In order to develop problem-solving skills, a child must (1) learn to control impulses; (2) understand what is a "right" or "wrong" behavior; (3) understand consequences to behavior; (4) think his choices and consequences through; (5) learn that there are not only "right" and "wrong" choices but many in between; (6) understand his responsibility in a choice; and (7) be encouraged to assess, review, and try again if necessary. Pre-school and kindergarten children can manage the first three skills; children age seven or eight can internalize and think about consequences; and by ages eight to twelve the last steps can be mastered. You should use words like "choice," "think," "responsibility," and "consequence" throughout your child's development.

When an impulsive child "reacts," you may "react" as well. The more your reactions are based on consistent plans and cues to teach your child control, the sooner your child will develop these skills.

Although punishment seems unavoidable at times, notice how often you do this. Punishment gives scant information to the child. Over time, this may result in a "bad boy" self-image and might increase undesirable behavior (which in turn means more punishment). Verbal explanations and a gradation of privileges and reinforcements teaches understanding, responsibility, problem-solving, and consequences for actions.

Activities

....

Activity #1: Starman/Starwoman
Materials: STAR technique (see pgs. 49 and 50), star stickers, cape
   or piece of material, chart
Age: 5–12
Vocabulary/Concepts: STAR, man, woman, stop, think, act right,
   practice, think for yourself (THINK-SELF)

....

An impulsive child responds quickly and without thinking; he acts on his first thought instead of considering alternatives or consequences. This activity is based on the "STAR" technique (see pgs. 49–50), which teaches your child to replace impulsive actions with a step-by-step process of thought. He is taught to tell himself (by signing or speaking) and then silently (with no gesture or voice) to stop, think, and then choose the appropriate action.

Begin by teaching your child the meaning of STAR. Use role-plays to show

how to employ STAR. Explain that for one day your child will become a STAR Man (or Woman). Throughout the day, look for STAR behaviors and give him a sticker in the shape of a star every time he stops, thinks, and acts right. Depending on your child's age and interest, you can make a cape for him to wear all day and use this cape to stick his stars on. Some children prefer the stickers to be stuck to their body. An older child may want to have his accumulated stickers put on a chart. Decide how many stars are needed for a reward. Ignore all impulsive behavior unless it is dangerous. Make the number of stars required correlate with your child's capabilities. When he stops and thinks for a second, stick a star on him and inform him that he is behaving like a STAR Man or Woman. You can use the star stickers preventively by positively reframing his actions and giving him a star before he does something impulsively. You could say, "Wow, I saw you stop for one second before you touched that vase!" Playact with your child future situations where a STAR Man handles frustration, crossing the street, and going into a toy store. Do this activity as often as necessary.

Activity #2: The Stop Sign

Materials: red construction paper, markers, scissors, large cardboard box, two soft pieces of cord, paint, aluminum foil
Age: 3–5
Vocabulary/Concepts: stop, car, stop sign, FINISH! (one-handed sign)

The most important concept of the STAR program for children ages three to six is to first get them to "stop." To get this point across you may want to make several red stop signs out of construction paper. Show your child stop signs on the road and have him observe what you do (stop, look around, and then proceed). Next, make a car for him by cutting out the top and bottom of an old box and putting two soft cords from front to back so that the car can fit over him with the two cords resting on his shoulders. Draw or paint doors, handles, a trunk and a hood. Make a mirror out of cardboard and aluminum foil and a wheel that your child can hold and turn. The wheel can simply be a circle cut from the remaining cardboard and left unattached to the car.

Have your child drive around the house, the yard, or with other car "friends." Hold the stop sign up randomly and praise him when he stops. Dropping the stop sign means he can go. Use the sign/word for "stop" to correspond with the use of the stop sign. You may want to post the stop signs up around the room and have your child independently navigate a course . If your child needs immediate reinforcers, reward him with stars (placed on his car) each time he stops on his course.

The next task is to transfer this concept to daily living. You may want to have the stop signs handy in various places throughout your house so that you can pick them up easily to playfully reinforce the concept. Good places to have signs available might be at the front door (stopping your child from running out of the house), in the kitchen (noting when your child needs to be careful), near his play area (stopping your child when he is being destructive), or in any area of your home that your child tends to exhibit impulsive behavior. As time goes on, just use the word *stop* to indicate the action. Before you admonish or redirect a child, always tell him you noticed when he was able to stop his action—even if it was only for a second.

Activity #3: The STAR Statue
Materials: STAR technique (see pgs. 49–50)
Age: 5–10
Vocabulary/Concepts: stop, think, decide, THINK-SELF, DO-DO?

Play the stop, think, and act statue game in which your child becomes a statue while he stops and thinks before he acts in an impulsive way. Have your child freeze or stop in place before he continues an impulsive behavior. Have him think out loud of what his choices are and then go ahead with an action. Practice different situations with your child. Use the phrase "STAR" as a part of your everyday language.

Remember to teach your child to reverse STAR to "RATS" (see pg. 50) to remind himself that a STAR Man makes mistakes and he can always try, try again.

Activity #4: Choices
Materials: masking tape or chalk, paper, markers
Age: 8–12
Vocabulary/Concepts: problem situation; DO-DO?; good, bad, or in-
    between choices; solutions; assess; try, try again; MULL-OVER

As adults, we have ways of problem-solving—but how do we teach these to our children? To successfully teach any concept, make the lesson playful, have visual and tactile structures, and create a cue for later reference.

You will need masking tape to tape the floor or chalk if you want to do this in your driveway. It is best to have at least five people involved in this game so invite family and friends. Entice your child by soliciting his help to tape or chalk a square on the floor and label it with a question mark. Next, draw or tape two lines going from this square five feet in a diagonal direction.

At the end of each line, write or tape a paper bearing the words "good idea" and "bad idea."

One person begins by standing in the question mark box, which represents a situation, problem, or confusing circumstance. The person names some topic that he would like some feedback on, such as, "I don't know who to invite to my birthday party." Half of the remaining people stand at the "good idea" side and half at the "bad idea" side. Their job is to discuss the situation and come up with an idea that is "good" or "bad" depending on where they stand.

The person with the problem then walks up the "good" line and hears many good ideas for solutions. Examples of good ideas might include "Invite family and friends in your class." He returns to the question box and walks up the "bad" line and hears some "bad" ideas. Examples of bad ideas might include "Tell people you will invite them if they bring you a big present." Children are often hesitant at first to give bad ideas, but then they get a kick out of it once they understand they are permitted to do this. By showing that bad ideas are options that a person can refuse or choose, you stress individual responsibility.

The person with the problem then returns and thinks about what he has heard and decides which advice he will use. He should be encouraged to think about and discuss the consequences of the suggestions. Ask questions or model asking yourself, "Which idea is a good one?"; "Which one will get me in trouble?"; "I would like to do the bad idea because . . . but maybe that would not solve the problem."

Variations on this game include switching bad and good idea teams, having two people who are sharing a problem seek advice together and decide on the best courses of action, playacting the ideas to see what the results would be, making situation cards to encourage ideas or to help those who don't want to admit problems, and drawing more lines in the middle ground area to highlight the concept that many decisions are not bad or good but simply require weighing options.

Later, you can cue your child to this activity by asking "Is that a good, bad, or in-the-middle choice?"; "Well, you tried one idea that did not work—can you go back to the question box and think of choices?"; and "That action was your choice; do you remember some of the other ideas or do you need a "good" idea helper?"

The Parents' Role in a Deaf Child's Education

•••••••••••

I. King Jordan

*T*here is universal agreement that the value of an education for all citizens is so great as not to be in question. The current movement to provide full access to education for all citizens, including the millions who are among the disabled community, speaks to our belief in this value judgment.

Thomas Jefferson termed education "the chief instrument" of progress essential to democracy.

Daniel Webster described education as "the great lever of all things."

Horace Mann, who was a leader in public education and a champion of special education in the 1800's, believed education to be "the great equalizer of the conditions of men—the balance-wheel of the social machinery."

It was Benjamin Franklin who said, "If a man empties his purse into his head, no one can take it from him."

On the lighter side, Mark Twain observed: "Training is everything. The peach was once a bitter almond; cauliflower is nothing but cabbage with a college education."

There is indeed an equalizer for deaf persons. That equalizer is education. Most of society's doors, which historically have been closed to deaf persons and

I. King Jordan, Ph.D., is a psychologist and the president of Gallaudet University in Washington, D.C.

other members of the disabled community, are now open. Recent legislation, especially the Americans with Disabilities Act, marks a final turning point in the achievement of these opportunities for access. To help our deaf children seize this moment is among the greatest gifts that parents can provide.

The axiom, "education commences at the Mother's knee" was never truer than for the deaf child. The role of family in the educative enterprise is crucial for all children. For the deaf child, the family and larger community should become major partners in education. A colleague of mine, Dr. Mervin Garretson, wrote a paper several years ago that he called "The Unwritten Curriculum," in which he described the extensive amount of time involved and the opportunities available in out-of-class learning.

Surprisingly, children spend only about eight percent of their time in specific classroom activity.

Dr. Garretson quoted the scholar, Henry Steele Commager, who wrote, "It is, after all, the community which performs the major part of education, not the schools; it performs through a hundred miscellaneous institutions from family to farm, from government to playing field, from churches to labor unions, from newspapers and journals to comics and radio, and, above all, television."

For the deaf child, too often the school must fill the void that, for the hearing child, is assumed within this unwritten curriculum provided by the community. The community is a physical presence but often is not communicatively accessible to the deaf child, thus these thousands of learning opportunities are lost and must be gained by other means. Of course progress is being made in this regard, largely through telephone, television, and computer technology, but much out-of-class time for the deaf child remains less productive than desirable.

As children, we all have our heros and role models. This is equally true for deaf children, but we must not overlook the importance of helping them identify deaf persons among those role models. It is the responsibility of both the school and family to ensure that deaf children have an opportunity to establish goals and explore possibilities for their future. Within this context a few fantasies are in order, to be sure. They have the right to dream of being police officers, firefighters, astronauts, brain surgeons, or anything they desire. Deaf children, however, must have the opportunity to meet and know successful deaf adults as a part of their educational experience, both at home and at school. In this regard, a personal experience comes to mind.

During my presidency of Gallaudet University, I have tried to visit as many schools and programs for deaf children as my schedule permits. Shortly after becoming president, I was visiting classes at a school for the deaf in Rhode Island. My visit had attracted a good deal of media attention and I was being accompanied by several reporters and a television crew. I entered a classroom of six-year-old students and sat down with them (on one of those tiny chairs that is so uncomfortable for adults but puts you on an appropriate level with the kids). As I chatted with the class, one little boy got up and walked over to my side. He leaned on my shoulder with his elbow. He looked at me and smiled. I looked at him and smiled. There was an instant bond between us, a bond that occurred because of our deafness. He didn't know who I was and probably had never heard of Gallaudet University. But he knew that I was deaf and, because of all the media attention, he knew that I must be someone important. It is hoped that many such opportunities will occur for this young man to meet successful deaf people as his education progresses and his future is shaped by family, school, and community.

Perhaps the most important educational decision you will ever be asked to make on behalf of your child is that of finding the right school placement. Fortunately, schools are becoming much more sensitive to the need for a partnership between school and parent on all major matters affecting our children. Both specific placement and the appropriate array of services needed by our children are finally becoming a negotiable set of decisions between school and family. It is, therefore, crucial that parents make every effort to be informed about those services that the school is capable of providing and the extent to which these fit what is known about the student's needs.

We should remember that schools are obligated to inform parents about all options available, both within the local setting and outside the home community, should the local setting be judged as inappropriate to meet the student's specific educational needs. We should remember also that no placement should be considered as "cast in concrete." If a placement doesn't work well for the individual student, change should be considered. We should not assume that a particular kind of placement is best for our child throughout the elementary and secondary years. Students should have opportunities for change in placement as their needs and desires change. For example, many students enjoy the atmosphere of a special school during their adolescent years when opportunities for social and recreational pursuits may be restricted in the mainstream environment. Some combination of special school and mainstream classes may be an appropriate option for others. It is becoming increasingly rare that a student spends an entire school career in the same type of school placement.

In my opinion, there is one ingredient to a good placement that is the number one priority: communication accessibility. When there is not open and meaningful communication between and among the student, peer group, and all persons who are a part of the educational team, everything else becomes relatively less important.

Parents have to contend with too much educational jargon in the process of working with the school setting. It is important to ask questions and to avoid being intimidated by terms that are unclear or confusing. One such term that we hear often and have wrestled with over the years is *least restrictive environment.* This term, along with *mainstreaming* and *integration,* frequently is used to define an approach to placement that presumably mandates placement of all disabled children in regular classes attended by non-disabled children within the local neighborhood school. More recently these terms are being used somewhat interchangeably with the term *inclusion.* Interestingly, these terms are not defined in federal and state laws and regulations. It is important, therefore, to be aware of more flexible, and equally credible definitions for these concepts. Inclusion, as well as Least Restrictive Environment, need not be defined as *place* oriented. Increasingly, inclusion is being defined as an idea that incorporates basic values that promote participation, friendship, and interaction in all aspects of education and community life. Organizations such as the Conference of Educational Administrators Serving the Deaf (CEASD) are defining *inclusion* as a philosophy that:

● Maximizes the child's abilities and potential;

● Facilitates direct communication access with other persons;

● Enables the child to function as an active, independent, and full participant; and

● Promotes the child's self-esteem, confidence, and competence in a natural and comfortable manner.

To be included, the child must actually feel included, thus the school that calls itself an inclusive school must meet these criteria. Recent federal policy guidance on behalf of services to deaf students has reinforced this notion about the concepts of *inclusion* and *least restrictive environment.* This places the business of program placement and service provision back where it belongs: at the level of individual need and preference.

School was never meant to be all excitement and thrills where new insights come quickly and with minimal effort. Much of school involves self-discipline and hard work on the part of all students, but the rewards of mastering a new concept, of meeting goals and deadlines, of contributing to a class enterprise are enough to satisfy the motivational needs of most students. The child who will thrive educationally is the one who enjoys a school setting where communication flows freely, where services are readily accessible, where there is an atmosphere of caring along with challenges, and where inclusion is evident through demonstrable attitudes and daily events. It is this process, not the location, that determines freedom from restrictiveness and that largely determines whether the child sees school as a daily chore or an opportunity. If the child feels empowered and has a large measure of ownership in the educative enterprise, rather than being only a passive participant, then the probability of success is virtually ensured.

For parents, the sometimes formidable task is locating that desirable school setting, especially when it doesn't already exist in or nearby the home community. Next is ensuring that a school/home/community partnership is forged. This requires much time and energy and thus is never easy, regardless of family structure and situation (i.e., traditional, single parent, foster, or other). Parents must become personally and directly involved with the school, assuming an equal responsibility with the school for assisting the deaf child to demonstrate her best effort and maintain a high motivational level.

The future for our deaf children has never looked better. Opportunities for them to participate fully in our society's occupational, civic, social, and leisure activities are improving rapidly. Barriers are coming down and in their place, bridges are being built: public policy bridges, technology bridges, and, most importantly, bridges to the hearts and minds of John Q. Public. Public sensitivity to and understanding of the needs of disabled persons, the final hurdle to equality and accessibility, is rapidly becoming a reality.

In view of this outlook for continued improvement within our society for opportunity on behalf of deaf people, let me return to my earlier premise. As opportunities improve, demonstrated ability becomes increasingly important. Education, then, is and will be the equalizer—the development of skills and talent through education will make the difference. If opportunity is denied it will be because skills are not in evidence, not because of deafness.

Finally, it is important for parents to know and appreciate that the profession of education of the deaf is not without controversy. There have been and continue to be issues on which no universal agreement exists. A colleague at Gallaudet University, Dr. Donald Moores, has identified the major controversies in the form of three deceptively simple questions:

- Where should deaf students be taught?

- How should deaf students be taught?

- What should deaf students be taught?

The Where question, of course, leads us to the placement issue, especially the various arguments relative to merits of mainstreaming vs. special schools.

The How question suggests the age-old oral/manual controversy as well as more recent discussions about the relative merits of one way of signing over another in the educative process.

The What question suggests the relative emphasis in curricular areas. For example, should schools include extra measures of instruction and practice in the areas of speech and auditory training, and more recently in sign communication and Deaf culture? If so, how can this be done while still giving adequate emphasis on basic subject areas?

Parents face the task of trying to understand these controversies as well as dealing with the prospects of conflicting advice from well-meaning professionals. There is no one right or wrong answer to these where, how, and what questions. Although education is conducted largely as a group process, it is very individual in nature. Accordingly, the Individual Educational Program (IEP) process is crucial to arriving at many of the decisions embedded in these questions. Parents must take an active role in the IEP development for their child. This is important in understanding the complexities of program decisions, being a part of those decisions, and ensuring that your child is protected from decisions made without adequate information or based on administrative convenience.

CHAPTER

13

School Problems
• • • •

The school can play an important role in a deaf child's communicative, social, and cultural development. This chapter covers specific problems in deaf education, such as those related to mainstreaming, handling learning disabilities, and helping your child adjust to a school's educational "style." We will also address more universal parenting issues such as having a child who does not do homework or lacks motivation.

Children are excited and eager learners; they want to know everything—why, how, and what for? They live for learning, loving, and pleasing parents and teachers. They seek mastery, control, and competence; yet so many children have difficulty in school with behavior, academics, and homework.

This chapter offers ways for you to encourage your child to become a better student, gain self-confidence, understand and state her needs, and navigate and succeed in a deaf-sensitive educational system. Remember that you are your child's first and most important teacher.

DIFFICULTIES RELATED TO MAINSTREAMING

The mainstreaming of deaf children into hearing schools can take a number of forms. The following listing of these forms was derived from the book, *Can't Your Child Hear?* (Roger D. Freeman, Clifton F. Carbin, and Robert J. Boese, PRO-ED Inc., 1981).

1. The child can be placed in a hearing classroom with some additional support.

2. The child can be placed in a hearing classroom and receive daily contact with a resource teacher who works specifically with deaf students.

The problems may look like:

● ● ● ● ● ● ●

- Child is struggling to keep up with all classes.

- Child has no stories about "special friends" and does not have after-school buddies.

- School has bad acoustics and lighting in classrooms, teachers do not set up the lessons for optimal visual pacing, teachers misuse the interpreter, and classroom has poor setup/seating.

- Parents do not feel they share the same experience with other school parents.

- Student studies on the floor, with the dog, captioned soap operas and visitors streaming through the room.

- Student waits until the last minute before bed to begin homework.

- Student breaks down in tears because Mom is not helping her with her project due tomorrow.

- Parents stay awake until 3:00 A.M. pulling the child's project together.

- Student teases, distracts, and jokes in class.

- Student makes no progress in academics even when trying hard.

- Student is angry, oppositional, and refuses to do schoolwork.

3. The child can be based in a specialized class while taking some academic classes in the hearing classrooms.

4. The child can spend a majority of her time in the specialized classroom and be mainstreamed into gym and art classes with hearing classmates.

Since deafness is a low-incidence condition (approximately one in a thousand children has a severe/profound hearing loss in early childhood), areas with smaller populations will have very few deaf children. In a small community, a school with a mainstreaming program may have only one deaf child in the school. If your child lives in a more populated area she may have a few deaf peers. Town educational departments have, at times, combined funds to create regional deaf educational programs.

In the 1960s there was an increase in the number of deaf school-age children due to the rubella epidemic. Day schools primarily accommodated this new group of deaf children.

There have been legal (Public Law 94-142) and social factors that have contributed to parents and educators favoring mainstreaming over residential schools for deaf children. Public Law 94-142 (The Education for All Handicapped Children Act, amended as The Individuals with Disabilities Education Act in 1990) was passed in 1975 and came as a result of court cases focusing on the public education of developmentally disabled children with a diagnosis of mental retardation. Prior to this law, many students with a mild/moderate deafness diagnosis were being served in public schools, while those with a profound/severe diagnosis were often in residential schools. Parents and educators had sought ways to make the residential deaf student become a more integral part of her family life. This move contributed to a prioritization of integrating deaf students into regular school programs.

Public Law 94-142 emphasizes provision of the "least restrictive setting" for disabled students. There has been much debate over what "least restrictive" means for deaf children. If a deaf child is isolated, lacks deaf peers, has teachers and hearing classmates who are insensitive to deafness issues, does not communicate directly with her teachers, and does not have adequate support, then we should question whether mainstreaming is "more restrictive" for this child.

If a child is mainstreamed and she is not a part of a specialized "deaf" program, the parents may find that they have a "different" status among other parents. The parents of a deaf child may have a difficult time finding parents and professionals who understand their position and needs.

The trend in educating deaf children at this writing is focused on public day school settings (approximately sixty percent) and publicly funded residential programs (approximately twenty-five percent). The obvious advantage to a day program is that the child (particularly in younger years) can live at home with her family. The advantage to a residential facility is that it gives the child a linguistic, cultural, and social network. Throughout a child's development, parents must monitor the deaf child's communicative, academic, and social gains. At all times, the school placement should match the child's developmental needs.

One of the obvious goals of mainstreaming deaf children is to integrate them into a hearing body of students. While a deaf child may show academic success in such a setting, she may also have difficulty making important social connections with hearing peers. This will become more apparent as the child reaches the ages of eight through twelve since peer contact, alliances, and approval become more important to the child at this time.

The deaf child who is comfortable using her speech and has enough residual hearing to carry on conversations with hearing students is likely to feel more socially comfortable among them than the child who cannot use speech. The child who does best in a mainstream situation is usually one who has

1. Residual hearing enabling her to follow spoken language in individual and group situations;

2. Speech that is understandable to hearing peers and teachers;

3. Average or better intellectual skills;

4. Good self-control;

5. Patience; and

6. Assertion skills allowing her to ask questions, obtain explanations, and demand support when needed.

When the school makes specific efforts to promote more interactions between hearing and deaf students, the deaf student's social experience improves. Simply adding more mainstream classes will not suffice. Any interactions must take into account the needs of the deaf child and support sensitivity (not sympathy) by hearing peers. One cannot expect social and communicative barriers to be acknowledged and overcome by students without providing them with appropriate vehicles for doing so.

Interpreters are an invaluable resource in mainstream settings. However, an interpreter cannot guarantee that a teacher will be sensitive to the deaf student's needs, and the interpreter does not take the place of intimate communication between teacher and pupil or among students. Nor is an interpreter always available, adequately trained, or a good linguistic match for a student.

Forming Your Relationship with Your Child's School

Once you have looked closely at your child's desires and her skills with regard to spoken and receptive English, patience, assertion, and learning independence, then you can make the decision to mainstream her and at this point you must prepare school personnel. As a parent you can insist on a number of things. At minimum, you can ask that all school personnel participate in an inservice about deafness; that those working directly with your child understand her communication needs, which might include their taking a sign language class; that teachers are well aware of how to use interpreters; that the classroom environments are conducive to your child participating to her fullest; that a person trained in deaf education be available to your child; and that hearing students are prepared and sensitive to deafness issues before your child arrives.

You may want to set up informal meetings (lunch at your home, for example) with your child and her primary teachers. Consider contacting a deaf adult who was mainstreamed to give you (and your child) feedback on what this was like. You may find such a person by contacting any agencies servicing the Deaf in your area or contacting NAD (National Association of the Deaf) to see if there is a local chapter in your area.

This kind of planning is best done early in your child's educational career. Later, if your child remains in a mainstream setting, she will likely adapt to many problematic conditions. Problems such as teachers standing behind a light source or permitting a very noisy classroom may be very difficult for your child who may choose to "go along" than draw attention to herself. Remember, from year to year teachers, students, and even school settings may change. Be sure to re-evaluate conditions each new school year.

Activities

Activity #1: The Mainstream Committee
Age: 7–12
Vocabulary/Concepts: mainstream committee, discussion, complaints, share, human rights, clear communication

This activity is useful in empowering your child and helping her to feel more capable of resolving issues that may arise in the mainstream school setting. Enlist the school's help in having your child either form or participate in a committee for mainstreamed deaf students. Participants might have weekly meetings at which they discuss topics of business, take time to socialize, and have opportunities to plan events. This committee can bring up both long-standing and new problems they might have in the mainstream situation.

For example, the committee might feel that the school should have sign language classes and this could be implemented. Other issues may include teachers uninformed about deafness who make simple but critical mistakes. Trainings would help to ameliorate some of these problems. Perhaps the students could put some portion of the trainings together. A teacher or school counselor might attend the students' meetings and educate the committee members on how they can bring their grievances to the administration.

The committee might also discuss their thoughts and feelings about being mainstreamed students. Discussions of this nature should be led by a qualified counselor. Certainly there should be time to socialize. If your child has an opportunity to meet with other deaf children, then it is more likely that specific issues of deafness will be raised. However, student suggestions of problem-solving mechanisms should not replace the training of school staff by a professional in deaf education. It is a real eye-opener for educational staff to meet a deaf adult who can explain the importance of attending to the deaf student's specific needs.

If your child is the only deaf child in her school, consider having hearing mainstreamed students join with her to create a committee. This type of group would allow for sharing and support; however, your child will have particular communication and identification needs that are different from those of other mainstreamed students. You might want to invite hearing students to participate in meetings from time to time. Of course, all hearing/deaf meetings should be interpreted unless the children request otherwise.

Activity #2: The Parent Committee

Start your own committee for parents of deaf children at the school. Meet other parents with mainstreamed children and take this opportunity to share thoughts and feelings as well as to work together on solving problems that concern all of you.

Activity #3: Mainstream Kit
   Materials: sign language books, pad, fun pens, notebook
   Age: 6–12
   Vocabulary/Concepts: mainstream kit, help communication, stuck,
      COMMUNICATION BREAKDOWN

Prior to starting your child in a new mainstream setting, help her adjustment by making her a special mainstream kit. Include any books written for children that address peer problems, mainstreaming, or learning sign language. For signing students, a pocket-sized sign language book is handy for helping your child teach other children some signs. You can also see that the school acquires a collection of sign language books (see the Bibliography for some suggestions).

Equip your child with a small note pad and attractive pens or pencils to carry with her at all times. Encourage her to use these when communication becomes unclear. Give her a special notebook to use to regularly communicate with her teacher. Encourage the teacher to write weekly messages in the book that require a response from your child. Show your child how to write messages to her teacher. Add a special gift for her first day of school.

HOMEWORK PROBLEMS

At times, homework can be redundant and boring, causing disinterest on the part of the student. Historically, deaf children often have been given highly repetitive school work as a substitute for rich communication. However, teacher-training programs, knowledge of language development, and understanding of issues related to deaf children have improved in recent years. School curriculum and homework should reflect these improvements.

The "how to" of learning is as important as the content. Children who have not learned good organizational and time-management skills tend to procrastinate. Well-intentioned and frustrated parents may find themselves doing their child's homework. Doing the work for the deaf child may be a parent's attempt to save time by minimizing communication frustration. Refrain from this. When your child does her homework independently, she can experience pride, responsibility, self-discipline, and a sense of accomplishment once the work is completed. Doing the work for your child dilutes whatever academic learning was intended and encourages your child's dependence on you.

Examine your child's homework/activity/bedtime schedule. A child deserves a break between school and homework (especially after a long bus ride). Most children respond best to the incentive of being allowed to play once the homework is finished. In some cases, however, children need a snack or play time before homework in order to focus. Together with your child, develop a homework/playtime schedule and help her stick to it. Develop a system for her to organize daily work. With structure, she will find it easier to focus, to feel motivated, and to complete the work sooner.

A child may use the homework struggle to displace feelings from other issues. Your deaf child may be experiencing socialization, communication, or interpreting problems at school. Or perhaps family problems have confused or upset your child. Set aside time unrelated to homework to discuss general school or home issues.

Support your child in fulfilling her homework responsibilities. Encourage her by helping with general organizing aids, study habits, and the homework environment. If your child is confused about instructions, help her get started by reviewing these with her. If she gets stuck help her to get back on track. Do not feel that you need to become your child's tutor, however. Often parents assuming this role do not understand the steps needed to master an assignment or they may not have the latest technical skills needed to understand the subject matter. They may become emotionally involved with the child completing the assignment in a certain fashion.

Children benefit from seeing the connection between academic learning and daily living skills. Help your child imagine real life applications of homework assignments. Use these opportunities to curb your child's fantasies about how easy it is to own and drive a car, to live on one's own, or to cook.

Above all, regularly communicate with your child's teacher. Having a communication book that goes back and forth between home and school is a great way to keep a daily log of current curriculum, social/emotional concerns, new vocabulary, and homework assignments. Have regular phone and parent/teacher conferences to assure consistent approaches to your child's learning. Together, develop ways to ensure that your child understands homework tasks and is held responsible for them.

Join your school's Parent/Teacher Organizations or help to develop one if this is lacking. You may find it comforting to meet with other parents who are raising a deaf child.

Activities

● ●

Activity #1: The Office

Materials: see list in activity
Age: 6–12
Vocabulary/Concepts: office, homework, study, appointment, SET-UP

● ●

Homework provides a child with an opportunity to practice and strengthen academic skills while also giving her valuable experiences in handling responsibility, managing time, acquiring independence, and completing goals. Most parents agree with this philosophy, but getting your child to agree is another matter. Kids do not see the overall benefit of doing homework, since it requires self-discipline and an ability to put off more exciting activities.

Work is more enjoyable if the work environment is attractive and comfortable. This activity creates an inviting personal work space for your child. First, set up a physical arrangement that defines your child's "office" space for doing homework. Make sure this is a private space away from public distraction (no TV nearby and minimal family traffic). Furnish the space with office equipment that makes doing homework more attractive. Here is a list of materials that might appeal to your child:

● A desk with lots of drawers, files, and compartments. Fill the top drawer with pencils, pens, markers, crayons, and art supplies (such as glue and scissors). Fill other drawers with writing paper, colored paper, folders, and index cards.

● A wall calendar that appeals to your child and has enough space for her to write "to do's."

● An age-appropriate children's dictionary and thesaurus.

● Special touches like a desk set with a pen holder and perhaps even a name plate for her or a schedule book.

● A lamp that provides ample light.

● A clock to help your child time assignments.

Once the office is set up, encourage your child to use it daily. Model this for her by setting up your own office for paying bills and doing paperwork at home. Let your child know that homework is her responsibility and that you will be supportive and give her help if she needs it. The best help you can offer is to assist in the planning and organization of homework assignments. Help her map out a week's schedule by writing homework assignments and times for doing homework in her schedule book. You may even want to write in times when you will be available to help with specific assignments. If she waits until the last minute to do a longstanding assignment she cannot expect you to come to her rescue without an "appointment" (the logical consequences of not taking responsibility for homework).

At first you may need to monitor or supervise your child's homework schedule and "office attendance." Give her a choice to "do your homework now or later, but you must definitely do your homework." Over time, as your child becomes more self-reliant, you can phase out your role as supervisor.

This activity works best if you provide a little incentive. Learning new things and completing homework is hard work. Rewarding your child for accomplishing these demands is similar to receiving a wage for going to work. We are not necessarily suggesting that you give your child a paycheck for doing homework, but consider setting up a "Homework = Learning Chart" to help your child feel that what she is doing is important and worth the effort.

Homework = Learning Chart

Name:_____

Date	Homework Task	Completed
	Brought homework home	
	Went to my office	
	Completed assignment(s)	
	Studied for a test	
	Worked on a long-range project	
	Brought homework back to school	
What I learned today:		

This chart requires that your child visit her office daily and organize and complete homework assignments. It also asks her to describe to you what she has learned. This is an important component of the incentive program because it encourages your child to associate homework with learning. We want our children to feel the power of knowledge and the satisfaction of comprehension. Your child can share new knowledge with you at a special time each day or at the time you give out daily points on her chart. You can add other school-related activities to the chart, such as good behavior in school or being on time for the school bus. Rewards might include supplies for the child's office, like a set of folders, a special calendar, or a fancy schedule book.

Activity #2: Ten Days to Go

Materials: bulletin board, paper, markers
Age: 9–12
Vocabulary/Concepts: days to go, TIME APPROACHING, TIME SOON

Using a bulletin board, post how many days your child has before homework is due. This is usually good for larger projects, such as a report. Announce how many days are left each time you change the day on the bulletin board. As the deadline approaches, mark and announce the hours "fifteen hours to go." This can be an alternative to nagging unless your child responds as if you were nagging, "Will you stop saying the time, Dad, I know!" If your child views your reminders as nagging then change the time without announcing it. After your child learns about this method, reduce the number of times you make an announcement and allow her to take responsibility by counting down the days herself.

Activity #3: The Study Break

Surprise your child with a little snack and a glass of milk during her study hour. Announce this as "the study break time" and let her know that you are very pleased with her study efforts. Take time to listen to your child. Ask questions about her school day and review homework with her.

Activity #4: Helpful Homework Hints

Sometimes children can become frustrated and overwhelmed due to an inability to prioritize, time, and pace assignments. If it appears that your child is getting bogged down with the concept of homework, it may be that she needs some help developing good study habits. When your child tries new study habits, notify the teacher to be aware and be flexible with assignments if need be; to offer study habit tutoring; or to give ideas and feedback. Here are some ideas for teaching studying skills:

1. With the teacher, have your child practice reading, restating directions in her own words, and then applying them. Use the same method for this at home. "OK, first they want me to read the story, right? Then I need to answer the questions at the end. And I can answer them with sentences from the story or my own words."

2. Prioritize which subjects or assignments are hard and which are easy for your child. Determine what order makes sense for her to tackle her work. For most children, doing the difficult subjects or tasks first while they are fresh is best—they then slide through the easy ones. However, children may waste too much time on the difficult subjects and become upset, discouraged, and unable to finish their other assignments. For these children, you might want to do one easier subject first, or alternate between easy assignments and hard ones so that she feels some sense of accomplishment. Also, the child can be taught to finish parts of the assignment and then return to other parts.

3. With the teacher, determine how much time your child needs to finish homework each night; how much time each assignment will require; and how much time should be spent on the specifics of an assignment (such as math problems). Have your child practice this. This may help uncover where your child needs more time or where she is being less efficient. A child might get stuck on one math problem for an hour when she has twenty more to do. This should not be a pressured experience, but a "let's-see-what-works" enterprise.

4. Remind your child that she can always go back to something she didn't understand and that she will feel better if she avoids getting frustrated and stuck on one topic. This is a good skill to practice and comes in handy when taking standardized exams.

5. Have your child plan breaks so that she becomes used to using breaks to reinforce working toward completion rather than as a way to avoid finishing. Use the priorities list to decide where a nice break would fit in.

6. Encourage physical movement breaks. Sometimes doing a few bends and stretches or a few push-ups can recharge your child's energy.

7. Help your child celebrate the completion of homework, even if she feels dissatisfied with the results—the efforts deserve a reward. Perhaps she can play outside for a half an hour, play on the computer, make a phone

call to a friend, play a board game with a family member, read a book, or watch a favorite TV show.

LACK OF MOTIVATION TO LEARN AND POOR BEHAVIOR IN SCHOOL

A disinterested student may have low self-esteem resulting in an "I can't" attitude. She needs challenging but attainable goals, motivation and support to develop an "I can" attitude, constant small successes, and deaf role models to give her hope for a successful future.

An unmotivated child may actually suffer from a fear of failing and thus exposing her inadequacy. She may believe it is safer not to try. Share with your child your investment and excitement in learning. Verbalize your own curiosities throughout the day by asking questions about how things work. Demonstrate acceptance of mistakes as a part of learning and model your willingness to be wrong or confused, such as asking for directions when you are lost.

Children who feel unchallenged or bored by schoolwork become disruptive and cause distractions and as a result are labeled as "troublemakers" and "unmotivated." Ironically, many of these children are bright and may even be gifted. If your child seems inadequately challenged, easily completes work, and is frequently told she is not reaching her potential, then have her evaluated by a specialist in deafness who can identify learning strengths and can recommend ways to enhance her overall education.

A child may feel unable to meet the standards and expectations of parents or unable to live up to the accomplishments of older siblings or peers and as a result she gives up. Help your child develop personal goals independent of others. Avoid comparisons to yourself, siblings, or peers.

Your deaf child's school peer group will likely influence the demands she places on herself. When schools have small groups of deaf and hard of hearing children in them, there may be a predominance of one group or the other. If a profoundly deaf child prefers ASL and is among hard of hearing children who switch between voicing and signing, the deaf child may begin to feel she has to fit in, yet cannot. Likewise, if a newly deafened or non-signing hard of hearing child is placed with strong ASL deaf signers, she may feel constantly overwhelmed. Discussions with classroom teachers, school administrators, and other parents might help in devising short and long-term solutions and policies to handle this difficulty. Explore alternate school placements if interventions do not seem to work and the child remains unhappy.

The child may feel pressure to assimilate with peers. To avoid being a "nerd," she may not achieve her academic potential or act out (taking the role of the "class clown" or "troublemaker"). Challenge stereotypes, both yours and your child's, which limit growth and potential. Support individualism while understanding the powerful pull to be like peers. For example, challenge distorted ideas such as "everyone will like me if I make them laugh" or "no one will like me if I get A's."

All children are naturally curious and born with the ability to learn. Children are more motivated to do well in school when the family environment supports education. Establishing a fun learning environment in your family is the key link between the desire to learn and acquiring a formal education. Parents are a child's first and most important teachers and can model a desire for knowledge, expose their children to a variety of learning experiences, support special interests, and teach organization and self-discipline skills.

Activities

. . . .

Activity #1: Family Fun Games

Materials: see suggestions in activity
Age: all ages
Vocabulary/Concepts: family games, learning, school

. . . .

This activity will provide your family with several fun activities that make learning an enjoyable family priority. Bear in mind that play is a child's most natural form of learning. The school curriculum and homework assignments can be enhanced by family learning adventures and games and can increase your child's motivation to learn.

Set up a communication system between school and home that keeps you informed of your child's curriculum, specific learning themes, and school agendas for the year. Have regular discussions with the teacher to learn about your child's progress and specific learning needs required for each subject. Turn your home into a learning environment of fun and games that dovetails with the school curriculum. Here are some suggestions:

1. *The Family Wheel of Fortune:* Create your own family TV game shows such as the "Wheel of Fortune," "Jeopardy," or "Where in the World is Carmen Sandiego?" Come up with questions for the game show that will reflect what your child is currently studying by using her academic calendar and homework assignments. Take turns being the contestants. Make the prizes be things the family wins together, like a trip to the Science Museum or ice cream shop. Use humor, modeling, "Try, Try Again," and lots of cheering and encouragement throughout the game. (See pgs. 67–69 for a list of catalogs that sell family learning games.)

2. *Family Learning Adventures:* Plan to take a family field trip that relates to your child's current studies. Seek out activities that are not scheduled school field trips. Three books by Peggy Kaye—*Games for Learning* (1991, Farrar, Strauss, Giroux), *Games for Reading* (1984, Pantheon Books) and *Games for Math* (1987, Pantheon Books)—have great suggestions for family fun and games.

3. *Family School Days:* Make learning a family affair by taking a class and studying a subject together. Make this learning experience a family ritual. Take a class in American Sign Language together (contact state schools for deaf children or agencies servicing deaf people to find information about this). Learn to play a team sport; take a course in astronomy; or learn a new craft like knitting, pottery, or painting. Most importantly, model for your child how to listen in class, ask questions, study, and be enthusiastic about learning. This is an incredible way to show your child firsthand how to have fun learning. If possible, plan vacations or weekend activities that are related to your "classes," for example, if you live in the city you might take a trip to the countryside to bird-watch or study wildflowers.

Activity #2: Happy Hobbies
Materials: see activity
Age: 6–12
Vocabulary/Concepts: hobby, EXPERT, SKILLED, smart

Teach your child good learning habits by investing time in a hobby. For example, if your child is beginning to collect stamps, support this by researching, going to collection shows, and helping her develop a personal collection theme. We suggest having your child share her knowledge with relatives and friends or take her hobby to senior citizens' homes and hospitals for children. This process teaches your child how she can learn about a subject and, through motivation and hard work, become an expert in her chosen field.

Activity #3: The School Picture Checklist
Materials: poster board, markers
Age: 5–10
Vocabulary/Concepts: need to do, improve, IMPROVE GRADUALLY

On a large poster board draw pictures down the left-hand side of school behaviors or tasks that your child struggles with daily. If your child has difficulty handling her behavior on the bus, draw a picture of a school bus; if she has difficulties getting along with her teacher, draw a picture of the teacher;

or if she is not getting her homework in on time, draw a picture of homework papers. For this activity, break a problem down into separate components, such as remembering homework, doing the homework neatly, and turning it in on time. In this way you will have more than one item to check off every day your child goes to school. Each time your child successfully accomplishes a task or manages a problem, she gets a check. Choose the desired number of checks she needs to receive her reward.

Activity #4: Teacher Time

When a child and a teacher have a problem with their relationship, encourage better communication by inviting the teacher out for lunch or dinner. Have your child write an invitation and plan the event. Make it special and stress the need for the two of them to get to know each other better. If your child has persistent problems with her teacher, do not push these aside until she gets a new teacher next year. Speak with the teacher or, if necessary, school administrators so that your child has the opportunity to resolve this difficulty during the present school year.

LEARNING PROBLEMS

A child who has difficulties in school may be suffering from an undiagnosed learning disability. Learning disabilities have been cited as the most prevalent additional obstacle for deaf students. The diagnosis of a learning disability in a deaf child is a more complex issue than the same diagnosis in a hearing child, especially if she has had to face many communication challenges.

If you suspect that your child has a learning disability, don't hesitate to get an evaluation from a specialist in deafness who is familiar with how language, environment, and emotions interconnect and who can compare your child to other deaf students. Many parents deny their own intuition for years, despite the fact that they are experts on their children. Careful testing and diagnosis can determine the presence of a learning disability and can assist you in addressing your child's real needs.

There are many types of learning disabilities, including attention deficits, both fine and gross motor skill disorders, and cognitive processing and communication problems. The cause of your child's deafness, such as maternal rubella, Rh factor, and prematurity may contribute to learning problems.

Emotional problems sometimes manifest themselves as learning problems. Simply, if the child is upset or preoccupied with an emotional difficulty, she will not be able to concentrate and perform up to her capabilities. In fact, she may prefer creating problems at school to confronting the pain or turmoil she feels in connection with problems she has at home.

A child with an undiagnosed learning disability will frequently feel frustrated, stupid, defeated, inadequate, and often scapegoated by her peers. When you clearly determine what the learning problem is, be frank with your child about that. When a child learns that she has a learning problem that can be remedied, she will most likely be relieved—she now has a reason for it and can feel reassured that she will receive support from her parents and teachers. When parents act as if the learning problem is not there, the child's imagination may run wild and she may identify herself as being dumb, slow, and a shame to her family.

A child with a learning problem might do anything imaginable to avoid confronting her weaknesses. She might lie about homework, throw tantrums, forget, defy, appear lazy, and blame others. While you may need to firmly address these behaviors (especially the more aggressive or destructive ones), be aware that your child should not be expected to give up these defenses overnight. As the child gains more support and begins to see that learning problems can be handled, the negative behaviors will begin to dissipate. Failure over time becomes a habit. Find times in your child's day when she is saying that she "can't." Gently, create and encourage "can" situations for her.

A deaf child with learning difficulties needs and has a right to specialized services in order to have a positive and fruitful learning experience. Even in the most ideal linguistic environment, a deaf child may show difficulties in learning that can result in her lagging behind peers, experiencing long periods with no academic gains, presenting behavioral problems and a lack of academic interest and confidence.

Visual learning is natural for a deaf child. Always assess whether your child is receiving a lot of visual input as an integral part of her learning (graphs, pictures, color coding). If your child has visual processing problems, she may need to have material presented in a particular manner for her to assimilate it.

Activities

. . . .

Activity #1: Child Teacher

Materials: this activity requires the cooperation of your child's
  teacher
Age: 8–12
Vocabulary/Concepts: child-teacher or tutor, help, skills, try again

. . . .

This activity can help your child to feel that she is a good and capable student. In order to successfully accomplish this activity, all involved teachers must be committed to your child succeeding in becoming a "Child-Teacher."

First, discuss this plan with your child's teacher and pick out a specific learning ability or disability the child has that can be positively reframed as a teaching skill. Your child will then have an opportunity to tutor a younger or more learning disabled student. In order to do this, she must be reminded of all of the skills she possesses—trying hard, social skills, physical skills, asking for help, and perseverance—anything that highlights her strengths. We suggest having your child become a child teacher to a student three or four grades below her to make the experience a guaranteed success.

With the help of her teacher and the teacher of the student she will be tutoring, have your child design a lesson plan. We suggest that you purchase a few inexpensive teaching tools, such as a weekly planner, flash cards, or folders, to make the activity attractive and to make your child feel "professional." Encourage your child to talk to either you or her teacher about strategies for helping others to learn. An example of a Child-Teacher lesson would be to have a learning disabled child who has problems with reading teach a younger child the alphabet.

Set up tutoring on a daily or weekly basis. Have your child share her thoughts about her student's progress with the teacher. Celebrate her success and invite teachers and students from both classes to an end-of-the-year or end-of-the-semester thank-you party.

This positive learning experience can demonstrate and have people take notice of your child's capabilities. Any small achievement made in teaching another student is truly an accomplishment to feel proud of. "Try, try again" if the Child-Teacher experience does not succeed. Your child may have been mismatched with her student. Encourage your child to try again just as her teachers do—they keep trying to teach even though a student may not learn right away.

. . . .

Activity #2: The Right Fit

Materials: boxes of varying shapes, unbreakable containers, plastic
    bags, random objects, aprons or old clothes
Age: 6–12
Vocabulary/Concepts: learning difference, personality, strengths,
    weaknesses, right fit, MATCH

. . . .

This activity visually shows the deaf child how learning and teaching must match. In other words, each person has a different learning style and must be taught appropriately. This explanation will help to normalize your child's learning disability for her since it demonstrates the way in which everyone learns differently.

Gather a number of boxes of varying shapes, unbreakable containers with different-sized mouths, plastic bags, and a wide variety of objects to try to fit into these containers. You can use fruit, marbles, dolls, shoes, paper, rocks, or liquids—virtually anything that is not made of glass or breakable parts. Begin by explaining that everyone learns in a different way and that the student and the teaching must fit. Take an item (an apple for instance) and put it into a small bag. Note how the apple fits, how you can tie the top, and how you can wrap the bag tighter to make it fit around the form of the apple.

Next, try to put the apple in a small-mouthed (plastic) jar. This should appear comical—push and tug and squeeze the apple until it bruises or scrapes open. Think of instances when your child may have felt pushed and bruised and had "hurt feelings" when she was being given information in a way that she could not understand it. Stress that no matter how hard you try, the apple is still an apple and you can't push it to fit without hurting it. Use liquids, small items, delicate eggs, playdough, or any item you feel will work to prove your point. (You may want to do this activity in the kitchen with old clothes on.)

When you have something that fits, ask the child what she imagines it feels like to have a good fit. Ask her when she had a teacher she fit well with. Connect this to any special services she is or will be receiving. Stress that the services are being provided not because she is dumb but because they fit her needs. She is like a beautiful shiny apple that will be smashed if she doesn't find a good learning-and-teaching match.

You can also do this activity by using a toddler's matching toy of the type where shapes must fit into matching holes (stars, squares, circles, and triangles). Again, use this to visually show the child what it means to be a good fit.

. . . .

Activity #3: The "Can" Equation for Success
Age: 8–12

. . . .

Teach your child to appreciate small gains and efforts as well as the final result. Remind her that people are often born with skills but if they don't use them they will not grow and become successful with them. What creates success is motivation and effort. There is always room for improvement even if only by a tiny amount. In fact, difficult conditions often inspire people to create new ways to do things.

To demonstrate this you can play a game of "can"/"can't." You begin by stating a "can't" and ask your child or other family members to come up with a "can" to counter that. Try using a hypothetical situation or one where someone you know has overcome odds. For example, you might say, "People in wheelchairs can't race in marathons." Your family then jumps in and states, "People in wheelchairs can race in marathons but they race in their chair rather than by running" or "I saw the marathon on TV and hundreds of people in wheelchairs raced."

Use examples of how people have had to overcome physical, emotional, political, and social barriers. Use examples of deaf people—"Deaf people can't talk on the phone"—"Yes they can! They can use interpreters, TTY's, or the relay service." Also, give examples of situations that have not happened yet—"A deaf person can't become the president of the USA"—"Yes, she can. If she has interpreters and TTYs she can communicate with anyone. Maybe she can even have other Deaf people in her cabinet!!"

Use historical examples—"People said that African-American slaves could not achieve; that Deaf people could not learn; that women should not vote." Again and again, with hard work and determination the "can'ts" turn into "cans." It is important to teach your child that wanting something and working hard does not necessarily mean that it will happen just the way you want it to—people have to change their goals and definitions of success all of the time.

Building Your Child's Self-Esteem

●●●●●●●●●●●●

Jack R. Gannon

*A*lthough I haven't seen him for more than three decades, I can still picture Willie as he moved slowly about the barber shop where he worked, pushing that long push-broom. Willie was the African-American bootblack in the barber shop on the town square where I grew up. He was tall, thin, and bony, and had slightly stooped shoulders and fuzzy grey hair.

His name was Willie, but the town folk called him "Dummy" because he did not speak. Willie was my friend and we had something in common. We were both deaf. As a young boy, I would frequently stop by the barber shop and visit with Willie and watch him work and do his funny jig as he entertained a customer while shining his shoes. Willie always wore a dress shirt and a tie and at the end of the day, after he had swept the shop, he would button up his blue striped vest, put on his jacket and hat, take his cane from the coat rack, and head for home.

I would watch him go. He would walk proudly around the square, then down South Main toward the hill over in the distance where he lived. He would walk with his head held high, a smile on his face, and the appearance of being the richest man in town, every bit the "businessman" that he was!

Willie did not have much of a formal education, but he was "life-smart"

Jack R. Gannon is Special Assistant to the President on advocacy issues at Gallaudet University in Washington, D.C.

and he taught me one of the most important lessons I ever learned. As I sat there in the barber shop, he would wag his long, bony, index finger at me in a scolding way as he towered over me, and sign: "Always be proud of who you are!"

As I watched him walk home after work, I could see him display his pride in who he was.

As a youth, I didn't have any ambition to become a bootblack like Willie, so I continued my education and eventually became a teacher. As I wended my way through school and college I had the good fortune to meet many wonderful deaf and hearing teachers, each of whom reinforced, in a different way, the valuable lesson my friend, Willie, had taught me: "Be proud of who you are."

Since the publication of my first book, *Deaf Heritage, A Narrative History of Deaf America,* I have received many invitations to give presentations around the nation and the world. This has given me the opportunity to meet and interact with deaf children and deaf adults in many parts of the world.

It is not unusual for me to encounter deaf individuals with low self-concepts. Many do not know who they are and are not aware of a proud heritage that is theirs. When I meet individuals with a poor self-concept, my thoughts invariably return to Willie and I see him again wagging his finger, admonishing me to: "Be proud of who you are!" and my heart sinks because I know many of these persons never had a deaf "Willie" in their lives.

Why do some deaf children have low self-esteem? As a deaf person and a former teacher, it is not hard for me to guess. I think one of the most important reasons is because they have no idea who they are.

What are some other causes of low self-esteem among deaf children? There are many causes. Let me cite some examples: paternalism; over-protection; poor communication between deaf child, parents, and siblings; exclusion and isolation; low expectations; lack of family's understanding of deafness; lack of involvement of the deaf child in family affairs; absence of positive deaf role models; inappropriate school placement; limited or no peer interaction; and more. All these contribute to poor self-esteem.

It is hard to believe, but it is a fact that many families do not bother to learn to communicate effectively with the deaf member in the family. Many claim that communication in the family is fine, but, in truth, it is not. Some parents even expect the deaf child to "do it their way" even when it is obvious that "that way" is not working. Often the expectation and the responsibility of maintaining effective communication are placed on the shoulders of the deaf child rather than assumed, at least in part, by parents and other members of the family.

In too many cases the deaf child is even ignored when it comes to family affairs and the child, in effect, becomes the family outcast. Deaf children must be involved in family planning, and they have a right to be asked and respected for their opinions. Deaf children must also be expected to shoulder their share of family responsibilities.

Many parents are still struggling to accept their child's deafness long after the deaf child has forgotten what hearing is all about or doesn't even think about it at all. Some parents display an outright rejection or hostility toward deafness and a refusal to admit their child has a hearing loss. Parents need to admit their child is deaf and sooner or later they must accept the fact and get on with life's important goals.

Then, of course, there are the parents obsessed with "fixing the problem." Most of my deaf friends and I have moved beyond those stages and are not interested in getting "fixed." We are more interested in being who we are and enjoying our lives as we are. There is a valuable lesson here for parents.

Too much paternalism and over-protection are other factors that contribute to a deaf child's low self-esteem. If we want our children to develop independence, as eventually they must, we must give them as many opportunities as possible to learn to be independent and to accept responsibility. The denial of these opportunities only contributes to a child's low self-esteem.

Low expectations of a deaf child are very common, but they are not healthy. Low expectations do not motivate or challenge a deaf child, and they often encourage him to be lazy, or to be satisfied with a mediocre effort. There are many deaf low-achievers today, I suspect, simply because they were never challenged or expected to do better as they should have been.

Isolation within the family, at school, and in the community are serious problems for deaf individuals. Lack of or poor communication is usually the leading cause of isolation and the lack of positive peer interaction.

These are just some of the contributing factors to a deaf individual's low self-esteem. What messages do all these examples send? The examples I have cited send a very powerful and clear message. They tell the deaf child: "You are not important." Or, worse, "You are nobody." And these unspoken messages begin to sow the seeds of low self-esteem.

All children need positive role models. Many deaf children are denied them. Parents are the child's most important role model and the child's first and most important teacher. The child would likewise benefit if the parents had at least one deaf adult friend. That would tell the child that the parents understand and have accepted deafness.

As parents and teachers we must set positive examples for our children to follow if we are to pass on to them the lessons we have learned and help them learn and grow and appreciate the fullness and the richness of their lives. They need someone to teach them that there are many options and many opportunities in this world and to remind them that the harder they work the luckier they get. They need to know that there is nothing wrong with being deaf and that, as deaf people, we live in two worlds—the world of silence and the world of sound—and that we have a right to expect the best of both.

As I think of Willie, lines from Douglas Malloch's poem "Be the Best Whatever You Are" come to mind. It is a message we need to pass on to our children:

If you can't be a highway, just be a trail,
    If you can't be the sun, be a star;
It isn't by size that you win or fail—
    Be the best whatever you are!

CHAPTER

14

Self-Concept

• • • •

This chapter offers problem-solving activities to counter low self-esteem, separation problems, and self-centeredness. A healthy self-concept is not something one achieves in an afternoon. It is a lifelong task and the result of growing and living in a nurturing and empowering environment. Deaf children must come to accept and, at best, feel proud of their deafness. Otherwise they will see being deaf as being lesser, bad, damaged, or as an excuse for not trying.

Positive self-worth is the foundation for the development of healthy reciprocal relationships, creativity, building on personality strengths, intellectual achievement, and responsibility. It is the glue that binds children's personalities so that they can become positive, integrated, and effective human beings.

We hope the activities in this chapter will assist you in improving your child's self-concept so that he will take pride in all aspects of himself, enjoy his accomplishments, act independently, assume responsibility, tap into his "personal power," confront challenges, accept mistakes, and feel satisfied enough to give to others.

If your child is extremely self-critical, experiences little joy or satisfaction from his achievements, and does not seem to benefit from the activities in this book, then consider consulting with a mental health professional.

LOW SELF-ESTEEM

A child with low self-worth minimizes his talents, avoids challenging situations, cannot accept losing, and feels that others don't value or like him. Help

The problems may look like this:

• • • • • • •

- Child often complains and puts himself and others down.
- Child constantly tries to control others.
- Child withdraws from new situations.
- Child avoids any disagreements, conflicts, or discussions.
- Child sleeps much more than usual.
- Child gains or loses weight (unrelated to body development).
- Child complains about being deaf and anything related to deafness.
- Child will say, "I can't, I am deaf."
- Child doesn't finish tasks and chronically says, "I can't."
- Child relies on others to do daily tasks.
- Child must win at all cost and breaks down if he does not.
- Child cries, complains, and moans about losing a game for days (and you wish they never invented Little League).

your child to appreciate his special skills, unique attributes, and positive traits. Teach him that being deaf is one these.

The child with low self-esteem often has a pessimistic outlook and feels powerless to change his situation. Conversely, a child who has the resources, capability, and opportunity to influence his life, feels a sense of control or "personal power."

Many environmental factors, alone or in combination, may contribute to low self-esteem.

1. *Rejection by loved ones:* Sometimes immediate and extended family members have mixed feelings about having a deaf family member who has different communication needs. Parental guilt, grandparents' discomfort, or a sibling's jealousy may be experienced by the deaf child as a personal rejection. Families do best when they share their feelings and parents do best when they have other adults to share their concerns with. A child with positive connections to friends and relatives will feel valued, needed, and wanted. He, in turn, mirrors these relationships and gains a sense of self-confidence.

2. *Rejection by peers:* Children constantly change allegiances and, at some point, unfortunately, your child may be excluded from a group. This may have nothing to do with your child's deafness, or with a group of hearing peers, the deaf child may be seen as different and easily scapegoated. He may reach an age at which he cannot keep up with his hearing peers' conversations and feels left out of the group. If your child has a small deaf peer group who have known each other for many years, they may have developed rigid roles among themselves. A child may have a different personality than his deaf peers and be excluded for that difference. In this case, exploring other social situations is a must.

3. *Parental withholding of love or conditional love:* If a parent has ongoing conflictual feelings about a child's deafness it may be difficult to love the child in an open and responsive way. Parents can learn to enjoy a child the way he is and not for who he might have been if they receive support in expressing feelings and struggle with the trials of communication.

4. *Negative comparisons to others:* Many adults use examples of other children to try to teach a child about aspirations. However, often the child just becomes defensive, angry, and at worst, gives up, when compared to others.

5. *Prejudice:* Deaf children are constantly confronted with a world that is designed by the hearing and with hearing values in mind. When the hearing majority creates an environment in which auditory exchanges are most valued, the deaf person is put into a dependent position. The message this sends to the deaf child is that he is not as important or as capable as his hearing counterpart. You cannot change the fact that your family may be primarily hearing. Yet you can create daily situations in which the deaf child is an active family member. He needs to feel acknowledged for his capabilities, he needs to know what is happening and for what reasons, he needs to have responsibilities and logical consequences, he needs to participate in family decisions and problems, and he needs to have his differences respected.

6. *Over-emphasis on appearance and performance:* Children do best when respected for their individuality. Having the expectation that a deaf child will "pass" for hearing is setting up a disappointment for both the parents and the child. A child who is loved unconditionally will come to believe that it is he, not his performance, that is loved.

7. *Being frequently ignored, ridiculed, or criticized:* Again, this can come as a result of your child being identified as "different" due to his deafness, behavior, or personality.

All people experience some of these negative influences at some point in their lives. If the child frequently experiences one or several of the above, then he is more likely to develop a negative self-concept.

The child with low self-esteem is sensitive to criticism and may even become defensive when given positive feedback (compliments). In your home, have the whole family practice giving respectful and constructive feedback. By gradually exposing your child to feedback in a loving manner that makes sense to him, you will help him become better able to accept it from others.

Most importantly, your child needs to learn that it is not what the feedback is, but how it is given. Teach him the difference between constructive feedback ("I don't like when you hit your sister like that. You broke a rule so you know what happens now—you need to apologize and no TV.") and damaging criticism, ("You are a real brat—get out of here now!!") Notice that this criticism usually requires less communication and explanation time. Get into the family habit of doing whatever it takes to establish detailed communication. This does not mean having lengthy conversations all the time—a simple "no" or "stop that" sometimes suffices as long as the child understands the reasons for your response.

A sensitive child needs to understand the notion that things are not just good or bad and that the process is as valuable as the results. Children tend to think in "good" and "bad" terms through age eight. However, you can introduce the concept of some things falling in the "middle" or being both a little good and a little bad to this age-group. As the child grows older (nine to twelve), he will benefit from a deeper understanding of choice, effort, steps in a process, consequences, evaluation, trying again, and how people's feelings affect their actions.

The following activities are specifically designed for the child whose low self-esteem stems from a lack of acceptance of his deafness. They will help him discover healthy ways to view his deafness.

Activities
. . . .

Activity #1: Deafinitely Wonderful Party
Materials: party invitations, activities, and decorations
Age: 5–12
Vocabulary/Concepts: party, together, fun, FOCUS DEAF, FOR-FOR?
. . . .

Celebrate and support your child's deafness by having a yearly "Deafinitely Wonderful" party. Every year, invite his friends, family, and school teachers to a party that celebrates deafness. Make sure that there are other Deaf people at the party who can equally celebrate their deafness with him. Have him plan the party and come up with activities designed to appeal to Deaf people. Invite a Deaf adult to the party who is an accomplished storyteller to entertain the children. Decorate with sign language pictures and pick a few interesting activities from chapter 6 to add a touch of Deaf culture to the party atmosphere.

Activity #2: 101 Reasons to be Proud of Being Deaf

Materials: paper, markers, crayons, pencil, cardboard, staples or yarn, hole puncher

Age: 7–12

Vocabulary/Concepts: proud, reasons

Make a special book with your child that elaborates on all the reasons to be proud of being Deaf. Have your child decorate the cover of the book in a way that shows his pride. This is a long-term project to be added to daily or weekly. For each entry he can either write a short comment like, "I know sign language" or "I'm very expressive," or he can draw pictures to illustrate these statements. Set a goal for your child to come up with 101 reasons. This will give you weeks of self-esteem building.

Activity #3: "Deaf People Can Do Anything Except Hear"

Materials: poster board or old bed sheet, available blank wall, fabric paint, markers, masking tape

Age: 8–12

Vocabulary/Concepts: I. King Jordan, can, skilled, CAN!

This important statement was made by I. King Jordan, president of Gallaudet University, a liberal arts university for Deaf people. Have your child make a large mural illustrating this statement. He can do this on a wall, paper, or even on a white bedsheet. Encourage your child to put his mural in a place where others can see it, such as in his school, library, church or recreational center. Consider having him do this project with other deaf peers.

These following activities are designed to address more general self-esteem problems not specifically related to lack of acceptance of deafness.

Activity #4: My Skill Sack

Materials: backpack, three-by-five index cards, pen, "Scarecrow" activity, "On My Own Kits" (see chapter 9)

Age: 7–12

Vocabulary/Concepts: can, skills, confidence, challenges, Try, Try Again

The contents of this activity's skill sack resembles the lists and cards used in the "Scarecrow" and "On My Own Kits" (see chapter 9). In this activity, however, you'll help your child define skills and relate them to a host of difficult situations.

Let your child pick out a backpack and carry in it a deck of three-by-five index cards noting his positive strengths (see Appendix G for a list of skills and capabilities). Have your child wear the pack. Explain that he can feel more confident in dealing with his feelings and handling daily challenges because the positive cards are "right behind him." Instruct your child to reach into his backpack and pull out several cards to help when he feels insecure. For example, if your child has a hard time meeting new people, role-play meeting a new person. Encourage him to pick out related skills (smiles nicely, a good listener, or funny) to help him feel more capable of handling the situation. Add new cards to increase your child's awareness of his skills.

. . . .

Activity #5: Honor Your Child Dinner

Materials: scrapbook, camera, plaque, written comments by guests
Age: 7–12
Vocabulary/Concepts: honor, guests, invite, positive, PRAISE

. . . .

Plan a special day or evening to honor your child for his accomplishments and unique personality. Ask friends and family members to attend and to think of something special to say about your child. For maximum strength, ask them to put their comments in writing. All negatives are left at the front door. Often, children are recognized on birthdays, at graduations, and at sports events. Rarely is a child recognized simply for being himself.

Your child will get a tremendous boost from seeing all these people honor him. Set up a situation resembling a real awards dinner. Serve a meal and place your child at the head of the table. One by one, each guest should make a speech praising your child. (Make sure your child can follow what is being said about him.) If necessary, hire an interpreter. Also, remind guests to be sensitive to including your deaf child in the dinner conversation—taking turns is essential and identifying who is speaking by having the speaker raise a hand or by passing a soft ball to the speaker will help your child follow the conversation.

Take pictures (or a video) and give your child a plaque (real or homemade) to recognize this day. Encourage your child to make a speech at the end of the event and to thank his guests. Using the photographs taken at the dinner, make a scrapbook and write in it the highlights of the evening. If your guests wrote their comments down then put them in the scrapbook. Review the nice things said about your child. Take out the scrapbook (or videotape) as a reminder when your child is feeling low. If you have more than one child, you will need to duplicate this and the following activity to show that all children are special for different reasons.

··

Activity #6: The Campaign Kid: Deaf Kid for President NOW!!
Materials: poster board, markers, paint, blank sheets of long paper for
 banner(s), pins, glue
Age: 8–12
Vocabulary/Concepts: campaign, president, candidate, vote, strengths,
 promises, rally, letter, Gallaudet University, DEAF PRESIDENT NOW!
 PAH! (An ASL expression that translates as "finally accomplishing
 a difficult task.")

··

A child with low self-esteem has often given up hope of succeeding and
tries to keep others from expecting too much from him. As a result, he continually speaks about himself in a critical and demeaning fashion, views things
pessimistically, and has a hard time handling compliments. In this activity, you
will playfully review his skills through "The Deaf Kid for President" campaign.

Start by explaining the definition of "campaign" to your child. Explain
how candidates campaign for the presidency by advertising their strengths
and skills. Use examples of class elections and local and national campaigns.

You can also provide a positive role model for your child by reading about
the current president of Gallaudet University. I. King Jordan was not elected
by public vote, but his appointment as the first deaf president of Gallaudet
University has been an inspiration to deaf people everywhere. (Look in your
local library or bookstore for a copy of *The Week the World Heard Gallaudet*
by Jack R. Gannon [Gallaudet University Press, 1989]; this is a photographic
day-by-day account of the Gallaudet student protest that lead to the selection
of I. King Jordan as president of the university). Use planful playing and creativity to manage your child's campaign for "Deaf Kid for President" (an imaginary president who makes important decisions regarding the welfare of deaf
and hearing children in the United States).

Use poster board, buttons, and banners to put together a campaign that
highlights your child's strengths. Have members of your family think of positive things to say about him and write these on the poster boards. Use the list
made in the "Skill Sack" activity to come up with campaign slogans that represent your child's skills. Have a campaign rally and put up the signs, stick on
the buttons, and tape up the banners. Help your child prepare a speech to
deliver to his "supporters" (family members and friends). Have him highlight
his abilities in a "Deaf Kid for President" campaign speech. Take pictures to
remember the campaign day.

Following his rally, vote your child into the Deaf Kid Presidency. Prepare
an inauguration with a special dinner and a swearing-in ceremony. You may
want to take this ego-boosting experience one step further and have your
child write a letter to the real President of the United States expressing his

desires and suggestions for helping children. You can even encourage him to sign it from the local Deaf Kid President. (The address for the White House is: The President, The White House, Washington, DC 20500.) Or perhaps he can send a letter to I. King Jordan at Gallaudet University stating his suggestions for educating and assisting deaf children. (This address is: Gallaudet University, 800 Florida Ave., NE, Washington, DC 20002–3695.)

Activity #7: Little Memos

On Post-it adhesive notes, write down little messages that state what is terrific about your child and leave them around the house, especially in funny places. Have your child collect them. See how many your child can remember by having him recall the messages at the end of the day.

Activity #8: Newspaper Front Page Headlines
Materials: large pieces of paper, markers, pens, computer
Age: 7–12
Vocabulary/Concepts: newspaper, headlines, success

Draw, illustrate, or use a computer to design the front of a newspaper. Announce in the headline something terrific about your child and together with your child write a story about what makes him so great. Project into the future five, ten, or twenty years and announce some great accomplishment he has achieved. Have a detailed story describe this accomplishment. You may choose to "publish" a monthly newsletter with headlines and stories to send to all your relatives, friends, and teachers detailing the latest news about your child. The headlines might read: "Sonny does all of his homework" or "Second-grader tries extra hard in math!"

Activity #9: Lunch Note/Parent Pen Pal

Receiving a surprise letter in the mail or a note in a lunch box can brighten your child's day. These can acknowledge your child's efforts, give your child a window into your own thoughts, or simply be acts of kindness to remind your child he is loved just the way he is.

SELF-CENTERED BEHAVIORS

An egocentric world view is normal and healthy in young children. It is a starting point for developing self-worth and security. When a child feels safe and valuable, he can translate these feelings to how he feels about and treats others. If he does not develop a sense of security and connection early, he will most likely feel empty and incapable of attending to other's needs and feelings.

Parental responsiveness is key for a child to develop a sense of safety and empowerment. Simple acts, accumulated over time, translate into important social-emotional foundations. For example, by simply following your infant's gaze you make a statement about the importance of these things that interest him and you teach him that he has some communicable control (empowerment). As your child grows, give him special attention when he has asked for it (at that moment or at some agreed upon time) as proof that you have heard his request and you respect his needs.

Sometimes a child asks for more than the parent can give. A child who won't take no for an answer frustrates a parent. Do not take it personally. It is not a sign that you've failed or neglected your child. Practice techniques such as effective listening, respect, and empathy; set firm and consistent limits; and seek your own support from a spouse, partner, friends, or family.

If you make some decisions for your deaf child that you later regret (like any normal parent), find a way to acknowledge these, make any changes possible, and move on. If you don't move on, you may find yourself succumbing to the temptation to alleviate your guilt by becoming too permissive or too liberal with your time and money when meeting your child's demands. In the long run this does a disservice to all involved.

While it is important to nurture a deaf child's sense of self, he won't learn to cope with frustration if his parents are overprotective, permissive, or all-giving. He may remain in an egocentric state of development and have difficulty accepting that he is not the center of the universe; sharing parental attention, time, and physical possessions; and recognizing that the needs of others will sometimes supersede his own.

Give your child opportunities to help others. Praise his efforts. Deafness is a difference, not an excuse. Your child requires that those around him make special efforts at communication but his deafness does not entitle him to be first in line, to have the biggest piece of pie, or to have different rules than the rest of the household.

A child who feels that his needs are not being met by his parents (perhaps due to a chronic or serious illness, prolonged or frequent absence of one or both parents, or divorce) may become more demanding or oppositional. It is also common for children to become more self-centered during difficult periods of transition or separation (beginning kindergarten, when the primary caretaker returns to work, or when the family moves from one house to another). If your child's behavior becomes more self-centered, oppositional, or demanding, reflect upon the last few months and ask yourself if any significant changes have occurred in your and your child's lives. Casually discuss these with your child—make sure he understands the reasons for these changes. Solicit his feelings, thoughts, and suggestions about how you can help him feel better about these changes.

A child may exhibit power-seeking behaviors if he feels he has no power to influence his environment or to make himself understood. A child feels in control when he can understand and be understood.

Seek opportunities for him to experience control and independence without engaging in a struggle. Defuse power struggles by picking and choosing your battles carefully and redirecting his desire to take charge. Offer him productive means for expressing his demands, frustrations, and unhappiness.

Teach your child to distinguish between his needs and his wants. Be patient; this is a slow and gradual process. Teach your child to value people over material objects, modeling this for him in your own actions.

Activities

· ·

Activity #1: Make Way for the King and Queen
Materials: paper, markers, construction paper, rhinestones, give
Age: 5–8
Vocabulary/Concepts: king, queen, nice, spoiled, sensitive, respect

· ·

Make your child king (or queen, as the case may be) of his palace. Explain to him that there are nice kings and spoiled kings. Provide examples of nice kingly behavior, such as asking politely for things, saying "thank you," and accepting "no" for an answer. Spoiled king behavior is selfish and demanding. Make a list of both nice and spoiled kingly behaviors.

Next, make a crown out of construction paper and rhinestones. When your child engages in nice kingly behavior, glue a rhinestone to his crown. When he shows demanding or selfish behavior, ignore him, use distraction, apply a logical consequence, or "TAP" yourself to resist his demands. Do not "bow" to the spoiled king's tantrums or whining. Help your child to "try, try again" when he makes a mistake. Use STAR/RATS to help him stop and think about his actions. Playfully remind him when he is being a spoiled king, "Excuse me, your Royal Highness, but did you want something?"

When your child has collected a considerable number of rhinestones on his crown, reward him (see Appendix B). If your child needs more time to decrease his selfish behavior, use a different color of rhinestone for each week. Plan ahead and prevent social disasters by reminding your child of nice kingly behavior before taking him from his palace and out in public.

Activity #2: The Sharing and Caring Project
Age: 5–12
Vocabulary/Concepts: share, give, SHARE WITH OTHERS

This activity asks everyone in your home to participate in a family caring project by giving time and energy to benefit others. We have successfully used this activity in dozens of families to lessen selfish behaviors in children.

Research local charity projects (churches, hospitals, children's centers, animal shelters, or nursing homes; especially those that serve Deaf people) and/or world organizations that address homelessness, health care, poverty, ecology, or educating Deaf people. Discuss what each organization does and pick one or two that will become your annual family "giving and caring project." It is important that you don't just send a check or give old clothes away as your only giving activity. Instead, learn about your chosen charity. For example, if your family chooses to do a project that benefits homeless children, learn about this problem and encourage your child to consider what it would be like to be in this situation.

Next, have your family outline a giving plan that allows for all members to contribute individually or collectively. Ideas might include participating in a "Walk for the Homeless" or sponsoring a car wash to raise money for a local shelter. Have your child donate some of his toys to a shelter to share his good fortune with others. Point out to your child that deaf children in other countries may not have the support available to them that your child has. Explore ways in which your family can contribute something to these children.

Create an atmosphere in your home conducive to daily discussion of the needs of others and model caring behavior. Create opportunities for your child to see the results or natural consequences of giving to others and to experience that wonderful feeling of helping and caring for others.

Below is a list of organizations you might choose to adopt for a family giving project. We have included a few organizations focused on deaf issues. We recommend that you contact The National Information Center on Deafness (V: 1-202-651-5051; TTY: 1-202-651-5052) for a Directory of National Organizations of and for Deaf and Hard of Hearing People in order to personally tailor your family giving project.

American Society for Deaf Children
814 Thayer Ave.
Silver Spring, MD 20910

World Federation of the Deaf
Ilkantie 4, PO Box 65
SF-00401 Helsinki, Finland

United Way of America
701 N. Fairfax St.
Alexandria, VA 22314

National Coalition for the Homeless
1621 Connecticut Ave., NW #400
Washington, DC 20009

UNICEF
3 United Nations Plaza
New York, NY 10017

Dream Factory
315 Guthrie Green
Louisville, KY 40202

(Dream Factory "brings smiles to the faces of chronically ill children.")

Environmental Action Coalition
625 Broadway
2nd Floor
New York, NY 10012

American Society for the Prevention of Cruelty to Animals
441 E. 92nd St.
New York, NY 10128

● ●

Activity #3: The Deaf Helpers Club
Age: 8–12
Vocabulary/Concepts: capable, help, SHOW OTHERS
● ●

The danger of viewing deafness as a handicap is that it causes many hearing people to feel sorry for deaf people. This activity challenges that assumption by having a group of deaf youngsters help others on a regular basis.

The group can be organized in school, through a parent-teachers organization, in partnership with deaf friends and parents, or through existing deaf youth groups. Introduce the concept of the Deaf Helpers Club as a way for deaf children to prove their capability by helping others. The members might tutor younger deaf children in day or summer camps, shovel snow for elderly neighbors in the winter, clean an area of a local park in the spring, or carry groceries for those unable to do so. You might end each helping activity with pizza and a movie. Consider having the local newspaper interview the Helpers Club once they are established. By combining giving and building self-pride, the club benefits all involved.

Don't forget that when the children become teenagers they could start a Deaf Babysitters Club that specializes in caring for deaf children.

Activity #4: Secret Buddy

A few times a month, have a secret buddy day. Each family member can pick a name out of a hat and become that person's secret buddy. Secret buddies leave little gifts, fun notes, and special surprises for each other. At the end of the day family members guess their secret buddy and thank them for their thoughts and kindnesses.

Activity #5: The Sharing Box
Materials: large cardboard box, markers
Age: 4–10
Vocabulary/Concepts: sharing box, together, SHARE WITH OTHERS

For some children, the concept of sharing means "taking something away from me" and for the deaf child this may become more exaggerated if explanations are not clearly understood. Try teaching the concept of sharing by creating a concrete visual place that means "sharing." On the front of a cardboard box write "Sharing Box." Fill the box with play items to be played with only if your child shares. Interactive toys, such as a ball, board games, and a long jump rope work well for this purpose. We suggest including desirable (solitary) play items, such as a doll or puzzle, to challenge your child to share something by taking turns.

Activity #6: The Giving Tree
Materials: *The Giving Tree* (Shel Silverstein, HarperCollins, 1964), large
    plant or branch, paper, pencils, markers
Age: 5–10
Vocabulary/Concepts: give and take, equal, fair, REPLACE

Read with your child *The Giving Tree,* which is a nice story about giving and taking. Talk with your child about how the tree gave to the man and the man reciprocated with his friendship. Make your own giving tree at home using a large plant or a large branch as your own tree. On small slips of paper, write things that parents give to children (love, time, material objects, hugs, help). Hang these slips like ornaments on the tree. Cut out slips of paper of all different colors and write on them things that children give to parents (love, chores, hugs, and going to bed on time) and put these items under the tree. Each time your child requests or demands from a parent, take the corresponding slip of paper off the tree. Have your child replace the empty space with a paper representing something a child can give to a parent, such as a "hug for a hug" or help with homework for help around the house.

. . . .

Activity #7: In Your Shoes

Materials: *one pair of shoes from each family member*
Age: *5–12*
Vocabulary/Concepts: *shoes, feelings, adult, child,* OTHER VIEW
. . . .

Collect several pairs of shoes from all family members. Have everyone try on each other's shoes. Ask your child what it feels like to wear the other person's shoes. Take turns trying on everyone's shoes and guessing what it feels like to be that person. Role-play a variety of situations in which your child acts as the parent and you act as the child to demonstrate to your child what it is like to be an adult when your child is acting selfishly or making demands. Show that you understand what it is like to be in your child's shoes when he is asking for or needing something from you. Tell your child how you feel in his shoes and encourage him to do the same when he is in yours.

. . . .

Activity #8: Empathy Antennae

Materials: *Pipe cleaners, fuzzy little pom poms, head band*
Age: *5–10*
Vocabulary/Concepts: *empathy, other's feelings, guess*
. . . .

Teach about the concept of empathy by making special antennae resembling insect antennae to be worn on your child's head. Explain that this special device can pick up "special feeling waves" of an other person. Have your child put on the antennae to help him pick up the feelings and thoughts of other people or how his behavior affects others. For example, if your child hurts another child's feelings by refusing to share his toys, have him put on his feeling antennae to see if he can pick up the "feeling waves" of that individual. Have him tell you what feelings he thought his "antennae" were receiving. Put on the antennae yourself when you want to model showing empathy for another person.

The Challenge of Socialization

• • • • • • • • • • •

Judith M. Gansberg

A friend of mine once said of his children, "Every child seems to be born with the innate knowledge of exactly what pitch to scream in that will drive his parents crazy, and he uses it!" It is no different for deaf children except that the language barrier between deaf child and hearing parent that exists during the first few years of the child's life means the child will become fluent in *the sound.*

For my second child, getting her point across means wailing in *the sound,* even when she is perfectly capable of expressing herself either in sign or orally (or both).

The sound may negatively color your view of deafness especially if your child is born deaf and you begin to hear *the sound* alarmingly often at about the time she would normally begin to talk, and before the deafness is diagnosed. And, it won't stop until she no longer needs the security of knowing Mommy can be manipulated by *the sound.*

There is no way to describe *the sound* to anyone unfamiliar with deaf children, but the expression "she makes *that noise*" receives nods of understanding from those in the know. *The sound* makes language issues overpowering for the hearing parents of a deaf child. In the case of my second child, she was diagnosed as deaf at four days old. She saw sign language from birth

---

Judith M. Gansberg, M.A., is the mother of two deaf children.

because of her older sister, and she has had hearing aids since the age of seven weeks and language and speech therapy since the age of nine weeks. Still, she often chooses to use *the sound* rather than language. It is a controlling device.

A friend of mine with a deaf son who is now a teen still recalls vividly those first two to three years when he had no language and communicated with *his sound* and assorted screeches. "We had had him in therapy for a month, first oral, then Total Communication (TC)." she recalls. "The language issue was tearing us apart. One evening at dinner, shortly after he started in the TC program, we had chocolate cake for dessert. After he finished his slice, he turned to me and signed 'more' instead of screaming. We were so excited, I gave him the whole cake."

Friends with hearing children and psychologists who have not worked with deaf children may give you the response about how the child is just exhibiting "age appropriate" behavior. "My son is doing that, too," is the standard reply. Or, "it's normal for a two-year-old to begin trying to take control of her environment." It is not the same. While your friend's child may indeed have reached the same stage of development, her child can hear. Yes, he is asserting himself just as your child is, but the hearing child does not have the added pressure of juggling understanding and being understood when learning nursery rhymes, lessons about right and wrong, how to talk back to his parents, and (add in an anxiety factor here) how to know when mom is warning if his behavior threatens bodily harm.

One mother laughs today, six years later, about the time her profoundly deaf seven-year-old was making herself a snack in the kitchen while acting up a bit for Mom's benefit. The girl managed to get her dress caught on some free-standing metal shelving full of books. As she left the room, the dress pulled the shelving. The mother stood frozen in horror with no way to verbally warn the child that she could get hurt. Luckily, the shelves fell safely behind the girl, who never even turned around, completely unaware of the loud, crashing disaster she had created. The mother could only breathe a sigh of relief that the girl was not hurt, and then replace the shelving with something bolted to the wall. Had this been a hearing child her behavior during and after the accident would have been unacceptable, but for a deaf child to walk away oblivious to the chaos she had caused behind her back is not unusual or odd at all.

"If I had a nickel for every time a hearing friend has told me how 'lucky' my deaf son is to have me as a mother because he's doing so well thanks to me, I could put all of my kids through college," the chocolate-cake mother reported. Every hearing parent of a deaf child has heard this "praise" from their friends (also possibly their pediatrician and the school psychologist if the child is mainstreamed). Though this is done with good intention, what parents of deaf children need is practical information and understanding. I have found information aimed at hearing children and parents often does not apply to my situation. No one understands what it means for hearing parents to have a deaf child like another such parent and a select group of trained professionals.

"I know my two older children probably have issues, but I'm so focused trying to solve all the problems of my deaf child, that the two older ones will just have to take care of themselves," said one burned-out mother.

Perhaps my husband and I are luckier than most. We have only two children and both are deaf. We don't have the added stress of balancing the needs and demands of hearing children versus deaf children. We just evaluate every possible family activity for appropriateness to us. Therefore, we don't go to the movies, we wait for them to come out on closed captioned cassettes. We don't have to make choices about whether to take the deaf child to the children's concert his hearing siblings want to attend in order to avoid family conflict, knowing it will be a frustration to the deaf child. We do go to lots of museums where Mom and Dad use Total Communication to make sure the children understand the exhibits. We go to ballet and dance performances (very visual), ballgames, and swim meets. If the historical site has a tour, we either avoid it or become interpreters (having studied the guidebook the night before to be knowledgeable). On occasion, we obnoxiously push our deaf child to the front so she can lipread the guide.

Simply put, having deaf children is a lot more work. For all parents, life with children is a true challenge. Everywhere you go with your children you must be alert and anticipate what the children will notice or react to that you take for granted, ignore, or don't begin to realize. Raising a deaf child presents additional challenges. For example, there are the sudden loud noises (which you barely notice) that the child's hearing aid turns into a sonic boom.

"What was that loud noise? Was it a bomb?" asks the child with a look of terror on her face.

"What noise?" you respond, desperately trying to recall what you heard, but didn't consciously process. The child's face indicates a panic that will surely lead to an upsetting and embarrassing scene.

You look around. "No, dear," you sigh. "It was that truck over there in the construction site."

Those are the obvious experiences. The ones you can solve quickly. But, there are others that make you think the child needs counseling, or else you do. When my older daughter was a toddler she refused to sit in her stroller. Every time I tried to take her anywhere it was a nightmare. All the other kids were sitting quietly being pushed along by their parents. Mine was screaming and writhing around, if I could wrestle her into the stroller at all. It was humiliating for me in front of friends, who sympathetically said "they all do that." But we all knew the child was either very spoiled or had a screw loose and I clearly had no aptitude as a mother. It wasn't until years later, while pushing my second child in her much smaller porta-stroller, that it hit me. My first child, in her large Aprica™ stroller, could not see me behind her. She couldn't see me and she couldn't hear me. In her mind, she was suddenly alone in a strange and frightening place. In her situation, I would have screamed, too.

Similarly, many parents of deaf children complain that the child screams when they put her to bed. It often takes an outsider to offer a solution. Turn off the light and she is not only deaf, but she cannot see anything. Imagine the terror you would feel. The solution—buy a night light.

While adjusting to the fact of the deafness, the parents must also learn to separate natural "age appropriate" stubbornness from the frustrations the child expresses because of communication issues. Stubbornness becomes exaggerated by the deafness because often the young child expresses both the frustration of not being able to get her point across and natural stubbornness with the same behavior. Plus, their language needs make them more dependent on you; thus they have more to prove with regard to their independence and ability to do things themselves.

My older daughter's first sentence was "I do it." And, indeed she did. She watched everything we did and learned to operate appliances and almost everything else in her world at home. (Result: she flooded the basement with the washing machine twice and murdered a stereo.) My younger child screams *the sound* as she asserts her independence (P.S. she just killed off the internal drive of a Macintosh™).

It is not surprising that deaf children find it easier to do things than to try to communicate with a hearing world. When the child tries to assert her independence in a way that needs to be controlled, is it stubborness or a natural adaptation to being deaf in a world designed for hearing people?

"I remember when my daughter was four. She had been in a school for the deaf, making excellent progress in speech and language, so we decided to put her in a mainstream summer day camp, which happened to have a deaf education student (who could sign) as a counselor," said a mother. "It didn't take a week before my child was bouncing off the walls at home. At the pediatrician's office she flitted around like a demented butterfly. He put her on daily doses of an antihistamine he said was being used to calm children who were mildly hyperactive. She took it for the summer and after that seemed fine. All we could guess was that for the first time she realized that she was different from the majority of children and was struggling to make the adjustment. The next summer she asked to go to the same camp, did, and enjoyed it thoroughly with no physical effects."

After a few years, reacting to the world through your child's point of view becomes more natural. You become more aware of sounds, sights, and the environment in order to protect and explain. You are always asking, "What is she perceiving now?" "Should I step in?" Perhaps you lose something of your own perceptions in the process. I think I've long since sublimated my own natural reactions in my effort to smooth out the world for my children. Do they appreciate it? They're children. Even though they need the assistance, they resent it and the potential for conflict abounds.

Even the best lipreader only gets about thirty percent accuracy. Most parents of deaf children soon learn to interpret. The other mothers sit on the sidelines knitting or reading and "watch" the swim practice or the Little League game. The mother of the young deaf athlete is on the deck/field doing the child's listening. The child needs the help—you know that. She does, too, but she's not about to admit it.

"Don't come into the bullpen again. It's so embarrassing. You're the only mother who does that," the child cries. I would hazard a guess that more arguments have begun in our family over a parent invading a child's "space" than for any other reason.

There is a major internal conflict for the parent here, too. On the one hand, it is difficult for a deaf child to integrate socially among hearing peers and you don't want to add to that, but on the other hand your child is going to miss some important information if you aren't the "only parent" who pushes in among the children and coaches. How do you know when to let go? At what point is she ready to go it alone?

The potential for conflict in a hearing family with a deaf child lurks everywhere. The family has to learn to live on its own level, different from any other family it knows, and different from the kind of family the parents grew up in.

Everything is different. Yelling at a child for bad behavior is out. As my daughter says: "When you're angry or when you yell you distort your face, so I can't lipread you. You're wasting your energy." Yelling with your hands in sign works a bit better—but creates an embarrassing spectacle in public!

There are also those unique moments that make my day in an odd way. My favorite of these is at swim meets when I sit in my seat in the stands talking quietly to my daughter who sits on the other side of the pool deck lipreading me (her chosen preferred mode of communication). Strangers sitting nearby eye me warily as I appear to be having a lively conversation with myself. It has become an in-joke among our team mothers. We smirk and enjoy ourselves as others slide over and give me a wide berth—as they would the man talking to himself on the New York City subway. No one else can do what my daughter and I do during meets—hold conversations from fifty feet apart without shouting!

Raising a deaf child, especially if you are hearing, is a completely different experience from what you expected or from what your hearing friends are having. Very little in your past can help you. Inevitably what will see you through is a lot of love and a truckload of energy.

CHAPTER

15

Social Skills

• • • •

This chapter focuses on improving your child's social interactions, her motivation to be sociable, and her resources for meeting other deaf friends. Social skills, from basic manners to initiating friendships, are learned through parental modeling and practice. You would no more want to send your child into social situations without adequate skills than you would send her into a swimming pool without the ability to swim. Therefore, you will want to equip your child with knowledge about relationships, etiquette (for both Deaf and hearing cultures), and making friends and keeping them.

Your child's first social relationships occur at home. Use your family as a training ground. Next see to it that your child has ample opportunity to make friends and to interact with them. Social skills improve as a result of participation in relationships with peers and adults, both deaf and hearing.

On the other end of the social skills spectrum is antagonistic behavior, such as aggression, teasing, and destructiveness. These differ from other social problems in that they not only cause discord between parent and child but may also bring the child into conflict with society. Parents can guide their children in using effective ways to control and vent anger. In addition, children can learn to make good use of power, the main ingredient in aggression and other antisocial behaviors.

SOCIAL SKILLS AND PROBLEMS WITH RELATIONSHIPS

A child with few peer relationships does not have the opportunity to develop skills to make and keep friends. Social skills are best learned in small steps, starting at an early age. Expose your child to a variety of social situations with

The problems may look like:
• • • • • • •

● Child constantly interrupts conversations.

● Child disappears in conversations and sits there blank-faced.

● Family has constant frustration in communicating.

● Child asks a question and is out the door, on the TTY, or at the computer before anyone answers.

● Child has few friends at home or in school and hangs out exclusively with parents or family members.

● Child has very few deaf friends nearby.

● Child does not know how to or shows no motivation to use the TTY or relay operators to contact friends.

● Weekends and summers are very lonely for the child and stressful for the parent.

● Child plays with children younger than herself.

● Child has only one set of friends.

● Child fights with parents and siblings often.

● Child flies through the supermarket with candy in her mouth, a cucumber in her hand, and people jumping out of the way.

● Child knocks things over, starts fights, or teases and then looks to see if you noticed.

● Family rules differ for different family members.

children and adults. She must have a circle of deaf friends and exposure to deaf adults.

Due to previous failures or inexperience, a child may withdraw from interactions with other children to avoid further failure, rejection, or anxiety. Another child, with the same feelings, might resort to extreme and undesirable behavior, such as aggression, teasing, or clowning.

Your child's withdrawal may relate to other struggles, such as school difficulties (academic, communicative, or social), attention problems, body-related issues (poor hygiene, overweight, or under-development), aggression, and low self-esteem. (Refer to the chapters in this book that specifically address these problems.) Or your child may simply be shy, desiring contact and friendships but finding socializing awkward, difficult, and, at times, even painful.

Reflect upon your child's school, after-school, weekend, and summer social network. For a number of reasons (communication, distance, transportation) many deaf children have friends in one of these domains and not others. For example, a child may have a comfortable set of friends at school while she is lonely and bored after school and during summers. While these problems are difficult to overcome, you will find it helpful to plan ahead (explore options for the summer and make plans early), contact other parents of deaf children to plan multi-family activities, and encourage ongoing hobbies and activities for your child (sports, martial arts, dance, swimming).

A child who has experienced multiple rejections from unkind peers may begin to internalize the belief that she is undesirable and unlikable. Explain to her that social skills can be practiced and improved, much like math, baseball, or art. Break down the process into basic, understandable parts to practice—making introductions, initiating conversations, listening, showing interest, expressing views, giving feedback, planning play, and ending conversations. Practice these skills at home. Next, make plans to gradually introduce her to safe social situations with her peers.

Keep an open door policy on visitors. This may mean a little more noise and commotion in your house, but the benefits clearly outweigh the bother. Encourage your child to use the TTY. When distance and transportation present a problem, plan weekend group activities (have your child meet her peers and their families at parks, beaches, bowling alleys, and skating rinks). Establish sleepovers as a common practice among a trustworthy group of children and parents.

Activities

. . . .

Activity #1: Eyecatchers
   Materials: see list in activity
   Age: all ages
   Vocabulary/Concepts: invite, friends, play
. . . .

Social skill problems are often rooted in a fear of taking risks. This fear may be intensified for your deaf child as she may have additional sensitivities related to being different from hearing neighbors and being excluded intentionally or unintentionally. This activity will give your child some suggestions to help "jump start" friendships by making her and her home more appealing. We call this activity "Eyecatchers" since you will make your home inviting and child-friendly. Before setting up any eyecatchers, review with your child appropriate ways to invite friends to her home and remind your child of the social skills she possesses. Model ways she can interact, be friendly, and share interests. Use role-plays to show her how to resolve conflict and communication problems. In our experience, the following activities have caught the eyes of children in many a neighborhood.

1. *The Tree House:* Good, old-fashioned tree houses are great for attracting children to your yard. Consider making one designed and built by the neighborhood children.

2. *Super Sandbox:* Younger children will flock to your yard if it has a big, oversized sandbox with interesting toys.

3. *The Big Games:* Using a large outdoor space, such as a driveway, design a big checkerboard game. Do this by making the checkerboard with chalk on the driveway and then using margarine tub lids as the game pieces.

4. *Carnival Times:* Make a backyard carnival, complete with games and prizes. Plan activities, such as throwing balls in buckets, hoop-tosses, bean-bag throws, and squirt-gun targets. You might choose to make the carnival a charity event and encourage your child to advertise at school, church, or camp.

5. *Sidewalk Art:* Paint the sidewalk and driveway with chalk or washable paint. Have plenty of art supplies ready for neighborhood friends to share.

6. *The Friendly Project:* Invite a few families in the neighborhood to do a project together. Your family can "sponsor" a neighborhood garden. Have the children help plant, tend, and eat an array of vegetables. Or set up a rabbit farm and have the children care for these friendly pets.

7. *Inside Fun:* Redesign a room of your home to be an attractive play area for children. Stock it with arts, crafts, games, toys, and good snacks. Or have your child invite friends over to bake a cake or cookies, to make a big bowl of Jello™, or to prepare any edible delight.

. . . .

Activity #2: Let's Party

Materials: invitations, food, materials for activities
Age: 6–12
Vocabulary/Concepts: party, invite, activities, socialize, play

. . . .

Throw a party as a learning opportunity for your child. Coach her on how to socialize with others. Explain to her that you will help her learn how to introduce herself and develop friendships at a special "friendship party." To make sure this party does not result in further rejection, make it a combined social gathering for both your adult friends and their children. The guest list should include deaf peers or, at a minimum, people who are sensitive to your child's communication needs; otherwise the party will be one more lesson in isolation for your deaf child.

Have your child help with the party invitations and organize the activities. You may want to think of a theme, like a beach party or a costume party, to make it more appealing to children. When an adult or child calls on the phone about the party, model how to talk appropriately, use the TTY, or access the relay operator in order to speak with that person. Beforehand, discuss with your child what kinds of activities children would consider fun to do at a party and plan to do some of these.

Explain how to introduce a game or an activity at the party. Have your child role-play being the party hostess by meeting people at the door, making introductions, and showing them around her home. Practice sticky social situations, such as how to share, clarify communication, deal with a bossy child, or handle an uncooperative friend. On the day of the party, remain near your child for support and guidance, while letting her "try, try again." Model good social skills, showing your child how to invite friends to return another time or making future plans. After the party, tell your child how well she did by highlighting some of the outstanding social skills she used at the party.

. . . .

Activity #3: "How to Make and Keep Friends" Video or Book
Materials: paper, pencil, cardboard or heavy board, scissors, markers, stapler, yarn, hole-puncher
Age: 7–12
Vocabulary/Concepts: make friends, keep friends, introduce, success

. . . .

Have your child write a book or produce a video on the topic of how to make and keep friends. Discuss together the steps a person takes when making a friendship and then have your child depict these in her book or video. Start the book or video with skills on how to introduce yourself and end with your child demonstrating a successful meeting and making a friend.

WHEN FRIENDS ARE FAR, FAR AWAY

While children may have deaf friends at school, because of geographic distances they do not have contact with them when at home. This becomes more stressful as the child grows older and wants to belong to a group of children, is interested in team sports, and likes to converse with peers.

Often, neighborhood hearing peers unintentionally exclude the deaf child as a result of their engagement in rapid group conversation. In less hospitable circumstances, the child becomes an easy target since she is different, her voice may seem odd to some, she may miss remarks made about her, and, in general, she may be either cautious or excessively active to make up for the discomfort of not feeling a part of the group.

To counter a deaf child's loneliness, a parent may find herself driving long distances to a friend's home. Some of the normal childhood interactions, such as bickering, might be cause for your child to want to come home early or to refuse to visit with a particular child. If the same children interacted daily in the immediate neighborhood, their fight would most likely last a brief period of time and would not cause a logistic or social nightmare.

Activities

. . . .

Activity #1: TTY Games
Materials: TTY
Age: 4–12
Vocabulary/Concepts: hello, good-bye, GA, SK, Q or ?, abbreviations
(reduce word size)

. . . .

When your child feels comfortable with her TTY she will have more contact with friends and family. You can help her become accustomed to using the TTY by helping her practice typing, decoding abbreviations, and using the etiquette. Play a game with your child in which you sit side-by-side and converse. You must first learn basic TTY etiquette and symbols, such as GA to indicate turn taking, SK to end the conversation, Q or ? to indicate a question, and using a polite greeting and sign off. Teach "Hi, GA" and "Bye, GA" to preschoolers. For your three-to-six-year-old, try expanding to: "Hi, Gia here, GA"; "Hi, Dad here, GA"; " Bye, SK"; and "Bye, SK."

The older child can practice spelling and abbreviations. For the child who has difficulty with spelling, make a list of important words and include pictures—proper names, places, "wh" questions, and words used to clarify communication (e.g., "understand," "again," "please slow," "sorry," and numbers).

If your child is comfortable with spelling, play with ideas about abbreviations. Teach your child to form abbreviations by omitting vowels. If she finds this confusing then show her some—e.g., problem=prblm or next=nxt. Take turns abbreviating whole sentences and guessing what they mean. Use this game to notice words that are difficult to abbreviate or to understand when abbreviated.

Because the TTY does not allow callers to view each other, the emotional quality of what is being said can be lost. However, Deaf people have adapted to this creatively. By using various emotional indicators (feeling words, visual indicators, capitalizing, punctuation, and drawing out a word), callers can convey the true emotions behind their words. Take turns speaking with your child, paying specific attention to adding words to color the tone of your message: e.g., "Guess you just woke up! hahahaha"; "Thank you (smile)"; "Ugh! I don't like that!!!!!!"; "I DO NOT WANT TO GO!"; "Ummmmmmmmmmm, well, hmmm, I don't know"; "Soooooooo, gotta go . . ." Guess what the other person feels or looks like based on the clues given over the TTY. Have your child create her own indicators.

Activity #2: Pen Pals

Materials: paper, pens, markers, cards, stamps, envelopes, padded
    envelopes, boxes
Age: 6–12
Vocabulary/Concepts: pen pal, letter, send, wait, conversation, story,
    far away, write, draw, surprise, card

Children adore receiving mail. Although getting a letter does not take the place of having a playmate, it can offer your child a weekly communication with a friend. Having the ability to read and write might make this activity more enjoyable; however, do not allow a low level of literacy to daunt your child. She can use whatever skills she has in written communication (and drawing). If she is self-conscious about her writing abilities, then consider coupling this project with school tutoring or an English class. Perhaps an older sibling might be willing to help.

The term "pen pal" has come to mean a person from far away (often another country) with whom a child exchanges letters. We use the word in a broader sense to mean anyone written to regularly; for example, an aunt or uncle in another city, a teacher, a deaf student in another school either in the area or from another region, a hearing student interested in learning about deaf people, a deaf adult, or a child who actually lives in another country. It would be a real treat if your child could find a foreign deaf child or adult with whom to correspond. Try contacting the National Information Center on Deafness, Gallaudet University, 800 Florida Ave. NE, Washington, DC 20002-3695 or the World Federation for the Deaf, Ilkantie, PO Box 65, SF-Helsinki, Finland to request lists of both American and foreign schools.

Introduce the idea of a pen pal to your child by asking her how she feels when she receives birthday cards, valentines, or letters. Explain that friendships develop in many ways, such as by phone, in letters, and in person. Discuss with her whom she might want to write to. See what strikes her interest. Initially she may prefer to practice writing letters with a reliable relative. Supply her with several options just in case some of them don't work out.

Have her use family cards (see chapter 7 on Family Unity); homemade stationery; or special store-bought writing paper. Give her some ideas about the variety of things she can do in a letter—draw, tell an ongoing story, send photocopies, tell jokes, and send small gifts or cards. Your child might wish to start a pen-pal club at school. Suggest this to your child's teacher as a possible class project.

Activity #3: The Family Network
Age: all ages
Vocabulary/Concepts: families together, fun activities, friends

Much as yourself, other parents are exploring ways to have their deaf children socialize with other deaf children. If your child is one of many deaf children at her school, talk with the other parents about having family activities together (picnics, beach events, sled-riding, or bowling teams). If your child has few or no deaf peers, seek out deaf schools in your area.

This activity depends on your interests, finances, transportation, and geographical area. In the Boston area, we have met families from a particular school that do activities together, such as hayrides and weekend vacations. We also know of a larger pool of families from a variety of schools who join together for monthly events, such as picnics, parties, and movies.

As you form relationships with other families, you can problem-solve and brainstorm together about other social events, how to handle transportation problems, child care exchanges, sleepover or weekend visits, respite needs, and how to encourage the children to maintain TTY (or pen pal) contact. You can also develop a wider support group of parents who have similar questions and concerns, some of whom may have more experience than yourself with particular issues.

Activity #4: Summer Sun and Fun
Age: all ages
Vocabulary/Concepts: summer, plan, families together, sleepovers, vacations, sports, team, activities, deaf camp, TTY, relationships, STAY IN TOUCH

This activity is an extension of the previous activity. Begin by having your family discuss what they would like to do for the summer. Next, use your family network to plan group activities. Find out what your child's friends will be doing over the summer and when. We recommend you do this as early as mid-winter for several reasons. First, summer often takes parents by surprise. Deadlines for camps are easily missed, summer day programs fill up, and family vacations may conflict with other activities. Secondly, once the weather starts to change people are often busy planting gardens, cleaning yards, and participating in spring events, such as weddings and graduations. And lastly, your children will enjoy the chance to plan and talk about summer.

To kick off the theme of summer, you may want to have a mid-winter beach party at your or another family's house. Grill hot dogs and hamburgers, wear beach clothes, and have a living-room picnic. Brainstorm summer activities. Consolidate resources, such as transportation, space, and supplies.

Your group of families can join together to make the summer active and fun, to minimize isolation for your children, and to lessen parental stress. Here are some ideas for summer plans:

1. *Camps for Deaf Children:* These are often some distance from home and require transportation, filling out applications, fees, and making sure that your child is ready for an extended stay away from home.

2. *Day Camps:* Sometimes municipal or specialized camps run on a school-day schedule. Schools will often organize activity-related summer programs if enough families show interest.

3. *Camping:* This activity can occur in state parks and provides a wonderful way for families to congregate.

4. *Trips:* Families can take mini-vacations together to the beach, lakes, water parks, or playing fields.

5. *Sleepovers:* These work well if regularly planned and if the site rotates so that no parent has more than one sleepover for the summer (Whew!). The children may find it more exciting to sleep in a tent than a bedroom.

6. *Picnics.*

7. *Vacation Pals:* Consider bringing one of your child's friends along on your vacations, and have your child accompany the other family on their vacation, in return.

8. *Cooperative Game Day:* For some ideas about fun, noncompetitive, outdoor games, refer to the following books: *Everyone Wins! Cooperative Games and Activities* (Sambhava and Josette Lurmour, New Society Publishers, 1990); *The Cooperative Sports and Games Book* (Terry Orlick, Pantheon Books, 1978); and *New Games for the Whole Family* (Dale N. DeFevre, Perigee Books, 1988).

9. *Team Sports:* Assemble family volleyball, softball, or frisbee teams. Make T-shirts for team members.

10. *Bike Trips:* Take short rides on a bike trail that ends up at a picnic site.

11. *TTY Calls, Pen Pals, and Relay Relationships:* Use the activities described in this chapter to help maintain contact with those children less accessible to your youngster during the summer.

12. *The Transportation Fund:* Consider sharing transportation costs with other families and even having fund-raisers to maintain a fund for emergency transportation needs.

13. *Saturday Night at the Movies:* Look for special captioned film showings of new movies. Meet friends and family at the theater and have a treat afterwards.

14. *YMCA, Boys or Girls Club, 4H Club:* Contact these agencies to learn what they offer in the way of summer activities and then develop a deaf contingent.

15. *Fireworks Displays:* Get a group together, prepare a pot-luck picnic, and attend a local fireworks display on the Fourth of July.

• •

Activity #5: Relay Relationships

Materials: TTY

Age: 8–12

Vocabulary/Concepts: TTY, relay operator, interpret, private, TAKE-
TURNS, wait

• •

Do you have many family and friends who don't own a TTY? Do not despair. You can teach your child how to use a relay service. This may not be feasible until the child is at least eight years old since she must understand the concept of an operator and will need to wait patiently for her calls to go through and for the operator to type. Trained specifically for this job, operators have a particular sensitivity to the varying written English capabilities of their clients. You might even want to find out if a local telephone company uses relay operators so you can take your child or family on a tour to see how they work. Explain to your child that operators must keep the information they transmit private.

MISBEHAVING IN PUBLIC

Children easily become either bored or over-stimulated in public situations (especially supermarkets, toy stores, restaurants, and family gatherings). You may find that your child loses control much more easily in public than when she is at home. This is especially true if a child has attention or sensory integration problems—she may feel bombarded with unwanted stimuli.

Have reasonable expectations for your child. Consider her age, maturity, and disposition. Always keep your child informed of her upcoming schedule to avoid unnecessary misbehavior due to her uncertainty.

Be prepared with toys, games, and snacks that will occupy the child when she is bored or tired. Find ways to include her in the activity (such as marking off items on the grocery list or finding them for you). When possible, you can use this time as a learning experience—the child can match pictures to coupons, use new signs, or learn to scan the shelves for particular items.

You will have a big problem if your child discovers that the consequences for misbehavior are different or nonexistent when away from home. Establish rules and expectations. For a child age five and older, mete out consequences that will be enacted later. Make sure these are clear to the child and she can make the connection between the behavior she exhibited in public and the consequence delivered at home.

Activities

∙∙∙

Activity #1: The "To-Go" Bag
Materials: large cloth bag, (games, crafts, and sitting-still activities),
    list of do's and don't's, portable "Think Chair" (see pgs. 51–54),
    paper, markers, "On My Own Kits" (see pgs. 191–192)
Age: 3–10
Vocabulary/Concepts: sitting still, do, don't, right, wrong, your choice,
    surprise, FORBIDDEN, THINK-SELF

∙∙∙

Activities such as grocery shopping and going to a fancy restaurant are not generally "child friendly." The child must sit still for an extended period of time and the social demands may prove too much for her energized personality. A deaf child will lose her patience even sooner as she tries to decipher what parents might be saying to cashiers, waiters, and salespeople. The parents' priority at these times is usually on completing the task, meaning accessible communication must take a back seat. All of this makes public outings a challenge for everyone. We do not suggest that you tolerate misbehavior, or that the child be left at home. However, parents need to "plan, prepare, and prevent" for these situations. We hope this activity will help you do that.

The "To Go" bag resembles the "On My Own Kits," with a few distinctions. First, the bag (backpack, briefcase, or large purse) should contain only "sitting still" crafts and activities. Second, include a list of "do's and don't's" in the bag outlining acceptable behaviors (sitting nicely, not arguing) and unacceptable behaviors (screaming, running, or fighting with a sibling). Include on the "do" list skills that your child has for keeping herself entertained, staying calm, and following directions. Tell her the consequences of exhibiting "don't" behaviors.

Set up an incentive program for behaving correctly. You may want to carry a "Think Chair" sign in the bag in case your child loses control and she needs to calm herself and think through her actions.

Add new, fun items to the bag occasionally and use these as rewards for acceptable behavior. Remember to TAP yourself to regain control of your actions in dealing with your child's negative behavior in public. Here are some suggestions for the bag: cards, bingo, travel-sized board games, "write-in" activity books, coloring books, little dolls, books, origami, needlepoint, three-dimensional puzzles, beads for making jewelry, and macrame.

●●●

Activity #2: The Time Machine

Materials: large cardboard box, buttons, paper, markers, paint,
    buttons, gadgets
Age: 5–10
Vocabulary/Concepts: time machine, fly, future, past, mistake, other
    way, goals, wish, think, right, wrong

●●

This activity allows you to model acceptable public behavior while your child has a chance to examine her behavior and to practice options. You and your child will make a time machine out of a very large cardboard box. The box should be large enough for your child to sit in it. Put buttons, gears, and gadgets in the box. Add a special window from which your child can look. Use this machine to travel backwards in time in order to review situations in which your child misbehaved and situations in which she exercised control. Make the machine travel forward for your child to practice social skills for an upcoming event or situation (a wedding or a party). She can also learn to deal with problematic situations that have previously given her trouble by practicing how to deal with these before they arise again. Take the time machine back to your own childhood and show your child mistakes that you made and how you learned to improve your behavior.

Use the time machine to help your child develop skills for making friends. Have her go back in time to meet some of her favorite heroes, such as Babe

Ruth or Laurent Clerc. Fly into the future to have her meet a new friend. Have a conversation with the new friend and invite the friend back home in the machine.

Here are other time machine travel ideas:

- Go back to a conflict which the child did not resolve well.

- Go to another country, planet, or universe.

- Go to a situation in which your child is apprehensive.

- Go to the past to figure out what really happened in a particular situation.

- Go to different points in history to find out what deaf people were doing at that time.

Activity #3: Restaurant Games

Materials: paper, pencil, menu, book, magazines
Age: 6–12
Vocabulary/Concepts: game, keep busy, quiet, understand, confusing

The goal of a restaurant game is to keep your children quiet and engaged in an appropriate activity. Keeping your child amused will prevent misbehavior in a restaurant. If your child enjoys word games, make up a story from words on the menu. Each family member can take a turn choosing a word from the menu and telling a piece of the story. Make sure your deaf child is able to follow the words, story, and turn-taking plan. Bring a book or magazine to use to continue this activity while waiting for your meal to arrive.

If you bring a pencil and paper, you can play any number of games. Play hangman. Try to guess words that family members can see or smell. Use words off of the menu. Or perhaps make up a story about the person who sat in your seat before you: what that person looks like, what she does for a living, and what she had to eat. Entertain your child with exotic stories about famous stars and mysterious people doing funny things. Have your child draw a picture of what these people look like.

Remember to assess your deaf child's comfort at mealtime. She may misbehave out of lack of involvement. If she often complains or misbehaves during meals at home, has a lot of trouble following conversations, or only communicates well with one family member, it is likely that restaurants will intensify these problems. Whereas at home she might leave the table, in a restaurant she may feel trapped.

. . . .

Activity #4: The Coupon or Shopping Detective
Materials: coupons, shopping list, pencil, discount ads
Age: 7–12
Vocabulary/Concepts: search, find, patient

. . . .

Give your child a stack of coupons, discount advertisements, or a list (with pictures) from the supermarket. The child's job is to search for the items pictured on the coupon or list. Explain to your child how the food is organized in your local supermarket and how to scan a shelf for an item (valuable independent living skills). If the child is developmentally able, teach her to check for the correct size. Ask questions to see if she knows the intended use for your purchases. At the end of the shopping trip, reward the child for her helpfulness by giving her a special coupon for a treat (this could be a real coupon or one that you made yourself to indicate a reward).

SOCIALLY AGGRESSIVE AND DESTRUCTIVE BEHAVIOR

There are four types of aggressive behavior: (1) provoked or reactive behavior (self-defense); (2) unprovoked (the need to dominate others); (3) aggressive outbursts (impulsive or explosive, in which a person is out of control); and (4) oppositional behavior (which is generally defiant, opposing authority figures and their demands).

Aggression is often used by a child who does not feel powerful or in control. An aggressive deaf child may not have the vocabulary to express her feelings, may feel overwhelmed by a host of frustrating (communication) situations, or may have learned to use aggression as a way of communicating needs and eliciting responses. Feelings of sadness, anxiety, confusion, and frustration might be communicated through aggression if a child does not have constructive alternatives for expression.

The aggressive child may have a problem discriminating feelings, interpreting all of them into "mad." Help your child identify and expand her feeling vocabulary—she will calm down if she discerns a variety of feelings and you will be better able to respond if you know more specifics.

Empower your child by offering useful methods for decision-making and expressing displeasure. This may take the form of challenging a parent—allow this to happen but teach her acceptable ways to disagree and state her point of view. If she has "power" to express herself and influence her environment then she will not need to control others.

Newspapers, TV, and video games often glamorize aggression. Your child may copy what she sees and not understand the context or consequences of the actions displayed. Curb your child's exposure to aggressive role models, TV, and highly competitive environments. Relate what she sees to your own family values and norms for behavior.

If a child is handled aggressively by adults she will learn to handle her problems with aggression. Lack of communication between parent and child can precipitate increased physical discipline of the child. Deaf children who are taught from early in life that asserting themselves through words will get them more positive results have less need to use aggression.

Teach your child to respect the bodies, belongings, and personal rights of others. Constantly model and explain these values to your child.

Activities

Activity #1: Appreciation Week

Materials: see activity for details

Age: 5–12

Vocabulary/Concepts: appreciate, thank you, enjoy, honor, fix, nice, help others

Set aside a week to increase your child's awareness and appreciation of people, property, objects, and the environment. Make a banner with your child announcing Appreciation Week. Explore the definition of the word "appreciation" by role-playing ways to show appreciation for people (saying "thanks" when you are given something) or property (walking on the sidewalk and not on someone's lawn). Choose from the following activities.

1. *My Home:* Do something nice for your home as a family. Plant a garden, fix a broken structure, redecorate a room, or buy a nice object. With an older child you can do something for a charitable organization that helps the homeless. Encourage your child to think of things a family or an individual does not have when lacking a home.

2. *Breakables:* Take your child to a factory where breakables (lamps, glass, dinnerware) are made to illustrate the effort, time, and expense that is put into making these items.

3. *The Letter:* Write a letter to a hero or heroine who represents your family's values.

4. *Thank-You Cards:* Design family thank-you cards to give to people when they have done something nice. Teach your child to send cards for no particular reason other than as a reminder that she simply appreciates a person.

5. *The UN:* An older child can learn about the harm of violence by becoming involved in a charitable organization that deals with domestic violence or violence against animals or the environment. Choose an organization, such as Greenpeace, the United Nations, the Anti-Defamation League, or a local crisis center as a place to get involved.

Activity #2: The Piñata Punch
Materials: papier mâché piñata, trinkets, small toys, candy
Age: 5–12
Vocabulary/Concepts: piñata, save, hold, express, anger, prize, win

This activity encourages your child to use constructive ways to handle angry feelings rather than hitting and breaking things. You will need a papier mâché piñata (found in stores that sell party supplies) and small trinkets for prizes. Cut a small hole in the top of the piñata to add more prizes gradually. Tell your child that you will give her a prize when she uses skills to refrain from hitting, to carefully handle an object, or to independently stop herself before breaking or damaging something. Put the prize into the piñata. Explain to your child that she will have the opportunity to express all of those angry feelings in an appropriate way with her piñata. After a few days, or at the end of the week, depending on your child's age and ability to delay gratification, allow her to smash open the piñata and retrieve her rewards.

It takes practice and effort for a child to halt the fury of the moment and refrain from hitting or destroying something. The piñata activity teaches children to stop and use good judgement (STAR).

Encourage your child to verbalize reasons for her anger of the previous week before breaking open the piñata. Remind her that the piñata is the only thing to destroy or hit. Of course situations will still arise in which you cannot ignore your child's behavior. If your child acts in an aggressive or destructive manner that calls for immediate attention, try using the Think Chair or Logical Consequences.

Activity #3: A Day in Court
Age: 8–12
Vocabulary/Concepts: court, lawyer, judge, jury, law, rule, break, victim, subpoena, restitution, pay-back, FORBIDDEN, FAIR

Set up a court system with your family. Take your child to a court house to observe the fundamentals of the process (the judge, witnesses, lawyers, and the expectation of telling the truth). If your child cannot follow the conversation, summarize it for her—don't expect your child to sit for a long time if she cannot follow the courtroom communication.

Bring the court structure into your home and take turns being the judge. Set up a court day. List out unacceptable behaviors that family members have exhibited during the week. Write down these behaviors prior to court day and give them to the perpetrators (subpoena). Have family members bring witnesses. After hearing the matter, the judge should make a fair decision and suggest an action for restitution. Do not use the court to mete out punishment but rather to suggest a way that the perpetrator can "make it up" to the victim (e.g., by doing something for that person). Here are some ideas for restitution:

- the child does another person's chores,

- the child raises money to replace an item she destroyed or damaged (by working, having a fund-raiser, or by saving her allowance),

- the child writes a formal apology on a card or poster.

Acknowledge when a family rule (law) has been broken. This reinforces the notion that all family members are expected to abide by the rules of the family. If your family chooses to do "A Day in Court," then all family members must agree to accept a subpoena when it is given to them. This may prove to be a successful way to empower your child to voice grievances with her parent's behavior. Suggest that your child's school take a trip to a court house (with an interpreter) for a more detailed understanding of the judicial process.

. . . .

Activity #4: Stomp Your Feet
Materials: plastic bubble wrapping
Age: 4–10
Vocabulary/Concepts: stomp, angry, express, let it out

. . . .

If your child needs an outlet for her aggressive energy, "bubble packs" will come in handy. Yes, those wonderful plastic sheets of bubble wrapping used for mailing breakables are great for feet-stomping angry children. Give your child a few sheets and instruct her to stamp out all of the bubbles or to stomp until all of her angry feelings have popped out of her feet!

. . . .

Activity #5: The Gentle Olympics and Games
Materials: as needed for chosen events—see activity suggestions
Age: 5–12
Vocabulary/Concepts: gentle, games or olympics, slow, carefully,
    teamwork, control

. . . .

Set up a "Gentle Olympics" in your home or backyard. Include games that require your child to win through gentle behavior. Some olympic activities could be carrying an egg from one point to another, having two people walk together holding a cooked spaghetti noodle between them, running up to a person without knocking or bumping into her, or tossing styrofoam packaging peanuts into a container. Make sure your child wins a gold medal for her success.

Play gentle games with your child. Make a house of cards with your child, carefully stacking the cards. Create a domino race by carefully standing dominoes next to one another; then top the end domino and watch the chain reaction happen. Throughout the game, comment to your child to show that you notice her gentle behaviors. Model feeling frustrated (knocking a domino over) and how to use self-talk to regain control, "Oh darn! Well, we all make mistakes. I guess I'll try again."

My Wishes and Wants Test

● ● ● ●

If I had three wishes, what would I wish for?

1.

2.

3.

If I had one hundred dollars, what would I buy?

1.

2.

3.

If I could do anything I wanted with my family, what would it be?

1.

2.

3.

My favorite activity is _____

_____

When I have special time with my parents, I like to _____

_____

When I play by myself, my favorite thing to do is _____

_____

If I could have special privileges, they would be _____

_____

201 Rewards Children Love to Work for

• • • •

[Ask children to put a check next to each item or privilege they would like to have.]

Toys

dolls

doll clothing

doll carriage

doll toys

doll house

doll furniture

stuffed animals

puppets

play kitchen

kitchen supplies

play make-up

dress-up clothes

board games

building blocks

large play items: playhouse, outdoor toys

play figures

puzzles

jump rope

jacks

marbles

swimming pool toys

sled

spending money for the toy store

bike

motor bike

Sports Equipment

balls

basketball

basketball hoop

surf board

ski equipment

sports-related clothing

soccer ball
baseball
baseball mitt
hockey gear
swimming gear
special sports shoes
ski poles/boots
ice skates
roller skates
golf equipment
skateboard
gymnastics mat

cheerleading accessories (pom-poms, clothing)
baton
boating gear (clothing, equipment)
volleyball
badminton set
horseshoes
sports bag
exercise equipment
fishing rod
windsurfer

Arts and Crafts

coloring book
crayons
markers
paints
easel
clay
ceramics
origami paper and instructions
fabric paint
jewelry crafts
yarn crafts (knitting, needlepoint)

ribbon/hairpiece crafts
sewing equipment
macrame materials
papermaking materials
pens
collage supplies
glues (in different colors)
holiday crafts
batik materials
tie dye materials
chalks

Special Classes

ceramics
swimming
dance
gymnastics
arts and crafts
music
sports (baseball, football, cheerleading camp)
sailing/boating

painting
horseback riding
drawing
calligraphy
cooking
tennis
martial arts

Foods

sweet desserts
special treats (candy, cookies)
making a favorite food
eating with his/her hands

cooking with a parent
gardening
theme picnic

Family Activities

bowling
ice skating
food outings (e.g., pizza, ice cream)
eating at a special restaurant
movie
picnic
flying a kite
trip to the playground
zoo
camping trip
play center outing
beach
museum
aquarium
roller skating
miniature golf
water slides
drive-in movie
build a tree house
sand box

playground equipment
play house
one-to-one parent time
concert
go to mom/dad's work
day at the mall
living room camp out
read book at night
go for a quiet parent-and-child walk
play cards with parent
play board game with parent
go shopping with parent
horseback riding
play pretend with parent
go out to lunch with parent
   business lunch at parent's work
   go out to lunch during school time
surprise day trip with parent
breakfast in bed

BIG Family Rewards

swimming pool
a vacation

computer
item for the home

Body Delights

new clothes
permanent/haircut
nails done
massage
new nail kit
make-up
perfume
lotions and powders
blow dryers

fancy brush
hair ribbons
hair gel
insignia of sports/star on clothes
rhinestones, buttons, pins
special shoe laces
baseball caps
sunglasses

Social Rewards

hugs and kisses
sleep over
a party
friend over for dinner
join a club (scouts, ski club)
story times
special ritual (e.g., piggy back)

tickling
personal letters written from you to
your child
phone calls
notes
visit to a friend's house
inviting a friend to a special activity

Special Items

surprise
jewelry
books
backpack
lunch box
computer game
telephone
records
tapes
bedroom accoutrements
   poster
   pillow design
   design and decorate own room
   lampshade
   stuffed animal
   new paint for the walls
   flowers
   plant
   new comforter
   furniture

telephone
television
stereo
camera
gift certificate
plaque
ribbon
trophy
money
television
pets
   fish
   gerbil
   guinea pig
   ant farm
   rabbit
   bird
   cat
   dog
   horse

Privileges

alarm clock
later bed time
later curfew
a day off from chores
TV time
stereo time
longer TTY/telephone calls
use of bike/motor bike
independent trips (e.g., to the store)
phone jack in bedroom
computer time
special TV shows
video game time
pool time
park time

outings with friends
   to the movies
   to the mall
   out to eat
allowed to sleep in one morning
be given own room
making choices about:
   wake up time
   sleep time
   homework time
   chores
   meals
cooking privileges

Token Program Chart

• • • •

Name: _____

My Goal is: Ask before I touch things that are not mine.

Day: _____

Morning: _____

_____

_____

Afternoon: _____

_____

_____

Evening: _____

_____

_____

Total Today:

Sample Contracts
● ● ● ●

Sample Contract #1

This contract focuses on one specific goal.

I agree to: do my homework every evening without getting upset.

I will help myself accomplish this by:
1) using my office.
2) doing my homework when I first get home.
3) asking for help in reviewing my work.

My parents will help by:
1) reminding me once.
2) helping me get organized.

If I do my homework all week I can choose one of the following:
1) go to a movie.
2) have a late bedtime one night.

Signed: Natasha   Date:
         Mom and Dad   Date:

Sample Contract #2

This contract focuses on a long-term goal and a new contract might be made once this contract's agreements are fulfilled.

Name:

My goal is: to tell people my feelings and get help instead of hitting people.

Agreement:
1) When I am upset, I will draw or write to express myself.
2) After I am calm, I will tell people what made me upset.

My dad, mom, and teacher will help me by:
1) Letting me know in a nice way when I look upset.
2) Reminding me to draw or write.
3) Not bugging me until I calm down.

I know that if I hit someone, then I will need to do an extra chore and do something nice for that person.

Signed: Bob   Date:
       Mom, Dad, Mr. Sunny (teacher)   Date:

Sample Contract #3

Use this kind of contract for a short period of time during which a child and parent/family work toward a goal.

Goal: To have a live Christmas tree.

Date Start: Date End:

Tanya: I agree to water the tree.
Mom: I agree to pick out the tree.
Dad: I agree to decorate the tree.
Nick: I agree to pick up the needles that fall.

Signed: Mom, Dad, Nick, Tanya

Chart and Reward Program

• • • •

SAMPLE CHARTS

Chart A
Use drawings of the tasks.
Name:

Must:	Sun	Mon	Tue	Wed	Thur	Fri	Sat
Pick up toys							
Feed cats							
Reward:							

Chart B

Must:	Sun	Mon	Tue	Wed	Thur	Fri	Sat
Make bed	✓	✓	✓	✓	✓	✓	✓
Do homework	✓	✓	✓	✓	✓	✓	✓
Take out trash	✓	✓	✓	✓	○	✓	✓
Bed at 8:30	✓	✓	○	✓	○	✓	✓

Total checks for week = 25

Total checks needed for bowling night = 24

A Sample Level Program

• • • •

Name: _____

Date: _____

Level 1

Total points needed for _____ weeks = _____

Responsibilities:
    1. Do one chore with one reminder = _____ points
    2. Do homework by 5:00 p.m. = _____ points

Privileges earned:
    1. Get an extra 15 minutes of play time
    2. Set bedtime 15 minutes later than usual

Level 2

Total points needed for _____ weeks = _____

Responsibilities:
    1. Do one chore with no reminder = _____ points
    2. Do homework by 5:00 p.m. = _____ points
    3. Walk the dog after school = _____ points

Privileges earned:
    1. Get an extra 30 minutes of play time

2. Set bedtime 30 minutes later than usual

3. Receive $.50

Level 3

Total points needed for _____ weeks = _____

Responsibilities:

1. Do two chores with no reminders = _____ points

2. Do homework by 5:15 p.m. = _____ points

3. Walk the dog before and after school = _____ points

4. Wash Dad's car = _____ points

Privileges earned:

1. Get an extra 45 minutes of play time

2. Set bedtime 45 minutes later than usual

3. Receive $.75

4. Choose a special activity to do with Dad

Level 4

Total points needed for _____ weeks = _____

Responsibilities:

1. Do three chores with no reminders = _____ points

2. Do homework by 5:30 p.m. = _____ points

3. Walk the dog before and after school and after dinner = _____ points

4. Wash Dad's car = _____ points

5. Help Mom garden = _____ points

Privileges earned:

1. Get an extra hour of play time

2. Set bedtime one hour later than usual

3. Receive $1.00

4. Choose a special activity to do with Dad

5. Choose a special activity to do with Mom

A Treasury of Children's Skills and Capabilities

● ● ● ●

Artistic Activities

cake-decorating
calligraphy
candle-making
cartoon-drawing
ceramics
clay-molding
coloring
crochet
cutting
doll-making
doodling
drawing lines, circles, squares
embroidery
fabric art
knitting

macrame
movie-making
needlepoint
origami
painting
pasting
photography
pottery
print-making
quilting
sculpting
sewing
tie-dying
weaving
woodcraft

Home Chores

cleans bathrooms
  bedroom
   closets

  dishes
  windows
helps clean up

Nature and Outdoor Activities

astronomy
back-packing
bird-watching
camping
collecting rocks
exploring
farming
gardening
hiking
mountain-climbing

playing on the playground
protecting the environment
protecting wildlife
recycling
rock-climbing
shell-collecting
studying butterflies
taking care of animals
traveling
whale-watching

Performance Abilities

costuming
dancing
  ballet
  jazz
  modern
  tap
dramatics
face-painting
improvisation

magic tricks, card tricks
mime
play production and direction
play-writing
puppetry
role-playing
set design
set production

Personality Traits

accepting
active
agile
alert
appreciative
artistic
assertive
athletic
brave
calm
careful
caring
charming
cooperative
creative
curious
determined
diligent
easy-going
empathic
excitable
fearless

flexible
focused
follows directions
forgiving
free-spirited
friendly
funny
generous
gentle
gifted
giving
good conversationalist
good in emergency situations
good memory
good problem-solver
good storyteller
gracious
great joker
happy
happy-go-lucky
hard worker
imaginative

independent
insightful
intriguing
joyful
kind
mature
motivated
negotiator
noncompetitive
observant
organized
patient
peacemaker
physical
pleasant disposition
polite
powerful
private

proud
quick learner
quick thinker
respectful
responsible
safety-minded
self-assured
self-confident
silly
smart
sweet
terrific laugh
thoughtful
trustworthy
truthful
understanding
well-mannered

Personal Appearance

brushes teeth well
cleans nails
combs hair nicely
dresses nicely
eats healthy foods
finishes a meal
has a friendly face
  a great smile
  cute dimples
  great freckles
  nice eyes
  nice hair
  nice nails

strong arms
  hands
  legs
  stomach
is petite
is muscular
is tall
knows when full
smells nice
takes care of clothing
tans nicely
uses bathroom right
washes self

Physical Abilities (fine motor)

carpentry
doing puzzles
drawing

handwriting
model building

Physical Abilities (gross motor)

balances well
catches well
climbs ropes
climbs trees
gallops

holds breath for a long time
hops
is flexible
is graceful
jumps high

leaps high
moves nice and slow
runs fast
skips

spins around
swings high
throws well
walks quickly

School Skills

answers questions in class
computers
concentrates
does homework
foreign language
geography
good attendance
good grades
good library skills
good presenter
good reports
handwriting
history
home economics
loves learning
math
turns in neat papers

participates in class discussions
punctual
raises hand in class
rarely absent
reading
religious studies
remembers to bring home books
research
respects teacher
science
spelling
stays in seat
studies hard
studies for tests
turns papers in on time
writing

Special Abilities

board games
crossword puzzles
cooking
video games
collecting baseball cards
   dollhouse furniture
   railroad cars
   stamps
fixing things
giving gifts

learning about cars
   dinosaurs
   electricity
map-reading
pet care
putting things together
reading directions
saving money
taking things apart
walking the dog

Social Skills

apologizes
follower
gives good hugs and kisses
good host
good loser
good pen pal
good phone skills
good sister/brother/cousin
good winner

has nice manners
helps others
introduces self nicely
is polite
leader
listens to others
nice party guest
participates in clubs
   earns badges

follows club rules
good member
joins activities
plays fair
plays nicely
plays quietly
remembers names
says "hello"

says "good-bye"
says "thank you"
says "you're welcome"
shares
sits nicely
supports others
talks nicely about others
waits turn

Sports Abilities

aerobics
archery
badminton
baseball
basketball
baton-twirling
bicycling
boating
canoeing
cheerleading
dart-throwing
fencing
field hockey
football
golf
horseback-riding
ice hockey
jogging
judo
jump-roping

karate
kite-flying
racquetball
roller-skating
sailing
self-defense
skateboarding
skating
skiing
soccer
softball
surfing
swimming
tennis
track and field
water-skiing
windsurfing
wrestling
yoga

Bibliography

$\bullet\ \bullet\ \bullet\ \bullet$

ACTIVITIES AND GAMES

Bornstein, Harry, and Karen L. Saulnier. *Sign Word Flash Cards*. Washington, D.C.: Kendall Green Publications, Gallaudet University Press, 1987.

Finger Alphabet Lotto. Eugene, Ore.: Garlic Press, 1992.

Hafer, Jan C., Robert N. Wilson, and Paul M. Setzer. *Come Sign With Us: Sign Language Activities for Children*. Washington, D.C.: Clerc Books, Gallaudet University Press, 1990.

Hoemann, Shirley. *Children's Sign Language Playing Cards*. Silver Spring, Md.: National Association of the Deaf, 1973.

Keep Quiet Reword Game. Stanhope, N.J.: Kopptronix Co., 1981.

The Manual Alphabet Poster. Washington, D.C.: Kendall Green Publications, Gallaudet University Press, 1980.

Miller, Ralph, Sr., Betty G. Miller, and Frank Allen Paul. *Sign Language Coloring Books*. Berkeley: Dawn Sign Press, 1985.

Schwartz, Sue, and Joan E. Heller. *The Language of Toys: Teaching Communication Skills to Special Needs Children: A Guide for Parents and Teachers*. Kensington, Md.: Woodbine House, 1988.

Shroyer, Susan P., and Joan G. Kimmel. *Secret Signing: PreK-1*. Greensboro, N.C.: Sugar Sign Press, 1988.

Shroyer, Susan P., and Joan G. Kimmel. *Secret Signing: Grades 1–3*. Greensboro, N.C.: Sugar Sign Press, 1988.

Stone, Rachel. *Let's Learn about Deafness: Classroom Activities*. Washington, D.C.: Pre-College Programs, Gallaudet University, 1988.

Van Den Berg, Patricia. *Activity Book for Deaf Children.* Roseville, Mich.: Patricia Van Den Berg, 1992.

BODY-RELATED ISSUES

Epstein, Leonard H., and Sally Squires. *The Stoplight Diet for Children: An 8-Week Program for Parents and Children.* Boston: Little, Brown & Co., 1988.

Exercise

Alter, Judith, and Pamela Wilson. *Staying Healthy: A Family Affair.* Washington, D.C.: Pre-College Programs, Gallaudet University, 1991.
Oliva, Gina, and Linda Crider. *Shape Up N'Sign.* Laurel, Md., 1991. Video.
Stewart, David. *Deaf Sport: The Impact of Sports Within the Deaf Community.* Washington, D.C.: Gallaudet University Press, 1991.

Sexual Development/Privacy

FitzGerald, Max. *Information on Sexuality: For Young People and their Families.* Washington, D.C.: Pre-College Programs, Gallaudet University, 1986.
Girard, Linda Walvoord. *My Body Is Private.* Niles, Ill.: Albert Whitman, 1984.
Minkin, Marilyn, and Laurie Rosen-Ritt. *Signs for Sexuality: A Resource Manual for Deaf and Hard of Hearing Individuals, their Families and Professionals.* 2nd ed. Seattle: Planned Parenthood of Seattle-King County, 1991.
Woodward, James. *Signs of Sexual Behavior.* Silver Spring, Md.: T. J. Publishers, Inc., 1979.

BOOKS FOR DEAF CHILDREN

Ancona, George, and Mary Beth Miller. *Handtalk Zoo.* New York: Four Winds Press, Macmillan Children's Book Group, 1989.
Andrews, Jean F. *The Flying Fingers Club.* Washington, D.C.: Kendall Green Publications, Gallaudet University Press, 1988.
———. *Hasta Luego, San Diego.* Washington, D.C.: Kendall Green Publications, Gallaudet University Press, 1991.
———. *The Secret in the Dorm Attic.* Washington, D.C.: Kendall Green Publications, Gallaudet University Press, 1990.
Andrews, Jean F., and Mike Allard. *The Ghost of Tomahawk Creek.* Aberdeen, S.D.: Northern State University, 1993.
Bahan, Benjamin J., and Joe Dannis. *My ABC Signs and Animal Friends.* Berkeley: Dawn Sign Press, 1992.
———. *Signs for Me: Basic Sign Vocabulary for Children, Parents, and Teachers.* Berkeley: Dawn Sign Press, 1987.
Baker, Pamela J. *My First Book of Sign.* Washington, D.C.: Kendall Green Publications, Gallaudet University Press, 1986.
Bellan Gillen, Patricia. *My Signing Book of Numbers.* Washington, D.C.: Kendall Green Publications, Gallaudet University Press, 1988.
Bornstein, Harry, Karen L. Saulnier, and Lillian B. Hamilton. *The Signed English Series.* Washington, D.C.: Kendall Green Publications, Gallaudet University Press.

Bove, Linda. *Sesame Street Sign Language Fun.* New York: Random House, 1980.

Bove, Linda, Tom Cooke, Anita Shevett, and Steve Shevett. *Sesame Street Sign Language ABC.* New York: Random House, 1985.

Chaplin, Susan. *I Can Sign My ABC's.* Washington, D.C.: Kendall Green Publications, Gallaudet University Press, 1986.

Charlip, Remy, and Mary Beth Miller. *Handtalk: An ABC of Finger Spelling and Sign Language.* New York: Aladdin, Macmillan Children's Book Group, 1987.

————. *Handtalk Birthday.* New York: Four Winds Press, Macmillan Children's Book Group, 1987.

Collins, S. Harold. *Finger Alphabet.* Eugene, Ore.: Garlic Press, 1992.

————. *Mother Goose in Sign.* Eugene, Ore.: Garlic Press, 1994.

Flodin, Mickey. *Signing for Kids.* New York: Putnam Publishing Group, 1991.

Lee, Jeanne M. *Silent Lotus.* New York: Farrar, Strauss, and Giroux, Inc., 1991.

Levi, Dorothy H. *A Very Special Friend.* Washington, D.C.: Kendall Green Publications, Gallaudet University Press, 1989.

Newby, Robert. *King Midas: With Selected Sentences in American Sign Language.* Washington, D.C.: Kendall Green Publications, Gallaudet University Press, 1990.

Newby, Robert. *Sleeping Beauty: With Selected Sentences in American Sign Language.* Washington, D.C.: Kendall Green Publications, Gallaudet University Press, 1992.

Rankin, Laura. *The Handmade Alphabet.* New York: Dial Books, 1991.

Schmidt, Diane E., and Karen Cameron. *Learning to Sign in My Neighborhood.* Silver Spring, Md.: T. J. Publishers, Inc., 1988.

Slier, Debby. *Animal Signs: A First Book of Sign Language.* Washington, D.C.: Kendall Green Publications, Gallaudet University Press, 1995.

Slier, Debby. *Word Signs: A First Book of Sign Language.* Washington, D.C.: Kendall Green Publications, Gallaudet University Press, 1995.

Sullivan, Mary Beth, and Linda Burke. *A Show of Hands.* Reading, Mass.: Addison Wesley, 1990.

COMMUNICATION

American Sign Language

Bahan, Benjamin J., and Joe Dannis. *Signs for Me: Basic Sign Vocabulary for Children.* Berkeley: Dawn Sign Press, 1990.

Bragg, Bernard, and Jack Olson. *Meeting Halfway in American Sign Language: A Common Ground for Effective Communication Among Deaf and Hearing People.* Rochester, N.Y.: Deaf Life Press, 1992.

Butterworth, Rod R., and Mickey Flodin. *The Pocket Dictionary of Signing.* New York: Perigee Books, 1992.

Eastman, Gilbert C., with Martin Noretsky, and Sharon Censoplano. *From Mime to Sign.* Silver Spring, Md.: T. J. Publishers, Inc., 1989.

Fant, Lou, and Betty G. Miller. *The American Sign Language Phrase Book.* Chicago: Contemporary Books, 1994.

Flodin, Mickey. *Signing for Kids: The Fun Way for Anyone to Learn American Sign Language.* New York: Putnam Publishing Group, 1991.

Greene, Laura, and Eva Barash Dicker. *Discovering Sign Language.* Washington, D.C.: Kendall Green Publications, Gallaudet University Press, 1988.

————. *Sign-Me-Fine.* Washington, D.C.: Kendall Green Publications, Gallaudet University Press, 1990.

Humphries, Tom L., and Carol A. Padden. *Learning American Sign Language.* Englewood Cliffs, N.J.: Prentice Hall, Inc., 1992.

Humphries, Tom L., Carol A. Padden, and Terrence J. O'Rourke. *A Basic Course in American Sign Language.* 2nd ed. Silver Spring, Md.: T. J. Publishers, Inc., 1973.

O'Rourke, Terrence J. *A Basic Vocabulary: American Sign Language for Parents and Children.* Silver Spring, Md.: T. J. Publishers, Inc., 1978.

Riekehof, Lottie L. *The Joy of Signing.* 2nd ed. Springfield, Mo.: Gospel Publishing House, 1987.

Shroyer, Edgar H., and Susan P. Shroyer. *Signs Across America.* Washington, D.C.: Gallaudet University Press, 1984.

Sternberg, Martin L. A. *American Sign Language: A Comprehensive Dictionary.* New York: HarperCollins Publishers, 1981.

————. *American Sign Language Concise Dictionary.* New York: Harper Perennial, 1994.

General Issues for Deaf Children and Their Families

Garretson, Mervin D., ed. *Communication Issues Among Deaf People.* Silver Spring, Md.: National Association of the Deaf, 1990.

Kannapell, Barbara. *Language Choice—Identity Choice.* Burtonsville, Md.: Linstok Press, 1993.

National Information Center on Deafness. *Communicating with Deaf People: An Introduction.* Washington, D.C.: Gallaudet University, NICD, 1987.

Schwartz, Sue. *Choices in Deafness: A Parent's Guide.* Kensington, Md.: Woodbine House, 1987.

Signed English

Bornstein, Harry, Karen L. Saulnier, and Lillian B. Hamilton. *The Comprehensive Signed English Dictionary.* Washington, D.C.: Clerc Books, Gallaudet University Press, 1983.

Gustason, Gerilee, D. Dfetzing, and E. Zawolkow. *Signing Exact English.* 3rd ed. Los Angeles: Modern Signs Press, 1993.

Shroyer, Edgar H. *Signing English: For Parents, Teachers, and Clinicians.* Greensboro, N.C.: Sugar Sign Press, 1988.

Speechreading

Deyo, David, Margaret Hallau, and Richard Chiarizia. *Speechreading in Context.* Washington, D.C.: Pre-College Programs, Gallaudet College, 1984.

Kaplan, Harriet, Scott J. Bally, and Carol Garretson. 2d ed. rev. *Speechreading: A Way to Improve Understanding.* Washington, D.C.: Gallaudet University Press, 1995.

CULTURE

Baldwin, Stephen C. *Pictures in the Air: The Story of the National Theatre of the Deaf.* Washington, D.C.: Gallaudet University Press, 1993.

Benderly, Beryl L. *Dancing without Music: Deafness in America.* Washington, D.C.: Gallaudet University Press, 1990.

Carroll, Cathryn. *Clerc: The Story of His Early Years.* Washington, D.C.: Kendall Green Publications, Gallaudet University Press, 1991.

Christiansen, Kathee M., and Gilbert L. Delgado, eds. *Multicultural Issues in Deafness.* White Plains, N.Y.: Longman Publishing Group, 1993.

Cohen, Leah Hager. *Train Go Sorry: Inside a Deaf World.* Boston: Houghton Mifflin Co., 1994.

Erting, Carol J. *Deafness, Communication, and Social Identity: Ethnography in a Preschool for Deaf Children.* Burtonsville, Md.: Linstok Press, 1994.

Erting, Carol J., Robert C. Johnson, Dorothy L. Smith, and Bruce D. Snider, eds. *The Deaf Way: Perspectives from the International Conference on Deaf Culture.* Washington, D.C.: Gallaudet University Press, 1994.

Gannon, Jack. *Deaf Heritage: A Narrative History of Deaf America.* Silver Spring, Md.: National Association of the Deaf, 1981.

Garretson, Merv, ed. *Viewpoints on Deafness: A Deaf American Monograph.* Silver Spring, Md.: National Association of the Deaf, 1992.

Glickman, Ken. *DEAFinitions for Signlets.* Silver Spring, Md.: DiKen Productions, 1986.

Glickman, Ken. *More DEAFinitions.* Silver Spring, Md.: DiKen Productions, 1989.

Greene, Laura, and Eva Barash Dicker. *Sign-Me-Fine.* Washington, D.C.: Kendall Green Publications, Gallaudet University Press, 1989.

Groce, Nora Ellen. *Everyone Here Spoke Sign Language: Hereditary Deafness on Martha's Vineyard.* Cambridge, Mass.: Harvard University Press, 1985.

Jacobs, Leo. *A Deaf Adult Speaks Out.* 3rd ed. Washington, D.C.: Gallaudet University Press, 1989.

Lane, Harlan. *When the Mind Hears: A History of the Deaf.* New York: Random House, Inc., 1984.

Mackinnon, Christy. *Silent Observer.* Washington, D.C.: Kendall Green Publications, Gallaudet University Press, 1993.

McCullough, Gayle, and Otto J. Menzel. *Feud for Thought.* Bristol, Va.: Life after Deafness, 1993.

Moore, Matthew S., and Linda Levitan. *For Hearing People Only: Answers to Some of the Most Commonly Asked Questions about the Deaf Community, Its Culture, and the "Deaf Reality."* Rochester, N.Y.: Deaf Life Press, 1993.

Neisser, Arden. *The Other Side of Silence: Sign Language and the Deaf Community in America.* Washington, D.C.: Gallaudet University Press, 1990.

Padden, Carol A., and Tom L. Humphries. *Deaf in America: Voices from a Culture.* Cambridge, Mass.: Harvard University Press, 1988.

Rosen, Roslyn, Barbara A. Kannapell, and Ivey B. Pittle. *Another Handful of Stories.* Washington, D.C.: Division of Public Services, Gallaudet College, 1984.

Sacks, Oliver W. *Seeing Voices: A Journey into the World of the Deaf.* Berkeley: University of California Press, 1989.

Schein, Jerome D. *At Home Among Strangers: Exploring the Deaf Community in the United States.* Washington, D.C.: Gallaudet University Press, 1989.

Van Cleve, John V., and Barry A. Crouch. *A Place of Their Own: Creating the Deaf Community in America.* Washington, D.C.: Gallaudet University Press, 1989.

FAMILY UNITY

Booth, Barbara. *Mandy.* New York: Lothrop, Lee, and Shepard Books, 1991.

Dicker, Eva, and Harvey Barash. *Our Father Abe: The Story of a Deaf Shoe Repairman.* Madison, Wis.: ABAR Press, 1991.

Greenberg, Joanne. *In This Sign.* New York: Holt, Rinehart and Winston, 1984.

Levi, Dorothy Hoffman. *A Very Special Sister.* Washington, D.C.: Kendall Green Publications, Gallaudet University Press, 1992.

Peterson, Jeanne Whitehouse. *I Have a Sister—My Sister is Deaf.* New York: Harper and Row, 1984.

FEARS AND ANXIETIES

Collins, S. Harold. *Can I Help? Helping the Hearing Impaired in Emergency Situations.* Eugene, Ore.: Garlic Press, 1993.

Gragg, Venita, Nancy B. Fones, and Richard M. Chiarizia. *What Is an Audiogram?* Washington, D.C.: Pre-College Programs, Gallaudet University, 1985.

Pace, Betty. *Chris Gets Ear Tubes.* Washington, D.C.: Gallaudet University Press, 1987.

HEARING AIDS

Simko, Carole Bugosh. *Ear Gear: A Student Workbook on Hearing and Hearing Aids.* Washington, D.C.: Kendall Green Publications, Gallaudet University Press, 1991.

Staab, Wayne J. *Hearing Aids: A User's Guide.* Phoenix, Ariz.: W. J. Staab, 1991.

Stoker, Richard, and Janine Gaydos. *Hearing Aids for You and the Zoo.* Washington, D.C.: Alexander Graham Bell Association for the Deaf, 1984.

Wayner, Donna. *The Hearing Aid Handbook: User's Guide for Children.* Washington, D.C.: Clerc Books, Gallaudet University Press, 1990.

HYPERACTIVITY, INATTENTIVENESS, AND IMPULSIVITY

Herigstad, Honi. *I Was So Mad!* Los Alamitos, Calif.: Modern Signs Press, 1986.

MOODINESS

Meadow, Kathryn P. *Deafness and Child Development.* Berkeley: University of California Press, 1980.

PARENTING BOOKS RELATED TO RAISING A DEAF CHILD

Adams, John W. *You and Your Hearing-Impaired Child: A Self-Instructional Guide for Parents.* Washington, D.C.: Clerc Books, Gallaudet University Press, 1988.

Atkins, Dale, ed. *Families and Their Hearing-Impaired Children.* Washington, D.C.: Alexander Graham Bell Association, 1987.

Ferris, Caren. *A Hug Just Isn't Enough.* Washington, D.C.: Gallaudet University Press, 1980.

Fletcher, Lorraine. *Ben's Story.* Washington, D.C.: Gallaudet University Press, 1987.

Forecki, Marcia C. *Speak to Me!* Washington, D.C.: Gallaudet University Press, 1985.

Fredrickson, Jeannette, and Janine Gaydos. *Life After Deaf: Impact of Deafness on a Family.* Silver Spring, Md.: National Association of the Deaf, 1985.

Freeman, Roger D., Clifton F. Carbin, and Robert J. Boese. *Can't Your Child Hear?: A Guide for Those Who Care about Deaf Children.* Austin, Tex.: PRO-ED, 1981.

Griffin, Betty F., and Irene Leigh. *Family to Family.* Washington, D.C.: Alexander Graham Bell Association for the Deaf, 1980.

Meadow, Kathryn P. *Deafness and Child Development.* Berkeley: University of California Press, 1980.

Mindel, Eugene D., and McCay Vernon. *They Grow in Silence: Understanding Deaf Children and Adults.* 2nd ed. Boston: College-Hill Press, 1987.

Naiman, Doris W., and Jerome D. Schein. *For Parents of Deaf Children.* Silver Spring, Md.: National Association of the Deaf, 1978.

National Information Center on Deafness. *Growing Together: Information for Parents of Deaf and Hard of Hearing Children.* 2nd ed. Washington, D.C.: NICD, 1991.

Schlesinger, Hilde, and Kathryn P. Meadow. "Emotional Support for Parents," In *Teaching Parents to Teach,* edited by D. Lillie, P. Trohanis, and K. Goin. New York: Walker, 1976.

―――. *Sound and Sign: Childhood Deafness and Mental Health.* Berkeley: University of California Press, 1972.

Spradley, Thomas S., and James P. Spradley. *Deaf Like Me.* 3rd ed. Washington, D.C.: Gallaudet University Press, 1989.

RESOURCES/DIRECTORIES

The American Annals of the Deaf. Washington, D.C.: Executive Committee of the Convention of American Instructors of the Deaf. Available from Gallaudet University.

The Broadcaster. Silver Spring, Md.: National Association of the Deaf.

Cagle, Sharon T., Keith M. Cagle, and Val Nelson-Metlay. *GA and SK Etiquette: Guidelines for Telecommunications in the Deaf Community.* Bowling Green, Ohio.: Bowling Green Press, 1991.

The Deaf American. Silver Spring, Md.: National Association of the Deaf.

Dubow, Sy, Sarah Geer, and Karen Peltz Strauss. *Legal Rights: The Guide for Deaf and Hard of Hearing People.* Washington, D.C.: Gallaudet University Press, 1992.

The Endeavor. Indianapolis, Ind.: Convention of American Instructors of the Deaf, Parent Section.

Frank, Steven A. *International Directory of Periodicals Related to Deafness.* 3rd ed. Washington, D.C.: Gallaudet University, 1992.

Gallaudet University, and National Technical Institute for the Deaf. *College and Career Programs for Deaf Students.* Washington, D.C.: Gallaudet University, and Rochester, N.Y.: National Technical Institute for the Deaf, 1991.

Gopen, Stuart, ed. *Gopen's Guide to Closed Captioned Videos.* Framingham, Mass.: Caption Database, Inc., 1993.

Myers, Peter C. *The ADA and You: A Guide for Deaf and Hard of Hearing People.* Washington, D.C.: The National Academy, Gallaudet University, 1992.

National Information Center on Deafness. *Clubs for Deaf and Hard of Hearing People.* Washington, D.C.: NICD, 1993.

———. *Directory of National Organizations of and for Deaf and Hard of Hearing People.* Washington, D.C.: NICD, 1990.

Telecommunications for the Deaf, Inc. *1995 International Telephone Directory for TTY Users.* Silver Spring, Md.: TDI., 1995.

The Volta Review. Washington, D.C.: The Volta Bureau, Alexander Graham Bell Association for the Deaf.

Willigan, Barbara S., and Susan J. King, eds. *Mental Health Services for Deaf People.* San Francisco: University of California, 1992.

RESOURCE TEXTS

Education

Moores, Donald P., and Kathryn P. Meadow-Orlans. *Educational and Developmental Aspects of Deafness.* Washington, D.C.: Gallaudet University Press, 1990.

History

Van Cleve, John V., ed. *Deaf History Unveiled: Interpretations from the New Scholarship.* Washington, D.C.: Gallaudet University Press, 1993.

Van Cleve, John V., ed. *The Gallaudet Encyclopedia of Deaf People and Deafness.* New York: McGraw-Hill, 1987.

Walker, Lou Ann. *Hand, Heart, and Mind: The Story of the Education of America's Deaf People.* New York: Dial Books, 1994.

Winefield, Richard. *Never the Twain Shall Meet: Bell, Gallaudet, and the Communications Debate.* Washington, D.C.: Gallaudet University Press, 1987.

Winzer, Margret A. *The History of Special Education: From Isolation to Integration.* Washington, D.C.: Gallaudet University Press, 1993.

Language

Baker, Charlotte, and Robbin Battison, eds. *Sign Language and the Deaf Community: Essays in Honor of William C. Stokoe, Jr.* Silver Spring, Md.: National Association of the Deaf, 1981.

Volterra, Virginia, and Carol J. Erting, eds. *From Gesture to Language in Hearing and Deaf Children.* Washington, D.C.: Gallaudet University Press, 1994.

Literature

Batson, Trent W., and Eugene Bergman, eds. *Angels and Outcasts: An Anthology of Deaf Characters in Literature.* Washington, D.C.: Gallaudet University Press, 1985.

Jepson, Jill, ed. *No Walls of Stone: An Anthology of Literature by Deaf and Hard of Hearing Writers.* Washington, D.C.: Gallaudet University Press, 1992.

RESPONSIBILITY

Deyo, David. *On My Own: Assistive Devices for Deaf and Hard of Hearing Students.* Washington, D.C.: Pre-College Programs, Gallaudet University, 1984.

Olsen, Harry, Jacqueline Maeder, and Martin R. Noretsky. *Skills for Living.* Washington, D.C.: Pre-College Programs, Gallaudet University, 1984.

Turk, Frank R., ed. *A Kaleidoscope of Deaf America.* Silver Spring, Md.: National Association of the Deaf, 1989.

SCHOOL

Communicating in School

Bornstein, Harry, and I. King Jordan. *Functional Signs: A New Approach from Simple to Complex.* Baltimore: University Park Press, 1984.

Collins, S. Harold. *Signing at School.* Eugene, Ore.: Garlic Press, 1992.

Piskula, Anita L., and Christine A. Watkin, eds. *Reaching Out with Sign: A Basic Sign Language Phrase Manual.* Elwyn, Pa.: Elwyn, Inc., 1994.

Mainstreaming

Bishop, Milo E., ed. *Mainstreaming: Practical Ideas for Educating Hearing Impaired Students.* Washington, D.C.: Alexander Graham Bell Association for the Deaf, 1979.

Collins, S. Harold, Kathy Kifer, and Dahna Solar. *Caring for Young Children: Signing for Day Care Providers and Sitters.* Eugene, Ore.: Garlic Press, 1993.

Davis, Julia, ed. *Our Forgotten Children: Hard of Hearing Pupils in the Schools.* Washington, D.C.: Department of Education, 1990. Available from SHHH.

LaMore, Gregory S. *Now I Understand.* Washington, D.C.: Gallaudet University Press, 1986.

National Information Center on Deafness. *Mainstreaming Deaf and Hard of Hearing Students.* Washington, D.C.: NICD, 1991.

Nussbaum, Debra. *There's a Hearing Impaired Child in My Class.* Washington, D.C.: Pre-College Programs, Gallaudet University, 1988.

Solit, Gail, Angela Bednarczyk, and Maral Taylor. *Access for All: Integrating Deaf, Hard of Hearing and Hearing Preschoolers.* Washington, D.C.: Pre-College Programs, Gallaudet University, 1992.

Starowitz, Anne Marie. *The Day We Met Cindy.* Washington, D.C.: Kendall Green Publications, Gallaudet University Press, 1988.

SELF-CONCEPT

Albronda, Mildred. *Douglas Tilden: Portrait of a Deaf Sculptor.* Silver Spring, Md.: T. J. Publishers, Inc., 1980.

Bowe, Frank, and Martin L. A. Sternberg. *I'm deaf too—Twelve Deaf Americans.* Silver Spring, Md.: National Association of the Deaf, 1973.

Bragg, Bernard, as signed to Eugene Bergman. *Lessons in Laughter: The Autobiography of a Deaf Actor.* Washington, D.C.: Gallaudet University Press, 1989.

Carroll, Cathryn. *Laurent Clerc: The Story of His Early Years.* Washington, D.C.: Kendall Green Publications, Gallaudet University Press, 1991.

Christiansen, John B., and Sharon N. Barnartt. *Deaf President Now! The 1988 Revolution at Gallaudet University.* Washington, D.C.: Gallaudet University Press, 1995.

Gannon, Jack R. *The Week the World Heard Gallaudet.* Washington, D.C.: Gallaudet University Press, 1989.

Hairston, Ernest, and Linwood Smith. *Black and Deaf in America: Are We That Different?* Silver Spring, Md.: T. J. Publishers, Inc., 1983.

Holcomb, Marjoriebell S., and Sharon K. Wood. *Deaf Women: A Parade through the Decades.* Berkeley: Dawn Sign Press, 1989.

Neimark, Anne E. *A Deaf Child Listened: Thomas Gallaudet, Pioneer in American Education.* New York: Morrow, 1993.

Nieminen, Raija. *Voyage to the Island.* Washington, D.C.: Gallaudet University Press, 1990.

Panara, Robert, and John Panara. *Great Deaf Americans.* Silver Spring, Md.: T. J. Publishers, 1983.

Robinette, Diane. *Hometown Heroes: Successful Deaf Youth in America.* Washington, D.C.: Kendall Green Publications, Gallaudet University Press, 1990.

St. George, Judith. *Dear Mr. Bell . . . Your Friend, Helen Keller.* New York: G. P. Putnam's Sons, 1992.

Stone, Casey, Janis Morariu, and Lois Dam. *Self-Esteem for Little Folk—S.E.L.F.* Washington, D.C.: Pre-College Programs, Gallaudet University, 1983.

Wiggins, Julius. *No Sound.* New York: Silent Press, 1980.

Zazove, Philip, M.D. *When the Phone Rings, My Bed Shakes: Memoirs of a Deaf Doctor.* Washington, D.C.: Gallaudet University Press, 1993.

Social Problems

Bradford, Tom. *"Say That Again, Please": Insights in Dealing with a Hearing Loss.* Dallas: T. H. Bradford, 1991.

Schloss, Patrick J., and Maureen A. Smith, with a foreword by Richard Stoker. *Teaching Social Skills to Hearing Impaired Students.* Washington, D.C.: Alexander Graham Bell Association for the Deaf, 1990.

Software

Interactive Sign Language Fingerspelling and Numbers, MS Windows and Macintosh. Seattle: Palantine, Inc., 1994.

Sternberg, Martin L. A. *American Sign Language Dictionary on CD-ROM,* MS Windows. New York: HarperCollins Interactive, 1994.

Videotapes

A Basic Course in American Sign Language Videotape Series. Silver Spring, Md.: T. J. Publishers, Inc.

Costello, Elaine. *Say It By Signing: A Video Guide to the Basics of Sign Language.* New York: Crown Publishers, 1985.

The Deaf Mosaic Videotapes. Washington, D.C.: Department of Television, Film, and Photography, Gallaudet University, 1992.

The Fantastic Videotape Series. Washington, D.C.: Kendall Green Publications, Gallaudet University Press, 1989.

Glickman, Ken. *DEAFology 101, Deaf Culture as Seen Through the Eyes of a Deaf Humorist.* Silver Spring, Md.: DEAFinitely Yours Studio, 1993.

High Five Fables and Fairy Tales Vols. 1–5. Burtonsville, Md.: Sign Media, Inc., 1994.

Humphries, Tom, and Carol A. Padden. *Learning American Sign Language Book and Videotape Set.* Englewood Cliffs, N.J.: Prentice Hall, Inc., 1992.

Once Upon a Time: Children's Classics Retold in American Sign Language Videotape Series. Retold by Benjamin J. Bahan, and Nathie Marbury. San Diego: Dawn Pictures, 1991.

The Rainbow's End Videotape Series. Burtonsville, Md.: Sign Media, Inc., 1993.

Sign Me a Story, with Linda Bove. New York: Random House.

Stories to Remember Videotape Series. Lightyear Entertainment, LP, 1992.

Supalla, Sam, and Benjamin J. Bahan. *ASL Literature Workbook and Video Series.* Berkeley: Dawn Sign Press, 1993.

Index of Activities and Parenting Techniques

•••

Activities

Parenting Techniques